Pandemonium and Parade

Pandemonium and Parade

Japanese Monsters and the Culture of Yōkai

Michael Dylan Foster

UNIVERSITY OF CALIFORNIA PRESS
Berkeley · Los Angeles · London

University of California Press, one of the most distinguished university presses in the United States, enriches lives around the world by advancing scholarship in the humanities, social sciences, and natural sciences. Its activities are supported by the UC Press Foundation and by philanthropic contributions from individuals and institutions. For more information, visit www.ucpress.edu.

University of California Press
Berkeley and Los Angeles, California

University of California Press, Ltd.
London, England

Library of Congress Cataloging-in-Publication Data

Foster, Michael Dylan, 1965–.
Pandemonium and parade : Japanese monsters and the culture of yōkai / Michael Dylan Foster.
p. cm.
Includes bibliographical references and index.
ISBN 978-0-520-25361-2 (cloth : alk. paper)—
ISBN 978-0-520-25362-9 (pbk. : alk. paper)
1. Japan—Folklore. 2. Animals, mythical—Japan. 3. Supernatural. 4. Spirits. I. Title.
GR340.F67 2009
398'.450952—dc22 2007050923

17 16 15 14 13 12 11 10 09 08
10 9 8 7 6 5 4 3 2 1

To my parents,
Joan and Jerry Foster

And in spite of all the pains I had lavished on these problems, I was more than ever stupefied by the complexity of this innumerable dance, involving doubtless other determinants of which I had not the slightest idea. And I said, with rapture, Here is something I can study all my life, and never understand.

Samuel Beckett

Contents

Illustrations

Acknowledgments

For a book concerned with listing, naming, and classifying, it is appropriate to begin with a list of names, variously classified, of the individuals and institutions to whom I owe thanks. There are many of them. Without a doubt, the first person on such a list must be Susan Matisoff, who was not only a wonderful mentor throughout my graduate studies at Stanford University, but who also generously continued to provide perspicacious guidance—both intellectual and practical—as this book gradually took form. I also owe a great debt of gratitude to Tom Hare and Jim Reichert for their keen insight, advice, and unstinting encouragement. Similarly, Bernard Faure and Miyako Inoue both inspired me with their inquisitive minds and scholarly passion.

In Japan I had the distinct honor of receiving guidance for a short period from the late Miyata Noboru, a scholar whose erudition was matched only by his magnanimity and eclectic sense of humor. My deepest appreciation goes to Komma Tōru of Kanagawa University, whose piercing creativity challenged me to look harder not only at my own project but also at all cultural processes and human communities. I am also profoundly indebted to Komatsu Kazuhiko of the International Research Center for Japanese Studies (Nichibunken) in Kyoto. Professor Komatsu inspired me constantly with his critical eye, his boundless curiosity, and his ability to cross and combine disciplines. He also generously provided me extended access to the resources of Nichibunken and to his "yōkai workshops," where I met scholars and writers who greatly influenced the direction of my work. In particular, I thank Jutta Hausser, Manabe Masayoshi, Takahara Toyoaki, Takeda Masaya, Tsunemitsu Tōru, Yamaguchi Masao, and Yasui Manami. I also extend special thanks to Ichiyanagi Hirotaka of Yokohama National University for his refreshing sensibilities and warm guidance.

My project benefited immensely from discussions with members of the Shingetsukai at Kanagawa University and the Chiba University Cryptozoological Association. I particularly thank Ariga Takashi for many exhilarating hours of perceptive humor and imaginative thinking. Although research I conducted on the island of Shimokoshiki-jima in Kagoshima Prefecture ultimately made no direct appearance in the pages that follow, in subtle ways the island is a presence in this text. I am especially grateful for the lasting friendship of Ozaki Takakazu, Shirasaki Hiroki, Hironiwa Yoshitatsu, and their families.

For research in Japan from 1999–2001, I was generously funded by a fellowship from the Fulbright Foundation, and while writing my dissertation I received financial support from the Department of Asian Languages, Institute for International Studies, and the Center for East Asian Studies, all at Stanford University. The munificence of the Geballe Dissertation Fellowship provided me a year at the Stanford Humanities Center, where my project benefited immensely from the critical insight of the other fellows, especially Michael Saler, Ethan Segal, and Jason Weems. As the dissertation developed into a book, my colleagues in the Department of Comparative Literature and Foreign Languages at the University of California, Riverside, supported me enthusiastically; I am particularly grateful to Sabine Doran, John Kim, Mariam Lam, Mimi Long, Henk Maier, Thomas Scanlon, and Dawn Whelchel. At UCR, I also benefited greatly from two quarters at the Center for Ideas and Society, and I thank my workshop colleagues there.

In the final stages of the project, the Freeman Spogli Institute for International Studies at Stanford University generously provided me with financial support and time away from teaching. I am indebted to Anne Allison for her thoughtful guidance as I sought a publisher, and Kären Wigen who shared her time, wisdom, and brilliant editing skills. At the University of California Press, two anonymous readers provided invaluable suggestions, and Reed Malcolm, Kalicia Pivirotto, Jacqueline Volin, and Bonita Hurd patiently and intelligently transformed my manuscript into a book.

It would be impossible to mention all the many others who showed support along the way, but my appreciation especially goes to Susan

Antebi, Ann Ayton, Christopher Bolton, Suzy Cincone, John Clayton, Claire Cuccio, Lisa Dipko, Adam Foster, Mark Gibeau, Hank Glassman, Gunji Satoshi, Hashimoto Hiroyuki, Kanazawa Kodama, John Katz, Annette Keogh, Naomi Kotake, Shu Kuge, Dylar Kumax, Kurihara Naohiro, Michele Mason, Miri Nakamura, Sayuri Oyama, Elizabeth Oyler, Kannikar Sartraproong, Shibuya Yōichi, Roberta Strippoli, Suzuki Ken'ichirō, Takeuchi Yuka, Tateoka Yōko, Kenji Tierney, Robert Tierney, and Leslie Winston. The ideas in the pages that follow were also shaped by innumerable encounters with individuals in big cities, tiny towns, restaurants, bars, buses, and trains—all those people, friends and strangers alike, who shared their thoughts and experiences made this book possible, though the responsibility for any errors rests solely with me.

My profound gratitude goes also to my family. The Suzukis, Tatsuo and Yumi, welcomed me into their home for many an evening of culinary enchantment and calm, insightful conversation. As for my parents, Joan and Jerry Foster, any words here can but dimly reflect my appreciation for years of patient support. Sadly, my mother did not live to see the completion of this book, but her boundless energy continues to inspire me.

Finally, how can I possibly express my appreciation to Michiko Suzuki? She has engaged tirelessly with my ideas, read and reread draft after draft, and challenged me to think and write with clarity. At the very least I can strive to do the same for her—although I can never hope to match the brilliance and grace she has shown throughout. Most important, though, she has taught me that mystery is not just a subject for academic inquiry but also can be found in the tranquil corners of everyday life, in quiet enchantments, such as the exquisite sense of inarticulateness I feel when trying to convey to her my gratitude.

Note on Japanese Names and Terms

Throughout this book, Japanese proper names are noted in Japanese order, with family name first. Where appropriate, I follow the Japanese convention of referring to certain writers, scholars, and artists by their pseudonyms or given names. For example, Mori Ōgai is called Ōgai rather than Mori. Japanese words and place-names that appear in standard English-language dictionaries are written in roman script with no macrons (e.g., Tokyo); other Japanese words are written with macrons to indicate long vowels. Japanese words used frequently throughout the text are italicized only on their first appearance.

CHAPTER 1

Introduction to the Weird

MYSTERIOUS BODIES

The bones were found in May 2000, in the small town of Yoshii in Okayama Prefecture. News of the discovery, according to one weekly magazine, "set off tremors throughout Japan." The skeleton was taken to a university to determine whether it really belonged to a *tsuchinoko,* a legendary reptilelike creature the existence of which had never been scientifically confirmed. After thoroughly examining the specimen, a professor of biology declared that the remains were not those of a tsuchinoko but rather of a malformed grass snake. This disappointing news did not dampen spirits in Yoshii. In fact, stimulated by the near-discovery, the town was experiencing a "tsuchinoko boom." A giant statue of the fantastic beast was set up at a neighborhood nursery school, local manufacturers began producing tsuchinoko wine and bean cakes, and a reward was offered for anybody who could actually find one of the elusive creatures.[1]

Meanwhile, at a major government-sponsored research institute in Kyoto, an interdisciplinary group of scholars had begun a series of bimonthly workshops to discuss Japan's culture of mysterious creatures, spooky tales, and strange phenomena. Participants came from academic fields such as literature, folklore, anthropology, history, geography, religion, and art. Along with several collections of articles, one result of these meetings was the establishment of a computer database with more than thirteen thousand entries on supernatural creatures culled from folkloric sources. Opened to the public online in 2002, the database received 180,000 hits in its first month of operation.[2]

A popular fascination with the body of a mysterious creature. A government-funded academic project to investigate the history and meaning of the supernatural in Japanese cultural expression. These two distinct but related manifestations of interest in the mysterious reveal that, at the turn of the twenty-first century, those things that defy established regimes of knowledge, remaining elusive and inexplicable, continue to stir both popular and academic imagination in Japan. I open with these two examples, not only because of their prominence in the media, but also because they demonstrate the multivalence of the mysterious and the weird, notions with the capacity to transcend the logic of local and national, popular and scholarly, belief systems and economic systems. Supernatural creatures negotiate the extremes, creating interaction between local commercial interests (tsuchinoko wine) and scientific study (a professor of biology), academic rigor (a computer database with more than thirteen thousand entries) and popular fascination (180,000 hits). Whether buried within the local landscape of a small town such as Yoshii or inscribed historically into the cultural topography of Japan as a nation, mysterious bodies and supernatural creatures operate variously as objects of belief, fear, commercial production, scholarly interest, and popular passion.

Such supernatural creatures, the weird and mysterious "things" that have been a part of Japanese culture (and perhaps every other culture) for as long as history has been recorded, are the subject of this study. In contemporary Japanese discourse, they are most often denoted by the word *yōkai* 妖怪, variously translated as monster, spirit, goblin, ghost, demon, phantom, specter, fantastic being, lower-order deity, or, more amorphously, as any unexplainable experience or numinous occurrence. I intentionally leave the definition open-ended, for the history of yōkai is very much the history of efforts to describe and define the object being considered. Because the meaning of the word changes with each attempt to limn its parameters, at the heart of this study are questions of signification and language. How do we talk of something ambiguous, continually shifting, a constant presence that is forever absent? How do we describe the mysterious body always on the verge of discovery, the apparition already disappearing in the mist? My objective is to explore some of the ways yōkai in Japan have been understood and interpreted through time, how they have played a role in vernacular practices, and how they have informed academic discourses that describe, explain, deny, or cherish them.

YŌKAI DISCOURSE

The yōkai, as has been said of the "monster" in the West, "is an embodiment of a certain cultural moment—of a time, a feeling, and a place."[3] In this study, I consider a long chronological swath, from the late seventeenth century to the late twentieth century, in order to explore discourses that imbue yōkai with specific meanings during different cultural moments. By unpacking such discourses, we can uncover the hidden philosophies and unconscious ideologies that circumscribe a category of things weird and mysterious. The notion of "discourse" I employ here involves an entire sociocultural web of written and oral forms of expression, ideas, beliefs, and traditions that are enmeshed and symbiotic and just as often contradictory and antithetical. Like many of the monsters in this study, the discourse of yōkai is hybrid: it weaves together strands from other discourses—encyclopedic, scientific, literary, ethnographic, folkloric—to create a discrete discursive formation of its own. Certain voices within this yōkai discourse are louder at certain times, but ultimately all the voices that coalesce dialogically at a given moment are "within the true" (as Foucault puts it). They are in conversation (though not necessarily explicitly or consciously) with one another; every articulation participates in the same discussion (or argument), and makes sense within the dominant episteme.[4]

To a certain extent, the discourse on yōkai is unusual not only because it incorporates voices from a diverse range of disciplines but also because its very object—that which is out of the ordinary—challenges ordinary discursive parameters. Yōkai discourse is always located at the boundaries of the other fields on which it draws. At any given moment, however, a range of "truths" is still accruing to the idea of yōkai itself, a certain pitch, as it were, in which the discourse of yōkai must speak in order to be heard.

As sociocultural contexts change, shifts in the conversation about yōkai are rarely the result of violent rupture: usually they are gradual, nuanced, overlapping, as one part of the discursive web centers on a particular idea, gathering mass until it becomes dominant. Epistemic changes are not absolute: more often than not, traditional understandings and articulations are refashioned within newly emerging ones. The mode by which yōkai discourse changes might be characterized as what archeological anthropologists call seriation, "a pattern of overlapping replication and innovation."[5] It is the replication or persistence of particular strands of discourse, their ability to link diverse cultural moments and reincorporate themselves differently "within the true" of the emerging episteme, that allows us to trace the mutable but somehow consistent notion of something called yōkai. While I am interested in both continuities and discontinuities, the real concentration of this book is on the areas of overlap and "in-betweenness." Rather than chart a neat genealogy of paradigms, I explore the untidy spaces where ways of thinking clash, collide, reproduce, and converge.

It is not my intention to trace all discourse related to yōkai. Rather, within the long chronology covered in the chapters that follow, I focus on four "moments" during which yōkai discourse was especially prominent and characteristic of wider cultural concerns, and in which we can clearly see the persistence of old forms even as new forms emerged. The first of these important historical junctures occurred during the Edo, or Tokugawa, period (c. 1603–1867), particularly from the 1660s through the 1780s, when yōkai made a name for themselves in both serious encyclopedic taxonomies and playful illustrated catalogs. The second moment came during the Meiji period (1868–1912), especially in the 1880s, as yōkai underwent a radical reevaluation in light of Western scientific knowledge. The third moment encompassed the first decade of the twentieth century through the 1930s, when yōkai were refigured as nostalgic icons for a nation (and individuals) seeking a sense of self in a rapidly modernizing world. And the fourth came in the 1970s and 1980s, as Japan asserted a new identity after its rapid recovery from the devastation of World War II. To a certain extent, my aim is to sketch out the contours of each of these moments and the role played by yōkai within them. More important, by unveiling a culmination of the influences, the incremental movements as one paradigm stutter-steps into another, I uncover a landscape characterized as much by discontinuity as by overlap and interaction.

Out of this ever-shifting terrain emerge the cultural practices on which this study is based. Such practices can be ritualized and institutional, or they can simply be everyday ways of being and interacting. Reading manga, telling ghost stories, playing games, collecting things: all of these are creative cultural forms that shape and are shaped by the signs that accrue around them, the visible, readable discursive threads by which we know of their existence. And ultimately it is these written texts that serve as the accessible material trace of thoughts or actions or events. Although one objective of this study is to read *through* written documents to get at the otherwise unknowable practices they encode, this mode of analysis must be complemented by consideration of the document itself as an object of interpretation—appearing in a specific situation, with a certain author (known or unknown) and a particular readership (known or unknown). Each text gives voice to the cultural practice under discussion but also speaks of the time, place, and ideological circumstances of its own production. And discourse is always heteroglossic: while academic, legal, or otherwise institutional texts so often become the dominant strands within a given discursive web, a whole set of nonelite, nonacademic popular texts are also part of the same web, often suggesting messages counter to the hegemonic threads. Especially by giving voice to oft-overlooked cultural products, such as games, urban legends, and popular weekly magazines, I seek to uncover the way yōkai are folded into everyday life experiences.[6]

THE INSTABILITY OF THE THING

Though *yōkai* is presently the word of choice in contemporary discourse on the subject, other terms are also invoked, such as *bakemono*, the more childish *obake*, and the more academic-sounding *kaii genshō*. In late twentieth- and early twenty-first-century Japan, however, *yōkai* remains the term most commonly associated with the academic study of these "things." Historically, the popularity of the word is relatively new. Although it has semantic roots in China and can be found in Japan as early as the mid-Edo-period work of Toriyama Sekien (chapter 2), it did not develop into the default technical term until the Meiji-period writings of Inoue Enryō (chapter 3), who consciously invoked it to describe all manner of weird and mysterious phenomena, naming his field of study *yōkaigaku*, literally, "yōkai-ology" or "monsterology."[7] Emblematic of the interplay between academic and popular discourses, Enryō's technical use of the word propelled *yōkai* into common parlance, where it remains today. The conscious use of *yōkai* by Enryō, and the word's rapid absorption into everyday speech, also reflects the absence of other words flexible enough to encompass the range of phenomena that would come to be considered under its matrix.[8]

The Tokugawa-period word that best approximates the broad meanings of *yōkai* was *bakemono*, which can be translated literally as "changing thing." This emphasis on transformation denotes powers traditionally attributed to such creatures as foxes, for example, which could take on different forms at will. The word *bakemono,* however, was not limited to shape-shifting things; it also signified a wide range of strangely formed, anomalous, or supernatural creatures.[9] Although explicit shape-shifting abilities may not have been intrinsic to many of the things that were called bakemono and later yōkai, the notion of *mutability* provides an important key to the ontology of the mysterious. In fact, deceptive appearances and instability of form can be found long before the advent of the Tokugawa period. During the Heian period (c. 794–1185), for example, it was believed that after death Sugawara no Michizane (845–903) transformed into a mischievous and spiteful spirit, an *onryō,* and caused a number of misfortunes, only relenting once he was deified as a sacred spirit, or *goryō.*[10] Death can change a human into something else, it seems, but even such an after-death manifestation is unstable and can be altered again—in this case from a demonic spirit to a deific one. Concepts of transmutation and transmigration lie at the core of Buddhist theology in Japan (as elsewhere), and it is not surprising that the form of the body would be understood as only a temporary lodging place in which a moveable and mutable spirit resides.

Michizane transformed into a troubled spirit after his death, but similar transmogrifications might occur even while the human in question was alive, the most notorious case being that of the living spirit (*ikiryō*) of Lady Rokujō in Murasaki Shikibu's *Genji monogatari* (*The Tale of Genji;* early eleventh century). In a series of disturbing episodes, the spirit of the still-very-much-alive Rokujō detaches itself from her body to haunt and torment her rivals—all unbeknownst to her. Even to the "changing thing" itself, corporeal appearance is deceptive; present in one place, she is also present elsewhere, simultaneously self and other, her form betraying a dangerous instability guided by an intensity of emotion beyond her control.

Although there were names for specific types of strange phenomena during the Heian period, an oft-applied term for all manner of mysterious and frightening experiences was *mono-no-ke.* The first graph of this term, *mono,* commonly denotes "thing," but as Doris Bargen explains, during the Heian period it was "not the tangible 'thing' it means in modern Japanese, but its very opposite . . . something unspecifiable, without a clear form, and therefore extraordinary, strange, to be feared as an outside force."[11] The second character in the construction, *ke,* is the same as the *kai* in yōkai (怪) and signifies a sense of the suspicious, the uncertain, the unstable. With the "thing" itself representing an unknowable external agency, *mono-no-ke* evokes both the danger and the mystery of this powerful and unpredictable thing; it might be creatively rendered along the lines of "the instability of the thing."

Regarding the strange phenomena in *The Tale of Genji,* Marian Ury implores us not to overlook "the fact that, on a literal level, the mononoke belong to a class of beings which Murasaki Shikibu's original audience thought of as actually existing and of which many of those readers must have had explicit conceptions." I would add to Ury's assessment that the difficulty of trying "to see the world through the eyes of people for whom supernatural creatures possess an independent and alarming reality" stems from the impossibility of transcending our own strict formulations of real and not-real.[12] That is, common contemporary understandings of "actually existing" or "reality" color our comprehension of the Heian period, when such notions were likely more fluid than our own. Mono-no-ke phenomena betrayed the instability and mutability of everyday existence, like ripples appearing suddenly in the solid-*seeming* surface of a dark liquid body. They were sudden, unusual, unpredictable—and therefore frightening. Though such phenomena were certainly not normal, they were always *possible.* Perhaps it is helpful to think of the occurrence of mono-no-ke as akin to a crime or an automobile accident—not an everyday occurrence but always a terrible, imaginable possibility capable of rupturing mundane "reality."[13]

From the Kamakura period (1185–1333) onward, one prevalent image of mono-no-ke was the *tsukumogami,* common household objects with arms and legs and an animated—even riotous—life of their own. According to "Tsukumogami-ki," a Muromachi-period (c. 1336–1573) *otogi-zōshi* ("companion book") tale, "When an object reaches one hundred years, it transforms, obtaining a spirit *[seirei],* and deceiving *[taburakasu]* people's hearts; this is called tsukumogami."[14] The word is thought to be a play on *tsukumo-gami,* with *tsukumo* indicating the number ninety-nine and *gami (kami)* denoting hair; the phrase can refer to the white hair of an old woman and, by extension, old age. The premise is that, when any normal entity—a person, animal, or object—exists for long enough, a spirit takes up residence within the form. Once more, transformation is critical here, particularly evident in household objects that do not simply alter their appearance but metamorphose from inanimate inorganic objects to animate living organisms. Yōkai-ified objects were particularly copious from the Kamakura period through the Muromachi, appearing in collections of *setsuwa* (short narrative) tales and a number of illustrated formats.[15]

The most famous visual representation of tsukumogami is the picture scroll known as the *Hyakkiyagyō emaki,* which comically portrays human-made objects—musical instruments, umbrellas, cooking utensils—as living things, with arms and legs, marching across the page. To be more precise, there are several related sixteenth-century versions of the picture scroll, all of which feature a similar parade of fantastic creatures and animated objects. These illustrations are infused with a sense of playfulness that turns out to be a critical, if unexpected, element of the yōkai image. Indeed, such lighthearted renditions of yōkai flourished during the Edo period and even into early Meiji, most famously in the work of the brilliant artist Kawanabe Kyōsai (1831–1889). As revealed by the various sixteenth-century picture scrolls, as well as later versions by Kyōsai and others, tension between the fearful and the comic, the repulsive and the appealing, has always influenced the construction of yōkai. The *Hyakkiyagyō emaki* might be interpreted as secular and lighthearted equivalents of Heian-period "hell screens," in which the demonic inhabitants and torments of hell are often portrayed with frightful seriousness. The characters of the *Hyakkiyagyō emaki,* on the contrary, are depicted with playfulness and wit, their purpose seemingly not to frighten or warn but to entertain.[16]

PANDEMONIUM AND PARADE

My comments here on pre-Edo-period yōkai are intended only to highlight the complexities of these constantly shifting conceptions, none of which are monolithic: at each moment in history, the construction of yōkai was shaped by specific religious, artistic, intellectual, and political contexts. The notion of the hyakkiyagyō, however, provides a metaphor that transcends historical contexts and serves as a useful optic through which to interpret many of the discourses encountered in this book. Hyakkiyagyō (alternatively pronounced "hyakkiyakō") literally means "night procession of one hundred demons."[17] In addition to its use in *Hyakkiyagyō emaki,* the term is found in medieval texts, including *Ōkagami* (Great Mirror; c. 1119), *Konjaku monogatari shū* (Tales of Times Now Past; early twelfth century), and *Uji shūi monogatari* (Collection of Tales from Uji; early thirteenth century), where it refers to a procession of demons passing through the capital at night. It was advisable to avoid venturing out on evenings when the hyakkiyagyō was known to be on the move. Such times and places represented danger: they were forbidden, unpredictable, beyond the control of humans or culture.

The hyakkiyagyō was a temporary but terrifying irruption of an otherworld into the present one, something that could not or *must not* be seen—in some cases, simply gazing upon the phenomenon could cause one's death. Though not a strictly accurate translation, one English rendering of *hyakkiyagyō* might be "pandemonium"—that is, a state of all or many (= pan) demons. *Pandemonium* was originally employed by Milton in reference to the capital of hell, but on a more terrestrial level it has of course come to refer to a condition of riotous disturbance, chaos, and danger: exactly what one would encounter on a hyakkiyagyō night in Kyoto.[18]

The visual taboo associated with the hyakkiyagyō is particularly significant in discourses on yōkai: there is an important relationship between that which *cannot* be seen (because it is invisible, indescribable, or numinous) and that which *must not* be seen (because it is terrible to look upon, frightening, or dangerous). The demonic pandemonium of hyakkiyagyō cannot be subjected to the human gaze, indeed converts the gaze into a danger to the observer. Ironically, through expressions such as the comical *Hyakkiyagyō emaki*, an inversion occurs, and that which should not be gazed upon is rendered visible—and gazed upon with pleasure. The unseen (unseeable) is transformed into spectacle; the mysterious spirits of untamed nature are transmuted into familiar everyday objects; terror turns into humor; pandemonium becomes parade. This movement—between a frightening, chaotic pandemonium and a lighthearted, well-ordered parade—provides a central metaphor for this study. My point is not that there is a single, irreversible change from one to the other at a particular time but that the constant lively movement between these two positions occurs in different ways during each of the historical periods I discuss.

TAXONOMIES OF FEAR AND TERATOLOGIES OF PLEASURE

Another overarching theme expressed differently during each period is the "disciplining" of yōkai. Since at least the seventeenth century, efforts have been made to define, describe, name, and categorize these creatures. In his classic preface to *The Order of Things*, Michel Foucault comments on Jorge Luis Borges's "certain Chinese encyclopedia" that divides animals into seemingly arbitrary categories, such as "embalmed," "tame," "innumerable," or "having just broken the water pitcher." This incomprehensible way of ordering, Foucault says, demonstrates "the exotic charm of another system of thought" and "the limitation of our own." While heralding the "wonderment of this taxonomy," however, he also notes that the encyclopedia "distinguishes carefully between the very real animals . . . and those that reside solely in the imagination," putting "them into categories of their own" ("sirens," "fabulous"), a move that "localizes their powers of contagion."[19]

In the various classification systems designed to order yōkai, we often do find them gathered into such categories: designations that always already presume a set of normative boundaries—real and imagined, truth and fiction—and a cultural imaginary in which such distinctions have meaning. But there are also spaces in the discourse of yōkai of mutual contagion, moments during which such boundaries are not so clearly distinguished and the division between fantastic and real is not recognizable (or desirable) as a marker of difference. In fact, the eventual creation of a separate category for yōkai marks a significant epistemological shift.

Whether they are mixed together with other "animals" or put in a private taxonomy of their own, the attempt to find a place for yōkai is an eerily consistent theme throughout yōkai discourse. Ordering a subject this elusive provides a profound challenge for the taxonomical impulse: to systematize and make comprehensible something that, almost by definition, cannot be captured. It represents a drive to render structure from chaos, to discipline the pandemonium and transform it into parade. In eighteenth- and nineteenth-century Europe, as Harriet Ritvo points out, "monsters in the aggregate inevitably resisted definitive systematic integration, no matter how earnestly attempted. Capacious, motley, irredeemably vernacular, the category 'monster' proved invulnerable to expert analysis."[20] As with the modern case of the tsuchinoko, however, often the very resistance of yōkai to classification makes efforts to organize and define them all the more robust—on both an earnestly scientific level and a more playful or commercial one. In some cases yōkai were an indigenous part of existing (or developing) classificatory systems, and in other cases they were set apart in their own distinct teratologies, but efforts to establish taxonomies were made during each period I investigate in the chapters that follow. Not surprisingly, the form of the taxonomy and the principles of classification reflect the sociohistorical context of the moment.

Scholars commonly stress the role of fear in the understanding of yōkai. Komatsu Kazuhiko, for example, notes concisely, "Transcendent phenomena/presences associated with fear—these are 'yōkai.'"[21] Accordingly the classificatory impulse of each historical period may well be associated with fear and the desire (or necessity) to fashion from a perilous landscape something concrete, a way of speaking of the dangers of an unknown environment. The birth of yōkai is the birth of a particular kind of language with a grammar and vocabulary for articulating a basic human emotion.

Geographer Yi-Fu Tuan describes fear as "a complex feeling of which two strains, alarm and anxiety, are clearly distinguishable. Alarm is triggered by an obtrusive event in the environment, and an animal's instinctive response is to combat it or run. Anxiety, on the other hand, is a diffuse sense of dread and presupposes an ability to anticipate."[22] Akin to this notion of anxiety, the unseen pandemonium of the Heian-period hyakkiyagyō inspires an amorphous, unarticulated apprehension of what might be lurking out there in the darkness. The naming of yōkai identifies the threat, specifying the nature of the danger, shining a light on the "obtrusive event." The "diffuse sense of dread" is sharpened into a focused alarm, and the individual can react appropriately. Whether this reaction is fight or flight—or some third possibility—at least the power to respond, the agency to determine one's own fate, returns to the subject. As a mechanism for contending with the unknown and its potential dangers, the concretization of fear into the icon of an individual yōkai is a satisfying way of contending with chaos. Accordingly, it is not surprising that yōkai taxonomies often include an inventory of the characteristics for each yōkai in question, an enumeration of just what sort of threat one is facing.[23]

In one sense, then, the creation of yōkai is actually a *rational* process. The translation of vague unreasoned fears into carefully individuated monsters reveals an imaginative form of ratiocination, a process similar to the production of metaphor. Indeed, the particular form assumed by a yōkai may be considered a "conceptual metaphor," a culturally and historically specific embodiment of a vague sense of fear.[24] Isolating and ordering these metaphors makes them less frightening: they can be put in their place. Not surprisingly, in contemporary Japan the question *What are yōkai?* often elicits not a definition but a list of examples. And ultimately, a list may be the only possible answer: the meaning of yōkai, their very existence, comes only with naming, listing, and organizing and the implicit interpretation such practices demand. With the movement from pandemonium to parade, these alarming monsters sculpted out of the anxiety of darkness take on distinct characteristics and a life of their own.

Nor is the articulation of their manifold forms confined to philosophical or scientific attempts at taxonomy. Popular art, games, and other playful cultural practices are similar to formal academic typologies in their methods of disciplining yōkai, revealing a profound link between fear and fun, horror and humor. As with the comical creatures of the *Hyakkiyagyō emaki,* frightening yōkai can become characters of mirth and entertainment: that which cannot be gazed upon is readily transformed into spectacle. A yōkai may signify something wild and frightening, but removed from its natural environment, it becomes sanitized and safe enough to be handled by children. Such different conceptions, however, are never mutually exclusive: the same yōkai can exist simultaneously as both a serious danger and a plaything, as an object of fear and an object of amusement. Belief and the toying with (and commodification of) belief are rarely far apart.

THE AMBIGUITY OF BELIEF

Accordingly, questions of belief implicitly inform yōkai discourse. It has been noted that anthropologists have often tended to take beliefs at face value and have "talked about them as if their elucidation were less problematical than the interpretations to be put on their contents."[25] In the examination of the beliefs of another culture or another time, an appreciation of the quality of those beliefs—their complexities, nuances, and inconsistencies—is too easily sacrificed for a holistic system or a satisfying narrative. From the outset, then, I note a profound ambiguity with regard to the ontological status of yōkai. During the Edo period, for example, when the existence of a traditional creature might be authenticated by an encyclopedia, new yōkai were simultaneously being invented, played with, and to some extent, believed in. With the advent of Meiji, belief in yōkai was explicitly criticized, but even a rationalist like Inoue Enryō recognized the possibility of what he called a "degree of belief" within the observer.[26] Even in the early twenty-first century, when "traditional" yōkai may have all but dropped out of the discourse of belief per se, new yōkai emerge to take their place and adopt many of their characteristics. At any given time, then, belief in yōkai is never a simple matter of yes or no but an unstable variable contingent on many other variables.

Even within the individual subject, belief is often ambiguously figured. The idea of "in-between believing" has recently been taken up by philosophers of mind like Eric Schwitzgebel, who makes "the case that philosophers and cognitive scientists interested in belief would profit greatly from an account of belief that allows us to talk intelligently about such in-between states of believing."[27] In twenty-first-century American culture, we can clearly observe in-betweenness in the way, for example, the question of whether one believes in ghosts or UFOs or Bigfoot often elicits an answer more complex than a simple affirmative or negative. A person may refuse to profess certainty about something but also refuse to deny its possibility. Scientific data may be invoked to "prove" certain things are real. Alternatively, students of cryptozoology, who seek "cryptids" or "hidden animals" (e.g., Sasquatch and Nessie), often consider anecdotal and legendary accounts as seriously as scientific findings.[28] Technology and superstition are not mutually exclusive: even today, many American airports avoid the number thirteen when labeling their gates. And in contemporary Japan too, it is certainly not just the devoutly religious or "superstitious" who select paper fortunes *(omikuji)* at shrines and temples on New Year's Day or avoid the number four because of its homonymic association with death.

I am interested not so much in stressing the persistence into the present of nonevidentiary beliefs—though this too is important—but rather in calling attention to the essential ambiguity of belief in yōkai.[29] In many cases, these creatures survive in the cultural imagination because of their very ability to pivot easily between the credible and the incredible. At times their existence is accepted unquestioningly, and at times it is denied avidly, but in most cases it is within the ambiguous ontological space between these two extremes that yōkai thrive. As scholars of the cognitive processes of belief have noted:

> In the competition among ideas for a place, so to speak, in the human mind, those ideas that strike an optimal cognitive balance between the intuitive and the counterintuitive are most likely to be given attention, to be remembered, and to be passed on to succeeding generations. Gods, spirits, and ghosts, for instance, are often depicted as anthropomorphic in various ways, and their conformance to our expectations respecting human capacities, purposes, and behavior renders them plausible. But it is the counterintuitive capacities and qualities assigned to them—their invisibility, their ability to pass through material barriers, and so forth—that render them memorable.[30]

Again, I would emphasize the *instability of the thing* as a defining characteristic, or at least a defining orientation, of yōkai. Flirting with both the "intuitive and the counterintuitive," yōkai allow room for doubt. In fact, both of the graphs that signify yōkai, 妖 and 怪, carry the meaning of "suspicious" or "doubtful."

But concomitant to the notion that something is doubtful or suspicious is a sense of possibility. While the semantic doubling of graphs denoting "doubt" or "suspicion" doubly emphasizes their meaning, perhaps it also inversely casts doubt and suspicion on the very certainty of doubt and suspicion. That is, the word *yōkai* can also be read as a sign indicating an instability of the "real," therefore invoking a sense of possibility; rather than fostering skepticism and disbelief, the word suggests a realm in which the imagination and the metaphors it creates are given some freedom. Certainly the world of play—the late-night telling of ghost tales, divination games played in a geisha house, the reading of spooky manga—allows this imagination to enchant the everyday landscape.

Often yōkai function through the ironic imagination, a concept that helps us think about, for example, the fact that enthusiasts of Sherlock Holmes are aware of his fictionality but persist in treating him as a real person—even to the point of publishing biographies. "Modern enchantments," the cultural historian Michael Saler explains, "are enjoyed as constructs in which one can become immersed but not submerged. Rationalist skepticism is held in abeyance, yet complete belief is undercut by an ironic awareness that one is holding skepticism at bay."[31] In contrast to naive imagination, ironic imagination describes a phenomenon associated with modernity; indeed, this is when it is most striking, when rationality and skepticism provide stark contrasts to "naive" beliefs in the "irrational."

At its most essential level, however, the ironic imagination also reflects the capacity of the human mind to simultaneously negotiate two (or more) different landscapes, the very mechanism that allows us to speak of any fictional character as if he or she is a living person with real-world agency. While notions of cognitive dissonance preclude the possibility of simultaneously embracing two contradictory points of view, we can also imagine cognitive resonance, whereby seemingly irreconcilable beliefs do not cancel each other out but actually prove to be, if not quite harmonious, at least productively resonant with each other. In the case of yōkai, such cognitive resonance allows belief and doubt, two sides of the yōkai coin, to happily cohabit the same space. It is no coincidence that a phrase arising frequently in yōkai discourse, *hanshin-hangi,* means exactly this: "half belief, half doubt." Not surprisingly, belief and doubt play out differently during the different periods I discuss. In a general sense, there may be movement from the naive to the ironic imagination, but the positivism of modernity does not always preclude the naive—some modern intellectuals express as much naive belief with regard to science as the people they are "educating" do with regard to yōkai.

Since the Edo period, yōkai have for the most part been treated as somehow distinct from—though related to—more sacred manifestations of belief known as *kami*. During the Tokugawa period, when popular kami, such as the seven deities known as Shichifukujin, the comically rendered Daruma, and the fox-related Inari, gathered cult followings, they were generally treated as something different from yōkai. To be sure, the distinction between yōkai and kami is a fuzzy one at best. A water spirit, for instance, may be simultaneously worshipped as a kami by families for whom the river provides ample irrigation and feared as a yōkai by families downriver who experience drought. As we will see, Yanagita Kunio famously characterizes yōkai as "fallen" kami.[32] And much more recently, Komatsu Kazuhiko has suggested that worship by humans may be the defining characteristic of the yōkai-kami distinction: yōkai are unworshipped *(matsurareteinai)* kami, and kami are worshipped *(matsurareteiru)* yōkai.[33] Not only do we find once more a continuum between the undisciplined pandemonic world of yōkai and the (somewhat) more ordered pantheon of the kami, but we also find that human mediation determines the identity of the supernatural entity in question.

Moreover, tempting as it is to categorize yōkai (like Western "monsters") as perpetrators of evil, in this regard too they are ambiguous. Certainly many yōkai are mischievous and even murderous, but at least since the Edo period, bad behavior does not seem to be a defining characteristic. The example of the yōkai/kami water spirit is instructive: in the zero-sum game of human survival, an act that benefits one person may very well hurt another. Yōkai defy definitive categorization—they are ambiguously positioned beyond (or between) good and evil.[34]

THE NATURE OF THE SUPERNATURAL AND THE AFFECT OF MYSTERY

As so much of the discourse on yōkai is bound up with the desire to articulate the inexpressible, it is important to clarify two of the English words that inevitably appear in the chapters that follow: *supernatural* and *mysterious*. *Supernatural* implies a dichotomy between the *natural* and something that somehow transcends nature; the premise for the supernatural is that there must be rules of nature against which its transcendent qualities can be evaluated. The limits of such categories, however, can be evaluated only through a cultural-historical lens. To most readers of this book, for example, it will seem "natural" for a creature such as a fox to be treated as an empirically viable entity—diagrammed by natural historians, described by biologists, listed in encyclopedias. But what of an encyclopedic entry that, along with a description of the fox's habitat and diet, also alludes to its propensity for bewitching people? Can some characteristics be considered natural and others supernatural? How do we express such things without imposing our own cultural and scientific classifications on people of another time and place?

To a certain extent such questions are moot. During the Meiji period, modern Western categories and scientific modes *were* imposed on native yōkai, and a natural-versus-supernatural dichotomy arose within hegemonic discourses. But during the Edo period, the division was less clear-cut. Durkheim notes that the supernatural refers to "all sorts of things which surpass the limits of our knowledge; the supernatural is the world of the mysterious, of the unknowable, of the un-understandable."[35] Though we may be able to ascertain what surpasses the limits of our own knowledge, it is much harder to determine the limits of others' knowledge: what is mysterious to *us* may be very well explained by *them*. Even so, during each period we do find things considered supernatural, mysterious, unknowable, or un-understandable by the people writing about them at the time. Within any given situation, it seems, there is a sense of what is considered standard and what is not. The transcendence of the everyday is critical here: rather than *supernatural,* perhaps a more appropriate, though awkward, coinage would be *supernormal.* Whether manifest as an unexplainable experience or the appearance of a monster, a breach occurs in the predictable everyday fabric of life: something happens that is beyond normal—and therefore worth remarking upon.

Or perhaps we can also think of the supernatural not so much as surpassing the natural but as having an excess of the natural—that is, too many or seemingly inappropriate natural characteristics bound incongruously into a single body. Corporeal context is important. Processes such as transformation certainly occur in nature (among amphibians and insects, for example), but when they appear in surprising proportions or in the "wrong" place (as when a fox transforms its shape), they become supernatural. By thinking of the supernatural as a weird convergence of natural elements in one form, we can at least make more complex the problematic dichotomy of natural versus supernatural. But however we define *supernatural,* the point is that, for any given historical period, a creature or phenomenon may be within the bounds of the "natural" but still be *out of the ordinary.*[36]

The Japanese equivalent of *supernatural, chōshizenteki,* is not common in discourse on yōkai. However, another word I use throughout this study, *mysterious,* has an equivalent that appears frequently even in Edo-period texts: *fushigi,* or *fukashigi.* On one level, *fushigi,* and by extension, *mysterious,* refers simply to the unexplainable. But its meaning with regard to yōkai is deeper than this—for there are many things beyond explanation for the average person that are not considered mysterious. The computer on which I am writing, for example, easily confounds my own powers of explanation. Even the basics of electricity—introduced for household use in urban centers (in Japan as well as the West) over a century ago—are outside the "limits of knowledge" for most nonspecialists. In one sense these are indeed mysterious things—but only when we wonder about them. And that is the important word here, *wonder,* for the notion of the mysterious is also bound up with a sense of wonder and awe.

Indeed, creatively translated, *fushigi* might be rendered as "that which cannot be grasped in thought." Mystery is the hollow core, the originary absence, the "thing" always just out of reach, always deferred. The distinct yōkai that emerge at different times are signs of this deference, metaphors for the impossibility of knowing. This is not to say that the excitement of mystery cannot be calmed; when mystery becomes commonplace and familiar, the wonder wears off and thaumaturgy transforms into the quotidian. As Stephen Greenblatt has noted, "The very words *marvel* and *wonder* shift between the designation of a material object and the designation of a response to the object, between intense, almost phantasmagorical inward states and thoroughly externalized objects that can, after the initial moments of astonishment have passed, be touched, catalogued, inventoried, and possessed."[37] Electricity was a wondrous, marvelous, and mysterious thing when it first appeared. But as it came to be part of the everyday landscape of modernity, it shed its aura of mystery and wonder. Mystery, then, is not a state of being: it is a quest, yearning, desire, affect.

UNCANNY, FANTASTIC, MONSTROUS

Since at least the Meiji period, research on yōkai has been a presence—albeit a spectral one—in anthropological, folkloric, scientific, literary, and religious writings in Japan. This scholarship has been all but overlooked in the growing discussion on the monstrous and the supernatural in the West. One purpose of this book is to contribute to the broader theoretical work on these issues by introducing Japanese scholarship into an English-language context. At the same time, however, I acknowledge that the meanings of yōkai in Japan and similar creatures elsewhere are always also bound to specific geographical, historical, and social contexts; any monolithic theoretical construct is destined to be as elusive as the monsters it seeks to capture.

Much Western discourse on supernatural themes in literature and film derives from Freud's seminal 1919 essay "The 'Uncanny.'" The word *uncanny* is a translation of the German *unheimlich*, described by Freud as "that class of the frightening which leads back to what is known of old and long familiar."[38] Linguistically, Freud explains, the two seeming opposites, *unheimlich* (unhomelike) and *heimlich* (homelike), develop toward each other until their meanings coincide. *Heimlich* refers to something of the home, "something concealed; secret" and therefore repressed (200). The uncanny, the *unheimlich,* refers to an experience that causes the return of this repressed, private, homelike something.

Freud teases out two related sources of uncanny experience: "either when infantile complexes which have been repressed are once more revived by some impression, or when primitive beliefs which have been surmounted seem once more to be confirmed" (226). This connection between the revival of the repressed and the reconfirmation of the surmounted creates an implicit correspondence between the development of the individual subject and the development of civilization. The second thread, in which ostensibly surmounted "primitive beliefs" are reconfirmed, often hinges on a sense of occult causality. Speaking of the recurrence over and over of a particular number, for example, Freud says, "Unless a man is utterly hardened and proof against the lure of superstition, he will be tempted to ascribe a secret meaning to this obstinate recurrence of a number" (214). Such superstitious thinking harks "back to the old, animistic conception of the universe. This was characterized by the idea that the world was peopled with the spirits of human beings; by the subject's narcissistic overevaluation of his own mental processes; by the belief in the omnipotence of thoughts and the technique of magic based on that belief; by the attribution to various outside persons and things of carefully graded magic powers." Just as humanity has evolved through this "animistic" stage, so too has the individual. But it seems "that none of us has passed through it without preserving residues and traces of it which are still capable of manifesting themselves, and that everything which now strikes us as 'uncanny' fulfils the condition of touching those residues of animistic mental activity within us and bringing them to expression" (216–17).

Freud's thesis has been remarkably influential among theorists of fantastic literature and the cinema of horror.[39] To a certain degree, my own discussion is implicitly informed by Freud's formulation—particularly in chapter 4, where I treat early-twentieth-century literary fiction and folkloric discourse. But Freud's easy application to this period is no coincidence: his own essay was written in the second decade of the twentieth century and must also be considered within the historical context of its production. His notion of human progress along a vector from the "primitive" to the "civilized" clearly reflects the dominant European discourse of the time, from social Darwinism to the ethnographic theories of Edward B. Tylor and James Frazer. The uncanny reconfirmation of the surmounted can be likened to the concept of a survival, a remnant of "primitive" times embedded in a more "mature" culture, or more mature psyche. Freud's teleological perspective is also remarkably similar to that of Yanagita Kunio and other early-twentieth-century Japanese thinkers who developed analogous evolutionary notions of civilization. My point is that Freud's is a theory of the *modern* uncanny; with respect to the conception of yōkai in the early twentieth century, it provides a valuable framework—but one that does not necessarily obtain at other times.[40]

Classic works on the fantastic, such as those by Tzvetan Todorov and Rosemary Jackson, are similarly only of limited use for theorizing yōkai.[41] Todorov, for example, posits the literary fantastic as that which causes a hesitation in the reader as he or she decides what to make of an occurrence in the text that does not seem natural, real, or plausible: "The fantastic occupies the duration of this uncertainty. . . . The fantastic is that hesitation experienced by a person who knows only the laws of nature, confronting an apparently supernatural event."[42] If the event turns out to be truly beyond the purview of explanation, then it falls under the rubric of the "marvelous." If it is ultimately explainable within the known laws of nature, then it is situated in the adjacent category of the "uncanny" (not identical to Freud's uncanny). We must remember that Todorov is interested in literary manifestations of the fantastic, in which the reader is assumed to express a drive to explain the mysterious event in question. Though we can see the development of this desire for explanation during the early Meiji period, it is ultimately predicated on a strict division between the supernatural and the natural, a division not always so clear in premodern or postmodern times.[43] Furthermore, in the case of yōkai, even when the drive to explain is strongly expressed in elite or academic discourse, it is not necessarily evident in common practice. The experience of "uncertainty" that Todorov posits may not demand a resolution; rather this uncertainty, the tension inspired by the ambiguous body, is often the very thing that animates yōkai.

Recently, a growing body of literature on horror films, with their paradoxical admixture of attraction and repulsion, has supplemented the discourse on the uncanny and the fantastic. Here again, as Andrew Tudor has pointed out, "by far the most common accounts of the appeal of horror are grounded in concepts drawn from Freudian theory."[44] James Twitchell, for example, complicates Freudian psychoanalytic models with a focus on the rite-of-passage function of the modern horror film, especially with respect to adolescent sexuality. Robin Wood posits a notion of "surplus repression" varying in type from culture to culture but resulting in the "projection onto the Other of what is repressed within the Self, in order that it can be discredited, disowned and if possible annihilated." Barbara Creed's work on the "monstrous-feminine" incorporates psychoanalytic theory (influenced by Lacan and Kristeva) into the analysis of gender in the horror genre; and Carol Clover's writing on slasher films highlights the critical relationship of horror, gender, and the gaze.[45] While the work of such theorists is invaluable for opening up discussions of horror as a genre of film (and human experience), such interpretations often tend toward a construction of the fearful and mysterious that does not do justice to the radical diversity of culture and moment. Tudor, for one, argues for particularity, concluding that the question we should be asking is not "Why horror?" but rather "Why do *these* people like horror in *this* place at *this* particular time?"[46]

Such a question, of course, also applies to yōkai: even if psychoanalytic conceptions of horror, the uncanny, and the fantastic resonate during the historical moment we call modernity (as I think they do), what exactly were the yōkai of the premodern period? In Todorov's framework, for example, mono-no-ke and hyakkiyagyō would be labeled "marvelous," a state of "the supernatural accepted."[47] Ultimately, whether accepted or rejected, the supernatural is understood within a specific historical construct (what was natural then may be supernatural now—and vice versa). The Heian period had its own laws governing the mysterious, laws that were complex and rigidly followed, but that allowed for Freud's "omnipotence of thoughts": the supernatural was factored into the structure of the natural. And yet even the fact that yōkai were accounted for—and there were institutionalized rituals to deal with their intrusion—does not lessen their supernormality and the sense of mystery and fear they were able to engender.

Similarly, modern science, industrialization, urbanization, and even psychoanalysis have not succeeded in banishing yōkai from the landscape. In the early twentieth-first century, not only do new uncanny and frightening phenomena continue to emerge, but there is also a resurgence of the yōkai of previous generations, now capable of provoking a powerful sense of nostalgia. Clearly one reason for the persistence of yōkai is their protean nature as cultural forms whose meanings can be adapted to succeeding historical contexts. In dealing with such constantly changing phenomena, then, how can we determine that they remain the same "thing"? What, if anything, unifies the conception of something called yōkai across historical periods? It is not just my own designation that identifies the concept: since at least the late Edo period, a notion of the "weird and mysterious" as a separate ontological category, like the categories Foucault alludes to in Borges's Chinese encyclopedia, was part of the cultural imaginary. In contemporary discourse all of these phenomena and characters are generally categorized together and treated academically by scholars of folklore, literature, history, anthropology, art, and film under the rubric of a new yōkaigaku, or more vaguely, *yōkai no kenkyū* (yōkai research).

As will become evident in the chapters that follow, despite all attempts to sort out its meaning the concept of yōkai remains vexingly diffuse. On one end of the spectrum we find phenomenal occurrences *(koto)*, strange events such as eerie sounds in a house at night or stars visible in the midday sky. At the other end are the somatic yōkai: material things *(mono)*, anomalous animal bodies, such as the tsuchinoko or the slimy green *kappa* water goblin sometimes still displayed in mummified form. Again and again there is creative tension between the mysterious occurrence and its fleshing out in the form of a weird body. This continuum between phenomenon and thing is also a movement from invisible to visible, spiritual to material, vague to specific: dynamics that coincide with the metaphor of pandemonium and parade. The energy between these two extremes, like an electric charge rippling between positive and negative poles, vivifies the yōkai concept. Even within a single yōkai, such as the fox, we find both these notions simultaneously manifest: the "real" physical body of the fox can be captured (in fact or in illustration), while the invisible spirit of the fox can bring about misfortune for a community or possess the body of a human. Likewise, both concepts are embodied in the notion of *yūrei*, or "ghost," its just barely visible, but ultimately untouchable, material substance fading into absent spiritual presence.

OTHER MONSTERS

This inclusive discourse on yōkai differs from many Western theoretical considerations of the "supernatural" and the "monstrous," in which there is often an implicit distinction between spiritual and material presences. In grappling with these issues, and seeking a transculturally useful way to discuss the continuum between "gods" and "spirits," anthropologists Robert I. Levy, Jeanette Marie Mageo, and Alan Howard suggest *numinal* to signify "spiritual beings." But they concede that "there are also many strange beings—giants, gnomes, fairies, phoenixes and the like—that fit uneasily into such a continuum because they have qualities we associate with neither gods nor spirits. They are on the fringes of the ordinary, at the outer edges of the uncanny zone, but unlike strange animals such as the orangutan cannot be captured, caged, and made, after a fashion, banal."[48] The concept of yōkai includes not only the "numinal" but also the other "strange beings."

As for these strange, nonnuminal creatures themselves, in recent years a growing body of literature has labeled them "monsters" and positioned them as corporeal manifestations of Otherness. They are the denizens of a so-called Goblin Universe, animals on the verge of possibility that taunt would-be discoverers with their repeated appearance in legend and anecdote.[49] If such creatures prove real, as did the platypus for European naturalists, they can lay bare the very foundations of established taxonomic systems. Not only do these monsters represent the potential to confuse standard zoological categories, but their very elusiveness—like that of the tsuchinoko—transforms them into objects of desire.[50]

One common approach operates from the premise that monsters are, as one scholar puts it, "supernatural, mythical, or magical products of the imagination." As such, monsters (or the people who tell of them) are ideal subjects for psychoanalysis, which "furnishes us with useful models of sublimation, projection, and displacement as tools for approaching the construction of monstrous images from human experiences."[51] Another monograph concludes that monsters "are images of the archetype of fear that lies deep in the unconscious" and symbolize "the struggle that confronts the psyche as it emerges segmented into consciousness, split down the middle by the contradictory endowments of its evolutionary history."[52] While such approaches may be thought-provoking, they are inevitably based on subjective (cultural and temporal) assumptions of real versus imaginary, assumptions that monsters are objects of fantasy rather than embodiments of (ambiguous) belief, which effectively excludes so many of the manifestations that fall under the rubric of yōkai.

Another common approach to the monster problem focuses on anomalous creatures as deformations or "monstrous" births. Monsters are not simply products of the imagination but are cultural constructions of the threatening Other that may, inexplicably and with no warning, appear in our midst. Conjoined twins, hermaphrodites, bearded women, two-headed sheep, and other "freakish" bodies challenge traditional categories not just within scientific taxonomies but also with respect to the basic moral and political structures of society. They blur genders, distort distinctions between "races," between animal and human, and even confound traditional understandings of personhood and individuality. The monster is the grotesque Other to be kept out of sight, the abject body through which difference is made manifest. By disrupting complaisant binaries, providing the unthought-of third possibility or excluded middle, monsters unearth the often disquieting ideologies at the foundations of social and cultural life.[53]

As transgressor of categories, questioner of values, turner-inside-out of standard assumptions, the monster—whether "real" or "imagined"—is a potent and persistent icon. Bakhtin's carnival provides a powerful lens through which such monsters can be understood: "a world of topsy-turvy, or heteroglot exuberance, of ceaseless overrunning and excess where all is mixed, hybrid, ritually degraded and defiled."[54] In the discourse of the Japanese otherworld, yōkai occupy this alternate space, the number one hundred, or *hyaku* (as in *hyak*kiyagyō), signifying their "heteroglot exuberance," the overflowing of their sheer numbers as they burst into the everyday world with a multiplicity of forms and polyphony of voices. Monstrous irruptions provide constant reminders of the instability of appearances and the arbitrariness of categories: they throw the parade of daily existence, with its hierarchies and ordered procedures, into a state of pandemonium.

YŌKAI AS OXYMORON

Monsters are never made from scratch. Assembled from the parts of other creatures, fastened together to fashion an original whole, a monster is a hybrid. But the monster is not constructed of just any mixture of features: rather, it is an oxymoron. The combination seems to be one thing but has a twist to make it another—yet it is not quite that thing either. Nor is it composed exactly of opposites: "Whereas the antithetical contradiction is unsurmountable tension," notes Michel de Certeau, the oxymoron has "the value of fullness." Building on de Certeau's ruminations on the oxymoron as a figure of speech, I suggest that the oxymoron as monstrous figure also stands for something beyond the combination of its parts, something that disregards the obvious, challenges simple description, and calls attention to its own weirdness. An oxymoron "is deictic," de Certeau says: "the combination of the two terms is substituted for the existence of a third, which is posited as absent. It makes a hole in language."[55] But the monster as oxymoron is often made up of the parts of more than two originals. It has numerous elements that complement and contradict simultaneously, so that its meaning comes not just from the pieces that have been combined to create it but also from the complement and contradiction of those pieces.

Similarly, the monster functions in discourse and practice as a sort of pun, like a play on words, speaking with a forked tongue so that the utterance always means one thing and simultaneously means something else. As pun, the monster is at once corporeal body and ethereal metaphor, concrete and abstract. The hole in language it makes is more accurately a kind of a trapdoor, an apparently solid surface that suddenly opens to reveal an army of dangers lying beneath. Through repeated usage, oxymoron or pun may fade into cliché, shedding its transgressive, category-confounding nature to take on a commonplace role with a stable function in the lexicon. In the same way, some "monsters"—such as the platypus—creatively shake up and remake the classificatory system, so that it makes room for them to settle in. But other monsters, because of their elusiveness, their refusal to be caught, never find their place: they remain forever outside existing categories, inhabiting a realm of persistent Otherness.

If a single notion can encapsulate the characteristics of the monsters I am speaking of, it is a sense of the *weird*. These oxymoronic creatures are askew. They have something missing or something extra; they stand out in a crowd and represent a crack in the veneer of the everyday—we are repulsed by their presence but stare nonetheless, fascinated, unable to look away. They are shape-shifting, unstable figures reflected in a warped mirror. The word *weird* not only invokes strangeness of form but is also bound up with the eerie and the supernatural—a related, though archaic, usage alludes to notions of destiny and fate. Historically, an unexplainable phenomenon or monstrous birth was often seen as an ominous portent.

Western discussion on the monster, as I have suggested, primarily concerns the tangible, bodily presence of the creature. In contrast, the yōkai represents an admixture of weird corporeality with something numinal or mysterious: yōkai bridge the intangible and tangible, spiritual and material, phenomenon and object. The mysterious is oriented toward what is beyond explanation, often beyond description: amorphous, confused, disturbing, or exciting, the pandemonium of the darkness with its uncontrollable, unseen forces. The weird is oriented toward the display of these things, the still unexplainable, but concrete, spectacles on parade. The mysterious generally has emotional impact, whether fear or wonder; the weird engenders a more intellectual response, expressed through curiosity, questioning, and categorizing. The invisible hyakkiyagyō of the Heian period were mysterious and frightening; their visible renderings—household items with arms and legs—were weird and comical. Again, these characterizations are nothing more than imagined ends of a spectrum, but if one were to define yōkai in some way that transcends the specific historical depictions in the chapters of this book, it would combine, oxymoronically, both the mysterious and the weird.

CHAPTERS, TROPES, AND SPECTERS OF NATION

Whether visible or invisible, yōkai always exist just outside the purview of history and, at the same time, reside at its very center. In different ways at different times, the *other* world of yōkai is instrumental in defining the *this* world of the Japanese nation. Yōkai are a constant absent presence in Japanese culture. Perhaps this is most apparent in the Meiji period, when belief in yōkai became the abject reminder (remainder) of prerationality to be sloughed off in the formation of a modern nation. But even during the early-modern Tokugawa period, the collection of disparate yōkai traditions from all over the Japanese archipelago contributed to a sense of shared heritage, a kind of national community imagined through a collective identity, of which yōkai were a defining element. We find here Benedict Anderson's notion of "homogeneous, empty time": yōkai are shared horizontally—differences between regions are documented, but they are documented as occurring simultaneously, within the same limited system of tradition.[56]

Perhaps even more striking than this synchronic otherworld of yōkai, however, is a diachronic continuum that creates through yōkai a historical continuity whereby a twenty-first-century viewer of yōkai films feels a sense of community, even simultaneity, with an eighteenth-century aficionado of yōkai line-drawings. This vertical, transtemporal dimension becomes a master yōkai narrative within which imagined communities made up of yōkai and yōkai practitioners (researchers, fans, collectors) also exist horizontally. Although it is tempting to suggest that both the vertical and horizontal axes of the yōkai otherworld might tell stories counter to the dominant narrative of Japanese (human) history, in most cases this otherworld is incorporated into (or co-opted by) the this-worldly structure it has the potential to critique—it is no surprise perhaps that the most extensive yōkai database is managed by a government-sponsored research institution.

I underscore the theme of nation here because, in a sense, this book follows the development of a quasi-nationalist discourse in which yōkai play an intimate role. During each of the four historical moments discussed, the otherworld of yōkai is imbricated in the way nation is imagined—whether through the collection and consolidation of disparate traditions during the Edo period, the rejection of the supernatural during the Meiji period, the preservation of disappearing customs in the interwar years, or the nostalgic commodification of yōkai during the late twentieth century and early twenty-first century. My focus is not explicitly on the question of nation, but the narrative of yōkai supplements, as an absent presence, the hegemonic narrative of Japanese cultural history. Yōkai may be marginal figures, but "what is *socially* peripheral is so frequently *symbolically* central."[57] During each of the historical periods I address, yōkai are specters haunting the nation, surprisingly lively metaphors for comprehending broader national-cultural paradigms. Shifts in the conception and perception of yōkai are played out within and between these paradigms, bound up with the particular tone of the fears, desires, and pleasures of the moment. The landscape in which yōkai reside alters with each successive generation, but every new landscape provides fertile terrain for the weird and mysterious to develop its own affective, aesthetic role in the story of the Japanese nation.

Each of the four major chapters that follow is loosely structured around an appropriate trope through which the yōkai-related discourse of the moment might be most pertinently characterized. These tropes are nothing more than metaphorical frames with which to better conceptualize and situate the particular historical instance: they are "within the true" of the particular moment, the best language for expressing the meaning of yōkai during the period in question. These tropes, however, are never mutually exclusive: they are all linked to each other and can be found to a greater or lesser degree throughout the three centuries I consider. By labeling each chapter with a single trope, I intend simply to stress that a given discursive mode seems to be fresher and more expressive of the cultural milieu of the specific moment.

For chapter 2 the most appropriate trope is natural history. This can be seen in the encyclopedic mode that developed out of neo-Confucian ideology and a burgeoning interest in pharmacology, botany, and zoology. This chapter explores how the earliest illustrated encyclopedias in Japan presented and classified mysterious creatures. Such academic taxonomies combined with a more popular interest in the weird and mysterious manifest in recreational practices, such as the gathering of strangely shaped items and the storytelling sessions known as *hyaku-monogatari*. In the 1770s, the artist Toriyama Sekien (1712–1788) skillfully fused the seriousness of academic encyclopedias with the playfulness of popular comic verse and storytelling to visually document the creatures of the invisible world. Sekien's four yōkai catalogs profoundly influenced how people conceived of yōkai, representing not only a culmination of encyclopedic and ludic practices but also the moment "yōkai" became an autonomous category. Just as the early encyclopedias created a sense of national community, Sekien's bestiaries contributed to the establishment of an explicitly Japanese otherworldly landscape.

Chapter 3 too focuses on the intersection of academic discourses and popular recreational practices. In the early- to mid-Meiji period, however, science provides the most appropriate interpretive trope. At the end of the nineteenth century, the philosopher and educator Inoue Enryō (1858–1919) created the discipline of *yōkaigaku* with a specific objective: to rationally explain away supernatural beliefs so that Japan could become a modern nation-state competitive with the West. Enryō developed an analytical framework to categorize yōkai and to scientifically sort out "superstition" from what he defined as "true mystery." In particular, I consider Enryō's treatment of a popular game, known as Kokkuri, that invoked traditional yōkai to divine the future. Surprisingly, the game was not indigenous to Japan; based on séance practices developed as part of the Spiritualist movement in the West, it raises questions of how a *foreign* method for communicating with the otherworld became a *native* practice. While Enryō applied newly imported scientific knowledge to debunk the "mystic" qualities of Kokkuri, other authors applied the new mystery of electricity to banish the traditional yōkai, a strategy that allowed the game to be simultaneously modern *and* enchanted.

Chapter 4 examines how writers and scholars in the first half of the twentieth century challenged Enryō's rationalizing objectives and contended with questions of what place yōkai were to have in a modernizing Japan. Here the central metaphor is the museum, as yōkai came to be defined as relics from the past to be cherished and displayed in the present. Canonical writers Natsume Sōseki (1867–1916) and Mori Ōgai (1862–1922) grappled with issues of supernatural belief in their stories, seeing yōkai as historical constructions still relevant to creating a sense of self for the individual as well as the nation. Academically, Ema Tsutomu (1884–1979) made the first explicit attempt to document not yōkai themselves but the changing meaning of yōkai in Japanese cultural history. Yanagita Kunio (1875–1962) further developed this mode of consideration when he appropriated yōkai for the burgeoning discipline of folklore studies *(minzokugaku).* One of modern Japan's most influential thinkers, Yanagita did not debunk yōkai beliefs as superstitions but set out to collect and organize them, listing them by name, place, and characteristic—as in a museum. To Yanagita and his followers, the collecting of yōkai represented a formal appropriation of their value as cultural commodities evocative of an ideal past. While their classification was a way to demarcate an "authentic" Japan, it also configured yōkai as lifeless historical relics, empty shells from another time.

Chapter 5 focuses on yōkai in the 1970s and 1980s, after Japan's period of rapid economic growth, as people struggled to come to terms not only with new modes of wealth and commodification but also with the personal sacrifices necessary to achieve them. The trope for this period is the media, by which I denote not only the role of yōkai within forms of mass media—manga, television, movies, and popular magazines—but also the continued function of yōkai as a medium through which past and present, rural and urban, real and imaginary, are constantly negotiated. In particular, this chapter focuses on the manga artist Mizuki Shigeru (b. 1922), whose popular illustrations, both narrative and encyclopedic, revitalized the image of yōkai in the cultural imagination, explicitly linking the late twentieth century with the Edo period. I also explore the advent of a new yōkai, Kuchi-sake-onna, the protagonist of a popular 1979 urban legend about a female yōkai with a horribly slit mouth. While academic discourse attempted to classify this creature, attributing to her a long *premodern* lineage, in the popular imagination she became a ubiquitous media icon, expressing very real *modern* concerns about women's roles in a patriarchal society.

The journey from the early Edo period to the late twentieth century is complex and sinuous. Accordingly, this study is unusually broad in terms of chronology and context, exploring successive landscapes through both close readings and distant viewings. Drawing on a wide array of academic and popular texts, I seek to elucidate critical but subtle threads of human consciousness. And by concentrating on the very things considered weird and mysterious, I hope the history of sensitivities I chart will also shed light on what is considered normal and explainable. Perhaps the pandemonium-parade metaphor is appropriate here too, as the book selects from the pandemonium of ideas, practices, and texts and arranges them into a paradelike narrative. Although by definition the mysterious must always remain unknowable, I hope to make visible some of the weird shapes and metaphors through which we strive to grasp it.

From the outset, I must also note the paradox of such an undertaking. Though my goal is to elucidate consciousness(es) with regard to yōkai of different historical moments, I am inevitably guilty of a teleological fallacy, for I write from within the limited consciousness of my own moment, constrained by a this-worldly grammar and syntax that can never be equal to the task of articulating the nature of mystery. Yōkai are shapeshifters: the instant they are pinned down and labeled, they transform into something different. The impossibility of articulation, of retaining the thing and speaking of it too, remains the central conundrum of this study, as well as the reason for undertaking it. Happily, I take comfort in knowing that my own inexorable failure of expression succeeds in preserving the object of inquiry.

The tsuchinoko mentioned at the beginning of this introduction embodies qualities pertinent to all yōkai. It demonstrates the coalescence of legend and narrative with the search for artifact and object. It highlights a reliance on the science of the time in determining the "reality" of the mysterious body. And ultimately it exemplifies a persistence of ambiguity and a longing for the unknown. In the final analysis, it is not the desire for explanation but a desire for the thing beyond explanation that ties together the various notions of yōkai explored in the pages that follow.

CHAPTER 2

Natural History of the Weird

Encyclopedias, Spooky Stories, and the Bestiaries of Toriyama Sekien

Among the native animals are a number of chimera introduced from China which exist only in the minds and writings of the Japanese, but not in nature.

Engelbert Kaempfer

THE DISCIPLINE OF YŌKAI

In the darkness, something is watching. You hear breathing, feel something brush against your arm. Yōkai are a presence characterized by absence; the quest for yōkai is driven by a desire to make concrete this abstract, absent presence, to make visible this invisibility. But how is this done? How is discourse constructed around something shaped by its own elusiveness? One way people have strived to concretize yōkai is by labeling and categorizing them. If you browse the shelves of any large bookstore or library in Japan, you can find compendia of yōkai, lists of their habitats and proclivities, illustrated catalogs featuring a different monster on each page. Some of these books are tongue-in-cheek, and others are serious ethnographic, historical, or literary studies, but one common feature is a tendency to name, list, and order these weird and mysterious phenomena. This discursive genre, the yōkai catalog, is indicative of the movement from pandemonium to parade, the carving out from the undifferentiated mass of mysterious things a controlled and ordered pageant with identifiable, named characters.

The oldest of these catalogs is the *Gazu hyakkiyagyō* (Illustrated Hyakkiyagyō) series: four illustrated sets of books published between 1776 and 1784 by Toriyama Sekien (1712–1788) and collectively documenting more than two hundred yōkai. Sekien's texts represent a watershed in the history of yōkai discourse and exerted an influence that reached beyond their own moment of production and continues to resonate in present-day conceptions and images of yōkai. In order to better appreciate the significance of his work, however, it is critical to first carefully consider the earlier part of the Tokugawa period, for during this time a dynamic set of popular and academic attitudes developed that would eventually set the scene for Sekien's bestiaries.

During the seventeenth and eighteenth centuries, Japan witnessed the growth of natural-history studies and the development of an encyclopedic culture in which collecting, naming, and describing became critical methods for comprehending the world. By seeking yōkai in the pages of several encyclopedic texts from this time, we can trace the contours of a complex discursive history and eventually arrive at a moment when yōkai commandeered an encyclopedia of their own. It also becomes clear that the Tokugawa period experienced the florescence of a very different kind of sensibility: a culture that placed value on recreation and play. It is from the convergence of these two seemingly contradictory modes of discourse, the "encyclopedic" and the "ludic," that Sekien's catalogs eventually emerged as bestiaries celebrating a distinct category of Japanese yōkai.

THE ENCYCLOPEDIC MODE

Before coming to the specific place of yōkai in the early-modern imagination, it is important to establish the intellectual and popular context in which they would play a role. During the first half of the Edo period, this context was informed by an approach I call the encyclopedic mode. The word *mode* here is purposefully broad—akin to *consciousness* or *mentalité*—and indicates an approach that informs writing as well as ways of acting. As a discursive and practical method, the encyclopedic mode signifies the serious undertaking of collecting and codifying, of pinning things down and labeling them. It emphasizes the presentation of an inclusive collection of knowledge about a subject; the compression of this knowledge into compact, self-contained units; and the listing and organization of these units. As "items" of knowledge are compressed into smaller and smaller units, they come to have a certain degree of maneuverability: they can be shuffled and manipulated as separate entities by those who have mastered them. Another characteristic of the encyclopedic mode is that the knowledge it provides is generally perceived as having a certain utility within a given society.

In Tokugawa Japan, encyclopedic expression was part of a broader development of a vibrant commercial book industry influenced by numerous factors, including new methods of production, rising literacy rates, urban development, and the growth of a reading public.[1] The encyclopedic mode was also intimately connected with neo-Confucianism and state ideologies. In particular, a belief that all things were worth investigation promoted a desire to record and order the natural world, fostering the development of indigenous natural history studies and guidebooks accessible to people in different social strata. While its roots may be found in government-sanctioned philosophies and programs, encyclopedic discourse reflected and inspired a popular curiosity about the natural (and supernatural) world and quickly became an intrinsic part of the cultural imagination of the Tokugawa period.[2]

I should stress here that the actual encyclopedias and compendia discussed in the pages that follow are certainly not the only texts that reflect the encyclopedic mode in scale, objective, and style. Indeed, Mary Elizabeth Berry has applied the label "library of public information" to the "enormous spectrum" of almanacs, manuals, gazetteers, calendars, maps, directories, travel guides, and dictionaries produced at this time. Their "common purpose," she explains, was "to examine and order the verifiable facts of contemporary experience for an open audience of consumers."[3] Formal encyclopedias and works of natural history were just one small part of this profusion of texts, but they provide an excellent window through which to observe some of the epistemological and rhetorical changes of the period. By tracing the development of these encyclopedias, and the place of yōkai within them, we also get a sense of the way yōkai fit into intellectual categories as well as popular playful ones.

Of all the strains of Confucian thought that entered Japan during the Tokugawa period, the philosophy of Zhu Xi (1130–1200) had the greatest overall influence. *Shushigaku,* as Zhu Xi's philosophy was known in Japan, was avidly promulgated by scholars such as Hayashi Razan (1583–1657), who would come to wield great influence on Tokugawa Ieyasu (1542–1616). Maruyama Masao argues that as a political advisor Razan was intimately involved in the establishment of the *bakufu* (shogunate), and that his family would eventually come to be the "custodian of the official philosophy of the regime." Although more recent studies have raised pertinent questions about the extent of Razan's power within the Tokugawa ascendancy as well as the "official" hegemonic status of neo-Confucianism, it seems clear that, by the second half of the seventeenth century, Shushigaku was the preeminent philosophy of the realm.[4]

Shushigaku extolled rationality, order, and pragmatism—its reach extended from issues of practical political governance and human morality to metaphysics and the structure of the universe. A critical element of this philosophy was the encouragement of intellectual curiosity and the "investigation of things" *(kakubutsu chichi)*. In theory, all things in the universe were originally one, and therefore humans and nature had to obey the same laws.[5] Through the careful examination of all things, we can understand these laws, and order can be achieved both personally and politically.

This promotion of investigation and order provided fertile intellectual ground for the development of the encyclopedic mode. One discourse that particularly flourished in this environment was *honzōgaku,* a term referring to materia medica and the research into pharmacology that was a vital part of traditional medical techniques in China. Although pharmacological studies in Japan had existed from at least the Nara period (710–784), the intellectual zeitgeist of Shushigaku and the importation of sophisticated Ming texts stimulated popular interest in the subject during the Tokugawa period.[6] The study of honzōgaku went hand in hand with scholarship in the arts and philosophy; many medical practitioners were well grounded in the tenets of Shushigaku and eager to reap the benefits of Chinese knowledge.

For all intents and purposes, the narrative of honzōgaku in Japan began in 1607, when Tokugawa Ieyasu dispatched Hayashi Razan to collect a shipment of books from the port of Nagasaki. Among them was the *Honzō kōmoku* (Chinese, *Bencao gangmu;* Compendium of Materia Medica) compiled by Li Shizhen and published in the late 1500s. Partially illustrated and containing some 1,903 entries, this fifty-two-volume work had proven extremely popular in Ming China and was reprinted numerous times. Ieyasu himself was interested in pharmacology, purportedly mixing his own medicines; the *Honzō kōmoku* became one of his favorite texts, and he kept it close at hand. Razan, too, took a keen interest in the massive work and produced a number of texts consisting of extracts from the *Honzō kōmoku,* with Chinese names and words transliterated into Japanese. As demand grew, versions of the *Honzō kōmoku,* with punctuation and reading guides *(kunten)* added to assist with understanding the Chinese, were produced in Kyoto and Edo.[7]

The *Honzō kōmoku* was not the only honzōgaku text imported from China in the early Edo period, but the others focused more specifically on the production of medicine and did not have the all-encompassing scale of Li Shizhen's work.[8] Although putatively a pharmaceutical manual for medical specialists, the *Honzō kōmoku* diverged significantly from previous works with regard to style, classification system, and the sheer quantity of entries (surpassing all other materia medica at the time). Unlike other texts, its classificatory scheme was not organized according to the properties of an object as a potential drug: rather, each object was examined "as an object in itself."[9] This focus dovetailed neatly with the "investigation of things" and fostered the development of a field of study even more wide-ranging than honzōgaku—what has come to be called *hakubutsugaku.* Hakubutsugaku, often translated as "natural history," connotes a general study of the natural world regardless of the medicinal values of the items being examined: as one scholar puts it, "Hakubutsugaku stems from the pure desire toward knowledge born of the curiosity humans have with regard to animals, plants, and minerals."[10]

In addition to the *Honzō kōmoku,* another, even more ambitious Chinese import greatly influenced the approach taken by scholars in this burgeoning field of hakubutsugaku: the *Sansaizue* (Chinese, *Sancaituhui;* Collected Illustrations of the Three Realms). Compiled by Wang Qi and Wang Siyi and completed in 1607, this 106-volume work divided the world into fourteen categories and treated each item of knowledge with a description and illustration. The information in the *Sansaizue* was not limited to the natural world but contained details of everything from geography to clothing to musical instruments. It was also remarkable for the richness of its visual images—so much so that it was "criticized for an excess of illustrative enthusiasm."[11]

The approach represented by hakubutsugaku in general, and the *Honzō kōmoku* and the *Sansaizue* in particular, is characterized by an attempt to consider a wide range of objects, to order them in some accessible fashion, and to reduce information about them into small units of description, often with a picture attached. In the Chinese case, such encyclopedic texts have a long history, but they became particularly prominent during the Ming period (1368–1644). In Japan, however, broad compendia of knowledge did not exist as such until honzōgaku and hakubutsugaku colluded with the neo-Confucian spirit of investigation.[12]

Berry argues convincingly that classification was "more than a practical tool for disciplining data. A form of logic, lodged in philosophical premises about the world, taxonomy did not so much assist as enable inquiry by positing the intelligible connection of phenomena within comprehensive structures."[13] The collection of parts implied a comprehensive, unified whole, and it is no coincidence that the development of an encyclopedic ordering of things came with the emergence of a unified

Tokugawa state. After the importation of the *Sansaizue, Honzō kōmoku,* and similar works, the stage was set, not only to transmit Chinese knowledge to a Japanese readership, but also to create an indigenous encyclopedia that would articulate knowledge found within the boundaries of a newly bounded nation—including knowledge of the creatures that would come to be called yōkai.

'*Kinmōzui*'

Considered the first illustrated encyclopedia in Japan, the twenty-volume *Kinmōzui* of 1666 was so widely circulated that an edition eventually made its way to Europe with the German physician Engelbert Kaempfer (1651–1716).[14] Consisting primarily of simple illustrations, each labeled with the Chinese name, Japanese name, variant pronunciations and sometimes a brief explanation, the *Kinmōzui* was an educational and enlightenment project originally intended for children. Its compiler, Nakamura Tekisai (1629–1702), was a Shushigaku scholar who believed the best way to reach a young audience was through clear visual images. The title itself reveals the agenda behind his efforts: Collected (*i* 彙) Illustrations (*zu* 圖) to Instruct (*kin* 訓) the Unenlightened (*mō* 蒙).[15] Tekisai's readership, however, was not limited to children: the breadth of information and accessibility of presentation appealed to readers of all ages and levels of literacy. As testament to its broad popularity, a second edition was released only two years after its initial publication.[16]

The *Kinmōzui* is deeply indebted to the *Sansaizue* but differs significantly in that, rather than quoting extensively, it simply emphasizes the names of objects and the differences between the Chinese and Japanese nomenclature. In scale the *Kinmōzui* is wide ranging, with sections on astronomy, geography, dwelling places, peoples, human bodies, tools, plants, animals, clothing, and more. Of the twenty volumes, nine are dedicated to plants and animals, with pictures so "accurate" and useful for everyday reference that they were in demand as late as the Meiji period.[17] Whether read by children or adults, Tekisai's *Kinmōzui* served to prescribe and popularize a certain world order, introducing people to things they might not otherwise know about and acquainting them with the "proper" names of things for which they might know only a local term.

Not only did the *Kinmōzui* go through numerous editions, with Tekisai himself supplementing various versions, but it also inspired a spate of related books. Many of these milked the popularity of the original, embedding the word *kinmōzui* in their titles but focusing on specific categories of knowledge: for example, *Bugu kinmōzui* (Kinmōzui of Military Equipment; 1685) and *Onna yō kinmōzui* (Kinmōzui for Women; 1688). And as late as 1807, the popular author Shikitei Samba (1776–1822) collaborated on a work titled *Gekijō kinmōzui* (Kinmōzui of Theaters). The popularity of the *Kinmōzui* also exposed it to parody; playful and sometimes satiric derivative texts appeared throughout the second half of the Tokugawa period.[18] Clearly the format and style of the *Kinmōzui*—the encyclopedic mode—struck a chord that would resonate for a long time in the popular imagination.

So how were yōkai—or those creatures that, from evidence found in contemporaneous or earlier texts, were thought to have mysterious abilities—treated within the *Kinmōzui*? Given the various works inspired by the *Kinmōzui* project, one might expect a separate encyclopedia, or at least a separate category within an encyclopedia, dedicated to things deemed mysterious, weird, or somehow out of the ordinary. However, this was not the case. While it is impossible to draw definitive conclusions, the fact that there is no separate category suggests that yōkai were *not* considered ontologically distinct from other phenomena. Or rather, the yōkai-aspect of a creature was not itself a determining characteristic for a separate category.

Take as an example the *tanuki*, most accurately translated into English as "raccoon dog," a mischievous yōkai for which there is ample evidence in pre-Edo texts.[19] Tanuki are real animals, but they were also notorious for their shape-shifting powers, including the ability to alter features of the landscape and cause people to lose their way in familiar territory. The *Kinmōzui* tanuki stands on its hind legs, a small furry creature with a sharp face; nothing about the illustration suggests unusual powers. The entry, too, is unremarkable, only noting the various ways of reading the character 狸 and saying nothing about the tanuki's behavior, mysterious or otherwise. The tanuki shares a page with the fox, or *kitsune,* an animal long associated with mysterious doings in Japan (and China). See figure 1. In fact, both the kitsune and tanuki together have become indelibly linked with mysterious phenomena, and the combined reading of the Sinicized pronunciations of their graphs, *kori,* has come to signify all manner of weird occurrences. Yet the kitsune entry also fails to make mention of any supernatural characteristics, providing only a somewhat innocent picture of an alert-looking fox and a denotation of the Japanese reading of the (Chinese) character.[20]

The *Kinmōzui,* then, offers no epistemological distinctions between "normal" animals and those believed to possess some sort of supernatural

Figure 1. Kitsune and tanuki from the *Kinmōzui*. Courtesy of the East Asia Library, Stanford University.

powers. It is possible that one reason Tekisai does not comment on the special powers of the fox and tanuki is that these powers were considered not supernatural but simply the nature of the beasts in question. More important, however, Tekisai's project was essentially one of visually figuring and naming, not of *describing*. His project equates the visual with the oral, showing what something looks like and glossing its articulation with little or no comment. Regardless of their special abilities, tanuki and kitsune are categorized alongside other animals similar in appearance.

How then does Tekisai contend with beings not so easily locatable in the natural world? One such creature is the *oni,* a demon figure well known in both China and pre-Edo Japan. Tekisai's oni image has numerous predecessors in Buddhist iconography and is not remarkable in itself. Worth noting, however, is the comparatively extensive commentary that accompanies the illustration: "Oni is *chimi,* which is the spirit of an old thing; *mōryō* or *mizuchi,* which is a water deity *[suijin];* and also the tree spirit *[kinomi]* or *kodama;* mountain demon *[sanki]* or *yamazumi.*"[21] The entry reflects the normative aspect of the text: by listing various related beings, Tekisai reins in local yōkai, placing them all under the single label of *oni.* He neither expresses a value judgment nor comments on whether the oni is a deity to be worshipped or a demon to be feared. He simply names the creature and informs his readers that, even though their familiar tree spirit or mountain demon might seem to be a distinct localized phenomenon, it has an established position in a countrywide framework. By subsuming regional variants and vernacular folklore into this single oni image, Tekisai links local signifieds to one authoritative centralized signifier, prescribing both appearance and pronunciation. The *Kinmōzui* was part of the broader Edo project by which almanacs, maps, and guidebooks "put together something emerging as a common social knowledge."[22] Naturalized in this way, yōkai became part of the body of information contributing to a burgeoning sense of Japanese identity.

Tekisai's classificatory scheme is notoriously bewildering. For example, he locates the oni in a category dedicated to "humanity" *(jinbutsu),* in which we also find images of equally elusive figures such as a Buddha, a bodhisattva, a Taoist immortal, and a giant. These "people" are grouped together with figures portraying court ranks, occupations, and residents of foreign countries. In Tekisai's scheme of the world, Ronald Toby suggests, "the human is a comprehensive ontological and epistemological category, to be ordered and imaged along with other observable phenomena."[23] But what allows such diverse beings—bureaucrat, butcher, nun, demon, fisherman, giant—to fit into the wider category of the "human"? In the final analysis, the determining commonality seems to be physical shape. To Tekisai, apparently, humanity is a matter of meeting certain requirements with regard to corporeal form: an oni, regardless of its unique qualities, is part of "humanity" because it shares a gestalt sense of anthropomorphism. Similarly, the tanuki and the fox, regardless of whatever special qualities they might possess, have four legs and fur just like the other animals in the "beast" category. Categorization in the *Kinmōzui,* therefore, is primarily decided by the corporeal shape of the thing portrayed.

This is actually not at all unusual in categorization processes. As a "basic-level" category, overall shape is fundamental for determining taxonomical divisions in so-called folkbiology of cultures around the world. Even Linnaeus, in naming genera, based divisions on differences in the shape of a plant's fruit. In other words, perception of overall shape, or "gestalt perception," turns out to be critical in the cognitive processes of categorization.[24] In a sense, then, it is only natural that Tekisai would create his broad zoological groupings through such readily observable characteristics. Ultimately the *Kinmōzui* project is visual: as an illustrated encyclopedia, pictures are most important. Perhaps yōkai, whether in animal or human shape, are not classified in a separate category because the unusual or supernatural abilities they possess cannot be seen (pictured) and, therefore, cannot be extracted as criteria for classification. Any unique quality would be subsumed by the physical qualities shared with others—be it human shape or four-leggedness. Yōkai-ness, almost by definition, does not denote a distinct shape or feature stable enough to fix in visual form. Beings that, in legends and local belief systems, were known to possess special powers and shape-shifting abilities were either simply left out of the equation or slotted into a position determined by (their most stable) physical appearance.[25]

'*Wakan sansaizue*'

The *Kinmōzui* was a normative effort to educate readers in proper Japanese nomenclature. We can only speculate how it influenced the way people conceived of real-world categories, how many of the names and categories reflected the popular imagination, and how many of them were imposed by Tekisai. Regardless of the actual contents of the text, however, the format of the *Kinmōzui,* its mode of expressing knowledge in small, nonnarrative visual units, became a standard method for conveying information as the Edo period progressed. A later encyclopedia, the *Wakan sansaizue* (Japanese-Chinese Collected Illustrations of the Three Realms), followed this same general pattern, but with an agenda less prescriptive than that of the *Kinmōzui.*

Commencing publication around 1713, the *Wakan sansaizue* was academic in style and sophisticated in commentary, a 105-volume encyclopedia so extensive it is hard to believe it was compiled primarily by a single person—an Osaka medical practitioner named Terajima Ryōan. Like the *Kinmōzui* before it, the *Wakan sansaizue* is illustrated, but the images are physically small and often overshadowed by text. Though the work derives its name from, and was greatly influenced by, the Chinese *Sansaizue,* it is much more than a Japanese translation of that work.[26] Ryōan quotes from dozens of Japanese and Chinese sources, appending his own comments and observations especially with regard to Japan and the Japanese natural world. His intent was apparently to include as much knowledge about the heavens, earth, and humanity as was available at the time of compilation. As a medical practitioner, he himself must have been well versed in pharmaceutical matters, and he frequently cites the *Honzō kōmoku* in his sections on plants and animals. Several other sections, particularly those concerning Japanese geography, contain original material and reveal a broad, concrete knowledge of the country.

The *Wakan sansaizue* is written in *kanbun* (Sino-Japanese), and though by no means a work for mass consumption, it proved enduringly popular among scholars and other literate folk. The information contained in its pages filtered into the cultural imaginary of the second half of the Edo period. Nishimura Saburō, a historian of science, suggests that its numerous republications through the Meiji period verify that the *Wakan sansaizue* was a "wellspring of knowledge" throughout the eighteenth and nineteenth centuries, and that "the circulation of such concrete, empirical, enlightenment works contributed to encouraging a broad interest in *hakubutsu* among the common people."[27] Part of the *Wakan sansaizue*'s lasting value lies in the fact that, far from being simply a Japanese version of a Chinese text, it made ample space for all sorts of native Japanese things, including yōkai. To be sure, Japanese yōkai were often forced into affiliation with Chinese counterparts and precedents, but unlike in the *Kinmōzui,* they were not subsumed under these labels; rather, their association with Chinese and historical authority legitimized them.

With regard to natural history in Europe, Michel Foucault has noted that, until the early seventeenth century, "the division, so evident to us, between what we see, what others have observed and handed down, and what others imagine or naively believe, the great tripartition, apparently so simple and so immediate, into *Observation, Document,* and *Fable,* did not exist."[28] Though directed at a different cultural context, Foucault's comment also obtains neatly for the *Wakan sansaizue:* with no explicit distinction between these three ways of knowing, many of the entries include observation, previous documentation, and fable (folklore). All three operate as vehicles for conveying knowledge to the reader, and creatures not native to Japan, such as elephants and tigers, are presented with as much authority as rats and rabbits. The "hearsay" of previous documentation, images, and legends serves as well as (or better than) empirical observation to legitimate an item. In the sections on fauna, Ryōan most frequently cites the *Honzō kōmoku* but also refers to other texts, his discursive style characterized by an interweaving of quotations from Chinese and Japanese sources, reports of legend, and his own observations and comments on the subject. The *Wakan sansaizue* project is one of amalgamation and compilation with a "desire for totality" akin to—but preceding by several decades—the vision of European works from Diderot's famous *Encyclopédie* of 1751–72 onward.[29]

Within this matrix, what does Ryōan do with the tanuki and the kitsune, animals we know are ontologically "natural" but who also have "supernatural" powers? As in the *Kinmōzui,* they are grouped together with creatures they resemble physically; in fact, the entry for the tanuki includes an image clearly derivative of the *Kinmōzui* illustration. Ryōan quotes the *Honzō kōmoku,* lists several types of tanuki, and details their appearance, eating habits, and even their odor. Finally he adds his own observations, in which he includes a casual reference to supernatural abilities: "Like a kitsune, often an old tanuki will transform into a yōkai" (1:445; 6:91–93).[30]

The section on kitsune also includes a picture almost identical to the *Kinmōzui* image, and Ryōan quotes at length from the *Honzō kōmoku* regarding appearance, habits, and the like. Finally he addresses some of the creature's more unusual qualities: "When a kitsune reaches the age of one hundred, it worships the Big Dipper, metamorphoses into a man or woman, and deceives people. Also, by striking its tail [against the ground], it causes fire to appear. . . . Also, it is said that, if you place the horn of a rhinoceros at a kitsune hole [den], the kitsune will not return home" (1:446; 6:94–95).[31] Ryōan then appends his own data: "In our country, kitsune can be found in all regions except Shikoku. For the most part, kitsune have a long life, and many have lived for several hundred years." He touches briefly on the kitsune as part of the Inari belief complex, noting that kitsune worshipped at Inari shrines have higher status than others. He then moves on to explain some of the kitsune's more profane biological characteristics and stranger propensities:

> When a kitsune is suffering, its call is very much like the crying of an infant; when it is happy, it sounds like [somebody] beating on a hollow container. By nature, kitsune are afraid of dogs; if chased by a dog, the kitsune will most certainly fart in its urgency. The odor is so bad that the

> dog cannot come closer. When a kitsune is going to transform itself, it always places a skull [on its head]. . . . It deceives people and will go after its enemies but also reward favors. Kitsune like rice cooked with azuki beans and also deep-fried foods. (1:446; 6:96)

Ryōan follows this passage with a rather long discussion of *kitsune-tsuki,* a frightening phenomenon in which a person is possessed by the spirit of a fox. He then adds more of his own comments and references to earlier texts that relate legends involving both shape-shifting and possession. In short, the entry on kitsune reveals two related aspects of Ryōan's methodology. First, he freely interweaves earlier documents, folklore (legends), and his own observations: the result is a compact but wide-ranging unit of information. Second, within this unit, no explicit distinction is made between characteristics that we would today consider biological (coloration, shape, call) and those we would understand as being supernatural, or at least supernormal (long life, ability to change shape and possess people).

Ryōan's entries on kitsune and tanuki characterize these animal-yōkai in terms of transformation or shape-shifting, indicated by the graph 化 or 變 or a combination of the two. After reaching a certain age, these animals have the ability to shift their appearance, to become something different. Whether or not this concept was inspired by observations of nature—flowering plants, butterflies emerging from chrysalises—the implication is that physical form lacks stability. Even the concept of fox possession presupposes a fox inhabiting and taking on the shape of a human body—that is, not *appearing* like a fox at all. Whereas the *Kinmōzui* works to stabilize the unity of name and image, the *Wakan sansaizue* problematizes this connection: pictures do not, in fact, speak for themselves. Overall shape is still the primary determining characteristic of categories in the *Wakan sansaizue,* but this shape has become much less stable. True to the characterization of yōkai as bakemono (literally, "changing things"), images that establish the appearance of kitsune and tanuki are undermined by a text that articulates the possibility of transformation.

Even so, the standard appearance of a kitsune or tanuki is not out of the ordinary: they can be grouped together with other animals similar in overall shape (furry and four-legged). Significantly, however, the *Wakan sansaizue* also creates a separate designation for a miscellany of weird and mysterious creatures that do not seem to fit in anywhere else. Located between the sections for mice and rats *(so-rui)* and birds *(kin-bu),* the category labeled *gū-rui kai-rui* derives its name directly from the *Honzō kōmoku* (and as in other sections on fauna in the *Wakan san-*

saizue, most of the entries in this category include direct references to the *Honzō kōmoku*). The category name itself is difficult to interpret concisely, and might be translated loosely as "fabulous/allegorical types and rare/mysterious types." I am wary of assuming, however, that the creatures subsumed under this rather vague designation are not considered "real." Although there is clearly a sense of indeterminacy associated with the label, the fact that the section is casually sandwiched between the rat and the bird categories gestures to an ontological veracity as viable as that for rats and birds. Ryōan presumably recognizes something out of the ordinary about these particular beasts, but he never explicitly questions their existence.

In general, the creatures in the *gū-rui kai-rui* category are monkeylike or even anthropomorphic: many of them are hairy and capable of walking upright. A number of the entries reflect an effort to reconcile (and legitimize) native beliefs and names with Chinese precedents. A case in point is the *mikoshi-nyūdō,* a tall, bald figure that would come to achieve prominence as a leader among yōkai in the late Edo period (figure 2). Ryōan says of the creature that it is "tall and has no hair. The folk *[zoku]* call it *mikoshi-nyūdō.* It is said that it leans over a person's shoulders from behind and stares him in the face. Could this be a kind of *santō*?" (1:459; 6:151) While Ryōan is recognizing a native yōkai known popularly as *mikoshi-nyūdō,* then, he is also linking it with a Chinese being, the *santō*—and the remainder of his entry is a quotation from a sixth-century Chinese text describing this santō creature. The effect is to authorize the native and vernacular by investing it with the authority and heritage of the Chinese and scholarly.

Several of the yōkai in this section of the text were also noted in the *Kinmōzui* half a century earlier. While the *mōryō,* for example, appears in the *Kinmōzui* as one of the variant beings included under the umbrella label of *oni,* in the *Wakan sansaizue* it is assigned a separate entry in which it is described as a creature the size of a "three-year-old child, black and red in color, with red eyes, long ears, and beautiful hair." Judging from the illustration, the mōryō looks very much like a human but for the elongated upright ears (figure 3). But Ryōan adds a sinister note, pointing out that this harmless-looking creature "likes to eat the livers from dead bodies" (1:460; 6:156–57). Immediately following the mōryō is another creature that the *Kinmōzui* also subsumes under the oni heading: the kodama, described by Ryōan as the spirit of a tree, not to be confused with the *yamabiko,* which is the "thing that answers [echoes]" the voice of a person walking in the mountains.

Figure 2. Mikoshi-nyūdō from the *Wakan sansaizue*. Courtesy of the East Asia Library, Stanford University.

The entries for mōryō and kodama suggest that Ryōan's *Wakan sansaizue* is in conversation not only with normative neo-Confucian ideology and Chinese texts but also with vernacular belief systems. Where Tekisai's *Kinmōzui* gathers up the disparate demons and deities of water, trees, and mountains and affixes the single oni label (and image) to them, Ryōan breaks them apart again, invoking the "original" Chinese sources to reinvest the mōryō and kodama with their distinct native identities. This is not to say that Ryōan simply identifies beliefs and lets them speak for themselves. In fact, often he is as prescriptive as Tekisai before him; his

Figure 3. Mōryō from the *Wakan sansaizue*. Courtesy of the East Asia Library, Stanford University.

reason for noting the difference between the kodama and the yamabiko, for example, is that they have been "*mistaken* as one and the same thing by the folk" (emphasis added). By pointing out such distinctions, however, his project represents an approach very different from that of the *Kinmōzui:* rather than simplifying and unifying, he is revealing the complexity of the Japanese "natural" world and opening a space in the cosmology for native yōkai.

In one case, Ryōan describes a local Japanese creature that seems to have no direct link with Chinese precedents or sources. This creature, called a *kawatarō*, is a version of one of Japan's most widely distributed and representative yōkai, now generally known as a kappa (figure 4):[32]

> There are many kawatarō in the valleys, rivers, and ponds of the west country and Kyūshū. About the size of a ten-year-old child, the kawatarō stands and walks naked and speaks in a human voice. Its hair is short and sparse. The top of its head is concave and can hold a scoop of water. Kawatarō usually live in the water but, in the light of the late afternoon, many emerge into the area near the river and steal melons, eggplants, and things from the fields. By nature the kawatarō likes sumō; when it sees a person, it will invite him [to wrestle]. . . . If there is water on its head, the kawatarō has several times the strength of a warrior. . . . The kawatarō has a tendency to pull cattle and horses into the water and suck blood out of their rumps. People crossing rivers must be very careful. (1:461; 6:159)

In the category of *gū-rui kai-rui,* the kawatarō is the only creature completely bereft of documentary evidence or links with a Chinese precedent. Ryōan himself makes no mention of this unique status; including the kawatarō here implicitly acknowledges the significance of native beliefs—a critical move that prefigures Sekien's creation of a separate catalog of Japanese yōkai and suggests the role played by yōkai in the early formation of a national identity.

Although Ryōan often distinguishes between Chinese sources and Japanese folk knowledge, in cases where there were no documents to reference he makes no distinction between his own observations and hearsay. His entry on the kawatarō, for example, never reveals whether his comments were based on conventional wisdom and folklore or derived from his own observations of kawatarō in the wild. This lack of distinction places folk belief on a par with empirical observation and previous documentation. By inscribing the creature within the scholarly format of the encyclopedia, he imbues it with epistemological legitimacy.[33]

Both the *Kinmōzui* and *Wakan sansaizue* highlight the visual: the former by relying almost entirely on illustration, the latter by using illustration in conjunction with detailed prose description. This admixture of image and word has meaningful ramifications: if we assume, for instance, that Ryōan himself never actually observed a kawatarō and that his illustration and description were based only on hearsay, then he has created for the reader a clear representation of something he has never seen. The authority embodied in the visual medium, along with the legitimacy invoked by detailed description, imbues the otherwise invisible kawatarō with a tangible physical presence. Ryōan's kawatarō is in fact considered the earliest illustration of a "kappa."[34] By converting hearsay

Figure 4. Kawatarō from the *Wakan sansaizue*. Courtesy of the East Asia Library, Stanford University.

into a visually bolstered compact unit of knowledge, the encyclopedic mode establishes the kawatarō as a classifiable thing that can be referenced and researched.

This move underscores both the legitimating powers of the encyclopedia and its potential to append to the knowable world a set of creatures for which there is no documentary precedent: both the ephemeral nature of oral folklore and its affiliation with a particular locale are transcended—and the kawatarō becomes part of the permanent Japanese record. Although the kanbun of the *Wakan sansaizue* may have rendered it difficult for common folk to access, the text became a vital source for scholars, authors, and artists, whose works would play an influential role in the popular imagination. It contributed to a wide diffusion of all sorts of knowledge—including knowledge of yōkai. Indeed, by making room for yōkai in an authoritative encyclopedic setting, Ryōan takes a critical early step toward the inception of a Japanese bestiary. Yōkai began to be endowed with their own natural history—a natural history that inscribed them within the discursive and territorial boundaries of an incipient Japanese nation.

THE LUDIC MODE: SHOW AND TELL

Honzōgaku and hakubutsugaku were serious pursuits: in the cultural milieu of mid-Tokugawa Japan, they represented a fresh way of thinking about the world and a new mode of representing and recording knowledge. At the same time, the Tokugawa period has also been characterized as a time of play, in which new forms of entertainment and recreation flourished. This sense of playfulness, which I call the ludic mode, also helped shape the way yōkai came to be interpreted.

Play is of course tricky to define, but for the present purposes I use the term *ludic* simply to denote cultural practices performed for fun or amusement—that is, practices not serving any explicitly *practical* purpose and not directly remunerated within the prevailing socioeconomic structure. Such practices, though often following complex rules and procedures, are generally performed outside the serious and productive business of life. "Work," in the words of one theorist, "is earnest effort toward some serious purpose deemed worthy of the pain involved, and play is nonearnest activity deemed worth doing because it gives pleasure."[35] Although play often ultimately has wider social and practical implications, the utility of the information and knowledge used in play is generally confined to the particular space in which it is performed.

The ludic sensibilities that developed during the Tokugawa period have been explained variously by such factors as the rise of a mass consumer culture, the extended "pax Tokugawa," and the growth of a leisure class. Timon Screech has noted that, "beyond flights from life, or ludic reenactments of it, the Edo sense of play *(asobi)* was a full rescripting of experience."[36] An underlying theme of play is indeed the creation of an alternate space with its own rules and patterns of relationships. One embodiment of this was the *ukiyo,* the so-called floating world of the pleasure districts, and the art, literature, and theater associated with it.

In contrast to a space of "earnest restraints and purposes," such a space of play allows the dynamic interaction of different realms of experience and discourse, permitting collusion and hybridization.[37] The ludic space acts as a medium, comfortably cradling contradictions and fostering negotiation among diverse discourses and between otherwise incompatible distinctions of status, occupation, and belief. Edo-period manifestations of this playful sensibility include the comic verse *(kyōka* and *senryū)* that developed toward the end of the eighteenth century, woodblock prints, *kibyōshi* (literally, yellow-covered books) and other illustrated texts, kabuki theater, and the carnivalesque atmosphere of spectacle shows *(misemono).*

Initially the levity of the ludic mode seems contrary to the encyclopedic mode's earnest pursuit of order and the serious work involved in documenting and organizing the world. If one expression of the ludic entails the creation of an otherworld, however, then it follows that, for this separate space to be fully rendered and inhabitable, it too must have an order complete with systems, categories, and relationships. As the encyclopedic mode developed throughout the middle of the Tokugawa period, it gradually became infused with a playfulness that colored the way its practitioners operated, what they chose as the objects of their investigations, and how they put these objects together. This convergence of the encyclopedic and ludic was vital to the collection and expression of knowledge regarding yōkai. In fact, the concept of yōkai as a distinct and autonomous category developed largely as a result of interaction between the serious cataloging work of the encyclopedic and the popular pursuit of entertainment manifest in the ludic.

Thus far I have focused primarily on the textual elements of encyclopedic discourse, but this mode of expression was by no means confined to the written word. Particularly in the nontextual manifestations of the encyclopedic mode, we can find the development of a ludic sensibility with regard to the mysterious and the weird. Both the *showing* of strange things and the *telling* of strange tales in a playful context helped develop a distinct category for yōkai and eventually made Sekien's bestiaries possible.

Showing the Strange: Product Conventions and Pharmaceutical Meetings

In 1716, with the rise to power of the eighth Tokugawa shogun, Yoshimune, and the advent of the so-called Kyōhō Reforms, honzōgaku and hakubutsugaku entered a new phase, in which the impulse to collect and categorize was encouraged by a political and economic agenda. To help alleviate the country's economic woes, Yoshimune instituted a nationwide project to develop native industry. Japan had been trading away indigenous silver and copper holdings for medicine from China, Korea, and Holland; now, in order to reduce the nation's reliance on imports, the government encouraged the growth of domestic pharmaceutical production. Accordingly, from 1720 to 1753, honzōgaku experts traveled around the country collecting information on all sorts of natural products and resources.[38]

Enthusiasm for natural history grew during this time and afterward, developing into a practice not limited to elite intellectuals but also pursued by a growing number of hobbyists. In 1757, commercial interests, academic specialists, and amateur enthusiasts began to organize meetings known as "product conventions" *(bussankai)* or "pharmaceutical meetings" *(yakuhin'e),* through which they could exchange information and display their products. For participants, one attraction of these meetings was the chance to have as many people as possible view their prized possessions. As honzōgaku developed into a more inclusive hakubutsugaku, many enthusiasts accrued large collections of strange and rare natural objects they were eager to show to an appreciative audience. There was a natural progression at this time from a narrow concentration on pharmaceuticals and related objects to attention to a "wider range of natural items in general, and the rare and strange *[chinpin, kihin]* in particular." This shift also encouraged an expanding interest among the common people *(shomin),* who were understandably more curious about strange natural objects than the technicalities of obscure pharmaceuticals.[39]

While product conventions were events—participants traveled to them and interacted with one another—they also generated textual artifacts akin to the encyclopedias. After one such meeting in Osaka in 1760, for example, the organizer, Toda Kyokuzan (1696–1769), produced a twenty-one-page illustrated catalog called *Bunkairoku* that recorded the items displayed at the meeting. In 1763, the great scholar Hiraga Gennai (1728–1779) published a six-volume catalog titled *Butsurui hinshitsu,* which included more than two thousand items presented at five Edo conventions. Gennai's work also reflects a fascination with the rare and strange: among the illustrations, for example, is an iguana (misidentified as a "caiman"), a creature not native to Japan that must have taken a circuitous route before arriving at the convention and finding its way into Gennai's text.[40]

Such textual (re)presentations further broadened the appeal of hakubutsugaku by making it accessible to those who could not attend the meetings. They also reflected the dynamic interplay of event and text: bound by neither, the encyclopedic mode as a cognitive framework became part of the popular imagination. "An interest in hakubutsugaku," Nishimura explains, "was already no longer confined to hakubutsugaku or honzōgaku scholars, nor to one group of enthusiasts or people who cherished academia, but had wrapped up the general public *[ippan taishū]* and deeply permeated all corners of society."[41] To be sure, whether samurai or commoner, one had to have a certain amount of leisure time, financial resources, and education to participate in product conventions or gain access to the catalogs they generated. Nevertheless, the wide interest they inspired reflects a popularization of the intellectual zeitgeist so critical in encouraging the investigation of things at the beginning of the Edo period, a mentalité that sought to collect and organize knowledge of the natural world.

Although both edification and amusement had always been inherent in the encyclopedic mode, amusement began to take on increasing significance toward the middle of the eighteenth century. Product conventions and pharmaceutical meetings thrived within a broader cultural context in which it was increasingly common for enthusiasts of a range of interests to gather together and display things. People enjoyed exhibiting not only natural or found objects but also products of their own making, such as flower arrangements, linked verse, and the comic poems known as *kyōka*. One "boom" followed another, as hobbyists of diverse status, occupation, and gender formed clubs to exhibit their findings or creations, comparing them and competing with each other. Such clubs were part of a cultural milieu in which the display of things (and of knowledge of things) became intertwined with popular entertainment and play—in short, a continuum between the encyclopedic and ludic modes of expression.

Certainly, as H. D. Harootunian has noted, the waning years of the Tokugawa period would witness a fixation with the weird as one of the "culture styles that characterize and shape the social, political, and economic transformations,"[42] but already by mid-Edo the strange and unusual were becoming fetishized. During the second half of the eighteenth century, the obsession with oddities generated an increasing interest in some of the more curious products of the natural world: people searched for rare trees and strange rocks, collected singing insects, cultivated bonsai, and raised goldfish, turtles, frogs, and even fleas. When devotees of a particular hobby gathered to compare collections, they would often choose the oddest items to be included in an illustrated record. This fascination with the unusual also greatly influenced the development of a lively culture of spectacle shows (misemono). An interest in strange living creatures—a major attraction of misemono was the oddly formed human or unusual animal—can be understood as an outgrowth of the product conventions and similar gatherings.[43]

Of course, the ultimate manifestation of the odd or unusual creature, the thing out of the ordinary, is the yōkai. Sometimes, as in the case of a two-headed snake, an anomalous natural specimen might be discovered and displayed with pride. Or in the case of mermaids or kappa, fabricated versions could be produced.[44] Located on the boundaries between the everyday and the impossible, these rare physical specimens encouraged a certain ontological ambiguity and play. The visual and the tangible complemented and confirmed the legends that accrued around a particular yōkai, reinforcing its existence; in turn, the legends complemented and confirmed the oddness of the thing on display, suggesting the possibility of other, even weirder things haunting the landscape. As we will see, the display of strange objects and the telling of strange tales worked together, legitimizing each other and eventually contributing to the formation of a distinct category for yōkai.

Telling the Strange: Hyaku-monogatari

The product conventions created a separate space in which to showcase things beyond the threshold of the ordinary. Surely there was an exciting, affective quality to such meetings—participants could come away having experienced something unusual, something on the edge of possibility. A similar dynamic, in which people immersed themselves in a space teeming with rare and extraordinary things, occurred in another form of popular entertainment known as *hyaku-monogatari.*

Literally "one hundred stories," hyaku-monogatari refers to a practice in which a group of people gathered together to exchange *kaidan,* spooky stories and tales of mysterious occurrences.[45] Whereas product conventions created a place for the display of strange *objects,* hyaku-monogatari provided a forum for the display and exchange of mysterious *narratives.* A 1718 text summarizes the hyaku-monogatari procedure: "First light one hundred lamps [wicks] with blue paper around them, and hide all weapons. Now, for each frightening tale, extinguish one lamp [wick]. . . . When all one hundred flames have been extinguished, a monster [bakemono] will most definitely appear."[46] In other words, after each story, a light is extinguished until the gathering is eventually thrown into blackness—and something mysterious is supposed to happen. The game's procedures reflect a penchant for collection and display combined with a sense that these acts in themselves can engender an experience beyond the realm of the everyday: "It is said that if one hundred stories of frightening or mysterious things . . . are collected and told, then certainly something frightening or mysterious will occur."[47] The appearance of a monster—or the expectation of its appearance—represents the transcendence of the bounded space of the storytelling game itself, and a conversion of supernatural *narrative* into supernatural *happening*. Saying induces the seeing; words create the wonder.

Originally, it is believed, hyaku-monogatari was a way for warriors to test their bravery, but by the early years of the Tokugawa period it had become a popular form of recreation. Participants in a tale-telling session would bring whatever stories they thought were sufficiently frightening: "something they had experienced themselves, something they had heard, something they had collected for the gathering from here or there, or something they had made up."[48] Each successive recitation ritualistically invoked the yōkai experience, gradually creating a mysterious space distinct from the real world, a space into which the otherworldly could enter. Because this otherworldly contact had no serious objectives beyond the thrills and chills of the contact itself, it was very much a space of play, and it is likely that many participants approached the experience with tongue firmly set in cheek.

As oral events, tale-telling sessions were ephemeral. Like product conventions, however, these gatherings soon became textualized: reflecting the popularity (and profit potential) of the practice, tales were gathered together and published. Varying widely in length and content, the collected narratives presented one enchanted possibility after another, sometimes with lighthearted humor, sometimes with pathos. Here, for example, is a brief story from a 1677 collection titled *Shokoku hyaku-monogatari* (Hyaku-monogatari of the Various Provinces):

> In Bishū, a samurai with a salary of two thousand *koku* had lost his wife. Every night she was all he could think about. Then one night, when he set down his light and nodded off, his dead wife, beautifully made up and appearing exactly as she had in life, came to his bedroom. She looked longingly and made to get under the covers. Surprised, the samurai said, "Is it possible for a dead person to come back?" He grabbed her, pulled her toward him, and when he stabbed her three times with his sword, she

> disappeared into thin air. His retainers rushed in, lit torches, and searched here and there, but there was nothing. When morning broke, they discovered a trace of blood on the hole of the door latch. Thinking this was very strange [*fushigi*] indeed, they searched and found a hole in a grove located at the northwest corner of the property. They dug this up and found an aged tanuki, stabbed three times and lying dead.[49]

The brief tale develops a subdued, spooky atmosphere of ghostly possibilities and draws on an implicit knowledge of the tanuki's shape-shifting abilities. In this fairly early example, the emphasis is on the mysterious event, and the tale is related in a straightforward and unembellished manner that retains an oral quality. One analysis of hyaku-monogatari collections posits a trajectory beginning with the oral sessions and developing toward an increasingly refined literary form, reaching an artistic apex with the publication in 1776 (the same year, coincidently, as Sekien's first catalogue) of the famous *Ugetsu monogatari* (Tales of Moonlight and Rain) by Ueda Akinari (1734–1809), a collection of nine spooky stories developed from a wide range of Chinese and Japanese sources.[50] The popularity of both the oral and written practices of hyaku-monogatari suggests that the weird and mysterious had a powerful fetishistic appeal for the Tokugawa-period populace, and that certain experiences were attractive precisely because they were rife with ambiguity and fear.[51]

A combination of factors during this period—namely, the recreational aspect of hyaku-monogatari, the rise of commercial publishing, and the popularity of the encyclopedic mode—contributed not only to the publication of mysterious tales in various collections but also to the extraction of yōkai, of weird or mysterious *characters,* from narrative or event. In many cases, the magical agent of a tale was an isolatable creature or being of some sort—or at least a phenomenon that could be named. As local phenomena and individual experiences were described over and over again to different people in different places, these namable yōkai gradually took on recognizable, identifiable features and behavioral traits. From a folkloric perspective, hyaku-monogatari tale-telling sessions were forums in which yōkai-related lore was actively traded; similarly, the written collections came to function as repositories of yōkai-related data.[52] The sharing of information allowed localized lore and legend to travel beyond particular settings. Little-known yōkai became better known, and certain similar yōkai became synthesized, as regional characteristics were attenuated.

In short, there is a twofold movement reflected here. First, the gatherings and written collections, whether serious or playful, represent an awareness of that elusive thing which somehow unifies all the tales: they are about mystery, the unexplainable, the *fushigi*.[53] The practice of hyakumonogatari confirmed the distinct category to which all tales of the strange belong. Second, the telling and retelling of these tales—set against a background in which the encyclopedic mode was developing and all sorts of things were being lifted from their natural environments—encouraged the extraction of yōkai as autonomous entities from the narrative context. These two movements, the coalescing of a category of the mysterious and the isolation of the corporeal icon of the yōkai, led the way to their coherent, encyclopedic cataloging.[54]

THE BESTIARIES OF TORIYAMA SEKIEN

In Japan, the earliest manifestation of the encyclopedic form with yōkai as the exclusive object of cataloging was Toriyama Sekien's *Gazu hyakkiyagyō* (Illustrated Hyakkiyagyō) series. Combined, these four sets of texts illustrate more than two hundred different yōkai, each one labeled and often including a brief description or commentary.[55] By extracting yōkai from their narrative contexts and cataloging them encyclopedically, Sekien allowed them to exist independently of the specific legend or experience in which they were first encountered.

Strictly speaking, this is not the first time yōkai were presented as a distinct category. In China, pre-Ming encyclopedic texts often portrayed weird phenomena. Most famous is the *Shanhaijing* (Japanese, *Sangaikyō;* Guideways through Mountains and Seas), originally compiled sometime between the fourth and first centuries B.C.E., a geographical compendium including descriptions of a variety of strange places and their unusual inhabitants. Such texts clearly influenced Sekien.[56] Similarly, Sekien's books derive their titles from the theme of the hyakkiyagyō, or "night procession of demons." As I noted in the introductory chapter, this monstrous procession became the subject of a number of sixteenth-century picture scrolls that portrayed, sometimes comically, a parade of misshapen creatures and animated objects raucously marching along. Sekien was also directly influenced by several Edo-period yōkai picture scrolls, such as the *Bakemono zukushi* (Complete Bakemono; artist unknown; date unknown) and *Hyakkai zukan* (Illustrated Scroll of a Hundred Mysteries; Sawaki Sūshi, 1737), that immediately preceded his own work. All these Japanese works, it should be stressed, are picture scrolls. They depict yōkai parading together, moving and interacting with each other in some way and implicitly embedded within a narrative structure (however simple). The famous Muromachi-period *Hyakkiyagyō emaki,* for example, concludes with the rising of the sun and the dispersal of the yōkai.

What makes Sekien's catalogs distinct is that, despite their reference to hyakkiyagyō, each creature is removed from the parade and presented separately, one on each page. The catalogs are nonnarrative; there is no storyline linking the pictures.[57] Nor do Sekien's yōkai interact with each other; each one is presented as a distinct unit of information. One reason for these changes is simply that the catalogs were in codex format: that is, they were not picture scrolls but were bound along a spine so that each page could be turned individually. Indeed, some 90 percent of books and manuscripts printed during the Tokugawa period, including the encyclopedias I have discussed, were bound in this *fukuro-toji* style.[58]

By choosing the fukuro-toji format and treating each yōkai as a distinct unit of information, Sekien explicitly replicates encyclopedic rhetoric; it is no coincidence that his catalogs emerged during the second half of the eighteenth century, when the serious encyclopedic work of hakubutsugaku scholars was being "played with" by amateurs and local enthusiasts. If the hyakkiyagyō is a parade of demons, then Sekien systematically freezes the procession, isolating, examining, labeling, naming, and (sometimes) describing each demon. He does to the world of yōkai what the honzōgaku and hakubutsugaku scholars did to the natural world. By extracting each participant in the pandemonic riot of yōkai, he makes yōkai manageable, fashioning order out of chaos. Moreover, by deploying the encyclopedic format already established in the cultural imaginary, he imposes an authoritative system on these elusive beings. Sekien's work is a natural step in the processes I have been tracing; dedicated to cataloging the inclusive panoply of monsters in the popular imagination, his catalogs are the first Japanese bestiaries.[59]

The extraction of yōkai from narrative is an extension of the fascination with the strange represented by product conventions and the catalogs associated with them. In this context, Sekien's own catalogs specifically present objects in the cultural imagination for which specimens or displayable relics were particularly hard to come by. His collections were influential in establishing later ideas about yōkai, not simply because of his individual creative genius, but also because they arrived at a moment of epistemological change. Against the backdrop of earlier encyclopedic documents, Sekien's catalogs reflect the crystallization of the concept of yōkai in Japan, the point at which an abstract sense of the weird and mysterious became, as it were, a basic-level category, observable through gestalt perception and presentable in its own encyclopedia. Things notorious for their shape-shifting took on recognizable shapes.

Furthermore, as we will see, in Sekien's work there is a progression from straightforward documentation to inventive, often parodic, manipulation of the encyclopedic form. The playful sensibility he infuses into his catalogs makes richer and more expansive the otherworld of yōkai. Not only does this playfulness eventually lead him to create entirely new monsters, it also transforms yōkai into multivalent metaphors through which he can talk of other things and implicitly question the boundaries of the real and the imaginary in ways that still resonate today.

Born in Edo, Toriyama Sekien was a member of the Kanō school of painting. It is believed that his family had served the Tokugawa bakufu for generations as priests; more than likely, Sekien himself was a priest, his interest in art originally a hobby rather than an occupation. Very little is known about his life, however, and aside from his four yōkai catalogues, little of his artwork remains. He is probably best remembered for the artists he influenced either directly or indirectly: he was an early teacher of the great Kitagawa Utamaro (1753–1806); he also taught Utagawa Toyoharu (1735–1814), who started the Utagawa line, of which the most famous painter, Utagawa Kuniyoshi (1797–1861), was the teacher of Tsukioka Yoshitoshi (1839–1892) and Kawanabe Kyōsai (1831–1889). All these artists were also known for their pictures of yōkai.[60]

Sekien's first catalog was *Gazu hyakkiyagyō* of 1776. Most of the yōkai in this three-volume set are fairly standard: many are found in the *Wakan sansaizue,* and most also were previously represented in the earlier Edo-period pictures scrolls, *Bakemono zukushi* and *Hyakkai zukan.* Each of these scrolls includes thirty yōkai, all but one of which appear in *Gazu hyakkiyagyō.*[61] In this first yōkai codex, Sekien labels the illustrations and does not append any further explanation. His kappa, for example, is a web-footed creature with a round indentation on the top of its head; it peers out from a clump of flowering lotus plants. In an inscription reminiscent of the *Kinmōzui,* the label says only: "Kappa, also called kawatarō" (figure 5).

His tanuki is an innocent-looking furry creature standing on its hind legs, its front paws somewhat awkwardly positioned in front of it.[62] It stands outside the gate of a house, and in the background is a small footbridge (figure 6). Perhaps Sekien's tanuki represents a link between the

Figure 5. Kappa from *Gazu hyakkiyagyō,* by Toriyama Sekien. Courtesy of Kawasaki City Museum.

natural and the human realms; indeed, the bridge disappearing at the edge of the frame hints at other worlds unseen by the viewer and figures into the liminal, shape-shifting character of the creature.[63] There is, however, nothing explicitly weird about the tanuki in the picture, nothing to suggest its mischievous proclivities; nor is there any written description other than a simple kanji graph glossed with the phonetic reading for *tanuki.*

This first catalog also contains a picture of a mikoshi-nyūdō (labeled only "mikoshi"), a long-necked, balding figure, emerging from behind a

Figure 6. Tanuki from *Gazu hyakkiyagyō*, by Toriyama Sekien. Courtesy of Kawasaki City Museum.

tree (figure 7). There is also a *nure-onna,* a snakelike creature with reptilian front legs, the face of a woman, long hair, and a very elongated tongue. This particular creature is absent from the *Wakan sansaizue* but does appear in the *Bakemono zukushi.* The yōkai included in this first set of illustrations by Sekien were already part of the popular imagination; no explication or description beyond the name would have been necessary. As with the *Kinmōzui* a century earlier, the pictures connected each discrete item with its proper appellation.

Figure 7. Mikoshi from *Gazu hyakkiyagyō*, by Toriyama Sekien. Courtesy of Kawasaki City Museum.

In some cases a seeming disjuncture between the name and the illustration reflects the juxtaposition of vernacular folklore and Chinese knowledge—and Sekien's familiarity with both. A good example is a yōkai called the *ubume,* whom Sekien portrays as a forlorn-looking woman naked from the waist up and clutching a baby (figure 8). The ubume of Japanese legend is a woman who died during childbirth; she returns to this world, her lower body covered with blood, appearing as evening falls at a crossroads or on a bridge, her baby in her arms. Accosting a male

Figure 8. Ubume from *Gazu hyakkiyagyō*, by Toriyama Sekien. Courtesy of Kawasaki City Museum.

passerby, she asks him to hold the baby until she returns. As he cradles the infant in his arms, however, it gradually gets heavier and heavier until he cannot move at all for fear of dropping the child. Desperate now, the man intones a Buddhist prayer *(nenbutsu)*. Finally the woman returns and thanks him for helping her baby "return to this world."[64]

The *Hyakkai zukan* and the *Bakemono zukushi,* which both preceded Sekien, label this yōkai *ubume* in hiragana. Today the standard graphs associated with it are phonetically appropriate characters that define the situation in which she died: 産女 (or 産婦), literally, "birthing woman."[65] Sekien, however, chooses characters with readings not readily associated with the pronunciation *ubume* or with the image of a ghostly woman holding a baby: 姑獲鳥, something along the lines of "mother-in-law hunting/acquiring bird." These characters, it turns out, are affixed to an entry in the *Wakan sansaizue* picturing a small bird perched in a tree and labeled as *ubume-dori* (ubume-bird). Citing the *Honzō kōmoku* as its source, the passage describes the bird as a creature that flies but becomes a woman when its feathers are removed. Moreover, the entry continues, "because this is the incarnation of a woman who has died in childbirth, she has breasts and likes to steal other people's children, raising them as her own." Ryōan himself adds several native Japanese legends relating to women, birthing, birds, and the disappearance of children (1:503; 6:342).[66]

When Sekien takes up this subject, he draws a picture of the woman from legend but labels it with the "bird" characters, simultaneously invoking both native and Chinese precedents. Like the compilers of the encyclopedic works we have looked at, he is cobbling together previous documentation, folklore, and his own observations to flesh out his entries. The ubume betrays a certain ontological instability—is it a woman or a bird?—and Sekien embeds this ambiguity in his text.

Through their powerful visuality, Sekien's catalogs also affect a movement in which yōkai progress from abstract phenomena to more concrete beings, from strange *occurrences* to strange *things*. The entry for *yanari,* for example, refers to the phenomenon of mysterious sounds emitted from a house (literally, "house sounding" or "sounding house"). Sekien's challenge was to visually represent an aural phenomenon. He has done this by showing tiny anthropomorphic creatures rattling the outer walls of a house, scratching and hammering away at its foundations: he has animated an ephemeral phenomenon, transforming a sound into something that can be seen and labeled (figure 9).

Sekien's first bestiary was popular enough to encourage him to produce sequels, and he eventually published at least four separate but related sets of fascicles. A close inspection of these texts reveals a progression from the simple illustrating and naming of common yōkai to a broadening of the category, and eventually to the creation of new yōkai. While remaining within the bounds of the encyclopedic mode, the four catalogs move from a straightforward scholarly accounting of yōkai to a playful experimentation with the format itself. As his work developed, the ludic element became more and more prominent; particularly in his later catalogs, Sekien mischievously pushed the limits of the encyclopedic

Figure 9. Yanari from *Gazu hyakkiyagyō*, by Toriyama Sekien. Courtesy of Kawasaki City Museum.

genre, playing with words and images to create meanings beyond the words and images themselves.

Gazu hyakkiyagyō, which contains fifty-one different yōkai, was followed in 1779 by another three-volume set, titled *Konjaku gazu zoku hyakki* (Continued Illustrations of the Many Demons Past and Present).[67] This second set, of fifty-four yōkai, differs from its predecessor in that each entry bears not only a label but also a short explanation of the creature in question. Once more, for example, we find the mōryō, this time

Figure 10. Mōryō from *Konjaku gazu zoku hyakki*, by Toriyama Sekien. Courtesy of Kadokawa Bunko.

with a description lifted almost exactly from the *Wakan sansaizue:* "Its figure is like that of a three-year-old child. It is red and black in color. It has red eyes, long ears, and beautiful hair. It is said that it likes to eat the livers of dead bodies." In contrast to the harmless-looking creature illustrated in the *Wakan sansaizue,* however, Sekien shows a monster with sharp nails and hairy ears pulling a body from the ground, a broken wooden stupa (*sotoba*; Buddhist grave-marker) indicating the disrupted burial site (157). See figure 10.

Though a number of Sekien's portrayals are derived directly from the *Wakan sansaizue,* his sources are exceedingly varied. Clearly he has combed through a wide range of documents—native and Chinese, scholarly and popular—and extracted creatures and phenomena that meet some criteria of the weird or frightening. The brief explanations he affixes to his illustrations describe what is in the picture, sometimes citing a source, sometimes citing hearsay ("it is said"), often simply explaining with a tone of objective authority.

While reflecting the pervasiveness of the encyclopedic mode in the cultural imaginary, Sekien's work is also firmly entrenched in the ludic tradition, providing entertainment for his readers. "Poetry," he writes in the epilogue to *Gazu hyakkiyagyō,* "is that which people feel in their hearts and express with their voices; a picture is a voiceless poem. It has form, but no voice. Through each one, emotion is awakened and feeling inspired" (92). This passage not only encapsulates Sekien's linking of form with voice, image with name, but also underscores the affective aspects of his work and the fact that his yōkai catalogs were very much associated with the Edo world of poetry.

More specifically, Sekien was conversant with a number of writers of kyōka (mad poetry or comic versification), and much of his own work can be understood as a visual form of this genre.[68] Though related practices had been around in one form or another for some time, during the Edo period kyōka and senryū developed in sophistication and became exceedingly popular—reaching an apex around the time Sekien published his yōkai catalogs. Comic versification provided a carnivalesque doppelganger of established poetic practice, replicating the standard short poem form known as *tanka* but playfully parodying traditional content and affect, often with complex puns and topical cultural references. Sekien's catalogs of the otherworld can be read as a visual counterpart of the kyōka genre—the encyclopedic mode dictating the format of presentation, but a playful sensibility informing the contents and introducing a humorous and poetic element to challenge the boundaries of encyclopedic expression.[69]

Sekien's engagement with kyōka and its lighthearted sensibilities is most evident in the visual references and word games of his two later collections, *Konjaku hyakki shūi* (Collection of the Many Demons Past and Present) of 1781 and *Hyakki tsurezure bukuro* (Idle Collection Bag of Many Things) of 1784. More verbiage accompanies the images, and the origins of each yōkai are often obscure, if identifiable at all. In fact, with all the obvious choices already portrayed, Sekien deftly begins to insert his own creations. This subtle inclusion of freshly fabricated monsters pushes the encyclopedic mode into a new level of sophistication, in which the authoritative format is used not just to document and record existing knowledge but also to bring new knowledge into existence, as Sekien playfully experiments with the representation of the "real."

The development of new yōkai begins as a creative movement from the abstract to the concrete, whereby the phenomenal (a sound, a feeling, a language game) is translated into a visible character. As we have already seen with the yanari, an ephemeral aural phenomenon can be transformed into a corporeal visual icon. Taken one step further, a yōkai, such as Sekien's *mokumokuren*, translates an affective phenomenon, a vague feeling or experience, into a visual image. Imagine you are alone, taking shelter in a dilapidated, abandoned country house. You have a troubling, unshakable sense that somebody or something is watching you. The mokumokuren embodies this feeling. Sekien's illustration shows the corner of a dwelling overgrown with weeds. The paper of the shoji screen is ragged and torn, and a set of eyes peers from each section (figure 11). Sekien animates the building, turning it into a living yōkai that keeps you under constant surveillance. He relocates causality from the inner feelings of the experiencer to an outside agent, transmuting a vague internal sense of panoptic surveillance into a vivid external expression.

But something more is going on here. Despite evoking an eerie feeling of being watched, the multiple eyes in the shoji are not particularly threatening; in fact, they look somewhat perplexed, almost comical. The description reinforces the levity: "No smoke, no mist remains; a house, in which long ago somebody lived, has many eyes. It must be the house of somebody who played go" (240). The joke here is that in the game of go the squares on the board are referred to as "eyes," and the designated counter for the playing pieces is also "eyes."[70] While creating a potentially frightening image, Sekien simultaneously undermines with wordplay the power of his own creation. His reference to the game of go is also significant because his own work is produced within the context of play. Not only does the reader need to be aware of the lingo of go in order to understand the wordplay, but Sekien is also gesturing to his own games, as seemingly simple but simultaneously as challenging as the game of go.

Sekien's visual and linguistic playfulness is often complex and requires detective-like unraveling and a fair dash of speculation. A creature called the *himamushi-nyūdō* provides a good example of Sekien's full immersion in the ludic mode. Featuring an ugly, long-necked anthropomor-

Figure 11. Mokumokuren from *Konjaku hyakki shūi,* by Toriyama Sekien. Courtesy of Kawasaki City Museum.

phic creature lapping up oil from a lamp (figure 12), the entry explains: "Life is work. It can be said that, when we have work, we do not fall into emptiness/poverty. A person who, while alive, spent his life uselessly, negligently stealing free time, [such a person's] spirit will become a himamushi-nyūdō after his death, licking the oil of the lamp, and interfering with the night work *[yonabe]* of others. These days, the incorrect saying of '*he*mamushi' comes from exchanging the sounds of *he* and *hi.*"

"Hemamushi," mentioned in the last part of the passage, refers to a

Figure 12. Himamushi-nyūdō from *Konjaku hyakki shūi,* by Toriyama Sekien. Courtesy of Kadokawa Bunko.

popular rebus in which the writing of the katakana graphs for *he-ma-mu-shi* (ヘ・マ・ム・シ), when inscribed in a set manner (often above the characters for nyūdō 入道), take on the appearance of a face in profile (figure 13).[71] The rebus creates a named "being" out of letters. Sekien pushes the word game one step further, implying that the game is based on the substitution of the katakana graph ヘ for ヒ; he inverts the origin, ironically suggesting that the rebus developed from an incorrect or accented reading of the name of the *real* yōkai (his own himamushi-nyūdō). A comparison of Sekien's image with the rebus reveals a visual similarity with respect to the position of the creature, the shape of its

Figure 13. Hemamushi-nyūdō. (Illustration by author.)

head and hands, and even the folds of its clothing—the corporeal form of the *hi*mamushi-nyūdō replicates the orthographic contours of the *he*mamushi-nyūdō (or vice versa).

Sekien's image and description of this yōkai not only are tongue-in-cheek but also serve as metacommentary: he is playing a game with what is already nothing more than a game. By suggesting that his own yōkai *preceded* the rebus with which his readers are already familiar, he also comments on the practice of wordplay and monster creation. And by highlighting the process by which monsters are created and named through the inscription of letters on paper, he gestures ironically to the hakubutsugaku project from which his own texts derive their form.

But Sekien's playfulness does not end here. *Himamushi* can also be read as *kama-mushi,* referring to the "insect of a *kama* [oven]." In the *Wakan sansaizue,* the cockroach is described as an insect born in the cracks of an old kama. Furthermore, cockroaches were notorious for feeding off the oil in lamps (fish oil was used during the Edo period) and interfering with people working by lamplight—in a sense, stealing profits. Not only is there a kama in Sekien's illustration but also a votive plaque *(ema)* with an image of a chicken, associated with warding off pests such as cockroaches. The sprig of *yomogi* (mugwort) next to the votive plaque is also an apotropaic for keeping cockroaches away. The suggestion, then, is that the yōkai known as himamushi-nyūdō is some form of metamorphosed cockroach that one tries (unsuccessfully) to keep at bay. Furthermore, another term for cockroaches and other insects, *abura-mushi* (literally, oil bug), gestures to the licking of the oil and was also a slang name for the permanent lover of a courtesan. *Yonabe,* or "night work," was slang for sexual activities. The implication is that the lover of a prostitute, by insisting on visiting at night (despite attempts to ward him off), interferes with the profit-making "night work" of his lover.[72]

Regardless of how far one pushes the interpretation, Sekien's adeptness at word- and picture play is evident: his work encourages the reader to engage playfully with the text. Moreover, his references to the world of the courtesan betray his own (and his readers') familiarity with this other profitable space of play, a world with which the publishing industry was in constant interaction during this period. The entry itself toys with the link between work and play, the serious and practical versus the frivolous and fun, showing them as two sides of the same coin: a man's night play is equivalent to (or comes at the expense of) a woman's night work. Indeed, the premise is that the himamushi-nyūdō steals away valuable "free time"—the very crime Sekien himself commits by providing readers with these entertaining word-image games. Ultimately, then, this was not a serious cataloging of folk beliefs but a complex, inventive, and commercially profitable form of recreation: Sekien and his readers were playing with pictures.[73]

It is worth noting a formalistic change in Sekien's descriptions in these later volumes. The two examples cited here reflect a trajectory away from straightforward description to circuitous and witty commentary. The preface to *Konjaku hyakki shūi,* Sekien's third book, explicitly reveals his engagement with parody as well as his invention of new monsters. His comments play on those of the great ninth-to-tenth-century poet Ki no Tsurayuki, who writes in his famous preface to the *Kokin waka shū* (Collection of Old and New [Japanese] Poems): "Poetry effortlessly moves heaven and earth, stirs to pity the invisible demons and deities."[74] Sekien's version signifies that his own work is not just the stirring of the invisible demons and deities but their creation: "Japanese poetry moves heaven and earth; this is the fabrication *[esoragoto]* of the invisible deities and demons through the movement of a brush, the derangement of the weird painted year after year" (185–86).

The lighthearted spirit with which Sekien approaches his subject may indicate the increasing urbanization and sophistication of his reading public. In the remainder of the preface quoted here, Sekien refers to the market-driven world of commercial publishing, noting that, despite his "embarrassment" at the "unworthiness" of his illustrations, he continues to present them to satisfy consumer demand. The desire for new demons and deities reflects a readership steeped in the discourse of natural history and encyclopedias but also conversant with the humor of comic versification and puzzlelike pictures. In fact, urbanization and the rationalism of academic hakubutsugaku did not banish traditional yōkai at all, for the fascination of the weird and mysterious continued to exist in both rural and urban contexts.[75] Nor did the invention of new yōkai and new renditions of old yōkai crowd out the established monsters of tradition. The late Edo-period consumer was willing to allow for some play—and the line between the real and the fabricated was not so seriously drawn. Scholarly form and playful content function together in Sekien's work, seamlessly blending tradition and invention in a text that challenges both.

PLAYING WITH MONSTERS

One breakdown of Sekien's work posits that, of more than two hundred distinct yōkai, the majority are derived from Japanese folklore or literature, fourteen come directly from Chinese sources, and eighty-five may have been fabricated by Sekien.[76] Of course, it is difficult to trace the origins of objects as elusive as yōkai, but whether he fashioned creatures from scratch or not, Sekien's creative agency both popularized yōkai that were not well known—making them an established part of the Tokugawa-period cultural imaginary—and synthesized the differing images of certain similar yōkai, lessening distinctions among local variations. The tension created through the collusion of the encyclopedic and the ludic infused his yōkai with a powerful sense of legitimacy and caused his work to resonate profoundly within the imagination of the period.

As catalogs dedicated only to creatures known for their ambiguity, shape-shifting, and elusiveness, Sekien's work is already parodic; his focus on the unstable, unknowable, and often invisible plays with the stability, knowledge, and visibility articulated by the encyclopedias. The authoritative framework of the encyclopedic mode operates as a sort of straight man to the comic antics of his images. This is not to say that Sekien is consciously attacking the authoritative order of things; but by packing each entry with puns and double entendres, he subverts—or at least plays with—the form, questioning the believability of any authoritative entry and destabilizing the link between word and image that lies at the very heart of the encyclopedic project. Whereas definition is the foundation of natural-history expression, Sekien's playfulness layers each entry with multiple meanings, making metaphors that work against stable definitions and break the bounded space of the categorization system.

As we have seen, the epilogue to Sekien's first work expresses an interest in replicating the affect of poetry through images. And in the prologue to his third set of catalogs, Sekien still talks of poetry, but in an explicitly parodic manner, cultivating the affect of humor. Indeed, in his latter two sets of catalogs Sekien fully embraces the ludic mode: sometimes with satire, sometimes simply with tongue in cheek, but always by alluding to something more than what is apparent at first glance. The effectiveness of his art depends on his adoption of the encyclopedic framework: having established himself in the first two sets of catalogues as an authority on the world of yōkai, he now has the liberty to play with his material.

What is most significant about Sekien's bestiaries is that he does not cobble together knowledge of something in the *known* world; rather, from folk tradition, Japanese and Chinese literature, earlier encyclopedias, and his own inventiveness, he assembles things linked only by a vague conception of the weird and mysterious. His yōkai are unified neither by physical shape, nor by shared characteristics relating to movement (e.g., flying, walking, swimming) or habitat (e.g., mountains, ocean, forests). It is difficult to pinpoint what connects, for example, the tanuki with a ghost, or yūrei; perhaps the only common attribute of such visually different characters is that they both appear in narratives as agents of mysterious events—for example, we can find a ghostlike figure and a tanuki in the same hyaku-monogatari tale related earlier. In the final analysis, then, Sekien creates a category whose members are affiliated not by overall shape but by a general association with the weird and mysterious, with being out of the ordinary.

In a sense, then, Sekien's work stands as a kind of marker signifying the crystallization of the yōkai icon and its subsequent release into the world at large. This move can be seen most clearly in the forms of entertainment that came after him. In the final one hundred years of the Tokugawa period, yōkai haunted the literature, art, and popular culture of Edo, Osaka, and Kyoto. They appeared in woodblock prints, in the popular literature and kibyōshi of Jippensha Ikku (1765–1831) and Santō Kyōden (1761–1816), and on the kabuki stage. Furthermore, Sekien's yōkai themselves—including mokumokuren and himamushi-nyūdō—became the subject of numerous parodies.[77] I am not claiming that Sekien's catalogs actually served as working lists from which artists and writers borrowed characters (though this sometimes might have been the case), but rather that the shift which made possible his separate encyclopedia of yōkai also established the creatures as free agents, pliable metaphors, to be used for all sorts of purposes.

Certainly yōkai in various forms can be found throughout Japanese history, but it was particularly during the latter third of the Edo period that they erupted with great vitality onto the popular cultural stage. To be sure, this was partially due to the creative florescence of a consumer culture in which books and prints and dramas portraying the lives of common folk reached unprecedented levels of popularity. The plethora of yōkai images was part of this vibrant media production. The adaptation of yōkai for popular purposes, however, represents a new way of conceiving of yōkai themselves. Although yōkai were used in earlier instances as metaphoric humans and employed in satire or parody, the freedom and frequency with which they were evoked toward the end of the Tokugawa regime suggests they had become particularly potent and versatile signifiers.

In addition to artistic, textual, and dramatic representations, games and other entertainments featuring monsters came in enormous variety—board games *(sugoroku),* yōkai shooting galleries, horror-infested misemono of all sorts, even a "bakemono candle" that would project the eerie flickering silhouette of a monster.[78] One playful cooptation (and commodification) known as *yōkai karuta* epitomizes the incorporation of the encyclopedic mode into the ludic. Yōkai karuta was a recognition card game in the tradition of *iroha karuta* (syllabary card) games, in which, for example, a famous proverb was read aloud from one card while players scrambled to find another card inscribed with the initial syllable of the proverb. Yōkai karuta, which became popular during the last third of the Edo period, developed this same idea but with a yōkai theme: the challenge was essentially to match a description of a yōkai on one card with the image of the same yōkai on another. Familiarity with the common characteristics and legends of each yōkai helped determine a player's success in the game.[79] Information about each yōkai was compressed into a single, discrete unit; the phrase describing the creature was associated with a visual representation. The yōkai became a tiny capsule of knowledge, as tight and self-contained as an encyclopedia entry. In effect, the linking of the image with its name that we observed in the *Kinmōzui* was now transformed into an association game, the work of connecting the two performed by the players, as the yōkai themselves were played with, literally shuffled and resorted, for the pleasure of the participants.

Significantly, too, the world of yōkai rehearsed in the game was a Japanese otherworld in which Chinese origins and documentation were irrelevant. Regardless of their place of birth, these yōkai haunted *Japan.* Berry demonstrates that encyclopedias, maps, gazetteers, and other publications helped establish a "cultural literacy . . . that ranged across the history, institutions, and mundane civility of Nihon."[80] Certainly knowledge of yōkai—whether embedded in the *Kinmōzui,* separately documented in Sekien's work, or toyed with in yōkai karuta—was part of this cultural literacy. And if, as Berry argues, this cultural literacy represented a "national knowledge," then yōkai also contributed to the cultural foundations of the early modern nation of Japan.[81] Through the gathering and creating of information about yōkai, beliefs from disparate parts of the land were drawn together (and distributed) under the auspices of a collective body of knowledge. All these creatures and phenomena were weird and mysterious, but they were also Japanese: the category of yōkai became, as it were, a national category.

EMBRACING AMBIGUITY

In discussing the long Edo period, we move from the early attempts of scholars to label and order the natural world to a game in which players win by demonstrating their knowledge of the labels and order of the *un*natural world. The work of Toriyama Sekien stands at the center of this dynamic collusion between the serious scholarly mode of the encyclopedic and the playful popular mode of the ludic. In the early twenty-first century, Sekien's catalogs are still referenced for the wealth of information they contain about the abstract but oddly tangible category of the weird and mysterious. Inversely, however, the ludic and creative element of his work—because it often plays off now forgotten cultural knowledge—is often undervalued, if not overlooked, in popular culture.

But Sekien's contribution goes beyond the specific figures he portrayed or created. Now more than ever, interest in yōkai is expressed through collecting, listing, categorizing, and displaying. The yōkai Sekien shaped or fabricated are members of a distinctly Japanese pantheon of weird creatures, specifically suited to the Japanese landscape, and the encyclopedic mode he toyed with has become the standard format for their articulation.

At the outset of this chapter, I suggested that one key element of the encyclopedic mode is that the knowledge presented presumably has real-world utility outside the confines of the text, while one characteristic of the ludic is that the utility of the play is generally confined to the context of the game itself. As autonomous entities, yōkai break the bounds of Sekien's playfulness: the encyclopedic form of his text ultimately takes on an encyclopedic function as well, and yōkai come to have a practical utility. Employable as floating signifiers, they emerge from their ludic space to find a place in the real world—be it in other forms of entertainment, as sociopolitical metaphors, or even through reimmersion in local folklore. The combination of encyclopedic authority and the widespread popularity of Sekien's illustrations worked to transform the fabricated into the real, releasing it from the confines of a book into the world at large.

In his famous story "Tlön, Uqbar, Orbis Tertius," Jorge Luis Borges relates the discovery of an encyclopedia from another world. The concepts outlined in this foreign encyclopedia gradually infiltrate the narrator's own world, altering and replacing existing knowledge: "Already a fictitious past occupies in our memories the place of another, a past of which we know nothing of certainty—not even that it is false."[82] Sekien's catalogs may not have replaced Japanese knowledge of the natural and supernatural world, but his creations have altered the way people understand and visualize the ghosts and monsters of their own folklore, literature, and local belief systems. By subtly blending invention and tradition, Sekien makes it difficult (or irrelevant) to determine which yōkai, which memories, are "real" and which are "false." Indeed, as Nakazawa Shin'ichi has pointed out, this mixing of yōkai with biologically real animals can also have the opposite effect, making natural history seem somehow unnatural: "Today, when we look at pictures of hakubutsugaku texts from this period, we are surprised by the strange sense of the fantastic they possess."[83] As a doppelganger of natural history, Sekien's work reveals an uncanny pantheon of creatures residing within the discursive realms of Japanese storytelling and history, and within the territorial boundaries of the archipelago itself. Yōkai become part of a collective national imagination.

In the final analysis, one appeal of Sekien's work is, perhaps, its ambiguity. Certainly it would be academically tidy to propose that after Sekien's pictures, as yōkai were co-opted for commercial and recreational purposes, faith in their ontological reality began to fade. This does not, however, seem to be the case: rather the playful use of yōkai and their adaptation as metaphorical tools flourished side by side with a persistence of belief and serious interest in their existence. The real and the fake, the serious and the playful, are anything but mutually exclusive.

Tōkaidō Yotsuya kaidan, the popular 1825 kabuki play by Tsuruya Nanboku (1755–1829), provides a vivid example of this complex interaction of the genuine and the made-up. Based on "real" local ghost stories, the fictional story of the frightening ghost of Oiwa-san thrilled Edo audiences. Meanwhile, fearful of being haunted, the actors diligently paid respect to the shrine and grave of the real woman upon whom the Oiwa-san character was based.[84] And in a wonderful metacommentary on the success of his own play, Nanboku's next production, *Kamikakete sango taisetsu* (1825), contains a scene in which the fear inspired by Oiwa-san's ghost is parodied when a landlord tries to take financial advantage of his tenants by disguising himself as a ghost. The ironic performance gestures not only to the commodification of the supernatural (in which Nanboku himself was implicated) but also to the power of its fabrication.

Similarly, while illustrated texts such as Jippensha Ikku's *Kappa no shirigodama* (1798) portrayed line-drawn kappa characters for parodic humor, hakubutsugaku scholars such as Takagi Shunzan (d. 1852) still produced detailed biological diagrams of the same creatures.[85] Nor did their role in the world of popular cultural production preclude yōkai from being a subject of serious discourse and inquiry, as seen most famously in the work of the nativist *(kokugaku)* scholar Hirata Atsutane (1776–1843), who invoked yōkai agents as he outlined his own vision of the otherworld.[86] Seemingly incompatible issues of "real" or "unreal" prove not only compatible but often symbiotic.

Neo-Confucian scholars in the early Edo period may have sought to subsume yōkai within an established cosmology, but there was no concerted effort to banish their mysterious agency from the human world. Indeed, Sekien's own work expanded the realm of the mysterious, creating a natural history of the weird that at once subverted and supplemented the taxonomy of the known world. Not until the advent of Meiji—and new rational and scientific theories from abroad—do we see efforts to explain away yōkai, to debunk the enchantment they inspire, and to create a new taxonomy in which the real is distinguished from the unreal.

CHAPTER 3

Science of the Weird

Inoue Enryō, Kokkuri, and Human Electricity

THE TRUTH ABOUT YŌKAI

On January 1, 1873, Japan officially changed from a lunar to a solar calendar and adopted a twenty-four-hour clock. This was a critical moment in the archipelago's transformation into a modern nation-state synchronized with much of the rest of the world. Implemented politically from above and reflecting the ideological stance of the new Meiji regime, this new way of understanding time signified (and caused) complex changes in everyday lives. Heterogeneous local temporalities, the cyclical rhythms of lunar time, and the relationship of holidays with specific seasons were superceded by the dictates of a mechanical instrument. As historian Stefan Tanaka explains, "The clock shows uniformity and regularity; it also begins the demystification of nature, nature as a machine rather than a place inhabited by spirits."[1]

Indeed, during the Meiji period (1868–1912), we find the first systematic and rigorous attempt to exorcize the spirits from the Japanese landscape. As we have seen, Tokugawa-period interest in yōkai focused primarily on collection and classification, organization and display; there was no explicit effort to sort out real experience from illusory. Meiji, however, with its influx of Western rationalistic thought and fresh scientific knowledge, spawned new attitudes toward the supernatural—at least as far as the intellectual and political leaders of the *bunmei-kaika* (civilization and enlightenment) movement were concerned. To be sure, with *rangaku* (Dutch learning) and the importation of European knowledge in the late 1700s, ideas concerning natural history and science had begun to shift much earlier.[2] But it was not until Meiji that these transitions reached a fever pitch, taken-for-granted assumptions were rethought, and class relations and social structures experienced unprecedented upheaval. From within this ferment a new discipline developed for approaching the mysterious, for not only sorting out the truth about yōkai but also purveying this truth to the common folk. The academic discipline was known as yōkaigaku, literally "yōkai studies" or "monsterology." It was developed by the Buddhist philosopher and educator Inoue Enryō (1858–1919).

In *Civilization and Monsters: Spirits of Modernity in Modern Japan*, Gerald Figal reviews Inoue Enryō's work, introducing many of the major themes of yōkaigaku and demonstrating the critical role played by yōkai in the ideology of the burgeoning nation-state. He shows how Enryō's discourse on yōkai, emerging during this moment of extreme sociocultural transformation, became intrinsic to Japan's modernity.[3] Against this intellectual backdrop, it is instructive to zero in on one of Enryō's earliest yōkaigaku projects, a particular yōkai called Kokkuri. A close reading of what has been written about Kokkuri—by Enryō and others—provides insight into the complexities of Meiji attitudes toward the supernatural that go beyond yōkaigaku's efforts to disenchant through rationalist logic and practical experimentation. Read through the intersection of intellectual discourse and popular recreational practices, Kokkuri reveals the complex ways in which the shift from superstition to science was fraught with contradictions and ambiguities. Ultimately we discover that the movement from a "mystic" landscape to a "scientific" one succeeds, not in destroying mystery, but in producing fresh modes of enchantment and modern sources of mystery.

Inoue Enryō and the Creation of Yōkaigaku

Born in 1858 in Echigo (present-day Niigata Prefecture), Inoue Enryō was a child of the Bakumatsu-Meiji transition; his life and interests typify the intersection of discourses that characterized this period. His father was the head priest of a Buddhist temple, and Enryō (or Kishimaru, as he was known as a child) was sent to study *kangaku* (Chinese learning) with the Western-trained medical scholar Ishiguro Tadanori (1845–1941). He later studied with the Confucian scholar Kimura Donsō, reading both Western and Japanese books on natural history and the sciences. This mixture of Chinese and Japanese learning tinged with Western scientific influences would remain a significant influence throughout Enryō's life.[4]

In 1881 Enryō matriculated in the Department of Literature and Philosophy at the University of Tokyo. A review of his courses reveals a wide range of interests, including various sciences, history, literature, Chinese philosophy, Indian philosophy, and a particular focus on Western philosophers, including Spencer, Hegel, and Kant.[5] His enthusiasm for learning, however, extended beyond the classroom; he was instrumental, for example, in setting up the Tetsugakkai (Philosophy Association), which would eventually produce the *Tetsugakkai zasshi* (Journal of the Philosophy Association) and is the predecessor of a group still active today.

Through examining various philosophical and religious positions, Enryō determined that, contrary to conventional wisdom, Christianity stood in opposition to the rationality of Western philosophy. In fact, he concluded, the one religion that could conform to modern Western philosophical thinking was Buddhism.[6] His unusual conviction that Buddhism could be modernized through Western philosophy inspired Enryō to establish his own school, Tetsugakukan, as the first educational institution in Japan to teach Western philosophy in Japanese (at the University of Tokyo, these subjects were taught in English). This school, which would eventually become modern-day Tōyō University, was opened in 1887, financed by donations Enryō had acquired by lecturing throughout the country.

At the heart of Enryō's ideology for modernizing Buddhism was the notion that one had to first eradicate the many superstitions and outmoded traditions that still haunted Japan. At least in part, then, it was this desire to explain away such obstructions that directed his attention to yōkai. However, Enryō's interest in yōkai was long-standing and had begun several years before he founded Tetsugakukan.[7] While still a student, he had been instrumental in establishing the Fushigi kenkyūkai (Mystery Research Society) to investigate strange phenomena of all sorts. Most likely modeled on the British Society for Psychical Research, the group consisted of members specializing in a variety of fields, from the biological sciences and medicine to literature and philosophy.[8] During this time Enryō first published an appeal for information on "strange dreams, ghosts, kitsune and tanuki, *tengu, inugami,* shamanism, possession, physiognomy, prophecy, etc.," so that he could research them from a psychological perspective and "consider and report on the facts of yōkai from each region."[9]

Although the Fushigi kenkyūkai met only three times, Enryō continued to advertise for informants on a wide variety of topics, and in 1885 he also began writing about his findings. These early works reveal that Enryō was searching for appropriate language with which to denote the object of his inquiries, and we can observe a gradual shift from *fushigi* to *yōkai-fushigi* and eventually to *yōkai.* Sometime around 1890 or 1891, Enryō used for the first time the suffix *gaku* (-ology/studies) to create *yōkaigaku,* though it was not until the publication of *Yōkaigaku kōgi* (Lectures on Yōkaigaku) in 1893 and 1894 that yōkaigaku became publicly established as an academic subject.[10]

More than two thousand pages long, *Yōkaigaku kōgi* presents Enryō's research on the subject of yōkai up to that point; it also locates his project within the trajectory of Japan's bunmei-kaika and the emergent discourses of modernization:

> Now, in our country, there are steamboats in the ocean, and trains on the land. Telegraphs and electric lighting have reached throughout the country; if we compare this to several dozen years ago, it seems an entirely different world has opened up. Our national subjects *[kokumin]* have truly acquired a great many conveniences. It irks me, however, that with regard to the many ignorant folk *[gumin]* still wandering astray and groaning in distress, we have not yet exhausted the powers of our academic disciplines. . . . This is because today's civilization advances in terms of tangible machinery but does not progress in terms of intangible spiritual developments. If the railroad of academic study could run into the heart of the common folk, and the electric light of knowledge shine, then we could claim for the first time the great accomplishments of Meiji. Therefore, in order to achieve these objectives, to actually apply these various academic studies, there is in particular the discipline of yōkaigaku. If through this [discipline], the light of a new heaven opens inside the hearts of the citizens, then is it too much to say that these achievements are just as important as the installation of railroads and telegraphs? Herein lies the necessity of the research and explanations of yōkaigaku.[11]

Enryō's rhetoric conflates the infrastructure of modernity—railroads, telegraphs, electric lights—with a new spiritual infrastructure to be developed through his own discipline of yōkaigaku. His project professes to enlighten the dark terrain of the common folk, disabusing the masses of old beliefs incompatible with the new landscape of a burgeoning modernity.

In spite of its massive scale, *Yōkaigaku kōgi* was produced relatively early in Enryō's career and served as a platform for his lifelong campaign against superstitious belief. Until his death in 1919, he continued lecturing throughout Japan (and China), pursuing his project with an almost missionary zeal and striving to reach a wider and wider audience. Certainly, Enryō's didacticism was informed by nationalistic objectives and a pejorative attitude toward the beliefs of the folk, but he was also the consummate educator, determined to share his knowledge and philosophy as broadly as possible.[12]

Along with his lectures, Enryō's written work was also accessible to a wide spectrum of the reading public, as evidenced, for example, by his serialized publications in the newspaper *Yomiuri shinbun,* later collected and reprinted as *Yōkai hyaku-dan* (One Hundred Yōkai Tales; 1898) and *Zoku yōkai hyaku-dan* (One Hundred Yōkai Tales Continued; 1900).[13] In one sense, these short articles might be characterized as a Meiji incarnation of the Edo-period hyaku-monogatari collections. Rather than gather together unexplainable stories of the supernatural, however, Enryō collected *explanations* of the supernatural. Read one after another, the stories present a daunting array of mystic possibilities, each one immediately smothered by Enryō's explanatory prowess as he systematically solves each riddle, removing the experience from the realm of enchantment and placing it into the realm of the mundane. Take for example the short episode recounted as tale number 41, "Dai-kaibutsu o torau" (Catching the Big Monster):

> Some years ago when I was staying at a particular school, a certain friend who was also staying there got up sometime after midnight needing to go to the bathroom. In the hallway he saw a large monster *[kaibutsu]* standing silently. The night was pitch black, and there was nothing to shed light on the situation. Facing this thing with suspicion, he asked, "Who are you?" but there was no answer. Nor did it make a move to run away. So summoning up all his courage and strength, he grabbed the thing with both hands. It was not a demon [oni], or a devil *[ma]*, or a monster *[kaibutsu]*, or a burglar; when he realized it was two straw containers of coal stacked one on top of the other and stuck in the corner of the hallway, he burst out laughing.[14]

While the game of hyaku-monogatari was said to have the power to inspire a supernatural occurrence in the real world, Enryō's *Yōkai hyaku-dan* would presumably have the opposite effect. The rationalistic explanations spill over from the text, making the seemingly supernatural seem natural, sometimes even comical, and inspiring readers to disenchant any mysterious phenomenon they might encounter in the real world. Having said this, however, I also suggest that, like its Edo-period counterpart, *Yōkai hyaku-dan,* complete with illustrations, was probably also enjoyed for its sensationalist and entertainment value. Although Enryō clearly took his project seriously, there is often a surprising sense of levity in his work, especially in later years. He may have considered himself a "peasant scholar" *(hyakushōteki gakusha)*,[15] but he was also a storyteller who lived up to his more notorious moniker, "yōkai hakase," or "Professor Yōkai." His almost obsessive lecturing throughout Japan and China speaks not only of his enthusiasm for education but also of his enthusiasm for sharing his knowledge of yōkai with others. These entertaining lectures also provided ample financing for his projects back home.[16]

Types of Yōkai

Toriyama Sekien and the Edo-period encyclopedists were intent on listing, illustrating, and commenting on yōkai, making them part of the cultural literacy of the period, but they never set out to explicitly define these strange and mysterious things. In contrast, Enryō expended a great deal of energy limning the parameters of his subject. Though his terminology shifted as his ideas developed, by the time he published *Yōkaigaku kōgi* he had settled on a fairly stable, if complex, classificatory scheme.

He explains that, in the universe, there are things *unknown*—these are fushigi, but they are not necessarily yōkai. We may be unable to explain familiar, everyday things such as fire and water, but this does not make them yōkai. On the other hand, there are weird *(ijō)* things we do not meet with on a daily basis; these more closely correspond with the definition of yōkai. But, Enryō goes on, if we strictly adhere to this designation, then a foreigner met in the marketplace—a weird, though not particularly unexplainable, individual—would also have to be considered a yōkai. He concludes, therefore, that a yōkai is not just the mysterious (fushigi) and not just the weird (ijō), but a combination of both. As to what is considered mysterious and weird, he admits that these are subjective categories based on knowledge and experience—and thus the definition of yōkai necessarily changes as human knowledge and experience also change.[17]

It follows that, because "scholars often understand those things which the common folk do not, they can point out that things are not yōkai." Enryō adamantly asserts, however, that, "if a scholar thinks therefore that there is no such thing as yōkai, then this is the scholar's error."[18] The goal of yōkaigaku is not to suppress *all* mystery but to sort out the *kakai,* or "false mystery" (or more accurately, "provisional mystery"), from the *shinkai,* or "true mystery." Through rational scientific explanation, we can systematically reject the kakai that interfere with recognition of the shinkai. As for concretely describing this shinkai, however, Enryō himself tends to skirt around this difficult undertaking. In one of his later essays, for example, he claims rather cryptically that "the grasping of the fushigi within the fushigi, also the probing into limitless time, the investigation into limitless space . . . these get to the very core. This is the real shinkai."[19] Ultimately Enryō's conception of shinkai is something akin to Herbert Spencer's "Unknowable": it refers not to the unknown that someday may become known but to that which cannot be known *(fukachiteki),* the limitless absolute *(mugen zettai).*[20]

Enryō's division of yōkai into shinkai and kakai, however, is only one fragment of his overall typology. Both of these designations are included in his category of *jikkai,* or "actual mystery," where they are defined in even greater detail. Kakai, for example, is explained as natural phenomena erroneously experienced as shinkai because the experiencer lacks the knowledge to understand that they are not truly mysterious. Another broad category is *kyokai* (empty mystery), under which fall *gokai* (mistaken mystery) and *gikai* (artificial mystery). The former refers to seeming mysteries that are actually caused by coincidence, while the latter refers to mysterious experiences created by human artifice.[21]

In short, Enryō's yōkaigaku elaborates a complex taxonomy of weird and mysterious objects and experiences. His view of yōkai was akin to the medieval European notion of "wonders" as "a distinct ontological category, the preternatural, suspended between the mundane and the miraculous."[22] Indeed, perhaps a more accurate translation would render Enryō's use of the word *yōkai* as "wonder." His *yōkaigaku* then becomes "wonder-ology," its mission to examine wonders so that the mundane and explainable can be put in their proper place, and the miraculous, the true mystery, can be appropriately cherished.[23]

Enryō's category of yōkai encompasses the same sort of "distinct ontological category" Toriyama Sekien helped create through his eighteenth-century bestiaries. However, whereas Sekien moves toward a more animate or character-based understanding of yōkai, in which weird and mysterious phenomena are visualizable as creatures, Enryō's usage of yōkai as "wonder" does not distinguish between experience and object, between phenomenon and creature. By drawing on new psychological and physiological knowledge, he situates the weird and mysterious inside the body and mind of the experiencer. No longer are yōkai external agents operating on humans; they are instead the internal imaginings of humans (mis)interpreting the external world around them. By ascribing *yōkai-as-creatures* to the human interpretation of *experience,* Enryō subsumes the object back into the experience, removes the mystery from the material world, and redefines it as a subjective production of the individual.

In his analyses, Enryō divides human history into three time periods, etiological categories each locating causality differently. The people of ancient times, he explains, believed that everything had its own spirit, and this spirit sufficed as the explanation for all sorts of strange doings. Next came belief in the existence of a separate ethereal body, a deity figure distinct from the objects over which it presided. But now, in the third epoch, advances in science allow us to find explanations in the rules *(kisoku)* that govern the natural world. Enryō himself, of course, writes from the front lines of this third time period, this moment of modernity, applying scientific knowledge to previously mystifying phenomena.[24]

But just as the study of nature necessarily requires the investigation of natural objects, Enryō's study of the preternatural must be informed by the study of preternatural objects. That is, in theory his definition of yōkai may encompass both experiences and animate creatures, but in practice much of his analysis begins with a focus on the creature and moves into abstraction from there. This also reflects the fact that, for the "common folk" into whose hearts Enryō would shine the "electric light of knowledge," the yōkai-as-creature was the dominant metaphor through which the experience of the weird and mysterious was conceived.

THE KOKKURI PHENOMENON

Enryō was dedicated to the project of ridding the masses of erroneous belief in false yōkai and superstition so that Japan could develop into a healthy modern nation competitive with the West. Although yōkaigaku was clearly an individualistic undertaking inspired by Enryō's own academic and ideological agenda, a careful examination of its application also provides insight into the broader experiences of people living within a context of critical cultural flux. Not only can we see the often-contradictory intellectual milieu in which Enryō operated, but also his data reveal the attitudes of many of the folk he sought to enlighten. What becomes clear, ironically, is that dyads of enchantment and disenchantment, mysterious and rational, old and new, native and foreign, were ambiguously experienced by the Meiji populace. Despite Enryō's best efforts to end the masses' fascination with the unexplainable, we find a persistent desire to seek out ambiguity and the infinite possibilities embodied by things that stubbornly resist illumination.

Nowhere is this more apparent than in the investigation of Kokkuri. In the 1880s Kokkuri was an extraordinarily popular divination game that neatly encapsulated the conflicting discourses of the moment. By exploring Kokkuri in some detail, we can see how yōkai, often in unexpected ways, persist in playing a role in intellectual discourse and common practices. More important, Kokkuri demonstrates that the Meiji trajectory from superstition to rational thought may have succeeded in changing traditional beliefs, but, at the same time, also helped generate new cultural products as mysterious as the ones it replaced. In Kokkuri, we see the resilience and adaptability of mystery within a shifting metaphorical landscape.

The setup for Kokkuri was simple: three bamboo rods were tied together to form a tripod, and a round tray or the lid of a wooden rice container was balanced on top. Three or four people would kneel around this tablelike structure, placing their hands lightly upon the lid (figure 14). In Enryō's account, the game begins with one person chanting: "'Kokkuri-sama, Kokkuri-sama, please descend, please descend. Come now, please descend quickly.' After about ten minutes of this invocation, the person says, 'If you have descended, please tilt towards so-and-so.' And with the lid balanced in place, the apparatus tilts, the bamboo leg on the other side lifting up. . . . Now any of the three people can ask questions" (22). Scenes similar to this were enacted throughout Japan as the practice spread rapidly; Kokkuri was an explosively popular fashion, a mass culture phenomenon that entered the homes of people throughout the nation. From the end of 1886 to the autumn of the following year, this divination game was so popular that, as the journalist and scholar Miyatake Gaikotsu (1867–1955) notes, it was played in "almost every household."[25]

Kokkuri was attributed to the workings of mysterious forces: it was, as Enryō himself asserted, "a kind of yōkai or mystery"(15). The name *Kokkuri* was ambiguous, variously signifying the practice, the spirit(s) invoked, and the apparatus itself. In fact, the vagueness of the name reflects the ambiguity inherent in the broader notion of yōkai, a name simultaneously denoting the experience of the supernatural, the mechanism for bringing it about, and the ghostly agents behind it. For the sake of concision, I refer to the phenomenon simply as *Kokkuri,* but it was also known as *Kokkuri-sama* or *Kokkuri-san,* the personifying suffixes

Figure 14. Photograph of Kokkuri from a 1912 book on hypnotism. Murakami Tatsugorō, *Saishinshiki saiminjutsu* (Seibidō shoten, 1912), n.p. Courtesy of the East Asian Library, University of California, Berkeley.

not only hinting at the respect it inspired but also bolstering the sense of an animated agent behind its operations.[26]

If we accept that Kokkuri itself can be labeled as a form of yōkai, then it was perhaps the most prominent yōkai of its time, arriving at a moment of critical transition in which the mystic knowledge of the past came head-to-head with the scientific knowledge of the future. It is not surprising that Inoue Enryō, leading the charge to banish superstitious belief, would choose Kokkuri as one of the first mysteries to grapple with as part of his yōkaigaku project. Dedicated to systematically investigating and explaining Kokkuri, *Yōkai gendan* (Yōkai Exegesis) of 1887 was Enryō's first monograph on yōkai and established a method and typology that would inform his later investigations of more "traditional" yōkai phenomena, such as tengu, ghosts, fox possession, haunted houses, and the like. More important, however, we can also analyze *Yōkai gendan* as one of many voices in the cacophony of discourses on the mystery of Kokkuri and its role within a broader cultural context. As a practice for contacting the otherworld, Kokkuri affords insight into how cultural change was manifest in the noninstitutional and mostly undocumented everyday experience of the Meiji populace, but it also offers an intimate glimpse into personal attitudes toward the spiritual and the supernatural in everyday life.

Kokkuri provides a space of overlapping and blurring boundaries during this period of cultural transition. As a modern practice calling on age-old spirits to forecast the future, it reflects both changes and continuities and demonstrates the negotiation of divergent worldviews as the nation embarked on a path toward modernity. On the one hand, Kokkuri represents a continuation of serious folk practices and systems of belief; on the other, it is a party trick, a carnivalesque ruse infiltrating mid-Meiji cultural life. As a site of both conflict and collusion, Kokkuri signifies in-betweenness. And because of this in-betweenness, it provides insight into the way a number of Meiji discourses played themselves out on the popular level.

What made Kokkuri so intriguing, troubling, and ultimately so appealing to so many people? Was it a mystical practice? A scientific procedure? A game? Of the many opposing discourses it channeled, perhaps the most evident are the "mystic"—by which I mean pre-Meiji practices of spirit possession and notions concerning yōkai—and the "scientific," specifically the elite Western-based normative ideology set on debunking superstition and disenchanting the mystic. Rather than moving cleanly from the mystic to the scientific, Kokkuri complicates the shift, and these two seemingly incompatible discourses come together within a third context, that of the ludic. By interrogating Kokkuri's place within these three worlds, we not only learn something of the lived experience of the Japanese during this moment of intense cultural flux but also witness the unfolding of a complex new way of understanding yōkai. And we see how yōkai, once again, are implicated in the formation of a national identity.

The Practice

Kokkuri was a technique through which a spirit was called down to inhabit a simply constructed apparatus.[27] Questions would then be posed to the spirit, which would answer by tilting the apparatus:

> It is asked, "Will there be a fire or similar disaster in so-and-so's house?" The leg does not lift up. Therefore they know there will be no disaster.
>
> It is asked, "Will there be good fortune in so-and-so's house? If there will be good fortune, lift this leg." The leg does not lift up. So they ask, "In that case, will good fortune not come?" But again, the leg does not

> lift up. "In that case, is it completely unclear at this time?" When they ask this, the leg lifts up. And so, they can judge that fortune or misfortune is not yet known. . . .
>
> Now, it is said, "If tomorrow will be a clear day, lift this leg." The leg does not lift. "In that case," they ask again, "Will tomorrow be a rainy day?" Again the leg does not lift. They ask, "In that case, will it snow tomorrow?" Now the leg lifts up just a little. And so they know that the next day will be snowy. (27)

Although his many examples give us some idea of how Kokkuri was practiced, Enryō also notes that, "according to the information I have received from various people around the country, the method of Kokkuri is not set, and varies from place to place" (22). Such variety suggests that Kokkuri was enjoyed by people from a range of socioeconomic spheres, and Enryō himself emphasizes that Kokkuri was a topic of conversation in both urban and rural settings: "With no distinction between city and country, high and low, people are talking about the mysterious phenomenon of Kokkuri" (15). A contemporaneous document also notes that "Kokkuri-sama [has] in recent years been popular throughout the city and the countryside, near and far."[28] Though such hyperbolic comments must be taken with a degree of skepticism, their invocation suggests that Kokkuri was at least *acknowledged* as having widespread popularity not identifiable with a single group or socioeconomic class.

The game was also particularly associated with geisha houses, significant because such places had clientele from different walks of life and were instrumental in the distribution of fads and fashions. Indeed, Enryō makes a point of noting that, with respect to Kokkuri, people from all socioeconomic circumstances were equally (though differently) deluded: "Those below the middle class, not knowing what [Kokkuri] is, attribute it to the doings of kitsune and tanuki [kori] or demons and deities *[kijin];* those above the middle class, not knowing the explanation, also classify it as one kind of yōkai or mystery [fushigi]" (15). While stressing Kokkuri's pervasiveness, however, Enryō also underscores distinctions with regard to both education and gender, noting, for example, that the game is more effective for "people who naturally have stronger beliefs, those poor in mental capabilities, and women and children" (41).

Kokkuri is variously written in katakana, hiragana, or kanji. Enryō and others make the same etymological argument: the name is derived from the word *kokkuri,* an onomatopoetic expression referring to the action of tilting or nodding. It describes, for example, the movement of a person nodding in agreement or nodding off to sleep; in the case of

Kokkuri, the expression denotes the tilting of the tray perched atop the three bamboo rods (35).[29] While the kanji characters chosen to denote this name may be phonetic equivalents *(ateji)*, they also signal how the practice was understood in the 1880s. By far the most common set of characters affiliated with Kokkuri are those denoting *fox* (狐 *kitsune* = *ko*), *dog* (狗 *inu* = *ku*), and *raccoon dog* (狸 *tanuki* = *ri*), three characters that became associated with the practice very early on.[30] The development of these particular characters to denote the practice reflects a certain mystic understanding of the game, and also must have promulgated and deepened this understanding as the game spread throughout Japan.

Each graph refers to a specific yōkai, all of which were known during the Edo period and represented in some fashion in Sekien's bestiary. As already noted in chapter 2, the fox has a long history in Japan and China as a mysterious, shape-shifting creature associated with kitsunetsuki, or "fox possession." Though not the only form of possession found in Japan, fox possession is one of the oldest recorded and most common.[31] The diverse supernatural qualities of the kitsune were no doubt evoked in the popular imagination by the inclusion of its graph in *Kokkuri*.

The second character in the compound denotes *dog*. Although dog deities or demon creatures known as *inugami* are associated with possession, the graph used in Kokkuri is commonly linked with the tengu, one of the most notorious of Japan's traditional yōkai and one illustrated in Sekien's first catalog. The word *tengu* literally means "heavenly dog," but the tengu is most often thought of as a sort of mountain goblin, sometimes depicted as being crowlike in appearance, sometimes depicted as a monklike figure with a red face and elongated nose. Historically, the tengu was often linked (negatively) with esoteric Buddhism and *yamabushi* (mountain ascetic) practices. Tengu are also held responsible for so-called *kami-kakushi* phenomena, in which they abduct a person (usually a young child) for several days or weeks.[32]

Finally there is the tanuki, the "raccoon dog" we have already encountered in the work of Sekien and many of the early encyclopedias. Though tanuki possession is not unheard of, the creature is more commonly associated with shape-shifting mischief. But again, the point here is simply that the use of the tanuki graph in *Kokkuri* alludes to an entire constellation of existing beliefs and legends. In a sense, the experience of Kokkuri becomes animated by distinct, visualizable yōkai characters—the odd behavior of the apparatus is explained by the manipulation of well-known, definable, encyclopedically documented creatures.[33]

One author suggests that the creation of the word *Kokkuri* represents nothing more than a kind of wordplay imposed on the practice by those who enjoyed it. Though he claims that the creatures indicated by the kanji have nothing to do with the workings of the game itself, he does astutely note that the graphs make the game seem "one level more mysterious *[kai]*."[34] Whatever the derivation of the neologism *Kokkuri,* then, this association of the kitsune, tengu, and tanuki transcends the name of the game and comes to be literally embedded in the practice. Enryō's informant from Miyagi Prefecture, for example, describes the construction of the apparatus: "Into the bamboo rods insert tags inscribed with the words *kitsune, tengu,* and *tanuki;* warm the mouth of the bamboo with a flame, and place a heated lacquer tray on top, covering it with a cloth" (26). And in Ibaraki Prefecture: "Trace the characters on the underside of a tray with the tip of your finger, and cover with a cloth" (24–25).[35] The inscription of these three yōkai endows the otherwise mundane structure with a supernatural quality. Operating through the principles of sympathetic magic, the graphs serve as metonymic representations, their presence a sort of lightning rod to call down the spirits they signify.

Once the ritualistic rendering of the name and the oral incantations to "Kokkuri-sama" worked their magic and a spiritual presence descended to inhabit the apparatus, the first order of business was usually to establish just what sort of spirit had arrived: "'If you are a fox, lift this leg . . . ' As the leg was not lifted, they knew it was not a fox. And again, it was said, 'If you are a tengu, lift this leg.' As again the leg was not lifted, they all knew that it was not a tengu" (28). Although the name may be derived from the movement of the apparatus, the kanji associated with Kokkuri not only infused it with an air of ritualism and mystery but also became an intrinsic element of the practice itself. Overdetermined and layered with meanings, the name works both descriptively and symbolically. By conjuring up images of powerful figures firmly established in the popular imagination of the Tokugawa period, Kokkuri calls on their supernatural authority and spiritual clout.

Contact with the Otherworld

It would seem, then, that Kokkuri represents the persistence of firmly entrenched Edo-period associations, traditions in stark contrast to new modes of knowledge imported from abroad during Meiji. But ultimately Kokkuri is a hybrid, one that confounds simple dualisms to act instead as a site of dynamic contact between oppositions. In fact, just as rationalistic theories, scientific procedures, and modern technologies were being introduced from the West, so too were "irrational" and "superstitious" methods for communicating with the otherworld: "Without a doubt," Enryō insists, "[Kokkuri] came from a foreign country" (33). As Ichiyanagi Hirotaka puts it, Kokkuri was "the trendiest of recreations [asobi] from America."[36] One reason for Kokkuri's popularity, therefore, was the opposite of its traditional associations: its exotic, nonnative origins. Although the practice (content) may have been grounded in the invocation of indigenous yōkai, the methodology (form) for summoning them was associated with newly imported ideas. Not only does Kokkuri represent a method of contacting the mystical otherworld of magical spirits, but it also signifies a very real point of contact with an otherworld outside Japan.

Several contemporaneous theories account for Kokkuri's introduction to Japan. One posits that it was a discovery of a New York scientist which became popular among young men and women in 1884. Arriving in Yokohama the following year, it made its way to the entertainment districts in the Shinagawa area of Tokyo, where it was accorded the "mysterious power *[kairiki]*" of kitsune, tanuki, and the like by the geisha living there.[37] Another author suggests it was introduced by a Japanese exchange student who had encountered it while studying physics in the United States.[38]

Enryō's hypothesis, however, is the most carefully fleshed out. He too purports that Kokkuri came from abroad, specifically from the United States. After first dismissing all other theories as "rumors on the street," he sets out to reckon the origins of Kokkuri by determining when the practice began in different areas and tracing the game's journey through Japan.[39] Concluding that it must have made landfall in the Izu region, he explains that, "last year, I journeyed to Izu and looked into the circumstances of [Kokkuri's] popularity in that region. I thus first came to know the truth of my hypothesis" (34). His explanation of Kokkuri's arrival on Japanese shores is compelling in part because of the detail he provides, and in part because it offers a lucid image of cultural exchange at a local level:

> Two years ago an American sailing ship came to the Shimoda area of Izu, and was damaged. Because of a torn sail, some Americans spent a long time on land; they passed on the method [of Kokkuri] to the people there. At that time the Americans called it by a name in English, but because the residents of the area did not understand English, the name was difficult for them to use, and it was given the name "Kokkuri." . . . So it is that this method came from the West, and it is clear that the vogue began in Shimoda. The boatmen who were in Shimoda at this time saw this strange thing all together with their own eyes. Afterward they went to the many ports from east to west and passed it along. (34–35)

We can imagine the scene: the American sailors playing their game surrounded by a crowd of curious onlookers mystified by the strange Western magic. The Americans demonstrate how to play, and the Japanese mimic their words, their actions. Then the Japanese try the game themselves: they watch dumbfounded as the tray tilts and nods in response to their questions, and they comment on the movement, *kokkuri kokkuri,* of this animated, yōkai-like, apparatus. Although apparently no independent records—either Japanese or American—exist to verify Enryō's account, his explanation adds depth to conventional historical images of the transfer of knowledge between the West and Japan. In contrast to formal exchanges with regard to education, government, technology, and the military arts, Enryō shows us a "spiritual" and yet very human side of Japanese contact with foreign—otherworldly—mysteries.

But what exactly were these American sailors doing? "According to what I have heard," Enryō says, "there is something in the West called table-turning. . . . This method is not the slightest bit different from Kokkuri-sama." Table-turning, he explains, entails a number of people sitting with their hands placed lightly on a table and causing it to revolve. They pose questions to the table, which responds by spinning or by lifting its legs off the floor (35). Enryō is clearly familiar with the so-called Spiritualist movement, which, for all intents and purposes, began in 1848 with a series of strange occurrences in the Hydesville, New York, home of the Fox sisters. Spreading across North America and into Europe, it rapidly became a popular religious and social movement.[40]

As modern Spiritualism developed, popular séances were performed by professional mediums who would cause tables to be rapped in response to questions posed by the sitters. Similar to this "table-rapping" was "table-turning," a procedure through which a table responded to questions by rotating and tilting. These movements were attributed to the influence of the spirits—that is, to the ghosts of ancestors or others called upon to provide information from beyond the grave. One reason for table-turning's particular appeal was that, unlike techniques such as table-rapping, it did *not* require a professional medium but could be practiced by anyone, allowing egalitarian access to the otherworld. Frank Podmore, an early British scholar of Spiritualism and prominent member of the Society for Psychical Research, records that, when an "epidemic of table-turning" made its way from the Continent to Britain in 1853, "it was found that not only would tables and hats rotate and execute movements of various kinds without apparent volition or control of those taking part in the experiments, but answers to questions—and even on occasion information not apparently known to any of those present—could be obtained by this method, a tilt of the table being substituted for the professional medium's rap."[41]

Given the general public's familiarity with table-turning, it would not be surprising for a group of American sailors grounded in Japan for a few months in 1885 to amuse themselves with some experimental turning of the tables: "The Americans who came to Shimoda knew this method from when they were in their home country in the past. In Shimoda they were unable to get hold of a proper table and so provisionally they imagined they could substitute bamboo and a lid [of a rice container]. And although these Americans told [the Japanese] that the method was called 'table-turning,' the locals, unaccustomed to Western languages, substituted the word *Kokkuri.* For this reason, I believe Kokkuri and table-turning are one and the same" (36). Enryō stresses here how a Western technology for spiritual communication was reinvented through makeshift construction with available materials and introduced to the mystified local populace. The Japanese proceeded to make the method their own: translating the name into one with meaning in the vernacular, and translating the spirits themselves into spirits with local relevance. In Western versions of the practice, participants tended to invoke spirits for whom there was a culturally accepted folkloric precedence—namely, the ghosts of dead family members. Not surprisingly the Japanese version also entailed a reliance on traditional representatives of the otherworld, especially kitsune, tengu, and tanuki (figure 15). One can imagine the game being passed on from place to place, accruing on its journey a richer and richer association with native yōkai.

The exchange Enryō articulates is an example of "transculturation," in which one group of people "select and invent from materials transmitted to them" by another.[42] While such exchanges are characteristically shaped by power politics, in the case of Kokkuri we cannot help but wonder which side, if either, would have dominated the practice. Indeed, as for table-turning in the United States and Europe, there was no agreement as to *why* the table moved. The Spiritualists, of course, argued that the movement was a clear manifestation of the spirit world. Scientists such as Michael Faraday and William Carpenter explained the movements in terms of involuntary muscular reactions triggered by unconscious anticipation. Others believed it was pure trickery. It is unlikely that the American sailors who brought the practice to Japan would have

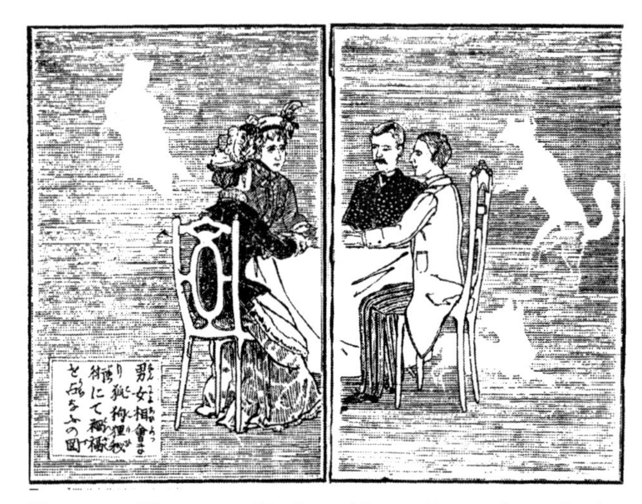

Figure 15. Westerners (?) play table-turning against a background haunted by fox spirits. The caption reads: "A picture of men and women gathered to divine fortune and misfortune through the secret method of Kokkuri." Ryōkū Yajin, *Seiyō kijutsu Kokkuri kaidan*, 1st ed. (Iiguru shobō, March 1887), 4–7; reproduced in Yumoto Kōichi, ed., *Zusetsu Bakumatsu-Meiji ryūkō jiten* (Kashiwa shobō, 1998), 316.

been able to explain the phenomenon to the Japanese, even if the two groups had better understood each other's languages. The picture nicely complicates the usual trope of "advanced" nations making contact with "unenlightened" natives and fascinating them with the magic of technology.[43] Ironically, although the natives were fascinated with this new technology, the representatives of the "advanced" nations were unable to enlighten them as to the process by which it worked; indeed, they themselves remained mystified by it. The advent of Kokkuri in Japan therefore represents not the transference of knowledge—as was the case with regard to education, political systems, economics, and military institutions—but the transference of mystery.

CREATING A NEW REFERENTIAL ECOLOGY

Although its importation from America would seem to define this mechanical structure as a new form of Western spiritual technology, we have already seen that the name *Kokkuri* soon came to have indelible associations with existing yōkai. Though it entered the country laterally from abroad, the practice found a home within already established modes of communicating with the otherworld. Specifically, Kokkuri was a form of spirit possession, in which the apparatus received into itself a spirit that responded to questions posed by the participants. Of course, spirit possession is manifest in many disparate forms; the literature on possession in Japan and elsewhere is vast. For our purposes, however, Kokkuri can be characterized as a form of "controlled" possession, in which a medium of some sort—a *kuchi-yose,* a *miko,* an *itako*—receives into herself the spirit of, for example, a fox.[44] Through employing a medium, a village might forecast events of the coming year or ascertain the cause of a problem that had been plaguing it. Mediums or shamans often passed through intense physical and psychological trials and training in order to develop the special skills required for their profession.[45]

The conflation of Kokkuri with mediumship pervaded the contemporary discourse. One author, for example, emphasizes the fact that Kokkuri very much "resembles" forms of Japanese shamanism known as "kuchi-yose" and "ichiko" (itako) and suggests that Kokkuri might be called a "Western ichiko."[46] As noted earlier, however, Kokkuri did not require professional mediums; rather, the apparatus itself *was* the medium, and it was a medium available to anybody. As Ichiyanagi puts it, "With no special connections or influence, you could easily have a supernatural presence dispatched to your sitting room."[47] To be sure, other forms of fortune-telling could be performed by nonprofessionals, and in this sense Kokkuri was not unique. But as a form of divination relying on outside spirits to *possess* something, Kokkuri may represent the first recorded instance in Japan in which possession as such became practicable by untrained participants.

With the advent of Meiji and the influence of Inoue Enryō and others, many Edo-period customs came to be viewed with suspicion and classified under the pejorative rubric of superstition *(meishin).* Not surprisingly, possession and the practice of shamanism did not escape the scientific gaze of the bunmei-kaika ideologues. After the introduction of Western-based medical and psychological practices, spirit possession gradually came to be defined in terms of mental illness: fox possession and related phenomena were increasingly diagnosed as nervous disorders or diseases of the brain. Those suffering from uncontrolled possession were no longer treated by religious or folk practitioners, but were confined to newly built psychiatric hospitals.[48] Moreover, the shamanic methods I have referred to as "controlled" possession came to be implicated not as folk practices but as criminal acts: by 1872, laws outlawing shamanism began to be promulgated throughout the country. Invoking the rhetoric of enlightenment, these laws strictly forbade miko and kuchi-yose from practicing their profession, warning that they deceived the common people and led the masses astray.[49]

Certainly, medical treatises and government edicts were not necessarily an efficient means of altering long-standing traditions and local practices. In fact, the issuance of edicts might be interpreted merely as an attempt by the new Meiji leaders to create an image of modern governance for public and international consumption.[50] At the very least, however, the psychological and medical concepts introduced during the bunmei-kaika period officially altered the discourse on possession, turning it into a deviant practice fueled by outmoded "superstitious" beliefs. Though it is impossible to assess the penetration of this intellectual zeitgeist into the popular imaginary, it is fair to say that the Meiji period—especially the several years following the Restoration itself—represents a time of disjuncture with respect to attitudes toward spirit possession. After the 1870s, shamanism could no longer be considered an "acceptable" or appropriately "modern" practice. "In modern Japanese society," Kawamura Kunimitsu points out, "the miko becomes a symbolic presence of that which spreads 'superstition' and leads astray the 'ignorant masses.'"[51]

In other words, Kokkuri emerged on the scene just as old "mystic" practices such as spirit possession and shamanism were being systematically suppressed by new "scientific" practices based on elite, usually Western-inspired, normative discourses. For Enryō and like-minded thinkers, confidence in the illuminating powers of modern science was set against a naive reliance on a premodern explanatory paradigm in which yōkai could affect the human world. The common folk were deluded, Enryō claimed; they were lost in a world in which people became possessed by foxes, and natural phenomena were attributed to the machinations of unseen spirits. Science could enlighten, driving away the darkness of mystery by revealing the "principles by which things work" (15).

Enryō is making a radical assertion here—he is suggesting that the Meiji populace, the common folk, have always been mistaken about the way they interpret the world around them, and that it is his responsibility, through the discipline of yōkaigaku, to lead them to a new interpretive paradigm. A useful tool with which to grasp the differing worlds of perception at stake here is the concept of "referential ecology," a notion originally introduced by Donald Campbell and later developed by sociologist Mark Schneider.[52] It goes without saying that every "thing" in the external world is understood through individual subjective interpretation, and that the nature of this interpretation is determined ultimately by a shared understanding of what the "thing" signifies within the particular culture of the interpreter. Referential ecology "invites us to conceive of phenomena, any and all phenomena, as constituting a system of 'niches' differentiated according to the ease or difficulty of developing referential consensus about them." Though in the case of certain objects and concepts people generally share a referential consensus, Schneider explains, "other phenomena, in contrast, are highly complex, irregular in their behavior, and observable only with the aid of expensive and perhaps undependable equipment, whether physical or conceptual."[53]

A physical object such as a tree is something for which referential consensus within and between cultures is fairly strong (though certainly not monolithic); in many (though not all) cultures, the "meaning" of a tree provides relatively limited room for disagreement. The possible symbolic, aesthetic, natural, and practical meanings that might be ascribed to a tree are *comparatively* circumscribed, and interpretations generally fit within a limited set of parameters. In contrast, something like an unusual occurrence or a particular action might be interpreted in fundamentally different ways. For example, the exact same behavior on the part of an individual might be interpreted as an indication of fox possession or of mental illness—depending on the referential terrain of the interpreter (or the interpretive community). That is, the same signifier can indicate a completely different signified, depending on which community is doing the interpreting. And some signifiers—those that have a stronger "occult" association—lend themselves to a wider range of interpretations.

For the transitional years of the 1880s, Kokkuri serves as just such an occult signifier, a cipher meaning something radically different to different interpreters. Explanations of the phenomenon could be phrased only in terms of the particular referents and metaphors available to the given interpretive community. For example, with the affixing of a Japanese word—*kokkuri*—to the movement, and then even more so with the connection of the yōkai-signifying graphs 狐狗狸 to the name, the practice came to make sense within the referential terrain of the people who played it. The movement of the apparatus could most effectively be explained through reference to otherworldly creatures acting upon the present world. Yōkai and spirit possession were ideas for which there was, at least in one interpretive community, what Schneider calls a "referential consensus."

Significantly, this idea of referential ecology also allows for a certain amount of "play" with regard to belief. Whether or not the people practicing Kokkuri actually *believed* in yōkai or were just *playing* with the notion is irrelevant; the point is simply that they shared the concept of yōkai as a referent with which to associate their observations. Yōkai provided a common language, a shared set of metaphors to explain otherwise unexplainable events. And not only were these metaphors readily available in the cultural imaginary, but they could also literally be referenced in Edo-period encyclopedias and Sekien's bestiaries.

Operations of the Spirit: Enryō's Exegesis

Enryō strove to reshape the referential ecology so that Kokkuri might be understood in terms of something *other* than yōkai; his desire was nothing less than to alter the landscape of perception by which people defined and gave meaning to the phenomena around them. The job undertaken by Enryō entailed shifting the set of references, from the easy ones already shared by many Kokkuri participants, to ones involving physiology and psychology and an entire set of referents foreign (in every sense of the word) to his readership. Such a transformation was not without its political motivations: as we have seen, practices such as shamanism and spirit possession were considered inappropriate for a modernizing nation-state.[54] In the preface to *Yōkai gendan,* Enryō not only explicitly states his broader objective of enlightening the common folk of Japan but also suggests that this can be done only through academic (scientific) explanation.

For the first major work of his yōkaigaku project, it is not surprising that he would choose Kokkuri, this new yōkai so conspicuous that it had even garnered the attention of foreign observers such as Basil Hall Chamberlain, who labeled it a "fashionable craze."[55] Kokkuri provided Enryō with a very visible case study through which he could begin to alter the metaphorical landscape: "I believe that, for the forward progress of civilization, it is necessary to illuminate academically the principles by which things work in order to make clear the way for those people who are lost; and so I will explain here the causes and circumstances of Kokkuri" (15). As we have seen, Enryō's goal in eliminating yōkai was not to destroy all conceptions of the mysterious but rather to weed out "false mystery" so that "true mystery" could be recognized. In Kokkuri he found no "true mystery" worth salvaging, but rather a complex nexus of internal psychological factors and external environmental factors that created the illusion of a mysterious force.

"To the oceans east and west, throughout the world old and new, of all the many forms of things and spirits in the universe," writes Enryō, "there are some which cannot be understood with normal reason *[futsū no dōri]*. These are known as yōkai" (16). Before tackling the specific issue of Kokkuri, he formulates a general rule for classifying and interpreting yōkai and mysterious (fushigi) matter of all sorts. His exegesis is complex, exhibiting a penchant for classifying and dividing that would continue throughout his work. Ultimately his inquiry moves increasingly inward, refashioning yōkai as constructions created deep within the human psyche and physiology. Rather than allowing yōkai to remain external phenomena that act on the individual, he shifts the agency of the yōkai *into* the individual and that individual's interpretation of matters observed.[56]

In the second half of *Yōkai gendan*, Enryō turns his attention to explaining the precise mechanism by which Kokkuri operated, mapping in detail the new referential terrain he wanted to promulgate. "When considering the causes of Kokkuri," he observes, "the common people *[tsūjō no hito]* believe it to be the doings of kitsune or tanuki; or, they profess it to be the workings of demons and deities [kijin]" (37). People who believed that the movement of Kokkuri was caused by a spirit "possessing" the apparatus were primarily "ignorant or uneducated." He goes on to assert that women and children with strong beliefs had particular success with the practice; moreover, Kokkuri responded correctly more often when posed questions concerning the past rather than the future, or when the question was "easy" rather than "detailed." Because Kokkuri did not work with equal success for all people, Enryō concludes, it could not be caused by a presumably objective phenomenon such as yōkai. "Furthermore," he continues, "if a demon or deity is really taking possession of . . . the tray, then it should not always be necessary for people to touch it with their hands." For these reasons, he asserts, there had to be a cause other than the workings of spirit possession (38).

In fact, Enryō explains, both external and internal factors caused the (mis)perception of Kokkuri (and other yōkai). The apparatus was constructed in such a way as to be delicately balanced and sensitive to the movement of hands placed upon it—factors Enryō characterizes as *external* causes (39). But these external factors combined with what he describes as *internal* influences, such as the fact that hands placed upon the tenuously balanced tray could not remain still indefinitely. Eventually at least one of the participants would move a little—and when even a tiny movement of the hands was transferred to the sensitive apparatus, a significant movement was generated. And when a single movement occurred, it gathered momentum until it eventually caused the apparatus to tilt or spin.[57] This combination of external and internal influences may account for some of the dynamics behind Kokkuri's movements, but Enryō acknowledges that we are still left with the question of why uneducated people with strong beliefs had more success with Kokkuri than educated people with weak beliefs (41). The answer "most necessary" to explain Kokkuri completely internalizes the process of causality, bringing the mysterious external "spirits" into the metaphorical ecology of the internal human "spirit," the realm of what Enryō calls *shinsei sayō*, "mental operations" or "operations of the spirit."

At this point, Enryō's exegesis becomes exceedingly complex: he is mapping a referential terrain foreign to his readers, and accordingly his explanation seeks to familiarize them with the details of this new topography. The two most important features of this landscape are *unconscious muscular activities (fukaku kindō)* and *expectant attention (yoki ikō)* (50). The former are automatic, or reflex, actions such as digestion and breathing. In order to elucidate the physiological functions here, Enryō outlines the "structure of the nerves" (composed of nerve fibers and nerve cells), the role of the brain and the spinal cord, and the synaptic connections created "between the nerve cells" in the brain. He explains that the brain is the location of thought, perception, will, and so on, while the spinal cord is the location for unconscious operations *[fukaku sayō]*. Some sensory impulses reach the brain, and the brain responds with a conscious command; other impulses receive unconscious responses from the spinal cord (44–47).

Enryō's discussion is remarkable for its physiological complexity as he takes the reader deeper and deeper into the internal workings of the human body and mind, and further away from any association with the workings of kitsune or tengu or tanuki in the external world. For Enryō, the truth about yōkai has a lot more to do with the impulses running through nerve fibers than with shape-shifting animals: "If a person already feels in his heart that Kokkuri should spin, then without his knowledge, his muscles will cause the movement to occur. In other words, without realizing it each person transfers the natural movement of his hands to Kokkuri. And the internal cause that produces this movement is *expectant attention.* Expectant attention occurs when one believes in advance that something should be thus, and so all expectations are focused in that one direction" (50).

Both of these key ideas, "unconscious muscular activities" and "expectant attention," are derived from the work of the American scientist William Carpenter, who explained table-turning in his *Principles of Men-*

tal Physiology. Whereas Carpenter's book is a broad scientific discussion *including* a critique of table-turning and like phenomena, Enryō adopts Carpenter's outline of the operations of the nervous system for the express purpose of debunking Kokkuri, explaining that, "as for movements that originate in the brain, there are those that are performed with awareness, and those that are performed without awareness. The latter is the cause of Kokkuri; in other words, it is [caused by] expectant attention and unconscious muscular activities" (50).[58]

Enryō goes on to elucidate how the ritualistic power of the name *Kokkuri* invokes expectant attention:

> As I have already pointed out, the public uses [the characters] 狐狗狸 to indicate *Kokkuri*, and when people hear this word, they think that the spirit of kitsune or tanuki is possessing [the apparatus]; the name *[Kokkuri]* has the tendency to encourage expectant attention. Moreover, the general public hears that Kokkuri is something that is possessed by kitsune and tanuki [kori], or demons and deities [kijin], and which makes pronouncements about good and bad fortune—and because they call Kokkuri a method to invite yōkai, they are really encouraging the expectant attention of most people. (59–60)

He also looks at his own data in order to draw some broader generalizations with regard to the power of belief:

> As for the rotation of Kokkuri, it follows through the laws of association that, since among all types of creatures the tengu is the strongest, [Kokkuri rotates] most forcefully when the tengu is summoned, and more weakly when weaker creatures are invoked. In other words, as for the tengu, since we know of its great power, we conceive of tengu and great power together; when we think a tengu is coming, we naturally *[mizukara]* apply great power, and it follows that Kokkuri responds by rotating more forcefully. On the other hand, when we think that a weaker type of creature is coming, we apply weak power, and we see that Kokkuri rotates weakly. (54)

Enryō recasts tengu and other yōkai as creatures of the imagination, transferring the mystic agency, the force that caused Kokkuri to move, from the external (other) world into the internal world of the self—into the physical and mental mechanisms of the human body. Kokkuri, it turned out, was a barometer connected to the mind, an instrument that measured the level of one's belief in the "false mystery" of yōkai. As Enryō explains elsewhere, "A person sees *kakai* and thinks it is *shinkai*. This is superstition."[59] It is only natural that "uneducated" participants, hindered by their inability to see beyond false mystery, demonstrated a much greater response in playing Kokkuri than did highly educated individuals. *Yōkai gendan* represents an effort to halt Kokkuri's movements completely through the promulgation of knowledge and the attenuation of supernatural belief. Enryō's goal was to transform metaphors from the mystic to the scientific, to shift the referential terrain of the Japanese people to one more befitting a nation on the cusp of modernity.

Human Electricity

To a certain extent, the new referential ecology of modernity had an effect on the way people interpreted the world around them; at the same time, however, it did not necessarily halt the movement of the Kokkuri apparatus. New and appropriately modern mysteries emerged from the very powers suggested by the scientific paradigm. Indeed, while asserting pejoratively that the "uneducated" classes attributed the operations of Kokkuri to possession, Enryō himself also notes that another theory circulated particularly among those with "a little bit of knowledge." These people claimed that Kokkuri was caused neither by "kitsune or tengu, nor by deities or demons, but by the operations of electricity." Enryō quickly dismisses this conjecture, pointing out that nothing in this regard had been made clear, and that, "recently, the public has overused this word 'electricity.' Whenever there is something difficult to explain through the physical sciences, everybody calls on electricity" (37). But the electrical paradigm had broad popular appeal. The attribution of Kokkuri's movements to the operations of electricity indicates that people were willing to rely on scientific explanation though not willing to fully commit to the difficult physiological and psychological paradigm Enryō was introducing. In a sense, electricity provided a middle ground—a new and foreign landscape to be sure, but one still shrouded in ambiguity and encouraging a magical transcendence of common experience.

The invocation of electricity to explain away all sorts of mysteries was by no means a distinctly Japanese practice. In the United States and Europe, electricity was at once scientific, magic, entertaining, and romantic, touted as a panacea for various diseases and as the secret behind numerous unexplainable phenomena.[60] Just as the discourse on Spiritualism dealt with profound philosophical questions in which nothing less than the structure of the universe was at stake, so too did the discourse on electricity. John Bovee Dods, a proponent of the "wonderful and mysterious science of Electrical Psychology," exemplified this attitude when he asserted that "electricity actuates the whole frame of nature, and produces all the phenomena that transpire throughout the realms of unbounded space."[61]

Given such hyperbolic claims, it is not surprising that those with a more scientific bent than the Spiritualists would summon the powers of electricity to elucidate the mysteries of the séance. In the 1850s, the egalitarian nature of the table-turning practice brought questions regarding the natural and the supernatural, the deity and the devil, into the middle-class parlor, allowing "one's dining-room table to become the scene of epic struggles."[62] Explanations of the table's rotation ranged from the devoutly religious to the rebelliously occult to a cunning form of legerdemain. One common conjecture, which refuted the Spiritualist attribution of the movements to supernatural forces but did not go as far as the scientific rationale of Faraday and Carpenter (and Enryō), posited that the rotation of the table was caused by magnetic or electrical forces.[63] Indeed, reportedly the impetus for Michael Faraday's famous 1853 investigation of table-turning was not its association with Spiritualism but rather his exasperation at the "great number of letters from experimenters demanding his confirmation that table-turning was produced by electricity generated by the group encircling the table."[64] But Faraday's assertion that table-turning was caused neither by spirits nor by electricity did not stem the tide of electrical worship (or, for that matter, Spiritualism), and electricity (and the related concept of magnetism) continued to be popularly associated with the workings of matter both physical and spiritual.

It is impossible to pinpoint how and when notions about electricity and its relationship to human physiology and psychology began to infiltrate popular culture in Japan. Though electricity, particularly in the form of the *erekiteru,* or "static electricity generator," had been a curiosity before Meiji, not until the 1880s, almost exactly coincident with Kokkuri, did it begin to garner mass attention.[65] In July of 1882, incandescent lighting was used to illuminate the graduation ceremony at the University of Tokyo. In November of the same year, part of Tokyo's Ginza shopping district was lit up, marking the general public's first exposure to electric light.[66] In 1883 the first electrical generating company was established in Tokyo and began supplying power publicly in 1887.[67] By the 1880s, then, electricity was becoming emblematic of Japan's nascent modernity and shifting urban landscape, and *electricity*, or *denki,* had become a trendy word used to name and market all that was new and special.[68]

Not surprisingly, when something new and mysterious appeared in the land, the electrical paradigm was immediately invoked as a "scientific" explanation. Electricity served as a substitute for what rationality had disenchanted; the very stuff that brought enlightenment became emblematic of a new mystery. In the opposition of mystery and science, electricity was a bridge between the two, simultaneously denying and confirming both.

Two surviving texts, produced for popular consumption, situate electricity at the root of the Kokkuri mystery. Even more than Enryō's work, these documents reveal a sense of how Kokkuri might have been understood by the nonelite classes of Meiji, who were feeling their way through a referential terrain in which the old metaphors were losing status but the new ones were not yet comprehensible or confirmed. It is impossible to assume the mind-set of an unknown readership, but these texts seem to reflect a general attitude toward Kokkuri held by members of the community who had no access to the elite education of Enryō but who were interested in understanding and taking part in the Kokkuri fad.

Seiyō kijutsu Kokkuri kaidan (Western Sorcery: Kokkuri Ghost Stories), "edited" by Ryōkū Yajin, is a forty-two-page monograph originally published in March 1887, several months before Enryō's *Yōkai gendan,* and revised and reprinted several times, including at least once (the third edition) after Enryō's monograph.[69] This later edition is explicitly in dialogue with Enryō's work, mentioning a "particular literary scholar" belonging to the "priesthood" and "possessing an academic degree" who did not venture into the Yoshiwara district, and who therefore did not discover Kokkuri until quite late.[70] Although much of Ryōkū's initial argument parallels Enryō's—such as his claim that education would enlighten the people to the fact that Kokkuri was not based on the machinations of yōkai—his text ultimately affords insight into a more popular response to the phenomenon than we get from Enryō's didactic stance.

Immediately apparent is the emphasis on Kokkuri as a Western *(seiyō)* import. Ryōkū makes clear that Kokkuri was not native to Japan but "was brought from America two or three years ago." The imposition of the three graphs for *kitsune, tengu,* and *tanuki,* he explains, established an overdetermined association with traditional Japanese "kuchi-yose" and "ichiko" fortune tellers and served to "move the hearts of the uneducated folk" (7–8). Like Enryō he also promotes the power of education and knowledge, but concedes that, even with learning, mystery persists: "Along with advances in human knowledge, the facts about that which is called mysterious [fushigi] or strange *[kimyō]* reach a higher altitude. As the mysterious and uncanny *[fukashigi kikai]* of the unenlightened world is vulgar and inferior, accordingly the mysterious and uncanny of the enlightened world is dignified and superior" (2).

Suggesting that progress in human understanding leads to a whole new level of mystery, Ryōkū removes Kokkuri from its common, mistaken association with yōkai, positioning it under this rubric of "dignified and superior" mystery and suggesting that Kokkuri's uncanniness "is not at all like sorcery, witchcraft, and the like." While lauding the powers of enlightenment, however, Ryōkū's own explanation of Kokkuri distinctly contrasts with Enryō's: "Through the energies of academic thought, the principle of its operations should become clear—its movement is caused by the workings of electricity [denki] within the human body (Human-electricity)" (15).[71]

The monograph goes on to present descriptions about how Kokkuri is played, including incidental commentary on the effectiveness of certain procedures for encouraging better electrical flow. Ryōkū explains, for example, that the tray should be round, because a square or angular tray does not permit good electrical circulation. And as for the color of the cloth placed on top of the tray, white or gold is most desirable, and "if you cover it with a blue cloth it won't move at all. For some reason the color blue interferes and stops the flow of electricity" (29–30). As for the workings of "animal electricity" and "human electricity," Ryōkū explains that, although some people consider them mysterious, they work on a positive/negative principle, like yin and yang, in which each person's body must possess the correct amount of electricity (38–39). "For instance," he explains, "if a healthy three- or four-year-old infant sleeps together with an old grandparent for two or three years, in the end it is said [the infant] will die. This is because the electricity from the infant's body will supplement the lack in the old person, creating a balance that the [infant's] supply cannot sustain" (39–40).[72] Thus, he concludes, the workings of electricity are based on this natural principle of flow from bodies of abundance to bodies of lack.

Ultimately, however, Ryōkū fails to elucidate the mechanism by which electricity operates in the practice of Kokkuri. He seems to suggest that the flow of electricity from one person to another through the apparatus is the force that makes the structure move, but he never actually states this. Nor does he connect the operations of electricity to Kokkuri's ability to answer questions and foretell the future. At first glance, such lacunae seem odd for a monograph that purports to enlighten the reader as to the workings of Kokkuri. But the insufficiency of Ryōkū's discussion indicates its position in the broader cultural context with regard to issues of the mystic and scientific. The positivist Restoration rhetoric denies the traditional spirits, embracing Western "science" in their place. Western science, however, ultimately does not diminish the mystery—it only transfers it to a "superior" plane of inquiry represented by the electrical paradigm. By shifting the focus from traditional rural yōkai to the modern urban yōkai of electricity, Ryōkū's rhetoric redefines the superstitious mysteries of the unenlightened past as scientific mysteries of an enlightened future: mystery is equated with progress.

Ryōkū concludes his argument by stating that his intention was to demonstrate "only that Kokkuri is not a mysterious [fushigi] practice." At the same time, however, he proclaims that "the operational phenomena of human electricity are subtle and uncanny *[bimyō kii]*" (42). In other words, he simultaneously enlightens (Kokkuri is not a mystery) and enchants (electricity is uncanny). Although Kokkuri can be explained by electricity, nobody can explain electricity, an intangible phenomenon whose operations are registered only through the movements of a machine. While electricity is different from "sorcery or witchcraft," it remains "something aptly labeled *fushigi*" (38). Kokkuri, and the "human electricity" through which it works, retains its magic, but it is not the magic of Edo-period superstition. Rather it is a scientific brand of magic, indicative not of a backward nation but of Westernization and progress: a rational, enlightened enchantment.

Ryōkū's approach betrays an acceptance of the in-between, an appreciation of—indeed a promulgation of—an ambiguous (and therefore appealing) solution to the Kokkuri mystery. In the final analysis, his monograph does nothing to disenchant Kokkuri; it only transfers the enchantment from the old to the new. If we recall Max Weber's famous comment that "the fate of our times is characterized by rationalization and intellectualization and, above all, the 'disenchantment of the world,'" Ryōkū's move is all the more intriguing.[73] Far from quashing enchantment, he broadens its realm to include the whole of intellectual inquiry, positing a certain irrationality within the sciences themselves: "If we are to judge by the use of the single word 'fukashigi,' then in all the phenomena of the universe, in everything around us, there is nothing that is not fukashigi. In astronomy, mathematics and science, there are a great many circumstances that are fukashigi" (36).

That *Seiyō kijutsu Kokkuri kaidan* went through at least three printings is evidence of its resonance with a curious public. Ryōkū's lack of conclusiveness with regard to the link between electricity and Kokkuri apparently did not deter people from purchasing his monograph. On the contrary, his transference of the mystery from the rural spirits of the past to the modern spirit of electricity may have attracted recently urbanized readers intent on sloughing off the pre-Meiji mysteries of their own pasts but reluctant to abandon altogether the possibility of the unexplainable. Another, shorter document published around the same time similarly reflects this profound ambiguity and also demonstrates a link between scientific rhetoric and the lively world of play. Published in 1886 in Osaka, *Jinshin denki no zuga* (Diagram of Human Electricity) pithily embodies a collage of discourses surrounding Kokkuri.[74] The cover itself draws on the cultural capital of Kokkuri's Western origins, catching the reader's eye with the mention of New York and the prominently featured English words *Human Electricity.* Here was a document that dealt with the trendiest of fads, filtered through the popular language of the West and of science.

Jinshin denki no zuga is essentially an instruction manual for the game. The author, one Kojima Hyakuzō, explains both Kokkuri's association with the entertainment districts as well as its *mis*-association with traditional yōkai: "Some geisha in the Shinagawa entertainment district imagined [these movements to be caused by] the mysterious powers of a kitsune or tanuki, and unreasonably applied the name 'Kokkuri-san.'" At first Kojima seems to dismiss the whole issue in commonsensical, Enryō-like, fashion: "Each person puts a single hand on the three-legged platter. When the hand of one of these people gets tired, the heaviness naturally causes the tray to tilt. . . . [When this happens] people unreasonably believe that Kokkuri-san has arrived." As we read on, however, we discover that Kojima is not in fact debunking the practice itself; rather, he is criticizing the form of play with *one* hand on the apparatus. The correct way, he notes, is to place *both* hands on the tray so that everybody's fingers are in contact. The linking of fingers presumably creates an electrical circuit causing the apparatus to move. Like Ryōkū, however, Kojima is vague about the details; though he claims that "the movements of this form of play known as Kokkuri are completely based on the operations of Human Electricity," he never actually outlines the dynamics of this relationship. In the end, he succeeds only in reenchanting the practice, noting that "the reasons why electricity works in this manner have yet to be discovered."

Kojima's equivocation resonated with a public willing to embrace manifold possibilities. A perfectly understandable explanation was not necessary to those playing Kokkuri—in effect, a "good" explanation would only diminish the excitement of ambiguity and the possibility of the undiscovered. Both Ryōkū and Kojima discursively construct Kokkuri as a hybrid, and such hybrids, as Richard Bauman and Charles L. Briggs note, "keep modernity from ever achieving the order and rationality that it is supposed to embody."[75] Kojima's readers were looking for an explanation that was modern in form, perhaps, but that in the final analysis would explain nothing at all. Such an explanation was not the sort of debunking exegesis Enryō provided, but rather one that elucidated how to make Kokkuri work more effectively—an explanation of *how to play* the game. Ultimately, Kojima situates Kokkuri as neither mystic nor scientific but a little bit of both and, mostly, a form of recreation. As an instruction manual for the game, his discussion gestures to the fact that Kokkuri, like Sekien's catalogs, is a site of convergence and overlap, a ludic space that allows negotiation between otherwise incompatible discourses, quietly subverting traditional mystic modes as well as new scientific modes by treating them all as entertainment.

THE SPACE OF PLAY

I have argued that the mystic practice of spirit possession, which had existed in one form or another throughout the Tokugawa period, was subjected to the critical gaze of the bunmei-kaika ideologues. Professional shamanism was criminalized, and spirit possession redefined as insanity. In this context, how could Kokkuri—in many ways a much more pervasive form of spirit possession than any pre-Meiji version—take hold? Constructed with readily available materials, Kokkuri granted everyone equal access to the spirits; in one sense, we can read the practice as a subtle defiance of Meiji attempts to legislate and medicalize traditional patterns of belief. In the post-Restoration context, the transference of shamanic agency from human to machine allowed people to escape both the legal framework and the discursive constraints of a medical vocabulary.

Such escape was made possible by Kokkuri's gamelike form and playful qualities. Kokkuri incorporated the unacceptable logic of the supernatural into the harmless grammar of play, assuming a form not only more accessible to the average person but also removed from the critical treatment afforded earlier, more serious varieties of spirit possession. Just as Kokkuri fits into a pre-Meiji epistemology with regard to the spirits, it also fits into the long lineage of recreational practices treated in the previous chapter. There I suggested that an underlying theme of play is the creation of an alternate space with its own rules and patterns of relationships. Such a space acts as a medium, cradling contradictions and fostering negotiation among differing discourses and between otherwise incompatible distinctions of status, occupation, and belief.

Kokkuri and more traditional (outlawed) forms of possession differ with regard to their respective objectives. The invocation of a fox spirit was commonly deployed for the purpose of determining some fact about the past or the future. The invocation of Kokkuri, on the other hand, rarely involved anything of great seriousness. On the contrary, the objective was simply the excitement of playing with something mysterious, the titillation of making contact with the otherworld. A "true" divinatory practice was utilitarian, providing practical insight into the past and future; Kokkuri was aesthetic, even sensual, providing a pleasurable experience of the strange. Even the questions posed to Kokkuri—Are you a kitsune? Do you like to dance? Will it rain tomorrow?—indicate that participants were primarily testing the accuracy of the apparatus, playing with the possibility of communication rather than trying to garner vital information about the future. As an oracle restricted to a binary system of "yes" or "no" answers, Kokkuri's guidance was inevitably limited in scope.

This lack of serious purport stands in distinct contrast to table-turning in North America and Europe. To be sure, some of the questions in the Western version of the game concerned verification of the connection with the spirit world and determining whose spirit was making contact. In Victorian drawing rooms, entertainment and thrill and even a hint of sexual titillation were certainly involved. And yet, the practice had serious ambitions: table-turning and the popularity of séances reflected a profound religious crisis. The motives behind the questioning of the spirit world conducted by followers of the Society for Psychical Research, for example, betray a powerful desire to get to the bottom of such issues as the immortality of the soul.[76] Although Enryō claims that there is "not the slightest bit of difference" (35) between Kokkuri and table-turning, even his own description of the Western version reveals an emphasis in the latter on philosophical concerns of more gravity than whether it will rain the next day: "The method is to face a table which is already turning and ask, 'Does God *[kami-sama]* exist or not? If God exists, stop turning.' And when this is said, sometimes the table will respond by stopping. And again, [they] will ask about the existence or nonexistence of heaven and hell, saying if they exist [the table] should strike the floor; in response to this, sometimes the table will lift a leg by itself and strike the floor" (35).

While the investigations of table-turning were embedded in the broader religious discourses of Spiritualism and movements such as Theosophy, Kokkuri had very little to do with institutionalized religion of any sort. The Bakumatsu-Meiji period did witness the rise of a number of new religious movements (such as Tenrikyō and Omotokyō) that developed from episodes of spirit possession and came to fruition through automatic writing and other occult techniques. Though Kokkuri relied on similar principles for its operation, it was not part of such religious and spiritual movements. Rather, as a recreational practice it represented a safe and secular manipulation of many of the same mechanisms that make religious experience possible.

This characterization of Kokkuri as a form of play also corresponds with contemporary discourse. Although Enryō emphasizes the danger of Kokkuri, labeling it "sorcery" *[genjutsu]* (19), even he alludes to its playfulness: "On holidays in the boardinghouses, students gather and play all night, asking all sorts of questions; in the city, people play music and sing songs while dancing along with Kokkuri" (20). In some cases the entertainment itself inspired Kokkuri to operate effectively: "Three women and children place their left hands lightly on top [of the apparatus]; when [the people] around them beat a drum or sing and make a commotion, the tray will begin to turn" (26).[77] Enryō's informant from Saitama Prefecture offers a scenario in which the apparatus itself joins in the revelry: "One person sings . . . and two of the bamboo legs match the tune of the song, moving up and down in turns. When the voice of the singer is pure and the tune is passionate, the legs move up and down one level faster, dancing in all directions throughout the room" (29–30). Just as one of the attractions of the pleasure districts was the excitement of a risqué atmosphere tinged with sexuality, so Kokkuri titillated with its sense of the otherworld so near at hand. It was an amusement to be enjoyed along with sake and laughter, akin to hyaku-monogatari and yōkai karuta, one game in a long lineage of mysterious entertainments.

Tsubouchi Shōyō's Banquet

One of Enryō's contemporaries, the novelist, translator, and literary critic Tsubouchi Shōyō (1859–1935), relates an anecdote about his own experience with Kokkuri.[78] His account highlights the way it operated in the contact zone between discourses of science and mystery. Most important, however, his vignette vividly illustrates the critical importance of the ludic in fostering the production of mystery. In the year 1886, Shōyō was invited by Konishi Yoshitaka,[79] the publisher of the *Konnichi shinbun,* to attend a party in a banquet hall with geisha:

> That was the time when the 'table-turning' known as 'Kokkuri-sama' was first brought to our country. As it is the way of the demimonde to be first in feeling a fascination for such [new] things, the three legs and round tray were brought into the banquet hall as part of the entertainment. Though it goes without saying that the various geisha [were excited], even our host, Konishi, made a fuss as they started the testing *[shiken]*. It was so accurate that even those who were half doubting *[hanshin-hangi]* in the beginning found it eerie and were duped to the extent that they were reluctant to place their hands on the tray.

Only Shōyō himself failed to be impressed by the new amusement, explaining, "Most likely the knowledge of mental physiology *[shinri seirigaku]* came from abroad first to the medical and literature departments of the University of Tokyo." Having studied there himself, and having read Carpenter's *Principles of Mental Physiology,* Shōyō was already familiar with the workings of clairvoyance, mesmerism, spiritualism, table-turning, and the like: "According to Carpenter's interpretation, the movement of the table is [caused by] the operations of 'expectant attention.' And because I believed this, no matter how hard everybody at the gathering tried to get the tray to tilt with me [playing], it ended in failure."[80] Shōyō implies that you must *believe* in one or the other—the scientific or the mystic. Since he believed Carpenter's explanations, the process was demystified: his scientific interpretation disenchanted the apparatus. In fact, the evidence he cites to prove his own interpretation is that Kokkuri refused to respond when he played—the power of scientific reason stymied the mystic. That is, while Shōyō's belief in science enabled him to cheerfully debunk Kokkuri, it also inhibited his suspension of disbelief so that he could not enjoy the game in the same way as his friends and the geisha.

The mysterious practice of table-turning, as well as the scientific knowledge that professed to demystify it, came to Japan from the West but entered through very different conduits—through the sailors in Shimoda as opposed to English-language texts and the professors at the University of Tokyo. Did Kokkuri belong to the uneducated lower classes (the courtesans) or to the educated elite (the publishers and writers)? Was it a "real" method for contacting spirits, or was it a parlor trick? A ritual or a game? Japanese or Western? The discourses that emerged to explain and promote Kokkuri positioned the practice itself as a hybrid nurtured within a ludic context. Furthermore, by inspiring a plurality of explanations, Kokkuri offered a subtle form of resistance not against Western knowledge itself but against the co-optation of such knowledge for a regime of disenchantment that threatened to infiltrate everyday life. Channeling the ghosts of spirit possession, Kokkuri refused complicity with new Meiji modes of ideological production that would banish the possibility of the mystic from everyday life.

This is not to say that Kokkuri presented a real threat to what Figal has described as "a network of national power that was being constructed through new knowledges manipulated and institutionalized by an elite caste who were formally and informally associated with the Meiji government."[81] As a form of homemade entertainment, Kokkuri seems to have flourished primarily in a space immune to official censure. Only when the commercial potential of the practice inspired its commodification did the authorities find a strategy for enforcement: according to an 1886 newspaper account, seven individuals were investigated by the local police in connection with the advent of a "Kokkuri teaching center" *(denjusho)* in a Kyoto neighborhood and the appearance of "numerous" outlets selling the Kokkuri apparatus.[82] To be sure, the results of this investigation are unclear, and Kokkuri does not seem to have been a major focus of police inquiry after this point, but its early configuration here as a crime attests to the implicit resistance represented by its practice and proliferation.

THE PERSISTENCE OF MYSTERY

While I hesitate to overemphasize Kokkuri's resistance to Meiji governmental policy, I do want to underscore the way Kokkuri and similar yōkai beliefs do not necessarily conform to the official trajectory of progress and modernity. Transitions on the level of mentalité, in the way people comprehend their worlds, occur gradually and inconsistently, full of clashes and contradictions and overlappings. In the 1880s, while Meiji intellectuals and oligarchs were charting a course for transforming Japan into a modern nation electrified and militarized and competitive in a world market, subtle transitions were also taking place in the lives of the populace.

The discourses surrounding Kokkuri reveal how political and ideological shifts are expressed on a cultural level, in everyday lives and experiences, in ways that make historical notions of premodern and modern much more nuanced. On the level of ideological production, new modes of scientific thinking may have produced discontinuities with regard to the mystic, but, in lived experience, continuities with regard to ludic attitudes helped bridge these contradictory positions. Kokkuri reveals that seemingly irreconcilable concepts were really quite compatible in the popular imagination—questions of mystic truth and scientific reality were less substantial than the aesthetic pleasure engendered by personal, playful experience with the unexplainable. This is particularly evident in the electricity paradigm—an explanation ornamented with scientific rhetoric but infused with the appeal of the unexplainable. Even while Enryō and others were implementing a rational regimen for the nation, Kokkuri offered a way for the Meiji-period layperson to translate the discoveries of science into a whole new world of mystery.

Ultimately, Enryō's discourse can be understood as an effort to remake the metaphorical or referential terrain, from one inhabited by the monsters of folk belief, the yōkai we find in Toriyama Sekien's work, to a landscape made up of muscles and nerves and synapses. These new physiological and psychological concepts came to serve a function similar to that of the old yōkai—they helped account for what was otherwise unexplainable. But, as Mark Schneider puts it, precise explanations "have a Spartan quality that is unforgiving of spontaneity and insensitive to the foggy or the strange."[83] With Kokkuri, the discourse of "human electricity" preserves this fogginess, shifting the causality of traditional yōkai to a different referential terrain, one haunted by the equally powerful (and equally elusive) concept of electricity. The imprecision of the public understanding of electricity not only allows the mystery to persist but also spawns new mysteries—couched in the rhetoric of science, but just as playfully confounding as the creatures of Sekien's bestiaries.

Although public excitement over Kokkuri seems to have peaked in the 1880s, the game never disappeared from the popular arena. In fact, its absorption into the cultural imaginary of Japan had become so complete that, in 1903, when the *Yomiuri shinbun* reported on the use of a "planchette" as a divination procedure in England, the article was titled "Seiyō no Kokkuri-san," or "Western Kokkuri," as if the Japanese version of Kokkuri had become the standard reference when alluding to techniques for communicating with the spirits.[84] More important, perhaps, the Kokkuri boom was a harbinger of the interest in hypnotism that would sweep the nation in the 1890s. Like Kokkuri, hypnotism would occupy an appealingly ambiguous position in the cultural imaginary, representing simultaneously a form of mysticism and the cutting edge of science.

Enryō's rationalism may have epitomized an extreme intellectual position not embraced by everybody, but it did powerfully affect the tenor of the discourse on yōkai. Not only did his voluminous collected data reinforce the Tokugawa-period process through which the weird and mysterious were gathered together into an autonomous category, but also his insistence on weeding out "false mystery" from "true mystery" inspired a new kind of categorization through which yōkai began to lose their living relevance. As we have seen, even discussions that encouraged a mystical appreciation of electricity tended to deny the agency of the spirits, relegating them to the unenlightened past.

By working so hard to remake the referential terrain, Enryō inadvertently inspired new mysteries and, in turn, imbued the older metaphors—kitsune, tengu, tanuki, kappa, and the like—with a patina of age and stability. In a sense, then, by promoting yōkai as that which opposes the modern, Enryō's polemics and the ideology of progress out of which they emerged helped fuse yōkai with the concept of "tradition." In contrast to Kokkuri and the hypnotism boom that would follow it, traditional yōkai took on a stability of form increasingly associated with a space of the rural and past and, accordingly, nostalgia. The taxidermic preservation of this past, and the yōkai that haunted it, loomed as a valuable modern project particularly within the burgeoning field of folklore studies (minzokugaku).

CHAPTER 4

Museum of the Weird

Modernity, Minzokugaku, and the Discovery of Yōkai

There is no place that is not haunted by many different spirits
hidden there in silence, spirits one can "invoke" or not.
Haunted places are the only ones people can live in.

Michel de Certeau

THE DEATH OF THE TANUKI

In the waning years of the nineteenth century and the beginning of the twentieth, Japan's modernization altered the metaphoric as well as the physical landscape. One quintessential feature of both of these new landscapes was the train. With thousands of miles of track laid down throughout the country, not only did the steam train transform the countenance of the land itself, but it was also part of a broader "transformation of perception."[1] The land became a series of vistas moving across the still screen of the train window, a picture scroll unfurling through time and space. And time and space themselves contracted as the transportation infrastructure transcended mountains and rivers, reaching into communities once thought inaccessible, linking country and city in an intricate network of communication.

Through the Meiji and Taishō (1912–1926) periods and into the early part of the Shōwa period (1926–1989), as trains came to be increasingly common throughout the land, the mystery of this mechanical form of movement clashed with the older icons of the mysterious represented by yōkai. At times, the two referential ecologies collided head-on:

> Now there's reclaimed land in the area around Shinagawa, but in those days the waves ran against the shore, making a sound like *pashan, pashan*. It was a lonely place, and there were a lot of tanuki and kitsune there as well. At night, when the train would run through, they would hear a sound—

> *shu shu po po po*—coming from the other direction, and they'd hear a steam whistle blowing, and they'd say, *A train is coming!* At first, even the conductor was thinking, *We're going to crash*, and he would stop his own train and have a look around.
>
> But the train from the other direction never came. *This is strange*, they'd think, and then one night as always, the *shu shu po po po* sound came, and they could hear the steam whistle, and this time they thought, *Let's not worry about it*, and they gave it more speed and went straight ahead.
>
> When they did that, everybody thought there would be a head-on collision—but they just went right on with no problem.
>
> When dawn broke, along the tracks at the foot of Mount Yatsu, they found a big tanuki lying there dead. Back in the days of the steam engines, there was only one track so there was no way a train could randomly come from the other direction. Well, of course, it was just that tanuki really enjoy imitating things.[2]

The confrontation between tanuki and steam train, a common trope during this period, gestures dramatically to the changing meanings of yōkai. The old forms of magic, the shape-shifting talents of the tanuki, still had the power to dazzle and deceive, causing the train engineers to proceed with caution through the lonely countryside. But the instant they stopped believing and plowed full speed ahead, the iron mechanism of technology could make the magic powerless, transforming a supernatural creature into nothing more than an animal body lying dead beside the tracks of progress.

The imagery here betrays a profound anxiety about the burgeoning infrastructure of modernity. Like the train, "progress" ultimately ignored such apprehensions and steamed on ahead, leaving tanuki dead in its wake. Were yōkai the victims of modernity? Did faith in the scientific repress or supersede belief in the mystic? As in Kokkuri, the relationship between modernity and yōkai in the early twentieth century rarely expressed itself in simple binaries. Whether reflected in common legends such as this one, in literary works by canonical writers, or in the discourses of new academic projects, attitudes toward yōkai were layered and complex and ambiguous.

We can see how these attitudes were expressed across different cultural forms and social strata by carefully reading a number of texts produced between 1905 and 1939, from the end of Meiji to the early years of the Shōwa period. In addition to the technological changes commensurate with an ongoing modernization project, these three and a half decades saw a critical range of political and cultural transitions. Japan's 1905 victory in the Russo-Japanese War (1904–1905) signified its emergence as a world power and fueled its continued colonialist incursions throughout Asia. At home, a populist, liberal sentiment developed into the short-lived period of "Taishō democracy." On the cultural front, the early years of the twentieth century witnessed the rise of popular movements toward self-betterment and self-cultivation *(shūyō)* and the modern lifestyle *(modan seikatsu)*, complete with modern girls *(moga)* and modern boys *(mobo)*. One theme that permeated this dynamic period was an introspective quest to establish an identity—for Japan within the world, and for the "self" within a changing Japan.

Attitudes toward the mysterious broadly reflected how Japan's past, present, and future were constructed within this shifting historical context. As Inoue Enryō had hoped, yōkai and the noninstitutional belief systems associated with them came to be thought of more and more in the pejorative, as something that (in both Freudian and political terms) must be repressed for the healthy growth of the individual as well as the nation. In the dominant intellectual discourse of the early twentieth century, yōkai were no longer considered part of the living present; rather, they were an embarrassing reminder of the premodern past—a dead tanuki rotting by the train tracks.

Part and parcel of their disappearance from the living present was the growing scarcity of yōkai in the lively world of play. This is not to say that nobody was playing with monsters—yōkai karuta and other forms of monstrous recreation were enjoyed through the Taishō period. But such games had become colored by nostalgia. Spirit possession and similar forms of mystic practice were marginalized, and the supernatural entertainments that took their place—such as the hypnosis craze that developed after Kokkuri—were subsumed within the expanding realm of the sciences and increasingly divorced from the yōkai tradition.[3] For their part, yōkai were characterized as constructs of the past. In a sense, the disenchanting rhetoric of Enryō and similar bunmei-kaika promoters had led to a discovery of yōkai: only when people found themselves in a modern landscape seemingly *devoid* of yōkai did they seek out the yōkai that had infested the Tokugawa period, and that were also in fact still lurking just beneath the surface of the modern.

The works of two canonical literary writers, Natsume Sōseki (1867–1916) and Mori Ōgai (1862–1922), often feature protagonists confronting this modern landscape and engaging in a struggle to define the self, what Tomi Suzuki has called "the privileged signifier of modernity."[4] For these characters, urban (Tokyo) intellectual men, subjectivity included the rejection of yōkai and the premodern beliefs they represented. All too often, however, these characters discover that the banished Other returns, causing them to anxiously question their modern ways of interpreting the world around them.

The individual struggle for identity portrayed in these literary texts also reflects a broader communal struggle to establish a sense of identity for the nation, a quest to define what it meant to be "Japanese." Whereas the literary fiction of Sōseki and Ōgai represents yōkai as the persistently reemerging Other repeatedly rejected by the Self, the scholarly discourses of Ema Tsutomu (1884–1979) and Yanagita Kunio (1875–1962) nostalgically incorporate the Otherness of yōkai into "tradition" and, by extension, into the communal Self of the Japanese nation. By tracing the history of yōkai and classifying their forms, both Ema and Yanagita transcend questions of belief; they map out an "authentic" otherworld of an idealized Japanese past. In their work, the anxiety about the ghosts of the past expressed by Sōseki and Ōgai is transformed into desire, and this desired past ultimately becomes an intrinsic element of the present: the Other becomes a part of an individual and national sense of Self.[5]

This nostalgic focus encouraged the sterilization of yōkai. Although Yanagita did not necessarily ignore the nasty habits and murderous proclivities of the monsters he dealt with, by documenting them historically he helped turn them into relics: tangible but safe reminders of a communal Japanese experience. Recall that, in the discourses and practices of both the Tokugawa and the Meiji periods, the notion of yōkai signified a broad continuum of phenomena, from ontologically extant creatures to unexplainable occurrences. Sekien's illustrations, Enryō's exegeses, and even the practice of Kokkuri, all developed from this tension between the tangible icon of the weird and the numinous experience of the mysterious. In their attempts to organize and construct taxonomies for these things, Ema and Yanagita also created a new meaning for yōkai, one from which the broad concept of the mysterious was somehow extracted from the weird body of the monster: the yōkai became divorced from the sense of mystery, or fushigi, that had once animated it. While the advance of the steam train may have extinguished the mysterious life force of the tanuki, leaving yōkai corpses in its wake, it also inspired the collecting of these corpses for study, taxidermic preservation, and display in a museum, lifeless perhaps, but still cherished.

AN UNWILLING SUSPENSION OF DISBELIEF

Natsume Sōseki and Mori Ōgai were arguably the two most important literary figures of the early twentieth century. Unlike some of their contemporaries, such as Izumi Kyōka (1873–1939) and Akutagawa Ryūnosuke (1892–1927), neither Sōseki nor Ōgai is particularly famous for treating yōkai-related themes. Yet a careful reading of several of their texts reveals that their realist storylines and complex psychological characterizations betray a troubling anxiety about the issues we have been dealing with. By interrogating one story by Sōseki and several works by Ōgai, we can explore how they illustrate a changing consciousness with regard to the weird and mysterious and how they reflect the nuances and ambivalences of this consciousness. These ambivalences, and the often contradictory desires constituting them, help shape a sense of what it meant to be modern in early-twentieth-century Japan.

Empty Sounds: Natsume Sōseki's 'Koto no Sorane'

As a novelist, essayist, satirist, and literary critic, Natsume Sōseki sensitively portrayed many of the private conflicts of his generation. One of these was the tension between old belief systems and new systems of rational thinking. His short story "Koto no sorane" (The Empty Sounds of the Koto; 1905) demonstrates the ambivalent relationship of a well-educated urban man with the superstitious ghosts of the past. The new landscape through which the narrator (literally) walks is a landscape colored by the discourses of Inoue Enryō, and the narrator himself is a modern, urban subject whose worldview is informed by new scientific and psychological discourses rather than by the "superstitious" customs of old. Yet his faith in the new paradigm is rattled by the persistence, and uncanny relevance, of "old-fashioned" beliefs and practices.[6]

The story opens with the narrator visiting his friend, a scholar named Tsuda, who is not only well-versed in psychology but also a student of ghosts.[7] The two men discuss the narrator's impending marriage, his purchase of a house, and his hiring of a housekeeper, an old woman whom he calls a "superstitious old hag" (97). The narrator complains that the housekeeper is constantly badgering him to move, insisting that his house is inauspiciously located. She has also interpreted the nightly barking of a neighborhood dog as an omen portending misfortune for the narrator's fiancée, who by chance has recently been stricken with influenza.

Upon hearing this, Tsuda tells the narrator about his own cousin's recent death from influenza. His words ring ominously, and the narrator, increasingly uneasy about his fiancée's well-being, responds, "Don't be so inauspicious—you're just frightening me. *Wa ha ha ha ha ha*" (102). His forced laugh here, uncomfortable and hollow, lies at the crux of the modern urban intellectual's uneasy relationship with the mysterious. Though he realizes rationally that there can be no contingent relationship between signs and misfortune, he slips easily into a less positivistic mode of thought. His anxiety is further nurtured by Tsuda's account of a strange occurrence associated with his cousin's death. Away in the army in Manchuria, the cousin's husband had peered into a mirror his wife had given him. Instead of seeing his own face, however, he saw hers, pale and sickly. This occurred on the very day she died—although he would not actually hear of her death for several weeks.[8] The story does nothing to assuage the narrator's growing concern for his fiancée; in fact, as old metaphors intrude upon the new, his entire worldview is rattled:

> My bachelor's degree was in law. I judge with common sense the thing as it is at the time of its occurrence; it is not so much that I am incapable of considering other ways of thinking, it is simply that I prefer not to. Ghosts [yūrei], hauntings *[tatari]*, karmic connections *[innen]*—what I hate more than anything else is thinking about such fantastic things. But I am a little bit awed by Tsuda's mind. And when this impressive teacher starts to tell ghost stories seriously, then even I am obligated to reassess my attitude. Truth be told, I had believed that such things as ghosts and palanquin bearers had permanently closed up shop since the [Meiji] Restoration. Nevertheless, to judge by Tsuda's appearance, it seems somehow that, unbeknownst to me, such ghostly things *[yūrei taru mono]* have made a comeback. (105)

Immersed in the new "common sense" of Meiji, a common sense that rejects the possibility of yōkai, the narrator is startled by the revelation that serious intellectuals such as his friend Tsuda are rethinking these things of the past. He agrees that the story of the dead wife's visitation is indeed "mysterious" [fushigi] and asks if "such things are possible." Showing him a book, Tsuda answers calmly that "these days there seems to be proof that such things are possible." The narrator reflects that, "when I think of how the psychologists have revived the ghosts, I can no longer mock them. . . . With regard to ghosts, the bachelors of law must follow blindly the bachelors of letters" (108). Soon after this revelation, he realizes it is already eleven at night, bids Tsuda farewell, and begins his journey home in the rain.

But the conversation has sensitized him, and as he walks through the urban landscape, the sights and sounds of the city taunt him with ominous forebodings. In Gokurakusui, an area of tenements *(nagaya)* inhabited by the poor, for example, he contemplates the eerie silence surrounding him.[9] Rather than considering with "common sense" that the residents are sound asleep, he reads the absence of activity as signifying an absence of life: "Perhaps, actually, they are dead" (110).

As he continues to walk, he encounters two men carrying a small box draped in white—the coffin of a baby—and he overhears one of them say, "There are those who are born yesterday, and die today." And the reply: "That's life. It's just life, so there is nothing that can be done" (111). For the first time in his life, the narrator contemplates his own mortality, wondering, "How had I been able to live so indifferently until now?" (112). The baby encapsulated in a coffin becomes a metonym for death—his own, his fiancée's, indeed for all death past, present, and future. What is important here is not simply that the narrator is suddenly obsessed with the possibility of death, but that he projects a kind of agency into the topography of the city, reading each feature and each encounter as a sign akin to the pale face of Tsuda's cousin in the mirror. The cityscape is no longer the quotidian here and now of the physical landscape: it has become the uncanny yōkai-infested terrain of a previous generation. The narrator experiences each landmark as a symbol in a mysterious code that, if correctly read, will reveal (or determine) something about his own future.

In a sense, a veil of modernity has been lifted from his eyes, and the city through which he walks has been made strange. The defamiliarized cityscape unfolds as if to torment him, each sign signifying something foreboding. At Kirishitan-zaka ("Christian [Martyr] Slope"), for example, a sign warns: "The steepest slope in Japan. Those who value life, beware, beware" (112). Only yesterday, the narrator thinks, this sign would have amused him, but now it signifies the terrifying truth of his own mortality and all the perilous obstacles that await him. Tonight his pedestrian sojourn through dark, rainy Tokyo is anything but pedestrian: it is an act of interpretation, a reading of a text that tells of the past (the Christian martyrs) and warns of the future ("beware, beware"). Just as it is possible to compare such "pedestrian processes to linguistic formations," so the narrator's walk is an act of reading/writing,[10] of inscribing subjective meanings into the landscape (the same process, of course, undertaken by the reader of Sōseki's text).

Central to this process of reading/writing is the relationship between a sign and an occurrence—a relationship that is not rational by the narrator's own commonsense standards. Just as the appearance of Tsuda's cousin's image in her husband's mirror signified her death, so the narrator reads the signs of his urban journey as omens of his own fiancée's demise. The specific associations created by the narrator are less important than the fact that he creates them at all: he is a well-educated, sensible student of law, making the sort of mystic associations so diligently explained away by the likes of Inoue Enryō years earlier. Though he is well aware that his thoughts are inconsistent with the grammar of modernity, he cannot avoid them. When he sees the flame of a lantern in the distance, for example, his thoughts inexplicably turn to Tsuyuko, his fiancée: "Even Tsuda, the psychologist, would be unable to explain the relationship between the flame and my future wife. However, there is nothing preventing me from thinking things that cannot be explained by a psychologist. Red, vivid, like the dwindling tail of a fuse, that fire caused me immediately to recall my future wife. At the same time, the instant the fire is extinguished, I cannot help but think of Tsuyuko's death. I stroke my forehead and it is slippery with sweat and rain. I walk in a dream" (113–14).

The confluence of sweat and rain as the narrator strokes his forehead is a minor detail to be sure, but one that emphasizes the inseparability of his own interiority from the exteriority of the landscape: self and city coalesce in a walk that is simultaneously dream and reality. By the time he completes his oneiric journey and arrives home, he is drenched and thoroughly disheveled. The old housekeeper greets him at the door, and in a comic exchange that directly alludes to the act of (mis)interpretation, the two inarticulately try to read each other's face. Not surprisingly, because of her belief in superstition (which requires, after all, the interpretation of signs), the "superstitious old hag" is the more "skillful at reading appearances *[ninsō]*" (115) and manages to deduce that the narrator has been worrying about his sick fiancée. She explains that no word has come from Tsuyuko herself, but that there have been mysterious howling sounds outside—signs that, according to the housekeeper, presage the worst.[11]

After a sleepless night full of ominous imaginings, the narrator rises at dawn and rushes off to Tsuyuko's home, arriving covered with mud, and so early that most of the family is still in bed. Tsuyuko, it turns out, has completely recovered from her illness. The narrator's concern quickly turns into relief and then awkwardness as he attempts to make excuses for his early morning visit. The scene is comic, as he is clearly embarrassed at succumbing to the same superstitious worries as his housekeeper. But here the reader's laughter echoes the awkward laughter of the narrator himself; it wells up from the gap between the "objective" worldview inspired by modernity and the "subjective" mystic interpretation of the world into which the narrator (and perhaps the reader with him) has slipped. Either interpretation seems somewhat ridiculous in light of the other—but it is the constant awareness of both, the persistent threat of the intrusion of one into the other, that creates the comic/anxious moment. Safe and secure with Tsuyuko's family, the narrator feels happy for the moment, but he has also become aware that his own interpretation of the world, and how he is located within it, is disturbingly, comically, unstable.

Upon leaving his fiancée's home, the narrator goes to a barbershop. As his hair is trimmed he listens to a lighthearted conversation that echoes the very concerns dealt with throughout the story: the clash of two different referential ecologies. The conversation seems at first to mock the narrator's own uncertainty, as suddenly the barber says, "Hey Gen-san, there really are some foolish people in this world, aren't there?" To this Gen-san replies, "That's for sure. Ghosts and specters—those are things from long ago! In this present day of electric lights, there can't be such outlandish stories" (126–27).

Sōseki craftily stitches together the dialogue so that the barber's interjections to the narrator about his hair are intertwined with his observations about the current state of the supernatural. The effect is to suggest that attitudes toward yōkai are as faddish and fickle as the latest fashions:

> "Isn't it too short?"
>
> "These days, everybody has it about this length. People think sideburns are foppish and silly.—Well, it's all a matter of the nerves [*shinkei*]. In your heart you think of them as scary, and then naturally the ghosts get cheeky and want to come out," he spoke once more to Gen-san, as he wiped the hair off the razor with his thumb and forefinger. (127)

Tongue-in-cheek though they may be, the comments reflect an ambiguous relationship to the supernatural, on one hand attributing the belief in ghosts to the "nerves," but on the other simultaneously retaining—at least rhetorically—the agency of the ghosts themselves (who "*want* to come out"). Playing out the joke, the youngest member of the group earnestly inquires, "Gen-san, these 'nerve' things—where are they?" To which Gen-san can only "vaguely" respond: "Nerves? Nerves are everywhere" (128). Just as yōkai had once populated the Edo landscape, so "nerves" have taken their place as a pervasive, but indistinct, metaphor of early-twentieth-century mystery.[12]

The conversation continues now in a vein that can be understood as a critique of Enryō himself or, at least, of the popularization of his ideas.

It turns out that the barber has been reading a book entitled *Ukiyo shinri kōgi roku* by Uyamuya Dōjin. The title, which might be translated as "Record of Psychology Lectures of the Floating World," makes satiric allusion to the popularity of the psychological paradigm for explaining the inexplicable. The author's name is also a satiric gibe: *uyamuya* signifies indefiniteness, vagueness, obfuscation—in a word, "ambiguity." *Dōjin* indicates a person who has embarked upon a particular *way* (often referring to Buddhist practice). Thus, the name Uyamuya Dōjin might mean "one who follows the way of ambiguity," and it reflects a distrust of the psychological paradigm's power to enlighten any better than the mystic paradigm it replaces.

As the men in the barbershop read from this book, the ambivalent overlapping of these two paradigms is further emphasized: "It is said that tanuki deceive [bakasu] people, but why would a tanuki deceive somebody? This is all done by hypnotism [saiminjutsu]" (128). The book, we gradually realize, is written from the point of view of a tanuki upset with Japan's embracing of a Western model of modernity:

> The modus operandi of the entire tribe of tanuki is the technique of hypnotism that is currently used by practicing physicians; since long ago we have employed these methods to deceive all sorts of honorable folk. The technique imported and directly passed along by Western tanuki has been labeled hypnotism—worshipping as "doctors" those who apply this technique is the foul result of an idolization of the West that those such as myself secretly find lamentable. Despite the fact that all sorts of native Japanese magical techniques *[kijutsu]* have been handed down, there is such a commotion about Western this and Western that. It is my humble opinion that the Japanese of today simply have too much contempt for tanuki; I speak for tanuki throughout the country in expressing the hope that all of you honorable people will reconsider these issues. (130)

The comic diatribe not only illuminates the shift in referential terrains—from the bakasu techniques of the tanuki to the hypnotic techniques of the West—but also pokes fun at the scientific pretensions associated with those who would be known as doctors. Although the explicit discussion concerns native yōkai magic versus foreign scientific magic, it must also be read allegorically, in a broader historical context in which Japan's old ways were already beyond recovery. Indeed, when Sōseki's text was published in 1905, Japan had embarked on its war with Russia and had irrevocably entered the world arena. In the rush to modernize, native goods and techniques of all sorts were being overrun by foreign imports. The tanuki, in his cry for respect here, represents the neglected native voice challenging the inevitable advance of the steam train and the machines of modern Western technology.

In this humorous rant purportedly written by an acolyte of "the way of ambiguity," the tanuki's voice sardonically critiques a conservative, antimodernity stance. On the other hand, by noting the commensurate nature of tanuki and "doctors," the text also questions the value of such "new" psychological techniques as hypnosis. Ultimately, Sōseki parodies both positions, demonstrating that they are two sides of the same coin. Indeed, "Koto no sorane" itself artfully straddles both referential terrains: Tsuda, the scholar and psychologist, tells an "objectively" true story of mystical omens and after-death visitations, while the narrator, a commonsensical bachelor of law, relates a "subjective" experience of omens that, in the end, prove false. In a period of shifting understandings, both stories ultimately have equal value, and Tsuda accordingly records the narrator's experience in his own thesis on ghosts *(yūrei-ron)*. Sōseki's tale reflects a multiplicity of voices—those of Tsuda, the narrator, the housekeeper, and the men in the barbershop—each one conscious of the shifting cultural landscape. Although this shifting was felt on many broader fronts (politics, education, industrialization), by focusing on issues of belief, science, and superstition, Sōseki locates these concerns at the very heart of the everyday experience of the Meiji populace and the individual's attempt to define the Self.

Mori Ōgai's Hollow Laughter

Like Natsume Sōseki, Mori Ōgai was a major literary figure and public intellectual at the turn of the twentieth century. His contribution to Meiji intellectual life included fiction, drama, poetry, biography, translation, literary criticism, and a constant engagement with medical, military, and political matters. His position as a prominent medical doctor gave him an unusual perspective on the cutting-edge sciences of his time and made his observations of the weird and mysterious all the more poignant.

Although as a doctor, soldier, and scholar he was very much involved in processes of Westernization and modernization, Ōgai differs from his contemporary Inoue Enryō in that, like Sōseki, he takes a position on these issues that is more nuanced and difficult to extract from his wide-ranging corpus of work. As with the lives of so many of his generation, Ōgai's life itself reflected a multiplicity of influences: he was born in the countryside but educated in Tokyo; he was grounded in the Chinese literary classics but also read Dutch and German scientific writing; and he studied abroad and read and translated Western literature, but spent his last years writing historical and biographical works concerning the Tokugawa period. If Ōgai's life was driven by the contradictions and ambiguities of his historical epoch, then, as J. Thomas Rimer has noted, his "reactions to these ambiguities have come to epitomize for later generations the spiritual realities of those times."[13]

Although Ōgai does not explicitly invoke images of yōkai, some of his fiction implicitly engages with the weird and mysterious. A brief look at three of his stories published between 1909 and 1911, shortly before he turned his attention to biographical and historical writing, reveals characters grappling with different knowledge formations—the mystic versus the scientific. A fourth story, which I consider in greater depth, overtly locates the past within the present by considering a modern version of the Edo-period game of hyaku-monogatari. Just as Sōseki's "Koto no sorane" illustrates a convergence and conflict of attitudes, Ōgai's stories reflect a sophisticated and sometimes contradictory stance. In all four stories, Ōgai's well-educated narrator contends with the overlapping of metaphorical landscapes, expressing a deep sense of unease about his own identity.

In "Hebi" (Snake; 1911), Ōgai seems to espouse the enlightenment rhetoric of Enryō a generation earlier.[14] Narrated by a "professor of science" *(rigaku hakushi)*, the story recounts a visit to an inn in the Shinshū area. The professor hears the sad tale of the master of the inn, about his mother's recent death and his wife's subsequent insanity. This insanity, it seems, was brought on by the continuous appearance of a large snake on the Buddhist altar where offerings are made to the soul of the dead mother—with whom the wife had never been on good terms. Upon consultation, the narrator decisively disenchants this ominous occurrence in simple natural terms, as Enryō might in one of his short exegeses, pointing out that the snake came from a nearby storeroom where rice was kept. "Animals are ruled by habit," he explains. "If it settles here once, it will surely settle here again. . . . There is nothing mysterious about it at all" (24). The story concludes with a further confirmation of faith in modern science: the narrator advises the master to have his wife seen by a specialist in mental health.

While this one story articulates a rationalistic creed reminiscent of Enryō, it is not Ōgai's final word on the issue. Rather, it serves as a foil, highlighting more nuanced and anxious literary explorations of similar concerns. Elsewhere, for example, Ōgai questions the very integrity of the kind of "specialist in mental health" the protagonist in "Hebi" recommends. Although science may provide hints as to how the mind works, he suggests, there are dangers in the application of this knowledge, dangers that reveal a still-hidden, mysterious dimension of the very mind that science professes to uncode.

Originally published in 1909 in the literary journal *Subaru*, "Masui" (Hypnosis, or literally, Enchanted Sleep) is related in the third-person perspective of a law professor named Ōkawa Wataru. As he prepares to leave Tokyo on a business trip, Ōkawa receives a visit from Sugimura, a medical doctor and old friend from his days as an exchange student in Germany. Ōkawa and Sugimura discuss another doctor, named Isogai, a specialist in "diseases of the nervous system."[15] Ōkawa's mother-in-law is ill and has gone to see Isogai—in fact, she and Ōkawa's wife are with Isogai as the two friends talk. The men conclude that Isogai is an excellent scholar, but Sugimura adds rather ominously that there is something strange about him: "I don't like to express judgments of people in the same profession, but as it is just between the two of us, I will say it. Whatever you do, just don't send your wife to Isogai" (190).

Ōkawa's wife soon returns home and, as if in response to Sugimura's warning, she does indeed seem upset. She explains that her mother had gone home after the examination, leaving her alone with Isogai to candidly discuss the mother's prognosis. Isogai had ushered her into his office and explained that her mother would be fine, but that her illness was a little difficult to cure and that she must be massaged. As if to demonstrate, he had suddenly taken hold of the wife's shoulders and begun to stroke her arms: "I felt disgusted by it," she explains to Ōkawa, "but he's such an important doctor" (197). She proceeds to describe how, although horrified, she could not take her eyes off his. She has no recollection of what happened next, but when she came back to herself, Isogai was sitting behind his desk.

Infuriated, Ōkawa tells his wife that she was in great danger, that she must not see Isogai again, and that they must never tell anybody about the incident. He then leaves for his business trip, and as he sits on the train, disturbed by what he has heard, we learn that he had immediately recognized Isogai's use of hypnosis, recalling the techniques of Mesmer and Braid when he heard his wife describe the doctor's suspicious behavior: "Among the many books the professor had read, he had had the misfortune of having read in some detail about hypnotism *[masui-jutsu]*. There is a reason for this. When the professor was a child, Kokkuri-san was popular in Tokyo. Then, when he went abroad, 'table-rapping' *[tsukue-tataki]* was popular in Europe. As he had already been interested in the mystery [fushigi] of Kokkuri-san, he thought to look into an interpretation of this similar [phenomenon of] table-rapping, and read a book about Spiritualism [Spiritismus].[16] And then he read books on hypnotism" (203). The story concludes at this unsettling, unresolved moment, with Ōkawa and the reader never certain about what occurred while the wife was under Isogai's hypnotic spell.

Ominous and quietly disturbing, "Masui" suggests the possibility of sexual violation and dangerous abuse of medical authority. Not only does the story accurately reflect contemporary attitudes toward hypnotism, but it is also modeled on specific events and people.[17] The spooky, suggestive quality of "Masui," as well as the sexualized subject matter, positions it as a forerunner of the so-called *ero-guro-nansensu* (erotic-grotesque-nonsense) genre that would flourish several decades later.[18] It is also worth noting here how "Masui" can be viewed in relation to my discussion of the changing face of the mysterious. First, we find the continued influence of Kokkuri and the milieu in which it flourished; this form of play popular in the 1880s was still present in the cultural imaginary of the early twentieth century and, at least to Ōgai's professor, was clearly connected to Western forms of Spiritualism and hypnotic techniques. More important, hypnosis is no longer associated with the mystic. Ichiyanagi Hirotaka has suggested that early-twentieth-century hypnosis "escaped a variety of binarisms, and, adrift on a sea of ambiguity . . . entered increasingly into the framework of 'science' with medical academism at its core."[19] In "Masui," hypnotism is a scientific technique practiced by an elite expert on nervous disorders. Just as Sōseki's tanuki had insisted, it had come to be a form of deception performed by doctors worshipped for their adeptness at Western science.

This negative view was part of an increasingly common attitude that recognized the potential danger of hypnosis as a device for controlling others and a "system through which latent male sexual violence was released."[20] Ōgai's short story reflects a very real anxiety about the powers of science and psychology. The mystery might reside no longer within the technique itself but in the motivations of those who would use it for nefarious purposes. Unlike "Hebi," with its seemingly straightforward faith in science and psychology as means for unraveling the mysteries of animal and human behavior, "Masui" betrays an apprehension about such trust. Through the dangerous character of Isogai, the brilliant revelations of modern science are transformed into an amoral power; like a deity or demon figure, science must be treated carefully, for it can bring either blessings or disaster. Reconsidered in light of "Masui," the professor in "Hebi" (particularly with his suggestion that the master's wife should see a mental health specialist) becomes a caricature of the potentially dangerous overconfidence placed in scientific interpretations. And the tanuki's fun-loving sorcery, supplanted by the sinister deceptive capabilities of hypnosis and its practitioners, seems indeed a loss to be lamented.

Despite, or perhaps because of, his own personal engagement with medical science, Ōgai's fiction during this period expresses a wariness of blind faith placed in any single mode of interpretation. In another story, for example, the author even more explicitly questions the confidence bred of psychological and rational understanding. "Kompira" (1909) tells of a professor of literature who, while in Shikoku for a series of lectures on psychology, finds himself near Kotohira Shrine, the home shrine of the deity Kompira. Despite being told by one of his local hosts that "it is said that Kompira is a wrathful deity, so if you leave without paying your respects, there's a possibility you will be cursed," the professor is anxious to return to his wife and young children in Tokyo, and so departs without visiting the shrine.[21] When he arrives in Tokyo, however, he discovers that—on the very day he left Shikoku—his infant son had been stricken with whooping cough; his young daughter too would eventually become ill. The remainder of the story relates, in heart-wrenching detail, the steady decline and eventual death of the baby boy.

Throughout, the professor is reminded guiltily of his failure to visit Kompira; his increasingly weak attempt to cling to his faith in rationalism is contrasted to his wife's desperate reliance on a talisman purchased at a local Kompira shrine in Tokyo and on a dream that portends the death of the son but the recovery of the daughter. Indeed, as his wife's dream had foretold, the story concludes with the daughter gradually recovering her strength. The wife, not surprisingly, develops increasing faith in Kompira. As for the professor himself, the last line of the story is provocatively ambiguous: "Let's hope that Professor Ōno, a philosopher, would not also become a believer in Kompira-sama" (435).

The parallels with Sōseki's "Koto no sorane," published four years earlier, are striking. Unlike Sōseki's narrator's walk through Tokyo, however, Professor Ōno's journey is not punctuated with forebodings and superstitious imaginings; only after his arrival home and the discovery of his child's illness does his failure to pay respect to the Kompira deity begin to haunt him. Ironically, for all his worrying, Sōseki's narrator learns that his fiancée is fine; for Ōgai's professor, on the other hand, it is as if his lack of concern causes the children to be stricken. But the similarity of the two stories speaks to the tenor of the times: both narratives present a modern intellectual who is grappling with the persistent and intrusive powers of premodern belief and trying to locate his own subjectivity within this changing referential terrain.

"Kompira" raises troubling questions about the faith in reason expressed in Ōgai's own "Hebi." The story is awash with detailed physical descriptions of the children's health—temperature, food intake, excremental functions—and replete with medical data, including not only the names of diseases but also the latest medicines. Yet the doctor's prognosis is wrong: although he tells them the daughter will die, she goes on to recover—as the wife's dream had foretold. Faith in modern scientific methods ultimately proves as tenuous as, if not feebler than, faith in the supernatural.

At the heart of the story is the professor's introspective reasoning in response to his wife's belief in the Kompira deity:

> Somewhere the professor had read a metaphor about stealing the ragged clothes of a poor person, but not being able to replace them with silk in exchange. No matter what the superstition, if you are going to say it is a superstition, you have to have some belief with which to replace it. As he did not have this himself, [the professor] could not scold his wife. But he felt that, to agree with her on this, he would be losing his position as a scholar; and so at such times he would laugh and tease her. (414)

We have seen this uneasy laughter before, in "Koto no sorane," and here too it arises at the anxious nexus of the mystic, to which the professor's wife clings, and the scientific, which the professor himself is unable to relinquish. It is the hollow laughter that reverberates through the contact zone of two overlapping yet incompatible landscapes; laughter is a symptom of the narrator's unease within this zone.

A desolate tone echoes throughout the story, stemming not only from the pathos of the infant's death but also from the professor's inability to replace his wife's "ragged clothes" with silk. Early in the story, he looks over his diary and bemoans its emptiness: "It was utterly lacking in interest. Form with no content. Or perhaps the professor's life itself was like that; when he thought about it, wasn't it too a thing utterly lacking in interest?" Even the lectures he had given on psychology, each one carefully researched and written, ring hollow; no matter how much effort he makes, he "cannot breathe life into them" (395).

In a later short story, Ōgai returns to this theme of hollowness, of form-with-no-content, and the sense of emptiness that pervades the modern landscape. Although the title of this story, "Hyaku-monogatari" (1911), explicitly refers to the spooky tale-telling game discussed in chapter 2, the story does not portray the fantastical experience typical of the Tokugawa-period practice. Rather, the first-person narrator soberly relates a mundane tale that culminates not in the occurrence of a supernatural event but in an artfully rendered anticlimax. The playfulness characteristic of the Tokugawa tale-telling sessions is strangely lacking, and there is a stilted, dead quality to the events Ōgai describes. The entire story is characterized by a detached and contemplative tone in which the narrator muses on his own role as an "onlooker" *(bōkansha)*. Throughout, Ōgai blends fact and fiction: although some of the characters are pseudonymous depictions of Ōgai's contemporaries, others are called by their real names—including novelist Ozaki Kōyō (1867–1903) and the kangaku scholar Yoda Gakkai (1833–1909). And indeed, the reader is led to believe that the narrator himself, though never referred to by name, is Mori Ōgai.[22]

In essence, the story portrays the disenchantment of the urban intellectual environment of late-Meiji Tokyo and the desire of the displaced individual, the onlooker, to find a role in this emerging society. Ōgai's focus on the hollowness of words and the hypocrisy of human interaction is a commentary on the dissolution of the old metaphorical landscape and the emptiness of the new, on the impossibility, that is, of replacing the old rags with silk. The banishing of the mystic from everyday life represents the hollowing out of words and the isolation of the individual; signifiers have come unfixed. The very title of the story refers to this disconnection, for *hyaku-monogatari* no longer means the same thing that it did for earlier generations.

In the opening lines of the story, the narrator explains that time has passed since the unfolding of the events he is about to relate, but that the impression they made on him remains strong: "As this is the first time such a thing has happened to me, and it doesn't seem as if it will ever occur again, it is fair to say that I encountered a once-in-a-lifetime event."[23] He then reveals that the event in question was his visit to a session of hyaku-monogatari. In light of what occurs (or does not occur) later, this rather dramatic buildup misleadingly primes the reader for a happening of supernatural proportions—once-in-a-lifetime and unforgettable—that is meant to come at the conclusion of a successful session of hyaku-monogatari.

Before proceeding with his tale, the narrator expresses his concern that hyaku-monogatari is associated with a specific time and place, and his readers in other countries may not understand the context:

> On the off chance this story is translated into a European language and it joins the ranks of world literature, readers from other countries will be at a loss, thinking I have put forth a ridiculous idea, and so I will promptly begin this story with an explanation. Hyaku-monogatari, it seems, entails the gathering together of a large number of people. They set up one hundred candles and, one by one, tell tales of monsters [bakemono], extinguishing a candle after each tale. In this fashion, after the one hundredth candle is put out, it is said that a true monster will appear. (121–22)

Of course, this explanation serves not only to familiarize foreign readers with the game but also to remind contemporary and future *Japanese* readers of a practice no longer in vogue—no longer a viable referent in modern Tokyo. Ōgai's description also establishes the game as a metaphorical lens through which all that follows in the story can be interpreted. Unlike the authors of the hyaku-monogatari collections from the Edo period, however, Ōgai goes on to consider the possibility of a psychological mechanism at the root of the phenomenon: "Perhaps, just as when a fakir intones, 'Allah, Allah,' and sees a deity in front of his eyes when he lowers his head, so too [with hyaku-monogatari] the nerves are progressively stimulated to the point of causing a temporary visual and aural illusion" (122). Ōgai has succinctly encapsulated the psychological paradigm, invoking the ubiquitous "nerves" and essentially describing the concept of "expectant attention" that Enryō had promoted some twenty-five years earlier. In the late-Meiji period, an introduction to hyaku-monogatari is incomplete without an accompanying scientific interpretation.

The narrator then relates how he was invited to attend the hyaku-monogatari session by a friend, a fashionable young dandy named Shitomi, who informs him that the event is being sponsored by a wealthy man named Shikamaya.[24] "Having no other obligations," and "enough curiosity to see what this thing is all about" (123), the narrator decides to join the party and duly shows up the next afternoon at a boathouse where all the guests have gathered to travel along the Sumida River to the site where the event will be held. Ever the onlooker, the narrator waits quietly, eavesdropping on shreds of superficial conversation. He realizes that he himself, were he to participate in these conversations, would sound as artificial and forced as everybody else—so he remains silent.

He concludes that everybody in the room "must be thinking his own thoughts," and that hyaku-monogatari serves as nothing more than an empty pretense for the gathering:

> It was for this thing called hyaku-monogatari that everybody had come, but hyaku-monogatari is a relic from a world that has now passed. Even

> if we call it a relic, the thing [mono] itself no longer exists and nothing more than an empty name remains. From the start, objectively a ghost [yūrei] was a ghost, but we have now lost even the subjective viewpoint *[shukan]* that in the old days could take something that was not [a ghost] and breathe life into it *[fukiirete]* so that it seemed to exist. All those things that we called ghost stories [kaidan] or hyaku-monogatari have become what Ibsen would call ghosts. Because of this, they no longer have the power to attract people. They no longer have the power to prevent people from thinking their own thoughts. (125)

Ōgai describes hyaku-monogatari here as a "relic," an *ibutsu*—that is, a thing *(butsu)* left behind from the previous generation. However, he continues, it cannot even properly be called a *thing* anymore; hyaku-monogatari has lost the *thing* itself, become only form with no content. As the word *monogatari* might be translated literally as the "telling of the thing," it is no coincidence that Ōgai describes hyaku-monogatari as an *ibutsu* without the thing; *monogatari* devoid of *mono* is nothing more than *katari,* an empty telling, the *langue* without the *parole.* And this is exactly what the narrator hears all around him at the gathering: "As a whole, the mass of people assembled on this second floor uttered few words, but when they happened to speak, everything they said rang hollow *[shirajirashii]*" (124).

Ōgai invokes the contemporary irrelevance of hyaku-monogatari as a comment on the emptiness and hypocrisy of such social gatherings, the lack of any shared feeling of community, and the paucity of *things* worth communicating. In the context of a game that deals with the supernatural, however, it is worth asking what he means by the *thing,* this content that has become divorced from the form of hyaku-monogatari. On one level, certainly, he is referring to the mystic *thing* we examined earlier—not necessarily the belief in something beyond the ken of human knowledge, but the readiness to believe in the possibility of mystery. The signifier *hyaku-monogatari* is no longer attached to that once-potent and meaningful referent, the ghost. His comment that "in the beginning, objectively a ghost was a ghost" refers to this signified as something that once seemed objectively real. By using the words *kyakkanteki* (objectively) and *shukan* (translated here as "subjective viewpoint"), Ōgai draws on a Kantian notion of subjectivity, implying that it is the observing subject who gives meaning to the phenomenon. The subject "breathes life into" that which does not possess the appropriate content *(sore ni nai naiyō).* Ōgai provocatively chooses a character meaning "lie" (嘘) to denote this process (fukiirete; 嘘き入れて) of breathing life into something. That is, not only does he invoke the filling up with life of an otherwise empty form—the very thing the doctor of philosophy in "Kompira" was unable to accomplish—but he also implies that this can be done only through telling tales, through fabrication and lies. As we saw in chapter 2, it is the telling of tales in hyaku-monogatari that invokes the mystic; it is the saying that causes the seeing. Ōgai's point is that the modern subject no longer believes (or wants to believe) in these things called ghosts—so hyaku-monogatari is nothing but a hollow form that can no longer be filled with the telling that once brought it to life.

Ōgai's allusion to Ibsen's 1881 play *Ghosts* is also significant.[25] These "ghosts" are not supernatural or spectral figures in the literal sense, as in the traditions of kaidan and hyaku-monogatari; rather, Ibsen refers metaphorically to the transgressions of earlier generations, as well as to the ideas, ideals, and rules of the past that "haunt" the present, hindering freedom and progress: "It's not only the things that we've inherited from our fathers and mothers that live on in us, but all sorts of old dead ideas and old dead beliefs and things of that sort. They're not actually alive in us, but they're rooted there all the same, and we can't rid ourselves of them. . . . I should think there must be ghosts all over the country—as countless as grains of sand."[26] Ibsen is lamenting the resilience of superstition and the "old dead beliefs" that impede social progress and modernity. The thrust of his argument, though very differently rendered, is reminiscent of Inoue Enryō's contemporaneous attempt to subdue the demons of Japan's own "superstitious" past. The beliefs and ideas of the past are walking dead.

By noting that "all those things that we called ghost stories or hyaku-monogatari" are now nothing more than ghosts, Ōgai's narrator suggests that the modern interpretive community does not respond the same way to the old texts: no longer does a spooky tale inspire a spectral play of the imagination; no longer does the subjective energy of belief infuse the telling of a story with the reality of experience. On the contrary, the mystic has lost its power to bewitch; like Ibsen's ghosts, it has become a pale shadow, symbolic only of the old ways that no longer have meaning. Hyaku-monogatari, in this context, can be nothing more than a relic.

As the story progresses, the emptiness of the experience is underscored. Traveling down the Sumida River toward the place where the game will take place, the guests come to a bridge on which some students are standing: "Just when the boat I was on went under the bridge, [the students] shouted, 'Fools!'" (127). The outburst poignantly, if ambiguously, comments on the party itself. Are the participants foolish for their conspicuous consumption on the boat? For feigning communication and community, when their interactions are stilted and hypocritical? Are they haunted by Ibsen's ghosts, refusing to relinquish the ideas of the past as they cynically recreate a practice no longer consistent with modern Japan? The silence of Ōgai's narrator allows the starkness of the comment to resonate throughout the story.

And once they arrive at the venue itself, the hollowness of the enterprise becomes even more evident. The narrator follows the others up a path toward the house where the game is to take place. As he nears the entrance, two serving women suddenly appear from a gap in the hedges. "Scary, wasn't it?" (129), one of the women says. Ōgai again reminds us that his own story, presumably, deals with the supernatural and frightening; the narrator inquires immediately of the two workers, "What is it?" But the women only stare rudely at him and disappear through the entranceway. The narrator decides to see for himself what lies between the break in the hedge:

> In a space set back a little, there was a small storage area that looked as if it was normally used for flowerpots and brooms. As it had already become a little dark in the shadows, it was difficult to see clearly into the back of the storage area; I made to peep in, and could make out a life-sized ghost with long hair hanging down, dressed in a white kimono, placed on a bundle of reeds or something, and peering out. It was a ready-made ghost that a ghost-story teller *[kaidan-shi]* in a theater would have taken around through the audience. Thinking, Oh, so this is a foretaste of the hyakumonogatari session, I felt somewhat as if I was being made a fool of, and I withdrew. (129–30)

Inadvertently he has stumbled upon the supernatural experience that was to serve as the climax of the hyaku-monogatari session. He has glimpsed the mechanism that makes the mystery possible, the backstage machinations through which the illusion is produced. And what he discovers is not impressive in the least—it is mundane, almost shabby, a doll shoved into the corner of a storage space. The serving woman's comment—"Scary, wasn't it?"—takes on a satiric tone now, as we realize that she must have been referring to something entirely different; she could not possibly have found this "ready-made ghost" frightening. Or, perhaps, what is scary is the very everydayness by which the illusion is produced. The narrator's discovery of the mechanism serves to foreshadow the (anti)climax, presaging the fact that there will in fact be no mystic revelation at the end of the story. Indeed, a sense of disinterest pervades the whole experience: when the narrator joins the other guests, he notes, "No matter which face I looked into, there was not one that showed the tension that comes from anticipation of something, or even just from curiosity" (130).

Finally the narrator sees Shitomi, the friend who had invited him, and Shitomi promptly takes him to meet Mr. Shikamaya, host and sponsor of the affair. Shikamaya's appearance is "different from the other guests." There is something out of the ordinary about him: "Although the room was quite crowded, around this man there were empty seats; when I stood at the entranceway, I noticed this immediately" (131). Shikamaya is a well-known social figure, notorious for his dissipated and extravagant lifestyle: "He had been in the newspapers, and I had heard my friends telling rumors about him" (133). In fact, the narrator admits, "from the beginning, my curiosity about what sort of thing hyaku-monogatari might be was fed by a certain amount of curiosity about what sort of man would put on such an affair" (132).

To the narrator's surprise, Shikamaya, a man of about thirty, seems not only detached but also somewhat melancholy and careworn. He is accompanied by Tarō, a famous geisha, who sits by his side like a nurse tending to a patient.[27] What, the narrator wonders, could have prompted this seemingly alienated and uninterested man to sponsor such an event? "He may have known very well that putting on the hyaku-monogatari session was a foolish thing from the beginning, and that the people who came were perhaps driven by the intention to devour his Western-style food; or perhaps, allowing the haze of superstition to shut out rationality, they were moved to come by a childish curiosity to experience the frightening *[kowaimono-mitasa]*. Wasn't he coldly watching all of this through those bloodshot eyes that appeared, the more I looked, to be malicious or demonic?" Reflecting the same coldness of observation he senses in the host, the narrator himself concludes, "I felt this man Shikamaya to be an interesting subject of study" (133–34).

The remainder of the story focuses on the narrator's observations of this enigmatic figure and on his musings on how his own personality reflects Shikamaya's.[28] The true mystery, we discover, is not a supernatural occurrence at the end of a session of tale-telling but rather the unknowable human heart of this curiously disinterested host. While all the guests speak with empty words, their conversations following formal conventions but lacking in content, Shikamaya does not speak at all; yet his appearance is, ultimately, the true yōkai at the conclusion of the one hundred tales. Or rather, for the narrator, the uncanny experience is his discovery of himself reflected in the yōkai-like figure of Shikamaya, a self strangely removed, defined by its lack of place. The doppelganger, Freud famously notes, is a trope often associated with the uncanny, in which "the double becomes a thing of terror."[29] In the enigmatic figure of Shikamaya, the narrator recognizes his own eerie double, the yōkai at the center of the affair. He has seen enough and, before a single spooky tale is told, takes leave of this "haunted house" (141).

Several days later the narrator finds out from his friend Shitomi that he had left at just the right moment: after several tales, Mr. Shikamaya had also disappeared, apparently taking Tarō upstairs to sleep. Shitomi mentions nothing about the content of the stories or the appearance of a yōkai: with the disappearance of the mysterious host, it seems, hyakumonogatari itself is forgotten. The gathering portrayed in "Hyakumonogatari" sits in stark contrast to the hyaku-monogatari games of old and even Shōyō's banquet discussed in chapter 3. For the guests in "Hyaku-monogatari," the game is already disenchanted and can no longer arouse even a playful sense of wonder. Rather the mystery that inspires the coming together of so many people is located in the heart of the enigmatic host, who in turn represents to the narrator the mysterious nature of his own personality. Ultimately for the narrator, the experience of mystery is the "appearance" of Shikamaya, the Other that reflects the Self: mystery resides within.

In one sense, then, "Hyaku-monogatari" represents a fulfillment of Enryō's yōkaigaku vision: the ghosts of the past no longer haunt. They have been filtered out and explained away, so that all that remains is the "true mystery" of the human heart. Already in Ōgai's text we find a sense of melancholic longing, a modern, disenchanted ennui. Somehow, it seems, the landscape of modernity, the trains and the psychologists and the doctors, are a pallid substitute for the yōkai of the past. Whether doctors of philosophy, science, or literature, Ōgai's protagonists express a sense of loss and disillusionment.

THE PRESENCE OF THE PAST

Each of the stories here is informed by tension between a present-day Self that embraces the new scientific ways of interpreting the world and an Other of the "past," operating within a mystic system in which supernatural forces have real and potent agency. The "old-fashioned" metaphorical landscape constantly threatens to intrude on the present and is repeatedly repressed by the protagonist seeking to define his place within a modern society. It is exactly this uncanny return of the repressed (or surmounted) monsters of Japan's past, the continuous reemergence of superstition and irrational thoughts, that indicates anxiety about the present and uneasiness with the hollow spiritual structures engendered by modernity. The protagonists in these stories by Sōseki and Ōgai incessantly slip between two worldviews, constantly longing for the one that has just begun to drift away. Never quite at home in either referential terrain, they suffer from a perpetual in-betweenness that breeds angst and uncertainty, the implacable homesickness of the modern subject.

If, as these stories imply, the modern self is form-with-no-content, then ironically it is the rejected Otherness of the past, signified by yōkai, that represents the breath that can fill the hollow form with content. The protagonists of all these stories are "professors" or at least university graduates; they exhibit an intellectual self-consciousness characterized by introspection and attentiveness to their particular place in a changing world. Because of their schooling in the sciences (psychology, medicine), society (law), or the arts (Ibsen), they are coiners of a new Japanese culture imbued with the common sense of the modern urban intellectual: the dominance of the steam train over the tanuki has become a given. Unlike Enryō, however, they cannot express triumph at this progressive achievement; rather, they exhibit empathy for the dead tanuki, lamenting their own inability to revive its lifeless form.

To be sure, Japan's experience was a distinct movement away from the past, an irrepressible forward trajectory marked by trains and electricity and fresh forms of governance. The Otherness of the past became more and more distant, the old metaphors increasingly absent from the modern landscape. Such a lack creates desire; disenchantment energizes aestheticization, transforming the past into a longed-for space of purity and authenticity. The empty staginess by which hyaku-monogatari is to be performed in Ōgai's text, however, gestures to the hollowness of such longing, the unattainable desire for the authenticity of the tale-telling game and the lost moment in which it flourished. Like the mundane solution to a mystery, the "fulfillment" of desire ultimately only highlights the illusive, constructed quality of the desired object. Recognizing the emptiness of desire for an experience that does not, and cannot, exist, Ōgai's narrator returns home before the absence of the authentic has a chance to play itself out.[30]

In the final analysis, the "desire for desire" takes the form of an almost pathological nostalgia:[31] a longing that does not destroy the thing it longs for, that is an end in itself. In early-twentieth-century Japan, that "thing" is an aestheticized past and its spatial counterpart, the pastoral—

both of which come to be increasingly associated with a lingering enchantment. Given the dangers of modern mysteries, such as the sinister use of hypnosis in "Masui," the yōkai of the old landscape appear increasingly desirable. Even as the tanuki's transformative powers are stolen by the technological magic of the modern age, nostalgia energizes a vigorous search for living samples of these fantastic creatures.

If yōkai reside in the past, then one must turn to the geographical equivalent of this authentic world: the countryside. While we have seen that even in the city yōkai lurk beneath a patina of new buildings and paved roads, these yōkai are particularly troubling because they are now out of place. It is no coincidence that they make themselves known to modern subjects—like Sōseki's narrator and Ōgai's professor in "Kompira"—who are experiencing emotional stress that defamiliarizes them with the mundane world to which they are accustomed. These extreme cases are the exceptions that prove the rule: for the modern intellectual subject, the cityscape had become a space in which yōkai could not openly thrive, a place where their comic complaints (Sōseki's tanuki) or shabby appearance (Ōgai's ready-made ghost) elicit only cynical laughter and a twinge of pity. Parallel to the loss of mystery in the modern cityscape—indeed, out of the very intellectual milieu that informed Sōseki and Ōgai—came an embracement of Japan's rural hinterlands as a repository for disappearing traditions.

Yanagita Kunio's Authentic Other: 'Tōno monogatari'

One scholar who overtly valued the countryside as a storehouse for a disappearing Otherness essential for defining modern subjectivity was Yanagita Kunio, the putative founder of minzokugaku, generally translated as "folklore studies" or "native ethnology."[32] A sense of the relevance of the past, latent in Sōseki and Ōgai, is fully wrought in Yanagita's work: minzokugaku might be characterized as a discipline driven by nostalgic sentiment, informed by a desire to incorporate aspects of the past into the construction of life in the present. "Yanagita's countryside," as H. D. Harootunian has pointed out, "was an imaginary, constructed from a discourse aimed at conserving and preserving traces of a lost presence."[33] Yanagita's discussion of yōkai not only provides an example of this approach but also contributed significantly to changing the meaning of these creatures.

Before I explore his explicitly yōkai-related texts, however, it would be helpful to consider the relevance of his most famous "literary" work—*Tōno monogatari* (Tales of Tōno).[34] Published in 1910, at a time when, as Marilyn Ivy notes, "it had become inescapably clear that western capitalism would not only bring civilization and enlightenment but would efface much of an older Japanese world,"[35] *Tōno monogatari* must be read as part of the desire for this return to (or discovery of) an authentic Japan. While Sōseki and Ōgai view the past and pastoral from the vantage point of the modern and urban, Yanagita leads the reader deep into that past and pastoral, to a land inhabited by tanuki before the corruption brought by doctors with their Western hypnotic techniques, to a place that—as his preface points out—the train has not yet reached.

Indeed, the now-famous preface conveys a sense of excited nostalgia, as if Yanagita has discovered something lurking at the heart of the nation that must be shared before it disappears: "Is there anybody who, after hearing these tales and seeing this place, would not want to tell them to others?"[36] Many of the 119 short entries involve mysterious deaths, rituals, and yōkai, otherworldly phenomena that Yanagita relates in a decidedly objective, nonjudgmental tone. Unlike the Sōseki and Ōgai stories, *Tōno monogatari* never questions the viability of the phenomena presented—rather, Tōno (the village) is presented as a nonmodern otherworld where tengu and kitsune and kappa are still conceivable. Yanagita records these things in a fashion sometimes reminiscent even of the *Wakan sansaizue* of two centuries earlier: "It is not uncommon to find the footprint of a kappa in the sand near the banks of a river. This is particularly true on the day after it rains. It is like a monkey's foot in that the big toe is separate, similar to the hand of a human. In length it is less than three *sun*. It is said that the imprint of the tip of the toes is not as easily visible as that of a human" (27).

Throughout *Tōno monogatari*, Yanagita employs this straightforward style known as "flat description" *[heimen byōsha]*, a literary choice that imbues his tales with a truth value similar to that of the encyclopedias of old.[37] Though he is inscribing the rumors and hearsay of a small community, there is nothing overtly pejorative in his attitude. His work is full of references to various yōkai, but he neither ridicules nor attempts to debunk these creatures. Nor does he convey a sense that scientific and rational thought holds any greater sway than does local belief.

Particularly revealing in this regard, tale number 82 tells of a man who sees a ghostlike apparition, which is described in vivid empirical detail. In the end, the apparition cannot be explained, and Yanagita concludes, "The man [who saw the ghost] is modern *[kindai-teki]* and intelligent *[reiri]*. Moreover, he is not a person to tell lies" (37). The passage is unique among the tales in the collection because of its implication that an explanation for such supernatural events should be required at all. Is it because the man in question is *modern* that he requires scientific justification? Significantly, however, no explanation is provided: logic in the village of Tōno, Yanagita acknowledges, is not the same as the logic of the modern. The man's modernity and intelligence are ultimately overshadowed by the weight of tradition.

I do not want to overlook Yanagita's own cultural investment in Tōno: he is an urban intellectual recording and rewriting the voice of an "authentic" rural subject. Specifically, his appropriation of the voice of his native "informant," Sasaki Kizen (1886–1933), has been meaningfully critiqued in recent years.[38] Yanagita's exoticization (colonization) of an internal otherworld (Tōno = past and pastoral Japan) is part of a broader, often problematic, valorization of "native" Japan during a period of intense migration to the urban centers.[39] In one sense, Yanagita's work only reinscribes established hierarchies of metropole and periphery; the Otherness he constitutes for Tōno is the product of the discursive hegemony of his own Tokyo-based academic, government, and literary community. On the other hand, *Tōno monogatari* also marks a distinct shift from the attitude of Inoue Enryō and the bunmei-kaika thinkers. Yanagita has traded Enryō's didacticism for a new voyeurism, a gaze that observes and reports, translating the murmurings of an internal otherworld into a flat-descriptive urban vernacular. Like the collectors of the Edo-period bussankai product conventions, Yanagita gathers up the things that seem strange and striking and puts them on public display, clearly labeled with their place of origin.

But how does Yanagita slough off the didacticism of Enryō and depict "objectively" the customs of Tōno? As Michel de Certeau notes, "The ethnologist and the archaeologist arrive at the moment a culture has lost its means of self-defense."[40] The violence wrought upon the beliefs and customs of "traditional" Japan by the practical antinostalgists such as Enryō makes possible the new violence of the nostalgists who would preserve the remnants of the disappearing culture for the benefit of the emerging culture. Such violence is inevitable when there is a shift in cultural understanding: "Any organization presupposes a repression," de Certeau reminds us, and "it is violence that invariably founds a system of knowledge."[41] The discipline of minzokugaku that Yanagita would go on to develop is one such system of knowledge, founded on the violence of an ethnography that appropriates the authenticity of the rural Other. It is a system of knowledge that, in Harootunian's words, "aimed at implanting an image of an unmoving social order at the heart of a society in constant motion, a historyless and classless community within the historical epoch of capitalism dominated by class relations."[42] Yanagita's early literary ethnography of Tōno is not only an indication that the organic culture of the region is actually in the process of changing; it also tells a story of the elite, urban imaginary, in which an originary rural past is idealized as a locus of the true heart of the Japanese people and nation.

Tōno monogatari is one step in this process of aestheticization: a series of snapshots of a place out of time. Yanagita's focus on the landscape of Tōno (the preface literally inscribes the terrain in his writing, noting how a particular mountain is shaped like a katakana ヘ) indicates his "awareness," as Karatani Kōjin suggests, "that 'landscape' was really a matter of language."[43] Yanagita preserves the landscape of a particular time and place, crystallizing it in a form that not only gives (textual) permanence to the ways of the past but also makes them, with all their odors and unpleasantness, safely accessible to the modern reader back in Tokyo. This drive to represent and preserve the disappearing rural—inchoate in Yanagita's early work but more explicit later on—is what James Clifford famously refers to as "salvage ethnography," in which the "other is lost, disintegrating in time and space, but saved in the text."[44] Certainly, as Harootunian notes, "Yanagita's discipline sought to make manifest what hitherto had remained hidden as an act of preserving endangered life-forms."[45] But with regard to yōkai, the elusive spirits lurking at the heart of the rural landscape, it is the very act of making visible the unseen, of stabilizing the shape-shifting, that causes the mystery to cease: only after modernity has shed the abject body of the yōkai, rendered its magic powerless, can scholars collect, examine, and put it in a museum. The tanuki can be studied only after the train has killed it.

THE MODERN STUDY OF YŌKAI

Although many of the legends in *Tōno monogatari* tell of mysterious phenomena, the monograph is not explicitly about yōkai. Rather, as a collection primarily of short narratives and experiences, it is akin to the hyaku-monogatari collections of old. It is likely that Yanagita himself intended this work to be a contribution to literature rather than to a systematic discourse on the mysterious. Not surprisingly, however, while Ōgai and Sōseki were grappling with questions of belief and disbelief,

Yanagita too was beginning to consider the place of yōkai within the logic of a modernizing nation. His essays on the subject constitute a conscious resistance to Enryō's ideology; Figal has even suggested that the discipline of minzokugaku itself was "originally formed in explicit opposition to *yōkaigaku.*"[46] Yanagita's own "science" of the supernatural was an attempt to go beyond—or perhaps sidestep—Enryō's conflation of yōkai with superstition and to look more carefully at the relationship between yōkai and human beings.[47] In contrast to Enryō—and even to Sōseki and Ōgai—Yanagita does not focus on *whether* yōkai exist; he assumes that if people believe, or once believed, in their existence, then they are part of an empirical record, a critical aspect of Japanese identity, and should be studied as such. He is not concerned with separating the "real" from the "imaginary"; rather, he would embrace the very ambiguity that makes them both possible.

Experiments with Illusion

One essay provides particular insight into his acceptance of the ambiguity of mystery, revealing Yanagita's own early struggles with questions of belief and empirical reality. In "Genkaku no jikken" (Experiments with Illusion; 1936), Yanagita recounts an experience he had some forty-eight years earlier, when he was a fourteen-year-old boy living at his brother's house in Ibaraki Prefecture. One day, while digging around in the dirt near a small local shrine, a bored Yanagita has a mysterious experience:

> I don't know why I did this, but from a crouching position, I strained my neck upward and looked to a point a little down and to the east of the middle of the sky. Even now I remember vividly, in the clear blue of the sky, about fifteen degrees from the orb of the sun, here and there I could see several dozen daytime stars *[hiru no hoshi]*. . . . Because I felt that this was so mysterious *[shinpi]*, I told nobody of my experience for some time. And I kept in my heart the belief that, if you only had the chance, stars were something you could see in the daylight.[48]

The experience resonates with a sense of the mystic and the sacred: Yanagita has been afforded a momentary glimpse into an otherworld, and it opens up in him a new realm of possibility, a feeling that if one "only had the chance" the invisible realm might become visible. Eventually, he does reveal his vision of the daytime stars to some medical students, and his confession is greeted with laughter; the young Yanagita is ridiculed for slipping away from the hegemonic rationalism of the period. Together with the medical students, he peruses books on basic astronomy, and he gradually comes to doubt the veracity of his own experience. Nevertheless, it has made an indelible impression, and several years later, when he relates it to his university friends in Tokyo, they tease him, saying, "You're a poet!" (331).

The reference to poetry is noteworthy because it gestures to Yanagita's minzokugaku methodology: it takes a poetic approach to probe the heart of the folk.[49] Reminiscent of Sōseki's narrator's comment that, "with regard to ghosts, the bachelors of law must follow blindly the bachelors of letters," the scene suggests that it is the poet's willingness to believe, to transcend the objective laws of nature, that allows him insight into the subjective laws of the supernatural. Like metaphors, the daylight stars signify something beyond themselves, and Yanagita's glimpse into the mysterious becomes a powerful affective experience, a rite of passage, that makes him privy to—or at least respectful of—the subjective experiences of others. As Harootunian notes, for Yanagita's minzokugaku, "understanding the folk required not interpretation but the exercise of empathizing with their experience. The investigator had to be in a position to recognize what constituted the fund of spiritual beliefs the folk took as second nature—beliefs forever beyond the powers of the outsider to grasp."[50] In contrast to the urban intellectualism of Sōseki's narrator, the young Yanagita offers no resistance to the mystic signs presented to him, but rather desires to learn how to interpret their meanings. As an adult writing the essay, he seems to be saying that even now his own heart is not aligned with the skeptical medical students but with the child he once was, oblivious to the restrictions imposed on the universe by the science of astronomy.

This short episode indicates how Yanagita will seek to find and secure the mysterious in everyday life. He is searching for the poetry imbedded in common speech, the hidden turns of expression that give a glimpse of meaning beyond the words, buried in the landscape—or concealed in the sky. It is significant that he recounts the tale in 1936, when minzokugaku as a discipline had achieved what many consider its apex.[51] In the years between the experience and its inscription, Yanagita had developed an approach for dealing with such phenomena as the daylight stars: while recognizing his university friends' distinction between science and poetry, he would make a concerted effort *not* to deny the poetic—or rather, to incorporate the poetic into the scientific. In fact, poetic and personal as the experience may be, Yanagita explains that he is offering it only as a single example: "If we make efforts to simply record this sort of episode as it is told, it will prove useful" (329), and if many such experiences were collected, "we could come a little closer to the truth" (332).

But what is this truth Yanagita seeks? Certainly it is different from Enryō's "true mystery." Or is it? In a 1912 essay, Yanagita had already suggested that the locus of truth is to be found within the very humans who seek to disclose it: "Why is it that such unthinkable imaginings can occur in the brains of human beings? As for such things, even if scholars spend ten thousand years, they will never be able to shed light on these secrets of humankind; when it comes down to it, I think the most exciting part of yōkai research is that it takes you into these superlative and poetic spaces. . . . And so in the end, all we can say is that human beings themselves are indeed the most mysterious [fushigi] thing in the universe."[52] Minzokugaku in general, and Yanagita's "yōkai research" in particular, would develop as a method for looking into these mysterious human secrets. Unlike Enryō, however, Yanagita would search for root causes not in the psychology and physiology of the individual but in the customs and narratives and codified behavior of everyday life. Through reading these bits and pieces of folklore, he endeavors to archeologically extract an authentic thing, a communal history, to which these scattered signs refer.

'The nameless common people of past generations . . .'

An early example of Yanagita's approach is found in the 1917 essay "Hitotsume-kozō" (One-Eyed Rascal).[53] The essay concerns *hitotsume-kozō*—a small anthropomorphic creature with one eye, one leg, and a long tongue—of which Yanagita notes, "with only a little variation, this yōkai has traversed most of the islands of Japan" (119). Particularly noteworthy, he points out, is that there is little evidence of its diffusion as a legend by word of mouth; rather, it seems to have emerged similarly throughout the country (a case of what folklorists would call "polygenesis"). Presenting a "bold hypothesis" (134), Yanagita argues that the tradition of hitotsume-kozō represents a trace of earlier customs involving human sacrifice.

Long ago, Yanagita explains, there were rituals in which a human being was sacrificed. A year before the sacrifice, the victim would be selected through divination, and "in order to distinguish him from the others, perhaps one of his eyes would be poked out. This person who was to work in a sacred capacity would be treated with a certain amount of hospitality and respect." Yanagita goes on to suggest that, although "human knowledge advanced and such bloody rituals came to a halt," the notion that a one-eyed person could receive sacred intelligence from the deities remained (134). Many generations later, this conflation of one-eyedness with the sacred, and with the status of a sacrificial victim as a doomed outcast, would survive in the form of the yōkai hitotsume-kozō. Yanagita sums up his argument:

> Like most obake, hitotsume-kozō is a minor deity that has become divorced from its foundations and lost its lineage. . . . At some point in the long distant past, in order to turn somebody into a relative of a deity, there was a custom *[fūshū]* of killing a person on the festival day for that deity. Probably, in the beginning, so that he could be quickly captured in the event of an escape, they would poke out one eye and break one leg of the chosen person. And then that person would be treated very favorably and afforded great respect. . . . At any rate, after some time, [this sort of sacrificial rite] came to an end, and only the ritual in which the eye was poked out remained. . . . And in due course, the time came when putting out the eye became a superfluous procedure . . . Meanwhile, it was long remembered that the sacred spirits [goryō] of the past had one eye; so when this deity became separated from the control of the higher gods and started to wander the roads of the mountains and the fields, it naturally followed that it came to be seen as exceedingly frightening. (151–52)[54]

Though he himself recognizes the audacity of his hypothesis—and fears rival scholars will assert that "saying such things is an insult to the country"—Yanagita suggests that, even if his conjecture is completely wrong, by reading folklore in this fashion he is taking a new approach (152).[55] Most important for us here, however, is his interpretation of the meaning of yōkai: they figure as signs that, when properly interpreted, provide a glimpse into the lives of "the nameless common people of past generations[,] . . . what frightened them, what troubled them, and what they thought about" (153). The premise of his argument is that, "when old beliefs were oppressed and made to surrender to new beliefs, all the [old] deities [kami-sama] were degraded *[reiraku]* and became yōkai. That is, yōkai are unauthorized deities *[kōnin serarezaru kami]*" (125).

This concept of yōkai as deities who have lost their official sanction would become a major tenet of Yanagita's yōkaigaku. Essential to this configuration is the ambivalent status of the yōkai: scorned and feared as an abject, outcast body, and at the same time desired and respected as a figure with intimate ties to the sacred. The yōkai becomes a site of both desire and disdain, respect and repulsion; as such it is subject to a certain fetishization. Degraded though it may be, the yōkai of the present is somehow linked to a sacred world of the past and signifies a powerful nostalgic connection to a lost authenticity. As Yanagita's discourse on human sacrifice suggests, that "authenticity" was not always altogether attractive or salutary, but critically it is part of a communal *Japanese* past, and as such it inspires a nostalgic sense of community and nation: "In the conduct of people long ago, there were many things that were modest and good. Or rather, perhaps it is just that we feel this way about them as they get older and older and more and more distant. Moreover, these are not the survivals of Ethiopians or Patagonians, but of the lifestyle of the parents of the parents of the parents of the parents of our own lost parents; as if we are grabbing onto a sleeve and clinging tightly to it—this is how nostalgic we feel" (152).

Yanagita's emphasis on the identity of the Japanese is not surprising. In Japan, as elsewhere, the folkloric project is always intimately engaged with questions of identity. For Yanagita, yōkai such as the hitotsume-kozō provide a key to accessing this identity: their ubiquity affords evidence of a past shared by common ancestors. The reality of this past may be unattractive, but as part of a collective experience it is also an essential part of the modern Self. The existence of yōkai as a trace of this communal history identifies the Japanese as Japanese.

Ultimately, however, Yanagita's conception of the past remains elusive. He alludes to a vague notion of an originary epoch before the degradation of deities into yōkai, a sort of primordial unified moment when the sign and its referent were still intimate and there was no need for metaphor. It was a time before written documents, so that the only records were those inscribed in the landscape and remaining in the oral lore of not-yet-modernized places like Tōno. That is, Yanagita's past is not so much a prehistory as it is "outside of history itself." By understanding the yōkai remaining in the present, he can, as Harootunian puts it, "provide a map for the present to recover the location of the 'real,' the 'true Japan,' and the meaning of the 'Japanese.'"[56]

Ema Tsutomu's 'Nihon yōkai-henge shi'

While Yanagita was developing his minzokugaku, another scholar, too, took up the challenge of yōkai—but from a different stance. Ema Tsutomu relied much more heavily on the written record and was concerned with locating yōkai within a historical context, specifically outlining the different "pasts" in which they reigned. Like Yanagita, Ema approached yōkai not as things to be explained away or repressed but as critical agents in defining the Japanese identity. Before considering Yanagita's later development of yōkai studies, then, it is important to look briefly at Ema's *Nihon yōkai-henge shi* (Japanese History of *Yōkai-henge*) of 1923, the first post-Enryō attempt to create a taxonomy of mysterious creatures and the first explicit comprehensive effort to document the changing meaning of yōkai in Japanese cultural history.[57]

Ema was the foremost scholar of *fūzokushigaku,* a discipline dedicated to studying the history of customs and manners. In many ways, fūzokushigaku is similar to minzokugaku, and the two often overlapped and influenced each other. Just as the subject of minzokugaku is amorphous and constantly changing, so too that which qualifies as *fūzoku* (most commonly translated as "customs") is difficult to pin down. Although the two disciplines focus on many of the same areas—clothing, rituals, foodways—fūzokushigaku seems generally oriented more toward documenting fads and fashion diachronically, paying special attention to differences between historical periods. Rather than, for example, examining how weaving and dying customs are passed from one generation to another through means of oral transmission, or how such customs exhibit variation by region, a fūzokushigaku scholar might document general trends in clothing fashions and how they differ with each successive generation. The discipline can perhaps be described as a cultural history of everyday life.[58]

Nihon yōkai-henge shi is a cultural history of yōkai that highlights how they differ during each successive historical epoch. In contrast to Yanagita, who remained vague, Ema clearly delineates these different pasts: the age of the gods; the period from the reign of Emperor Jinmu (660 B.C.E.) to the introduction of Buddhism (mid-sixth century C.E.); the period from the introduction of Buddhism to the Ōnin War (1467–1477); from the Ōnin War to the end of the Edo period; and from Meiji onward (p. 370). For each one of the pre-Meiji periods, Ema draws on numerous literary, folkloric, historical, and religious texts, including the mythohistories of the *Kojiki* (712) and *Nihonshoki* (720) and the setsuwa tale collections of the *Nihon ryōiki* and *Konjaku monogatari shū*. For the Tokugawa period, he relies heavily on hyaku-monogatari collections and Sekien's catalogs, with which he amply illustrates his own essay.

Like Yanagita, Ema sets out to document yōkai without treating his subject matter pejoratively. Yet he also anticipates the modern reader's resistance to this method:

> The reader will probably say the following: in the past as in the present, there is only one logic. Things such as yōkai-henge [yōkai and shape-shifters] cannot exist in the world; or perhaps even if they exist subjectively, they do not exist objectively, and therefore in this world where there are such things as cars and airplanes, delusions are no longer worth listening to. Generally speaking, this is correct. However, I want to make clear from the start that my stance is fundamentally different from that of the reader who raises such an argument. The present essay works on the premise that yōkai-henge actually exist, and looks at how humans interacted with them in the past; put another way, I will look into the way our ancestors saw yōkai-henge, how they understood them, and how they dealt with them. (367–68)

With this caveat, Ema goes on to outline his own classificatory schema of mysterious creatures and beings. One fundamental way in which he differs from Sekien, Enryō, and Yanagita is in his terminology—specifically the distinction he makes between *yōkai* and *henge*. The latter is a term sometimes used interchangeably with yōkai, but Ema attributes a different set of associations to it:

> If you look at most dictionaries, you will see that *yōkai* is melded with *henge*, and *henge* is melded with *yōkai:* the two words are given the same meaning. However, for some years I have been researching this aspect, and it is clear that there is a difference in the definitions. So, if I were to give the definitions of both words that I have been considering for a long time, I would say *yōkai* is an ungraspable mystery, a nondescript *[etai no shiranu fushigi na mono]*; whereas *henge* is something that has externally changed its identity *[gaikanteki ni sono shōtai o kaeta mono]*. (367)

In its erudition and attention to detail, Ema's typology is reminiscent of Enryō's systematic discourse of a generation earlier.[59] Unlike Enryō's purpose, however, Ema's objective is not to debunk yōkai or to show the psychological dimensions behind the illusion but rather to create a taxonomy of the many forms the illusion can take. He contends, for example, that generally those things defined as "henge" are characterized by their ability to shape-shift *(bakeru)*, a technique that can itself be classified into two broad types: "this-worldly" *(gense-teki)*, and "transmigratory" *(rinne-teki)*. The former refers to creatures such as the tanuki and kitsune, which can alter their physical appearance in their present existence. The latter refers to changes made after death, when, as a result of some sort of tie or obligation, the body takes on a different form to reappear in the world—ghosts (yūrei) are an example of this type of henge (368–69).

As for corporeal appearance, yōkai-henge tend to take one of five basic bodily forms: person, animal, plant, material object *(kibutsu)*, or natural thing *(shizenbutsu)*. Ema defines *yōkai* (as opposed to *henge*) as something with a stable appearance whose form resembles one of these five types (368) but is not quite the same as these things: "Though its appearance may be like that of a human, it is not a human; though like an animal, it is not an animal" (392). He goes on to introduce increasingly complex distinctions of "singular" and "compound" body types (422–23); his essay is an experiment in describing nondescripts, of referencing known bodies to categorize bodies that defy categorization.[60]

But his analysis is not restricted to physical form. He also pores through literary and historical texts to determine exactly *where* and *when* yōkai-henge made their presence known, suggesting that "there is generally a set time and place depending on the type" (414). Evening is the most common time for yōkai-henge to emerge, and they have been known to show up in a wide variety of locations, including mountains, shrines, houses, and the ocean (414–18). Ema also carefully registers trends in the age and occupation of yōkai-henge as well as their gender: "Before the Muromachi period, males were the most common. But, since the Ōnin War, female figures have become more common, reaching approximately two and a half times the number of male figures. . . . During the early modern period, those yūrei that appeared for love or yearning were mostly female. Perhaps this is because the jealousy felt by females is stronger than that felt by males. . . . Furthermore, during the early modern period, even if an animal, plant, or object changed shape, it would generally transform into a woman" (442). Although he refrains from postulating the social function of mysterious creatures during different historical epochs, Ema's presentation opens possible avenues for critically reading the power dynamics of gender and the supernatural.

His thoroughness and taxonomical approach may be similar to Enryō's, but Ema accepts yōkai as real cultural phenomena, bringing them into the light of a careful academic scrutiny that is not designed to negate their existence. In the conclusion of his monograph, he reiterates that, "since the beginning of time in Japan, our ancestors have had a close relationship with yōkai-henge." The study of these creatures has a lot to teach us, he suggests, and they "should be given special recognition for the countless moral lessons they have contributed and their great efforts on behalf of people's self-cultivation [shūyō]" (450–51). In Ema's hands, yōkai are historical artifacts that can speak vividly about the culture(s) that created them. Unlike Yanagita, Ema does not study the present incarnation of a yōkai for its insight into the past; rather, each past incarnation is plumbed for its connection with the period in which it existed.

Ema's analysis ends with the advent of Meiji, to which he attributes a distinct shift in the role of yōkai-henge: "Since Meiji, along with the advances of academia, the secrets of the mysterious otherworld have unfolded beneath the clear lens of learning; yōkai-henge have, inversely, come to be threatened by humans, come to be frightened of humans." With modernity, it seems, yōkai-henge have learned to "hide themselves away and rarely torment humans." Although Ema admits that they may refuse to go away entirely, and that "the sublime world of the mysterious [shinpi] transcends science" (451–52), his point is that the onset of Meiji brings with it a reversal of the relationship between humans and yōkai: now it is the humans who seek out the monsters.

Yanagita's Approach

Yanagita's analysis begins where Ema's leaves off: with the present. Yanagita's gaze is trained on what he sees as a disappearing part of Japan, a *present in the process of becoming past.* Yōkai are survivals, like scattered shards of pottery that must be collected and glued together, with a liberal amount of imagination, in order to reconstruct the belief systems of the past. Yanagita had already begun to grapple with yōkai in "Hitotsume-kozō" and elsewhere, but his later writing on the subject was probably directly inspired by Ema's 1923 *Nihon yōkai-henge shi.*[61] He would go on to write a number of important essays that, considered together, suggest a theoretical framework.[62] His approach stresses three primary points: collection and categorization of yōkai; distinctions between obake and yūrei; and a theory of degradation, in which yōkai are understood as reduced or fallen deity figures.[63]

As with any process of archeological reconstruction, the first step is to gather up the scattered fragments. In many of his essays, Yanagita not only provides numerous examples of yōkai experiences and legends but also reasserts the need for further collection. The most systematic expression of this collecting process is his "Yōkai meii" (Yōkai Glossary), published over several months between 1938 and 1939 in the journal *Minkan denshō.*[64] Essentially a catalog of seventy-nine different yōkai, the glossary is made up of entries culled from local gazetteers and folklore collections (including his own *Tōno monogatari*), and each entry contains short descriptions of the yōkai in question. Often, the mysterious thing noted is less a creature than a phenomenon, such as the *nurikabe:* "Found on the coast of Onga County in Chikuzen [present-day Fukuoka Prefecture]. When [you are] walking along a road at night, suddenly a wall appears in front of you, and you cannot go anywhere. This is called nurikabe and it is feared. It is said that, if you take a stick and strike at the bottom of it, it will disappear; but if you hit at the top part, nothing will happen" (431).

The more famous yōkai—such as tanuki, kitsune, and mikoshi-nyūdō—do not require separate entries; they are mentioned only to better describe local manifestations that resemble them. Yanagita notes, for example, that a yōkai called *nyūdōbōzu* is the same as mikoshi-nyūdō, and that "there is a story of somebody meeting this in Tsukude Village in Mikawa. At first it looks like a small monk of about three *shaku,* but as [you] get closer it becomes seven or eight *shaku* and one *sun* tall. It is believed that if you are first to say 'I saw you,' then everything will be all right, but if it says this [first], then you will die" (433).

Although there are no subheadings or divisions in the catalog, a close reading reveals an organization rather loosely based on associations—*things that suddenly obstruct your passage at night,* for example, or *things akin to mikoshi-nyūdō.* In his introduction Yanagita does not mention this vague organization; rather, he stresses the difficulty of categorizing these things that are already disappearing from the landscape and even, he fears, from memory: "I still have not established a method for categorization, and I think the main reason for this lies in the insufficiency of words *[goi].* Now I would like to draw a little on the memories of readers. But perhaps it is already too late" (424).

Despite his pessimism, Yanagita does tentatively suggest two principles for categorizing yōkai. The first concerns the place in which they appear—roadways, dwelling places, mountains, and water—with roadways being the most common. The second principle focuses on "the degree of belief *[shinkōdo no nōtan]*": "For the most part these days, confidence [in the existence of yōkai] is rare, which indicates a tendency [of legends or beliefs] to turn into folktales.[65] In between [those who believe in yōkai and those who do not believe in yōkai] are those who don't believe in their existence but, upon hearing a story, experience an eerie feeling. This [group] is situated next to those who, though they normally reject the existence of yōkai, regress somewhat in their way of thinking when they see something mysterious [fushigi]" (424).

Yanagita's recognition of the continuity of belief and nonbelief—that even those who do not believe in yōkai can "regress somewhat"—is very much reminiscent of the Sōseki and Ōgai stories. His notion of "degree of belief" also recalls Enryō. Significantly, however, Enryō's focus was on the women, children, and less-educated folk whose belief encouraged the movement of Kokkuri—that is, for Enryō, "degree of belief" was an indication of relative levels of education and psychological disposition. For Yanagita, "degree of belief" becomes, ironically, a measure of Enryō's success, as belief in yōkai is attenuated by an increasing degree of belief in scientific rationale.

Ultimately, Yanagita does not actually employ his own taxonomical principles in the text, stressing only that "Yōkai meii" is a reference source to which he hopes others will add. Notwithstanding this hesitancy to classify, however, Yanagita's most famous contribution to yōkai studies is the distinct division he outlines between obake and yūrei in another short essay, "Yōkai dangi" (Discussions of Yōkai; 1936).[66] He prefaces his discussion by lamenting the confusion brought on by modern urban existence, noting that, until recently,

> there was a pretty clear distinction between obake and yūrei that anybody would have realized. To start with, obake generally appeared in set locations. If you avoided these particular places, you could live your entire life without ever running into one. In contrast to this, yūrei—despite the theory that they have no legs—doggedly came after you. When [a yūrei] stalked you, it would chase you even if you escaped a distance of a hundred *ri*. It is fair to say that this would never be the case with a bakemono. The second point is that bakemono did not choose their victims; rather they targeted the ordinary masses. . . . On the other hand, [a yūrei] only targeted the person it was concerned with. . . . And the final point is that there is a vital distinction regarding time. As for a yūrei, with the shadowy echo of the bell of Ushimitsu [hour of the bull; approximately 2:00–2:30 A.M.], the yūrei would soon knock on the door or scratch at the folding screen. In contrast, [bakemono] appeared at a range of times. A skillful bakemono might darken the whole area and make an appearance even during the daytime, but on the whole, the time that seemed to be most convenient for them was the dim light of dusk or dawn. In order for people to see them, and be frightened by them, emerging in the pitch darkness after even the plants have fallen asleep is, to say the least, just not good business practice. (292–93)

I quote this passage at length because it has become a critical, oft-cited element of Yanagita's writing on yōkai. As scholars realize when they pursue concrete folkloric examples, however, Yanagita's distinctions simply do not hold up. One ramification of his work, then, has been the continued effort of subsequent researchers to refine and amend his playfully outlined, and perhaps even tongue-in-cheek, classifications to make them better fit the existing examples.[67]

More significant than Yanagita's actual distinctions is his fear that such distinctions have been lost. "Without exception," he grumbles, city dwellers "confuse obake with yūrei." And it was not just urban folk who had lost their grip on the subtleties of the invisible world: conducting research on monsters had become increasingly difficult because the authenticity of informants had been corrupted. Some people in remote villages seemed to feel his queries were condescending; they berated him for thinking that country folk still believed in things such as yōkai. Yanagita's point here is not that the belief in the mysterious had disappeared; rather, he complains, plenty of "women and children" were still frightened, but they had "not received sufficient education to express what is inside of them" (292). In other words, "progress" had eliminated the old metaphors—the yōkai—for expressing fear and awe but had yet to adequately replace them. To invoke Ōgai's analogy again, it seemed that the folk who had lost the old rags of yōkai belief were worse off than before—with no clothes, silk or otherwise, to dress their fears.

Ironically, Yanagita longs for *(natsukashii kurai)* what he calls the "yōkaigaku era" (292), by which he means a time when the referential terrain was less murky, when yōkai were the dominant explanatory paradigm and, therefore, yōkaigaku (Enryō-style) had a clearly determined mission. Now, it seemed, the simple binaries had been muddied, and people could no longer even find the words to express the wonders and fears around them. It was during this critical moment as yōkai were vanishing that we had to listen to their fading voices: "Certainly, in recent years they are the most neglected element of our cultural record *[bunka etsureki]*; accordingly, when we as a people undertake a course of self-reflection, they are a resource that will provide a particularly surprising number of hints" (291–92). The rapidly disappearing Other of the yōkai could not be overlooked in defining the culture of the Japanese people.

This brings us to the third major aspect of Yanagita's approach, what we might call his degradation theory, in which he describes yōkai as a deterioration of ancient systems of belief. As in "Hitotsume-kozō," his conjecture is that once-serious beliefs had been degraded (reiraku), stripped of their sacred nature, to appear as yōkai.[68] In "Bon sugi medochi dan" (After the Bon Festivities: Tales of Medochi [Kappa]) of 1932, Yanagita outlines the three steps of a process he characterizes as the "foundational principle of our yōkaigaku." Citing the kappa as an example, he notes that in stage one the creature is respected and kept distant: we avoid places where it is known to lurk, and if we see a kappa we run away in fear. The next stage is when we begin to think that it is silly to avoid a particular place because of a kappa; we challenge our own fears, though inside we are still rather uncomfortable. Every person is different, Yanagita concedes, but "as for society, this is a period of half-belief-half-doubt [hanshin-hangi]." Finally we come to the third stage, when society has "evolved" and the number of doubters begins to increase. Accompanying this stage are stories of the subjugation of yōkai, in which they are made to swear never again to cause mischief. Yōkai have, at this point, fully left behind the realm of legend and belief to enter the world of folktale and entertainment (350–51).

Yanagita reiterates his understanding of this process in a number of different essays. In "Tanuki to demonorojii" (Tanukis and Demonology; 1918), for example, he notes that three distinct periods of "demonology" accompany the progress of civilization. In the first stage, the agent (yōkai) has the ability to possess *(tsuku)* people; in the second stage, it can derange *(kuruwasu)*; and in the third stage, all it can do is surprise *(odorokasu)*. These periods of progress, according to Yanagita, are also geographically determined—with the rural areas still in the earlier stages, while the urban centers of Japan have entered the third stage.[69]

Yanagita's conception of progress is based on a unilinear evolutionary model reminiscent of Ema's five epochs and Enryō's three time periods. The evolutionary paradigm, with social Darwinism at its core, was common currency in Japan at this time, and it is not surprising that all three authors viewed yōkai through this optic. Yanagita's particular reduction of cultural evolution is distinguished by its focus on different stages of development existing simultaneously, with progress along the evolutionary trajectory determined by geography—the distance of the periphery from the center. This notion of temporary regional differences works with the burgeoning idea of a broader "Japaneseness," in which, as Tessa Morris-Suzuki puts it, "local differences, rather than being the products of distinct local histories, were redefined as different evolutionary points along a single line of national history."[70]

Yanagita charts the process of human evolution by concentrating on the concurrent *devolution* experienced by yōkai. As humanity progresses and modernity increasingly informs everyday life, the yōkai's "fate" entails a gradual degeneration from an object of serious belief to one of comical entertainment (341). Ultimately, yōkai will be available only in the museums of modernity, displayed at different devolutionary stages for the appreciation of enlightened Japanese across the country. In other words, if yōkai are degenerated avatars of the deities of a shared, mythical past—before the advent of local differences—then their complete devolution will once again dissolve such differences and result in a unified Japanese culture. As the study of yōkai, a metonym for Yanagita's minzokugaku, continued to develop throughout the interwar years, a nostalgia for a unified, authentic past came to be translated into a longing for a unified, authentic future.

ECHOING VOICES, HOLLOW FORMS

As disparate as their agendas were, both Sekien and Enryō treated yōkai as living phenomena—to be collected and illustrated (Sekien) or, alternatively, gathered up and exterminated (Enryō). Yanagita and Ema, however, approached yōkai only as a link to the past (and the future). Yanagita in particular was not a biologist but a fossil hunter, discovering remains buried in the landscape, in the place-names, the dialects, and the local names for monsters. What unites these traces thematically is that they are words, most often *spoken* words: he searched for the contours of the past by listening to the sounds that echo through the present.

In several essays, for example, Yanagita focused on words denoting "twilight," such as *tasogare* and *kawatare*. These, he contended, derive from expressions meaning essentially "Who are you?" uttered at dusk, when the face of the other could not be recognized. The response would signify whether the passerby was a villager, outsider, or yōkai. Thus, it is with voice that the boundaries of the community are reconfirmed and proper order is maintained.[71]

Similarly, Yanagita informally surveyed children at play, asking them, "What sound does an obake make?" and suggesting that the voice of the yōkai becomes the name of the yōkai. By locating these words geographically, he divided Japan into three distinct regions. Through this sonar cartography, he superimposed on the modern landscape a map of the terrain in which yōkai once reigned.[72]

When Sekien was writing, a century and a half earlier, the sounds of yōkai suggested a simultaneously existing otherworld hidden within the present; Sekien's creativity could encourage the evolution of an aural phenomenon—such as the yanari—into a visualizable icon. Though Yanagita too listened for these sounds, for him they were the lingering echoes of an otherworld that no longer existed—the creativity involved in his own work did not entail envisioning "new" yōkai but linking present traces with incarnations from the past. In one essay, he maintained that tanuki, famous for their shape-shifting abilities, were much more talented at imitating sounds than transforming themselves visually.[73] Perhaps, then, it was not surprising that tanuki were particularly prominent when it came to challenging—with their *shu shu po po po* sound—the progress of the steam engine. The tanuki's voice was a plaintive cry expressing both its impending doom and, paradoxically, its permanent preservation in the discourse of minzokugaku.

Throughout the first several decades of the twentieth century, Japan's experience was colored by this effort to come to terms with these lingering voices of yōkai echoing through the modern landscape. Yanagita's project was one response to a sense of loss: akin to an archeologist, or a psychoanalyst, he purposefully dug up the buried monsters of the past in order to heal the trauma of the present. Whereas Sōseki and Ōgai sought to define the Self on an individual level, Yanagita grappled with a similar problem on a national scale. His study of folklore became a nostalgic effort to salvage the old metaphors and incorporate them into a communal identity for a new Japan. In contrast to the disconnectedness and disenchantment of Ōgai's urban tale-telling session, Yanagita's *Tōno monogatari* is steeped in a sense of connection and enchantment, where fantastic events are real because everyone in the community participates in the telling.

For Yanagita, then, the rural hinterlands concealed disappearing traces of the past: words were encoded references to yōkai, and yōkai themselves were fallen avatars of more awesome deities. The voices that could still be heard if one listened carefully (to legends, folktales, place-names, and children's games) were echoes from a "primordial moment prior to historical time,"[74] when yōkai could also be seen. But the intellectual milieu of the early twentieth century no longer had space for visible, living yōkai. Minzokugaku would collect and reassemble the remnants of the past, but ultimately the yōkai image that emerged was historical, lacking a sense of mystery in the present, real world.

Certainly, Ema, Yanagita, and even Enryō acknowledged that the unexplainable and mysterious—the fushigi—will survive as long as humans continue to ponder the world around them. Indeed, the drive to comprehend the mysterious goes hand in hand with modernity's advance: as Terada Torahiko (1878–1935), physicist, writer, and student of Sōseki, noted in 1929, the desire to understand yōkai operates as a catalyst for scientific innovation, stimulating inquiry into realms as varied as physics and meteorology. As each bakemono is explained away, it does not disappear but simply changes shape: "As human beings evolve, bakemono cannot help but evolve along with them."[75]

Terada's analysis, indisputable as it is, does not account for the discarded shell left behind when the mysterious takes up residence in something more appropriately modern. But it was empty shells such as these that were collected throughout the nation. If the pre-Meiji yōkai was a dynamic admixture of the mysterious and the weird, then in early-twentieth-century discourse the mysterious content was extracted from the weird form, the power to enchant lodged in more modern constructs, such as steam trains, nerves, and hypnotism. Through the backward-searching project of minzokugaku, yōkai became associated primarily with the weird form, the discarded shell, the tanuki dead by the tracks. While the fushigi continued to evolve—as part of science, psychology, and organized religion—yōkai themselves were cast off along the evolutionary path.

To be sure, fossilization was never complete. Yōkai could still, for instance, be appropriated for vivid social satire, as in Akutagawa's short novel *Kappa* (1927), in which the kappa community represents a parodic allegory of 1920s society.[76] And yōkai would also, to a certain extent, continue to have some function in local belief systems, legends, and folktales. But Yanagita's prediction that they would decline into comicality was not without validity. Like a self-fulfilling prophesy, the folkloric quest to document and textualize the survivals of a living tradition relegated yōkai to the taxidermist's workshop, physically preserved but devoid of life or mystery. Conversely, the wonders of science and the human mind assumed the role once played by fantastic creatures: the frightening, unpredictable thing one meets up with in the twilight. Sexual "deviance" and criminal violence became the monstrous subjects of ero-guro-nansensu, "the prewar, bourgeois cultural phenomenon that devoted itself to explorations of the deviant, the bizarre, and the ridiculous."[77] This genre, typified by the fiction of Edogawa Ranpo (1894–1965), explored such issues as eugenics, physical deformity, and criminal psychology, often in a sensationalistic manner. Within this context, yōkai inversely became safe and reassuring, comforting symbols of a shared national history, no longer vital participants in the horror stories of a modern nation preparing for a modern war.

Ultimately then, early-twentieth-century discourse on yōkai is characterized by a bifurcation, in which yōkai and fushigi came to follow two separate trajectories. While the fushigi continued to evolve, yōkai were increasingly portrayed as weird historical artifacts lacking direct relevance to the present. Although, of course, superstition and unexplainable occurrences would persist through the war years and afterward, yōkai were not commonly called upon as the default explanation for such phenomena. As Komatsu Kazuhiko has suggested, in times of war, people have no need to invoke yōkai to express their confusion and horror.[78]

Archaic figures such as the kappa or tanuki became incommensurate with the weighty concerns arising from the terrors of modern warfare and atomic weaponry. Not until the late 1960s through the 1980s did the old yōkai begin to find a home in modern media and new yōkai emerge to frighten, entertain, and breathe new life into the relics of the past, reuniting weird form with mysterious content.

CHAPTER 5

Media of the Weird

Mizuki Shigeru and Kuchi-sake-onna

NOT GODZILLA

Less than a decade after its devastation by American firebombing, Tokyo was destroyed again: this time by the rampages of a gigantic fire-breathing lizard known as Gojira, in the eponymous 1954 film. A deep-sea monster awakened from its slumbers by atomic weapons testing, Gojira (or Godzilla as the creature would be called in its American incarnation two years later) provided a powerful metaphor for the terrors unleashed by the nuclear age and the unforeseeable forces—political, environmental, technological—that would influence everyday lives in the decades after the war. In the darkness of the movie house, the gargantuan creature is drawn to the lights of Tokyo and devastates the city with its massive footsteps and fiery breath: the eternal conflict of nature and culture played out in a landscape being rebuilt after a cataclysmic war.

Gojira has certainly not been overlooked in discussions of film and popular culture.[1] But in the current field of yōkai studies, the fifty-meter lizard is generally relegated to a different category of analysis, most commonly labeled *kaijū,* a word often translated as "monster" or, more literally, "strange beast."[2] To be sure, the difference between a kaijū and a yōkai is a murky one at best, but the relative invisibility of Gojira within the modern discourse on yōkai highlights the way yōkai came to be defined in postwar Japan. Does Gojira's fictional birth somehow set it apart from the yōkai we have been looking at? Is it different because of its genesis within the medium of popular cinema?

These questions are intimately bound up with the ways "traditional" yōkai are understood. As noted in chapter 4, in the early twentieth century yōkai came to be associated nostalgically with the pastoral landscape of a disappearing Japan. Regardless of whether the origins of a particular yōkai are ultimately traceable to an individual creator or have been obscured through generations of telling and embellishment, the subjects of Ema's and Yanagita's investigations are historical: they are linked to the past, to the land, to a sense of tradition. As if in recognition of this, a backstory is created for Gojira in the film—he is a creature of local legend, emerging from the depths to fulfill his destiny. Regardless of this invented legend, Gojira is physically modeled on a dinosaur rather than any of the creatures in, for example, the *Wakan sansaizue* or Sekien's catalogues.[3] Perhaps he is simply too big to be a yōkai, too massive to lurk in the twilight shadows on the outskirts of town. Alternatively, Gojira might be considered to be, like a cyborg, a creature enhanced or mutated by technology, born from a violent fusion of culture and nature. Whatever the case, Gojira, both monster and movie, emerged not from layers of tradition but from a tragedy of violence and suffering: Gojira was made possible—necessary—by the war itself. He is a scar, a marker of trauma, "burdened," as historian Yoshikuni Igarashi puts it, "with contradictory missions: to simultaneously re-present the traces of history and to be erased from the surface of the earth."[4]

Gojira's popularity spurred numerous sequels and even a new genre, known as the monster movie, or *kaijū eiga*. One reason for the fascination of these films may have been a longing for the era *before* Gojira made his appearance, a desire to return to the lost innocence of a world before the national cataclysm of war and occupation made the destruction of entire cities a nightmarish possibility. Later monster-movie creations, such as Gamera and Gappa, did not possess the same gravity as Gojira, but throughout the 1960s many of the stories followed a similar narrative pattern: an ancient slumbering beast is brought to life and violence through inadvertent human intervention, be it technological carelessness (*Gamera;* 1965) or commercial ambition (*Gappa;* 1967). In most cases, the kaijū in question comes from somewhere offshore, either a distant Japanese island or foreign lands or waters.[5] In this context, Japan's own native yōkai seem quaint and anachronistic, safely secured on the shelves of the folkloric museums established through early-twentieth-century discourse.

In one sense, Gojira and his followers are foils for these traditional yōkai, postlapsarian embodiments of nuclear terrors that only intensify the idealization of a past further and further out of reach. Not until the 1968 release of *Yōkai daisensō* (dir. Kuroda Yoshiyuki; English title: *Yōkai Monsters: Spook Warfare*) do yōkai appear in a movie that could be labeled a kaijū eiga. The movie follows a normative kaijū eiga narrative; significantly, however, the yōkai remain in their own historical setting and represent not the monster to be destroyed but the soldiers defending the nation.

Set during the Edo period, the action begins when non-Japanese treasure hunters in "Babylonia" inadvertently awaken a monster that has been slumbering for thousands of years. The monster, a tengu-like creature with the ability to grow into a Gojira-sized behemoth, somehow ends up on the shores of Japan. There it exhibits vampiric tendencies, biting the neck of a local official *(daikan)* and commandeering his body. In the guise of the body-snatched official, the monster proceeds to destroy all manifestations of Buddhism and Shintō (Japanese indigenous belief) within the official's residence. Eventually various local yōkai—beginning with a comical kappa—take it upon themselves to assist the hapless humans in ridding themselves of this foreign invader.

The film is kitschy and often humorous, displaying a panoply of rather cheaply costumed yōkai derived from the pages of Sekien and his successors. With its foreign monster rampaging through Japan, it is similar to many kaijū eiga; this time, however, the defenders of the nation are a ragtag troop of traditional yōkai, and the action is set in the past. Significantly too, the film has a distinctly nationalist tinge to it: the invading foreign monster explicitly attacks symbols of Japanese religion, and it is *Japanese* yōkai who muster from all over the country to defend the land. Indeed, the rhetoric of nation permeates the film: after their victory, not only do the yōkai themselves proudly exclaim, "Japanese yōkai have won!" (Nippon no yōkai ga kattan ya zo!), but the phrase is later reiterated by the appreciative humans too.

I mention *Yōkai daisensō* here because it bridges a divide between monster movies and the yōkai anime that would be popular in the years to come, and also because the late 1960s seem to mark the beginning of a rediscovery of yōkai as an affective symbol for the nation. By 1968, when *Yōkai daisensō* was released, Japan was in the midst of its postwar economic rise. The Olympics had been held in Tokyo four years earlier, and most households could now afford refrigerators, washing machines, and televisions. It is not surprising that the pathos of the war years was no longer represented in monster movies, and was replaced instead with a sense of a national community capable of overcoming challenges from abroad: in *Yōkai daisensō,* the traditional yōkai represent this unified Japanese family. If the prewar work of Yanagita and others transformed yōkai into metonyms of an unspoiled past, then the aura of purity and innocence encircling them becomes all the more salient as this past is devoured by a sprawling, polluted, urban present. In 1971, a monograph on yōkai would open by characterizing the word *obake* as "this nostalgic, dream-filled word."[6]

Post-Godzilla Landscape

From the mid-1950s to the early 1970s, Japan experienced a period of rapid economic growth, reasserting itself in the world market with remarkable vigor. The extraordinary industrial development of this time also indelibly altered the national landscape: urban centers expanded both laterally and vertically with rows of concrete apartment buildings *(danchi);* new factories belched out smoke, driving the engine of economic revival and blackening the skies; and rural communities experienced unprecedented depopulation. In cities and suburbs, patterns of everyday life were shaped by new or revitalized media, such as the ubiquitous television and a reenergized popular publishing industry that produced inexpensive books and magazines and manga for a seemingly insatiable consumer base.

But as this period of rapid growth came to an end in the early 1970s, marked by an energy crisis and an overall economic slowdown, the sacrifices that had been required to fuel the national recovery became increasingly evident: widespread environmental destruction, diseases brought on by unfettered pollution, and a populace living in tiny anonymous apartments that, in 1979, would be facetiously labeled "rabbit hutches."[7] Akin to Gojira, the national economy had risen from the depths of the war only to wreak havoc on the traditional landscape and older ways of living. Although antiauthoritarian movements, such as the student demonstrations of the 1960s, were not new to Japan, the 1970s continued to witness resistance to governmental control with violent protests against the U.S.–Japan Security Treaty and the expansion of Tokyo International Airport at Narita. A sense of loss and of lost innocence inspired new dreams of the past, a longing for the rural communities and ways of life that had been abandoned in the reckless drive to industrialize. Accordingly, the 1970s and 1980s were also characterized by a renewal of interest in folklore and folkways, by a desire to reconnect with the past and find (or construct) a lost hometown space—a mission that became official in 1984 with the notion of *furusato-zukuri* (hometown-making) as "the affective cornerstone of domestic cultural policy."[8]

An essential part of both the sense of dislocation and the desire to reconnect was a resurgence of interest in weird and mysterious phenomena of all sorts. Among schoolchildren the horror manga of Umezu Kazuo (b. 1936) caused sleepless nights, and the early 1970s even saw a revival—in an altered form—of the Meiji practice of Kokkuri. But in shaping the popular imagination with regard to yōkai, two particularly prominent phenomena stand out, and reflect both an anxiety about monsters and an insatiable longing for them. The first is the (re)discovery of the yōkai as pop-culture icon. Specifically, the work of the manga artist Mizuki Shigeru represents a recommodification of Toriyama Sekien's creations—not only the images themselves but also the sheer abundance and variety of the yōkai on parade. Mizuki invests yōkai with a fictional life as "characters" in his narratives while, at the same time, drawing on their historic lineage and nostalgic energy. The popularity of his work both reflected and inspired the increasing presence of yōkai in the cultural imaginary.

The second critical phenomenon is the Kuchi-sake-onna, or "Slit-Mouthed Woman," a new yōkai that emerged at the end of the 1970s as Mizuki's creations were becoming an indelible part of popular culture. If the early twentieth century saw the image of the weird creature separating from the evolving and ever-present possibility of the mysterious thing, then Kuchi-sake-onna represented a coalescence of these two notions. The very real, frightening image presented in this contemporary legend breathed life into the nostalgic media character that the yōkai had become. Kuchi-sake-onna herself soon became a media star, placed by Mizuki and others into a long lineage of female monsters. Yet she was also simultaneously a living being, at once modern *and* authentic. Her brief but influential appearance proved that yōkai could still haunt the late-twentieth-century urban landscape. In the works of Mizuki and the phenomenon of Kuchi-sake-onna, we witness the emergence of a new kind of yōkai, who, like earlier ones, helped define Japan as a nation.

MIZUKI SHIGERU

For almost anybody who grew up in postwar Japan, the word *yōkai* conjures up an image created by Mizuki Shigeru (b. 1922). Mizuki not only produces manga, some of which have been made into popular television anime series, but also researches and writes extensively on yōkai. He has also published numerous illustrated yōkai catalogs explicitly reminiscent of the work of Toriyama Sekien some two hundred years earlier. In many ways, in fact, the yōkai phenomenon comes full circle with Mizuki's work: like Sekien, he exploits the popular media of his time while carefully treading the line between commercial entertainment and the encyclopedic mode. Of course, the Sekien-Mizuki comparison can be taken only so far, as the radically different historical and cultural contexts of the mid-Tokugawa and late-Shōwa periods endow their yōkai with distinct functions and meanings.

One notable aspect of Mizuki's popularity is the cult of personality that has developed around the artist himself. He has created a persona intimately linked with the nostalgic image of yōkai and Japan's rural past. In the mid-1990s this association became inscribed in the landscape of his hometown, Sakaiminato in Tottori Prefecture, with the creation of "Mizuki Shigeru Road," a downtown street festooned with more than one hundred bronze statues modeled on his yōkai. The road is a sort of three-dimensional picture scroll, a frozen yōkai parade, through which visitors can stroll.

One character who appears frequently in Mizuki's manga is a somewhat comical-looking bespectacled man representing the illustrator himself. By inserting this self-deprecating image of himself (often referred to as "Mizuki-san") into his own narratives, Mizuki at once infuses them with a lighthearted self-referentiality and contributes to a biographical narrative that is as much a part of his personal mystique as the yōkai world he illustrates. Along with the manga, Mizuki has also published a series of memoirs detailing his childhood in a rural village, his experiences as a soldier during World War II, and his life in the postwar manga industry.

Mizuki was born Mura Shigeru in 1922 and grew up in the rural Tottori village of Sakaiminato. Although his own memoirs (and biographical blurbs on his books) often identify his place of birth as Sakaiminato, apparently he was actually born in Osaka, where his father was employed, returning to Sakaiminato with his mother one month after his birth.[9] This rewriting of his birthplace from a major urban center to a small rural community is a minor point, but it underscores Mizuki's self-inscription as a person with authentic roots in the yōkai-haunted countryside. During the war, Mizuki saw combat near Rabaul in Papua New Guinea, where he suffered the loss of his left arm. After returning to Japan, he studied at Musashino Art School and worked as an illustrator of *kami shibai* (picture-card shows) and *kashi-hon* manga, cheaply produced manga that could be rented for a small price at shops throughout Japan.[10]

Mizuki first garnered critical acclaim and popular success with his 1965 manga "Terebi-kun" (Television Boy), which received the Sixth Kōdansha Jidō Manga Award. The narrative tells of a boy, Terebi-kun, who can enter into a television set and participate in the world beyond the screen. Appropriately, in this period of rapid economic growth, Terebi-kun seems exclusively to infiltrate commercials for new products—from ice cream to bicycles—acquiring the advertised item before its release on the market. But he does not use his special skills for personal gain: he gives many of the objects he acquires to a classmate whose family is too poor even to own a television. He then disappears for parts unknown, traveling with his portable "transistor" television and providing newly marketed products to needy children throughout Japan. Although "Terebi-kun" does not concern yōkai explicitly, it is worth noting how Mizuki reads the tenor of his times with regard to the mystifying new medium of television, playing with the notion of another world that interacts with our everyday existence while also highlighting the intensely commercial nature of the medium.[11]

Fittingly, Mizuki's own continued success was tied to the rapidly developing television industry: in 1968 (the same year as the release of *Yōkai daisensō*), his manga *Gegege no Kitarō* (Spooky Kitarō) was made into a black-and-white animated television series. Subsequently the series, in color, ran from 1971 to 1972, 1985 to 1988, and 1996 to 1998, with numerous reruns, and a new version started in 2007. Mizuki also continued to publish extensively in the manga form, most famously with *Kappa no Sanpei* (Sanpei the Kappa) and *Akuma-kun* (Devil Boy). He has been involved with filmmaking ventures and more recently has worked with Internet and computer technology. Indeed, Mizuki's popularity has never waned, and Japan is currently in the midst of a particular surge of Mizuki-mania with the national release of a live-action film version of *Gegege no Kitarō* (2007; dir. Motoki Katsuhide). By their promulgation through a variety of media, Mizuki's images and narratives have become very much a part of the popular imagination of children growing up in late-twentieth- and early-twenty-first-century Japan.

The *Gegege no Kitarō* narratives concern the adventures of a yōkai named Kitarō and his cohort of yōkai characters. Kitarō, the progeny of a ghost family, looks like a normal boy but for a shock of hair covering his left eye. His name, written with the character for demon (oni), might be translated as "demon-boy," a not so subtle reminder of his monstrous origins; with his single eye, he is also reminiscent of Yanagita's hitotsume-kozō, delicately balanced between demon, deity, and human. Another

Figure 16. Kitarō with Medama-oyaji. Mizuki Shigeru, *Chūkō aizōban Gegege no Kitarō* (Chūōkōronsha, 1994), 4:508. © MIZUKI Productions.

character, Medama-oyaji (Papa Eyeball), represents the remains of Kitarō's dead father. Medama-oyaji is portrayed as a small disembodied eyeball, but one that has arms and legs and a voice. He serves as Kitarō's protective familiar and can often be found sitting atop his head or shoulder, proffering advice (figure 16).[12]

The self-referentiality of the *Gegege no Kitarō* character starts with the fact that Mizuki's nickname as a child was Gege or Gegeru (his own childish mispronunciation of Shigeru).[13] Furthermore, Mizuki lost his left arm during the war, and one might posit a correlation between this missing arm and Kitarō's missing left eye; the mystical presence of that lost limb may be an invisible guide in Mizuki's work, just as Medama-oyaji supervises Kitarō in his various pursuits. More to the point, Medama-oyaji's monocular vision provides Kitarō with critical insight into the world of yōkai. One common theme in the *Gegege no Kitarō* series has Kitarō teaming up with his father and other familiar yōkai as a team of superheroes fighting for the survival of good yōkai and good humans against the forces of evil. In this way Kitarō also serves as a corollary to Mizuki himself, struggling to protect yōkai and the (super)natural world from fading into irrelevance.

Kitarō, Medama-oyaji, and other characters, such as the often devious Nezumi-otoko (Rat-man), are original creations of Mizuki. But many characters in the series are derived directly from earlier yōkai documented by the likes of Sekien and Yanagita. In particular, *Gegege no*

Figure 17. Nurikabe. From *Zusetsu Nihon yōkai taizen,* by Mizuki Shigeru (Kōdansha 1994), 337. © MIZUKI Productions.

Kitarō visually presents a number of the creatures listed in Yanagita's "Yōkai meii" glossary. In one short entry, for example, Yanagita explains that the *suna-kake-baba* (literally, "sand-throwing old woman") is "said to be found in various places in Nara Prefecture. [She] threatens people by sprinkling sand on them when [they] pass through such places as the shadows of a lonely forest of a shrine. Although nobody has ever seen her, it is said that she is an old woman."[14] Mizuki makes seeable this yōkai that "nobody has ever seen," removing her from the relative obscurity of Yanagita's academic writings to thrust her under the bright lights of popular culture.

Another regularly featured yōkai from the *Gegege no Kitarō* series, Nurikabe (plastered wall), similarly exemplifies this creation of character. As will be recalled from chapter 4, Yanagita's glossary explains that *nurikabe* refers to the troubling phenomenon of walking along at night and suddenly being blocked by a wall.[15] Like Sekien two hundred years earlier, Mizuki converts a phenomenon, in this case the experience of mysteriously being prevented from making forward progress, into an embodied visual representation. In his manga and anime, the nurikabe is illustrated as a large rectangular block with eyes and legs. Whereas Yanagita simply states that a wall "appears," Mizuki creates the wall's appearance (figure 17), and an invisible local phenomenon is transformed into a nationally recognized character.[16]

Redrawing the Encyclopedic Mode

Gegege no Kitarō, *Kappa no sanpei,* and other Mizuki manga are creative narratives; they fit into what I have been calling the ludic mode and are very much a product of the postwar commercial publishing and entertainment industry. At the same time, however, Mizuki labels himself a "yōkai researcher" and has made a project of seeking out and illustrating yōkai from around Japan. As with Sekien's Tokugawa-period codices, Mizuki's work often assumes an encyclopedic format: his catalogs and dictionaries come in a dazzling variety of sizes and shapes, some in color, some in black-and-white. Illustrated with the same creative levity as his manga, these encyclopedic texts stand as autonomous collections but also interact with and supplement his narratives. I suggested in chapter 2 that Sekien's illustrations work to extract yōkai from narrative context, transforming them into iconographic entities that can be reinserted into subsequent narratives. The same process occurs with Mizuki, many of whose yōkai circulate in and out of different expressive forms, sometimes presented as individualized characters in his manga and anime, other times presented as "real" yōkai in his catalogs.

I should reiterate that not all of Mizuki's yōkai are derived from tradition; Kitarō and his father, for example, are original creations and accordingly do not generally appear as entries in his catalogs.[17] The ontological status of other creations—such as Nurikabe and Suna-kakebabā—is more ambiguous. Although they appear in his manga as distinct characters with individual personalities, they are also documented as "real" entities to be collected and displayed encyclopedically. In an entry for the nurikabe, for example, Mizuki first duly references Yanagita, noting the specific location where the belief was collected in Chikuzen (present-day Fukuoka Prefecture) and then relating a personal experience with a nurikabe-like encounter that occurred when he was away in the "dark jungles" of the south *(nanpō)* during the war.[18] As an admixture of scholarly reference and personal anecdote, there is nothing particularly definitive about Mizuki's entry, but its inclusion in a book titled *Zusetsu Nihon yōkai taizen* (Illustrated Complete Compendium of Japanese Yōkai) lends it an unimpeachable sense of authority. Significant too is Mizuki's linking of a specific Japanese location in the past (Chikuzen) to a non-Japanese place (the dark jungles). That is, the nurikabe signifies a local, past experience as well as a universal, present experience, both of which somehow fit under the rubric of *Japanese* yōkai.

Central to Mizuki's entry is the illustration, in which an invisible phenomenon is made into a visible creature. In one of his many short essays, Mizuki addresses this critical issue of rendering the invisible world visible, suggesting that yōkai and similar spirits "want to take shape *[katachi ni naritagatteiru]*. That is, they want to show their appearance *[sugata]* to people." Even as he elaborates the mechanism by which this works, Mizuki infuses yōkai with independent agency:

> As something that tries to take form, they hint by knocking on the brain of the artist or the sculptor (in other words, this is the thing we call inspiration). We often hear, "Yōkai and kami are created by humans," but the funny thing is that the instant you believe this, the yōkai or the kami will stop knocking on your brain.
>
> You have to believe that yōkai and kami *do exist*.
>
> It is just that they are rather elusive because their forms are difficult to discover, difficult to feel.[19]

Mizuki suggests that one must possess a certain sensitivity to the invisible world, a "yōkai sense," in order to capture them and endow them with form for all to see. Ultimately, it seems, yōkai are affective phenomena; illustrating their appearance is akin to articulating a particular feeling.

Not surprisingly, along with Yanagita's descriptions, Mizuki's other major source is Toriyama Sekien. He portrays, for example, the mokumokuren, adding a frightened samurai to the picture of an abandoned house dotted with gazing eyes. Although Mizuki acknowledges Sekien's earlier image, and he notes the explanation of the eyes as the playing pieces in the game of go, he also adds several brief stories of his own, set in the Edo period, concerning this particular yōkai.[20] These stories are unreferenced, and it is likely they were fabricated or at least adapted by Mizuki. If, as suggested in chapter 2, the mokumokuren itself was invented by Sekien, then Mizuki is simply following in his long-dead mentor's footsteps, creatively playing with the "truth" of his entries and, in so doing, bolstering the believability of his picture with anecdotal "evidence."

Regardless of the truth or fictionality of Mizuki's entries, it is significant that his yōkai tend to be located in the past. Unlike Sekien, but clearly in the spirit of Yanagita and Ema, Mizuki situates yōkai in a historical setting, though often expressed in a tongue-in-cheek manner. Redrawing Sekien's himamushi-nyūdō, for example, he is attentive to details such as the kama and the sprig of mugwort. His text particularly focuses on the himamushi-nyūdō's penchant for licking lamp oil, joking that "with electricity so widespread, and [oil] lamps no longer used, even if the yōkai wants to come out, he probably won't appear. Therefore, we can say that this is a yōkai in danger of extinction." He suggests that perhaps the himamushi-nyūdō could travel as a migrant worker to the "Arab countries," where oil is plentiful. "Depending on the time period and the circumstances," Mizuki continues, "even yōkai must alter the places they haunt. It's a tough thing. Perhaps there will appear something such as an 'Organization for the Preservation of Yōkai.'"[21]

The jest is meaningful because Mizuki's own work functions as just such an organization, with many of his narratives featuring a struggle by yōkai against their own extinction. Furthermore, by illustrating Yanagita's collection, and redrawing Sekien's yōkai, Mizuki reintroduces the subject into the popular imagination. In both his manga and his catalogs, he presents creatures that are not born of the atomic age like Gojira, but that are products of the prewar and pre-Meiji imagination. Ironically, by fashioning them within predominant modes of popular media—manga and television animation—the very modernity that would cause the himamushi-nyūdō's extinction allows it to flourish and receive a wider distribution than ever before.

As with this tongue-in-cheek refashioning of the himamushi-nyūdō, often Mizuki reinserts yōkai into a context more relevant to his readers. Take, for example, one of Sekien's creations, the *tenjō-name,* literally, the "ceiling licker." Sekien draws a tall bony creature, seemingly suspended in midair, licking a wooden ceiling with its extraordinarily long tongue (figure 18). This strange creature appears in his *Hyakki tsurezure bukuro* of 1784; the title of the collection and the tenjō-name entry both reference Yoshida Kenkō's famous *zuihitsu* (literary miscellany) essay collection, *Tsurezure gusa* (Essays in Idleness, 1330–1331). In entry number 55 of this text, Kenkō suggests that "a room with a high ceiling is cold in winter and dark by lamplight."[22] Sekien's tenjō-name entry plays with this comment: "It is said that if the ceiling is high, [the room] will be dark and in winter it will be cold; but the reason for this does not lie with the design of the house. It is entirely through the machinations of this yōkai [kai] that you feel a chill in your dreams."[23] In other words,

Figure 18. Tenjō-name. From *Hyakki tsurezure bukuro*, by Toriyama Sekien. Courtesy of Kawasaki City Museum.

it is not the architecture that creates the darkness and chilliness, but the haunting by the tenjō-name.

The same yōkai is found in Mizuki's catalogs, illustrated in a remarkably similar fashion. But Mizuki's description is notably different:

> There is a yōkai called "tenjō-name." You would think that it would be a great help for neatly licking clean the ceiling, which normally does not get cleaned—but this is not the case. It is fine that this "ceiling-licker" licks the ceiling without being asked, but it actually causes dirty stains to adhere.

> When there is nobody around in an old house, temple, or shrine, it comes out and licks with its long tongue. . . . It seems that if they found stains on the ceiling, people in the old days thought it was the handiwork of the tenjō-name.

Not only is there no mention here of Sekien (or Yoshida Kenkō), but Mizuki also transforms the tenjō-name into a traditional yōkai which "people in the old days" invoked to explain the stains on their ceilings. In addition to inserting the creature into the discourse of tradition, Mizuki also goes on to enshroud the tenjō-name in a veil of personal remembrance, with a concomitant note of nostalgia. "When I was a child," he explains, "there was an old woman in the neighborhood who was particularly knowledgeable about yōkai. On occasion, she used to stay at our place, and she looked at the stains on the ceiling of our house and said, 'Look! The tenjō-name comes out at night and makes those stains.'"[24]

Through Mizuki's reinscription, the tenjō-name is transformed from a Sekien invention (and playful riff on Kenkō's canonical text) into a traditional yōkai lurking in the rural hinterlands and embedded within the corpus of lore possessed by old people before the war. By inserting his own childhood memory into an encyclopedic compendia of yōkai, Mizuki underscores his folkloric authority as somebody with an explicit personal connection to the traditions of the past. His own history is informed neither by scholarly familiarity with texts such as Sekien's and Yanagita's, nor by his many years of activity within the urban world of the postwar mass media industry, but rather by a childhood spent in rural Sakaiminato before the war. It was there and then, in an innocent, almost mystic atmosphere, that yōkai and the stories surrounding them inspired the imagination of old and young alike. Mizuki constructs his own hometown as an authentic and idyllic space representative of all hometowns; his manga, anime, catalogs, and personal memoirs bind postwar Japan to this desired prewar moment in much the same way that Yanagita's writings linked early-twentieth-century modernity with a mystical pre-Meiji imaginary.[25]

In one of his early autobiographical texts, Mizuki establishes this nostalgic world and his own position as a child within it. The old neighborhood woman mentioned in the tenjō-name entry, in fact, is one of the most memorable and lasting characters of his experience. She is called Nonnonbā (Granny Nonnon); her name, along with her knowledge of the otherworld, becomes indelibly linked with Mizuki in the title of his book, *Nonnonbā to ore* (Granny Nonnon and Me), originally published in 1977.[26] The memoir relates anecdotes of Mizuki's childhood in Sakaiminato, stressing his somewhat dubious performance as a student, his struggles to become a leader among the village children, and his relationship with Nonnonbā. In the first section of the book, sentimentally titled "Childhood Years Living among the Yōkai," Mizuki tells how he heard about the tenjō-name for the first time:

> Along with knowledge of annual events and ceremonies, Nonnonbā also knew all sorts of obake and mysterious [fushigi] stories.
>
> She would look at the stains in the dim light of the kitchen ceiling, and say with a serious expression on her face that they were made by an obake called "tenjō-name" that would come in the night when everybody was quietly sleeping. I would look at the ceiling carefully and think, well, yes, those stains seem to be from that. There was no room for doubt [figure 19]. (20–21)

This passage raises important questions about memory, both personal and cultural. It turns out, in fact, that Mizuki is not the only one to recall tenjō-name as an item of local folklore; a description similar to Mizuki's appears in a work by folklorist Iwai Hiromi (b. 1932), who comments that "nobody has ever seen the figure of this yōkai. But people have imagined it as having a very long tongue and being tall enough to reach the ceiling."[27] Komatsu Kazuhiko points out that both Mizuki and Iwai have, of course, seen the tenjō-name—Sekien's version—and it is not surprising that they would both describe it as a tall creature with a long tongue. It is impossible to assess whether the tenjō-name was actually fabricated from scratch by Sekien and introduced through his texts into oral tradition, or whether he fashioned it out of a local tradition for which there happens to be no extent record.[28] Whatever the case, however, his work certainly solidified it into a named, visualizable representation. And, if we are to believe Mizuki's comments, it seems that this image, shorn of its association with Yoshida Kenkō, entered into the cultural imaginary of rural Japan, elegantly morphing into an explanation for why ceilings become stained over time.

Mizuki's portrayal of the creature removes it (or confirms that it has been removed) from the realm of wordplay and classical literary allusion and locates it firmly in local folklore. By giving voice to Nonnonbā as the bearer of tradition, Mizuki links himself to a premodern Japanese authority—indeed, it is significant that Mizuki receives this knowledge, this indoctrination into the world of mystery, not from his parents but from an even older member of the community. Nonnonbā is portrayed as somehow involved with the otherworld: *nonnon,* Mizuki explains, was a local expression for somebody who "attends to the spirits" (16).

Figure 19. Nonnonbā explaining about tenjō-name. Mizuki Shigeru, *Komikku Shōwa-shi* (Kōdansha komikkusu, 1994), 1:57. © MIZUKI Productions.

Nonnonbā acts as a medium between an older or other world and Mizuki's; she is reminiscent of Sōseki's "superstitious" old housekeeper in "Koto no sorane," somebody who reads seemingly invisible signs. Rather than disparaging her, however, Mizuki lionizes her for the knowledge she transmits to him: "I came to have a sense of belief that there was another world in addition to the human world. As an interpreter of this other world, Nonnonbā was an absolutely indispensable person."

When one night his house begins to make strange sounds, for example, she deftly identifies the culprits: "Nonnonbā said that it was 'yanari.' Little demonlike creatures cause the noise" (60). Nonnonbā translates sounds and signs into oral pictures that the young Mizuki can imagine, and that he will eventually render visually for others to see.

Or so the autobiographical narrative would have us believe. Strictly speaking, in fact, many of Mizuki's illustrations, including those of hima-mushi-nyūdō, tenjō-name, and yanari, are overtly derivative of Sekien's images, throwing into question the extent of Nonnonbā's influence on Mizuki's visual imagination. In a biography of the manga artist, Adachi Noriyuki reports that, according to Mizuki's older brother, "she [Nonnonbā] was just a completely normal rural old woman. As for outstanding abilities, or special knowledge concerning spiritual matters, she had nothing at all of the sort."[29] Adachi suggests that, like all people of his generation, Mizuki encountered mysterious phenomena as a child—strange sounds at night and stains on the ceiling—but it is doubtful whether there was such a person as Nonnonbā "who would attribute these things to the machinations of yōkai, teach him their names, and interpret each one." Furthermore, although Mizuki's classmates recall hearing spooky stories as children, these were usually about more conventional yōkai, such as kappa and yūrei, with most unexplainable local phenomena attributed to the mischief of kitsune.[30]

In other words, whatever mystical knowledge Nonnonbā imparted to the young Mizuki, it seems unlikely she ever specifically enumerated the details of the tenjō-name and other peculiar characters. Even if she did, of course, Mizuki's visual images of these creatures are undoubtedly derived from, or at least related to, Sekien's.[31] By retelling the story of Sekien's monsters through the authenticating voice of Nonnonbā, complete with explanations suited to a rural village, Mizuki reinscribes these yōkai into the life-fold of the countryside. Just as Nonnonbā becomes the symbolic medium through which he is made privy to the secret workings of the supernatural world of the past, Mizuki himself serves as medium between the lost world of a country town and the (often) urban or suburban world of his readership.

My point here is not to challenge the "authenticity" of Mizuki's recollections but simply to note that, by sharing his personal memories, whether fabricated or not, Mizuki participates in the postwar construction of a communal memory of a premodern referential ecology. Whereas a century earlier Inoue Enryō worked to efface the topology of the supernatural, Mizuki's manga and yōkai compendia redraw the map of this nostalgic landscape. The figure of Nonnonbā acts as a guide through this terrain, reading the traces and trails of the invisible creatures that have passed before them, teaching Mizuki to interpret signs, such as stains on the ceiling or rattling screens, and connect them with their hidden meaning. Nonnonbā is an old woman who has already lived out her time: her stories, like the ravings of Sōseki's "superstitious old hag," have no resonance for "rational" adults. But to the prerational Mizuki, Nonnonbā's teachings make perfect sense. The knowledge of the mystic skips a generation (and social class)—the skeptical modern generation (and educated elite) of Enryō and Sōseki and Ōgai—to be imparted directly to the innocent young Mizuki. And Mizuki, as an adult, passes on this knowledge to the reader, presenting it invariably in a sentimental haze as something already-no-longer available—and therefore, all the more desirable.

Mizuki's illustrations helped repopulate the prewar countryside with the monsters of the past. Along with standard images of kappa and kitsune, he rediscovered the abundance and variety of yōkai in Sekien's catalogs, filling his own childhood with the copious images suggested by the hyakkiyagyō motif. Just as Sekien's inscription of yōkai in the encyclopedic format blurred distinctions between reality and invention, so Mizuki's repaints Sekien's yōkai onto the canvas of the prewar countryside: as Borges would put it, "A fictitious past occupies in our memories the place of another."[32] Mizuki creates a referential ecology for the past that is robust and encyclopedically complex; he transmits to his readers an image of a yōkai-infested world that may be richer and more varied than ever existed in the cultural imaginary of prewar, or even pre-Meiji, Japan.

Ethnography, War, Other Worlds

The public persona Mizuki created through his autobiographical writings complements the world of his manga and illustrated catalogs. His own life became paradigmatic of Japan's twentieth-century experience—or at least the experience of the "common" man in twentieth-century Japan. Raised in a country village, Mizuki was a reluctant conscripted soldier who suffered—as did Japan—irreparable damage from the war. And yet, through his ordeals, he discovered inner resources and otherworlds that fortified his future creativity. On his return home, Mizuki struggled through poverty like the war-ravaged nation itself, ultimately succeeding in a competitive market.

One of Mizuki's manga, not related directly to yōkai, is titled *Komikku Shōwa-shi* (Manga History of the Shōwa Period). Commencing publication in 1988 as the Shōwa period was coming to a close, this eight-volume illustrated history includes accounts of political and military events as well as social and cultural movements. But Mizuki, who was born on the cusp of the Shōwa period, has also interspersed scenes from his own life, renarrating his childhood in Sakaiminato and his relationship with Nonnonbā.[33] The history of the Shōwa period is also the history of Mizuki Shigeru: his personal memories of his hometown and wartime experiences have become part of the collective memory of the nation. To some extent, Mizuki's popularity developed out of this self-narrativization—he himself represents the transcendent experiences of the nation, and therefore he has the authority and the insight to re-present them for popular consumption.[34]

In *Tōno monogatari,* Yanagita portrays himself as a medium between the urban intellectual world of early-twentieth-century Tokyo and the rural otherworld of Tōno. He assumes the persona of ethnographer-hero, venturing into a distant realm and returning to report his experiences. Mizuki can be viewed similarly: not only does he construct a persona for himself as interlocutor between Sakaiminato and his readers, but he also centers his non-yōkai related work on this motif of alien or otherworldly experience. Unlike Yanagita, however, Mizuki's audience is not the elite intellectual of Tokyo but the everyman manga-reader of postwar Japan, and Mizuki is an ethnographer-hero only by accident: an ordinary man who has stumbled upon extraordinary people and places. This is particularly evident in the way he characterizes his wartime experiences. His memoir, *Musume ni kataru otōsan no senki* (Papa's War Diary Told to His Daughters), rhetorically positions the reader in the place of Mizuki's children—that is, Mizuki's personal account of the war becomes a public account, his individual memories retold for the sake of the family and nation.

The memoir recounts Mizuki's career as a soldier and also describes in detail his encounter with some of the native people of Papua New Guinea. Recovering from the loss of his arm, and suffering repeated bouts of malaria, Mizuki notices some indigenous children passing by the field hospital. Realizing there must be a village nearby, he duly sets off to find it. His first impression of the natives' lifestyle evokes a utopian otherworldliness and a desire for an unspoiled Japanese past, harkening all the way back to Japan's Jōmon period (c. 13,000–300 B.C.E.): "The natives were like the Jōmon people, all of them living in a place with a nice vista. Looking out at the ocean in the distance and eating a banana, you couldn't tell if you were fighting a war or in heaven. That is how much

Papa liked the atmosphere of the native village." He describes the village houses and observes flowers he has never seen before: "These gave me the sense all the more that I had come to an otherworld *[ikai]*. With a feeling as if I had somehow come upon a fairyland *[tōgenkyō]* or the Jōmon period, I moved toward where some natives were preparing food and getting ready to eat."[35]

Mizuki goes on to relate how he became friends with the villagers and spent more and more time with them. Echoing his veneration of Nonnonbā, he finds another old woman at the spiritual heart of the community: "It would seem that all the doings of the village were directed by the old woman, Ikarian" (152). Mizuki feels at home in "Ikarian's village," as he calls it, and spends all his free time there, eating and relaxing with his new friends. At one point, in a villager's home he comes across a Christian Bible; jokingly he reads several passages aloud, and the villagers begin to call him Paulo. Mizuki himself never elaborates on this choice of names, but it is impossible to overlook the reference here to the New Testament apostle who changed his name from Saul to Paul upon his conversion. For Mizuki has undergone a kind of conversion and spiritual rebirth, discovering in this small village the same innocent happiness he experienced in Sakaiminato before the war. Immediately after his informal christening as Paulo, he notices a strange odor emanating from the stump of his healing arm: "It was the smell of a baby. The smell of something reborn anew. Somehow something like hope was springing forth" (153–54).

Notably absent from Mizuki's portrayal of his war experience are sympathetic Japanese characters; his fellow soldiers usually remain nameless and his commanding officers tend to act in a mean-spirited and incomprehensible fashion: "I was bullied (your Papa had the lowest rank, so he was regularly beaten by the soldiers), and in every instance, they would say, it's the emperor's command, so *die*." In contrast, the residents of Ikarian's village are individually named and described, their "wonderful lifestyle" praised in hyperbolic terms (174). The disparity between the two worlds is made all the more vivid when Mizuki is forbidden by his military superiors to visit the village and then suffers a life-threatening bout of malaria. Emaciated and unable to move, he is gazing absentmindedly outside when one of his native friends walks by. Mizuki signals to him and asks him to bring fruit. Later that evening something cool brushes his hand; he opens his eyes and sees, barely visible in the darkness, the outline of a native child holding a dish of banana and pineapple. These ghostly visitations continue for several months, until he gradually recovers (178–80). Not only does the episode vividly illustrate Mizuki's faith in the life-restoring powers of the natives and their utopian lifestyle, it also portrays the natives themselves as otherworldly inhabitants with special powers, appearing at twilight and visible only to Mizuki.[36]

While the comparison between the otherworld of the native village and the invisible otherworld introduced to him by Nonnonbā is not explicit in this particular text, elsewhere Mizuki writes, "I found these mysterious *(kikai)* natives to be rare and interesting. . . . In later years I came to draw yōkai, but this was probably nothing but giving form to the agreeable atmosphere of these people."[37] The otherworldly realm, whether at home or abroad, is visible only to those willing (or naive enough) to experience it. Just as he was the child most receptive to Nonnonbā's teachings, so too Mizuki is the only soldier to care deeply for the invisible natives living around him. In both cases, Mizuki is an accidental ethnographer who ventures into these other realms and returns to tell about them. When the war is finally over and he is to be repatriated, it is with great sadness that he informs the villagers he must leave. They suggest he stay; considering this seriously, he consults with one of his doctors, who replies, "There are one hundred thousand soldiers here, and you are the only one who wants to be discharged locally" (190). In the end, Mizuki decides to go back to Japan, but he promises to return to the village in seven years.

Some thirty years later, he does return. The last section of his war memoir, titled "Little Heaven," describes this journey back. Ikarian, the old matriarch, has long since passed away, but some of his other friends are still alive, and their reunion with "Paulo" is joyful. In the afterword, Mizuki explains that he returned many times, eating with the villagers and staying overnight in their houses. This afterword, and indeed much of the second half of the memoir, ignores the fighting and suffering Mizuki experienced as a soldier—and avoids completely the politics of Japan's Pacific War. It seems rather that what Mizuki wants to pass on to his daughters (and the rest of the nation) is the story of the discovery of a little heaven on earth, an otherworld where one can be saved, reborn, and nurtured.

It is fitting that, in the thirty years between his war experiences and his joyful return to the village, Mizuki had created an entire encyclopedically inscribed otherworld of yōkai. "I can't say it in a very loud voice," he admits, but "Kitarō's world is similar to theirs."[38] In musing on the pristine "primitive lifestyle" *(genshi seikatsu)* of the natives in Rabaul, he wonders what went wrong with the modern way of life: "Instead of enhancing the good aspects of the primitive lifestyle, humankind had advanced in a strange direction. . . . The proof of this is that worries have increased at a ridiculous pace and we are so busy rushing around that we are left with nothing. I passed my days thinking about whether it would be possible to somehow improve upon this wonderful primitive lifestyle and discover a 'modern primitive lifestyle' really worth living" (174–75).

Mizuki's re-creation of Sekien's and Yanagita's yōkai against the backdrop of his childhood in Sakaiminato is an attempt to do just this: to imbue modern life with a sense of the primitive and mystical. He is attempting to breathe life back into the "nothing" of modern existence, to make real once more the characters of the old game of hyaku-monogatari. Taking Yanagita's ethnographic project one step further, Mizuki does not simply map the yōkai topography of the past but directly channels this past—suitably enhanced—into his manga, anime, and illustrated compendia. His project aims to keep the past relevant for the present, to create a "modern primitive" world for children living in the expanding suburbs of the second half of the twentieth century.

Through his manga and anime, Mizuki reintroduces and reanimates the museum pieces shelved and ordered by the folklorists before him, marketing them as toys, as moveable characters extracted from a communal past and suggesting the existence somewhere of a mysterious otherworld, a still vital "primitive lifestyle." But while he succeeds in making yōkai a constant playful presence in the lives of children growing up in the 1960s and 1970s, ultimately Mizuki's reinvigorated creatures are akin to the childhood memories of the nation itself. They derive, as Komatsu puts it, "from a profound regret, and are illustrated exactly as if they were memorial photographs."[39] Mizuki's pictures, and with them the predominant image of yōkai in postwar Japan, are memorials for a past now gone, a landscape eradicated by the destructive war as well as by the recovery that followed it.

Medium and Media

Mizuki Shigeru acts as a medium, channeling from one world to another, translating and negotiating different realms of experience. He stands between Sakaiminato and the world of his readers as a direct link with the ancestors of the modern Japanese, a liaison between the oral and the visual, the then and the now. Mizuki himself seems to cherish this mediator role, and notes facetiously that he is often thought of as a "yōkai-human."[40]

The notion of the medium, or rather its plural *media,* is appropriate to Mizuki in another sense too: his entire career has been built through agility within various modes of commercial media, from kami shibai, manga, television, films, and books, to video games and interactive computer technologies. Like his own Terebi-kun, Mizuki co-opts the modern technology of the media to enter other worlds and bring back rare and exciting gifts to an appreciative audience. In fact, Mizuki demonstrates an uncanny prescience with regard to modern media (and its inherent intertextuality): some eight years before *Gegege no Kitarō* was made into a television series, for example, he drew a manga in which he predicted that Kitarō would be "dragged" into television and cinema.[41] To a large extent Mizuki himself is a media construct: his public character has morphed, yōkai-like, from the innocent adventurous child (Gegeru), to the bumbling sincere soldier (Paulo), to the absentminded and irreverently wise old man (Mizuki-san) of his most recent memoirs.

Perhaps there is nothing at all surprising about the proliferation of Mizuki's yōkai in the mass media. After all, yōkai find a home in whatever means of articulation is most relevant and resonant—whether the local legend of a village community, a catalog by Toriyama Sekien, or a short story by a canonical novelist. The popularity of Mizuki's yōkai, however, does reflect a critical shift with regard to the type of media: manga, television, and the other commercial forums in which Mizuki's creations found their voice were venues with much broader national exposure than was possible in prewar Japan. The yōkai Mizuki claims to have learned about from Nonnonbā are no longer localized to Sakaiminato, but have become metonyms for the weird and mysterious that once haunted all of Japan: they are the yōkai of a national landscape.

THE SLIT-MOUTHED WOMAN

"If we look at yōkai," Mizuki writes in a 1974 compendium for children, "we can well understand the mood and feelings of people from long ago."[42] Emblematic of his larger project, this illustrated encyclopedia is written in clear, simple language, presenting each yōkai as a relic from the past and even including a chronology that fittingly ends in 1865, just before the Meiji Restoration. In other words, this is a history text celebrating the nation as it once was, one that introduces children to a communal past through which they can feel a sense of unity with their ancestors. Mizuki exhorts his young readers to understand the feelings that spawn yōkai and to use yōkai as a tool for accessing a sympathy with people from long ago: "When we feel frightened, people's faces seem to look like yōkai; people of the past must have experienced frightening things quite often. Therefore, the feelings of these people from long ago gave birth to so many yōkai."[43] While Mizuki's rhetoric admits that the yōkai era has passed, and the yōkai he reinvigorates are nothing more than historical figures, he also hints that the human dynamic by which yōkai are created—the alchemical reaction of imagination and fear—is still possible today.

And his words proved prescient: fear did indeed make people's faces appear like those of yōkai. As the 1970s drew to a close, a new monster emerged to haunt the urban and suburban landscape. Known as Kuchi-sake-onna, literally "Slit-Mouthed Woman," this demonic female yōkai resonated powerfully within the cultural imagination of late 1970s and early 1980s Japan, not only reflecting very real fears but also fitting neatly into the otherworld according to Mizuki. Japanese consumers, both children and adults, were intimate with yōkai as popular characters and playthings. Within this context, Kuchi-sake-onna served as a bridge between the nostalgic but harmless yōkai of the rural past and the hard-edged mysteries of the urban present; she was a catalyst for the reassociation of the weird yōkai icon with the frightening but desired possibility of the mysterious. Indeed, Kuchi-sake-onna very ably fulfills the role of medium, providing—at least to those who have searched for her historical origins—the missing link between the mystical past and the workaday present. She connects the prewar yōkai-haunted landscape with the freshly risen cityscape of the late 1970s.

The excitement caused by Kuchi-sake-onna was reflected in and amplified by her appearance in a number of popular media venues. In a sense, the prominence of Mizuki's yōkai in the postwar media world paved the way for this new monster, the first yōkai produced within the context of a national community linked by television, radio, and nationally distributed print media. While this broad exposure ensured that Kuchi-sake-onna would speak with many voices, most critical discourse placed her in a folkloric heritage, usually ignoring her salient meaning within the cultural imaginary of the 1970s and 1980s. It is important, however, to focus on the fact that she is the product of a very specific sociocultural context, and that, like the kuchi-yose shamans of old channeling the voices of others, she speaks of the hidden and voiceless concerns of the present place and time. If we listen carefully, we discover that she has something to say about the fears of children, the dangers of rapid industrialization, unchecked pollution, and most viscerally, the role of women in a hegemonic male social structure.

The Heteroglossia of Hearsay

> I have very scary memories of the Kuchi-sake-onna story from third and fourth grade of primary school. . . . This woman with a white mask and long hair would come from behind and tap you on the shoulder. When you turned to look, she would ask, "Am I pretty?" *[Watashi kirei?]* If you said, "Yes, you're pretty," she would say, "Even like this?" *[Kore demo?]* and remove the mask and threaten you. Or if you said, "You're not pretty," she would come chasing after you. When I parted with my friends on the way home from school, and it was getting dark, I would be frightened when I thought about it.[44]

This is just a single version of the contemporary legend that, in one form or another, made its way throughout the Japanese archipelago, terrorizing elementary and middle school students and stimulating discussions among older children and adults in every prefecture. Having initially appeared in December of 1978, by the summer of 1979 the story of the woman with the slit mouth was a nationwide phenomenon, a fine example of what folklorists term a migratory legend. The narratives associated with Kuchi-sake-onna are rarely fully wrought or logical: they are always contextual, a tidbit of experience, a personal memory recalled informally—the type of disçursive artifact so often overlooked, or underestimated, within cultural interpretation.[45] As hearsay, something *heard* and *said* (and heard and said again), there are as many versions of the legend as there are people who transmit it, and every telling is a performance with its own individual, particular context. The difficulty of unpacking a tale told in so many registers and for so many reasons is reflected in the way Kuchi-sake-onna has been interpreted by Japanese scholars. Her story has come to be considered the quintessential rumor or contemporary legend of late industrial Japan, and the slit-mouthed woman herself has become the quintessential modern yōkai.

One remarkable thing about the Kuchi-sake-onna legend was the breadth and speed of its diffusion. The first documented appearance was in Gifu Prefecture in December of 1978; by June of 1979, there were reports in every prefecture in Japan, including Hokkaido and Okinawa.[46] According to one set of statistics, in 1979 some 99 percent of children in Japan knew the legend in one form or another.[47] Although word of mouth was critical to her popularity, clearly one mechanism by which news of Kuchi-sake-onna traveled was the mass media—she was featured on television and radio, and also in small, localized media venues known as "mini-komi." Within several months she also appeared in a range of national print media, including popular weekly magazines and the tabloidlike "sports newspapers" *[supōtsu shinbun]*.[48] Excitement about Kuchi-sake-onna peaked in 1979, but there is no doubting the rumor's lasting impact and resonance: even among younger generations in Japan today, she remains a salient cultural icon needing little introduction. She is mentioned in the blockbuster horror movie *Ringu* (Ring; 1998, dir. Nakata Hideo), appears in Studio Ghibli's animated feature *Heisei tanuki gassen Pompoko* (Tanuki Battle of the Heisei Era: Pompoko; 1994, dir. Takahata Isao), and is explicitly thematized in a short film titled simply *Kuchi-sake-onna* (1996, dir. Ishii Teruyoshi) and recently in a full-length feature film also titled *Kuchi-sake-onna* (Carved: The Slit-Mouthed Woman; 2007, dir. Shiraishi Kōji).

Like any contemporary legend, the story of Kuchi-sake-onna is characterized by variation over time and space; it is reinvented with each telling, simultaneously palimpsest and pastiche. As it journeyed discursively through the country, the story accrued different elements, which filled out the narrative. Not only did Kuchi-sake-onna have a slit mouth, but she also carried a knife or a scythe. She was particularly fond of a hard candy known as *bekkō-ame*. She could run one hundred meters in several seconds, her tremendous speed often attributed to her having been an Olympic athlete. There were numerous ways to escape her, such as running into a record shop or intoning the word *pomade (pomādo)*, often three times.

Many versions of the legend also came to include explanations for the slit mouth, attributing it most often to a horrible accident during cosmetic surgery: "Due to a mistake in cosmetic surgery, Kuchi-sake-onna had her mouth slit up to her cheeks. Because of that, she would always wear a mask covering half of her face. She would approach people from behind, tap them on the shoulder and say, 'Am I pretty?' And if the person said 'Yes,' she would say, 'Even like this?' and remove the mask."[49] From Tochigi Prefecture:

> Kuchi-sake-onna came into being because there was this very beautiful woman, but she was concerned that her mouth was too small so she went to a certain cosmetic surgery clinic and had an operation. But there was a mistake with the operation to make her mouth larger, and the instant she saw her face after the operation, she went insane and became Kuchi-sake-onna. Usually she wears a large mask, and asks people "Am I pretty?"

> If they say, "Yes," she will remove the mask, say, "Even like this?" and show her mouth. If you see that and try to escape, she will come after you, and kill you with a scythe. She is exceedingly fast and can soon catch anybody, but she has the weakness of not liking the odor of pomade, so if you say "pomade," it is said that you can escape her.[50]

And from Kanagawa Prefecture:

> There are three sisters. The oldest had cosmetic surgery and, mistakenly, her mouth was slit open. The second sister was in a traffic accident and her mouth was slit open. Because of that, the youngest sister went insane, slit open her own mouth and was put into a mental hospital. She escaped and has appeared in town. Her hair is long; she always wears a mask and holds a scythe in one hand. If you give her candy [bekkō-ame], she won't chase after you. Or if you say "pomade," you can run away.[51]

Despite rapid urbanization and the breakdown of traditional village communities—or rather because of these things—the rumor had a profound effect on Japanese life in the first half of 1979. Apparently, children were afraid to walk home from school alone;[52] in Ibaraki Prefecture, children were warned to stay away from people wearing masks; and in Fukushima and Kanagawa Prefectures, police cars were sent on patrol.[53] Unlike the ghosts of the past haunting Sōseki's and Ōgai's urban landscape, Kuchi-sake-onna was born of the modern world, part of a new and potentially terrifying referential ecology.

But is Kuchi-sake-onna a yōkai? Strictly speaking, most of her attributes are not exclusive to yōkai. She might just as easily be characterized as a deranged woman disfigured by a tragic accident or quirk of fate, who does not display the most socially acceptable behavior with regard to young children—but a *human* nonetheless. Even the explanations provided for her defining feature—the slit mouth—are generally human, such as cosmetic surgery gone awry, a traffic accident, or a self-inflicted wound. In fact, many early children's accounts of the legend do equate her more with a kidnapper figure than with a yōkai.[54] And yet, very soon after the legend burst onto the scene, the "yōkai" label was affixed to this threatening woman. In contrast to attempts by Enryō, Yanagita, and Ema to delineate the physical and supernatural characteristics that make a creature monstrous, there seems to have been very little inquiry into why Kuchi-sake-onna should be considered a yōkai. Her immediate identification as yōkai in the popular media reveals a nostalgic desire for continuity with the premodern referential landscape; there was a longing for monsters, and Kuchi-sake-onna provided the perfect connection between the past and the present, the rural and the urban, the local and the national.

A Yōkai Is Born

Kuchi-sake-onna emerged at a moment of social transition and upheaval, and although this does not in itself explain her appearance, it certainly contributed to her ready transformation into a yōkai. The unprecedented economic growth of the late 1950s and the 1960s brought with it mass migration to city centers and a corresponding depopulation of rural communities. By 1972, Prime Minister Tanaka Kakuei lamented this loss of a pastoral home, prefacing his famous policy for "remodeling Japan" by pointing out that "the rapid rise in urban population has caused an increase in the number of people living in the big city—with no mountain in which to chase a rabbit, no river in which to catch small carp, and only a tiny apartment to call their hometown [furusato]. In such a situation, I expect it will be difficult to pass on to the next generation the excellent nature and traditions of the Japanese people."[55]

The 1970s and 1980s were characterized by the desire to rediscover the abandoned countryside and both the familiar and the mysterious lurking within it. In the 1970s, for example, Japan National Railway sponsored its "Discover Japan" campaign, followed appropriately by "Exotic Japan" in the 1980s.[56] The federal government funded local programs for "hometown-making," and Yanagita himself was reembraced both by intellectuals and the popular press. Nostalgia for the past, and an understanding of its political and financial potential, played a major role in both commercial and governmental policy through these two decades.

This was the mise en scène into which Kuchi-sake-onna arrived as though to demonstrate that monsters were not lost forever. Labeled "yōkai" rather than criminal, she proved that industrialization, modernization, and urban sprawl had not forever separated people from the deep mysteries of their furusato roots. Just as migrants to urban centers had transformed their lifestyles to accommodate the spaces of city and suburb, so too the mysteries of the past could refashion themselves to be compatible with anonymous streets and concrete apartment buildings. Indeed, Kuchi-sake-onna's emergence coincided with the discovery of the city as a site of folkloric generation and a valid subject of study: ethnography was no longer confined to the rural Other of Yanagita's day. The "common" folk living in apartment complexes could be haunted by a new generation of specters.

Kuchi-sake-onna's authenticity was ensured by demonstrating how she fit into a family tree of yōkai, with its roots in the past and its branches extending into the present and (like the Japanese population) into the cities. In early articles in the popular press, scholars and writers almost invariably linked Kuchi-sake-onna with folkloric precedents. Seki Keigo, for example, a Yanagita disciple famous for his extensive work with folktales, suggested that Kuchi-sake-onna was "probably a rumor *[ryūgen higo]* based on the tales of demon women *[kijo]* found throughout the country." He went on to tell of a narrative that had circulated sixty years earlier and which featured a female ghost asking questions of passersby.[57] Similarly, in another popular weekly, the folklorist Matsutani Miyoko pointed out that Kuchi-sake-onna's desire for candy "might be the influence of the 'candy-buying ghost' legend."[58] Although there are no explicit connections with Kuchi-sake-onna here, the presentation of the older rumors positioned the newer legend in a venerable lineage of mysterious women.

In establishing Kuchi-sake-onna as a legitimate yōkai, scholars sought out motifs to link her with traditional folklore and imbue her with a patina of age and authenticity. As noted earlier, for example, one common motif was the intoning of *pomade* three times. This men's hair-styling gel (produced domestically in Japan by the 1970s) became endowed with the same apotropaic powers as certain plants, such as mugwort, used traditionally to ward off evil spirits and pests. Furthermore, repeating *pomade* three times infused it with the ritualistic potency often associated with the number three.[59] Similarly, Kuchi-sake-onna was given a scythe as a weapon—a tool much more associated with the countryside than with a twentysomething woman standing on the corner of a city or suburban street. The scythe is a metonymic appropriation, a tool emblematic of the pastoral world transposed to an urban or suburban setting and imbuing its possessor with an association of the past and the countryside.[60]

The search for traditional influences reveals a signal desire to associate this very modern woman with the yōkai of the prewar and pre-Meiji periods. Folklorist Miyata Noboru, for example, draws a correlation between the image of Kuchi-sake-onna and the *yamamba* (old woman of the mountains), noting that, in Kumamoto and Oita prefectures, there is a belief that the yamamba will descend from the mountains and appear in the village when in need of assistance in giving birth. Miyata also suggests a connection between Kuchi-sake-onna and the ubume because of the particular powers of femaleness—birth and motherhood—associated with both yōkai.[61] It is not that Kuchi-sake-onna *is* the ubume, he explains, but rather that she is similar because "the relationship between mother and child is at the foundation of the way in which Kuchi-sake-onna is expressed." She represents the "latent fear" a child feels toward his or her mother and, through the constant attention she pays to children, she also articulates the profound desire of a mother to raise her child well. As a warning to the "human world" regarding the relationship of mother and child, Kuchi-sake-onna "draws on the lineage of yamamba and ubume."[62]

Historical sociologist Satō Kenji has noted that the tendency to seek historical connections with earlier yōkai can obstruct the analysis of contemporary legend and rumor.[63] The idea that a modern yōkai "draws on the lineage" of earlier yōkai is premised on a vague sense of mystical transmission. Folklorist Nomura Jun'ichi, for example, explains that, when young people tell of Kuchi-sake-onna, something traditional that remains latent *(senzai)* in their consciousness reemerges.[64] While notions of "latent memory" are clearly problematic,[65] heuristic tools such as the idea of memetic transmission, in which "memes," or units of imitation, are passed from one generation to the next, might be useful for exploring certain consistencies over time—and perhaps might remove some of the mysticism from the notion of the traditional.[66] Motifs such as the number three are (for whatever reason) an established part of the grammar of storytelling; they get passed along to children through folktales and jokes and other stories related by their parents (or received from books or television), and the children naturally imitate these motifs in their own subsequent narratives. Similarly, motifs that came to be part of the Kuchi-sake-onna legend—the scythe, the chanting of apotropaic invocations, superhuman speed—are transmitted to children through, for example, the manga and anime images of Mizuki Shigeru.

Indeed, the familiarity of both children and adults with Mizuki's otherworld contributed a great deal to Kuchi-sake-onna's rapid incorporation into the panoply of existing yōkai. Popular culture was saturated with images of yōkai, and urbanites were intimately familiar with the words *yōkai* and *obake.* When the rumor of a dangerous deformed woman appeared on the cultural stage, it was placed in a ready-made discursive framework.

An example of this dynamic can be observed in a five-page spread in the June 29, 1979, *Shūkan asahi,* a popular entertainment weekly. Although clearly written for a popular audience, the article features a stylized chart demonstrating the legend's progress across Japan and is complete with references and quotations from scholars in various fields, including psychiatry, communications, and juvenile psychology.[67] Most significant, however, are the accompanying illustrations by Mizuki. The

Figure 20. Mizuki's rendition of Kuchi-sake-onna. Mizuki Shigeru, *Zoku yōkai jiten* (Tōkyōdō Shuppan, 1984), 79. © MIZUKI Productions.

first two pages are adorned with a somewhat comical picture of a large woman ripping off her mask to reveal a huge fanged mouth while two children fall back gasping in horror. This illustration—or a reworked version of it—would later become the picture Mizuki would include for the "Kuchi-sake-onna" entry in his various yōkai catalogues (figure 20).[68] Appearing when the legend was still very much in circulation, Mizuki's illustration helps label and authenticate Kuchi-sake-onna as a "real" yōkai. Bold letters on the first page of the article credit Mizuki with the illustration, legitimating the phenomenon as one worthy of the attention of Japan's greatest yōkai artist.

The spread also contains other smaller illustrations—such as one of the *iso-onna* (woman of the rocky shores), with the caption: "Iso-onna = one of the classic *[kotenteki]* yōkai with a slit mouth. Haunts the ocean and eats people." These illustrations, also penned by Mizuki, establish Kuchi-sake-onna as part of a tradition stretching back into the rural origins of the country. Mizuki himself is "impressed" with Kuchi-sake-onna because "folklorically" she has all the characteristics of the classical yōkai: "At the root of yōkai is the big mouth opened wide as if to say, 'I'll bite you!' She appears at the time one meets demons; that is, you meet her in the evening after school. She has a tool that can give you a shock, such as a scythe, and words such as 'pomade' are the protective spell *[mayoke]*. She has everything [necessary to be a yōkai]." Mizuki further establishes continuity between Kuchi-sake-onna and the documented yōkai of Japan's past, describing a mystical history in which yōkai were part of a shared imagination: "During the Edo period, some three hundred kinds were made into illustrations by Toriyama Sekien. The Japanese lived together with yōkai. But however much we say they had charm, there was always the fear of not knowing what they were going to do. While feeling this fear, the Japanese enjoyed this world of communal illusion *[kyōdō gensō]*."[69]

Mizuki goes on to draw a parallel between the hierarchical structure of the Tokugawa period, which demanded taxes of the farmers, and the intensely competitive contemporary social structure that puts pressures on children to get into first-rate schools. Such a comparison rhetorically links the contemporary situation to the notoriously yōkai-haunted Tokugawa period and neatly situates Kuchi-sake-onna in the age-old family tree of yōkai. Also, by invoking Toriyama Sekien, Mizuki parenthetically identifies himself as Sekien's modern-day successor. Kuchi-sake-onna's treatment by the popular press demonstrates the interplay of popular culture and academic discourse—each one feeding off the other, with Mizuki Shigeru, manga artist and yōkai expert, policing this intersection.

A Star Is Born

By the summer of 1979, Kuchi-sake-onna's rapid diffusion throughout the country, and the fear she instilled among children, had become an important news story in itself. The entertainment industry did not miss its chance to capitalize on the popularity and profit potential of this "beautiful" female yōkai: by August of 1979, King Records had cut a pop track titled "Catch Kuchi-sake-onna" (Kuchi-sake-onna o tsukamaero), featuring a trio of young female singers all wearing white masks.[70] One commentator has lamented that the media's interest in the legend effectively destroyed the rumor as a form of "play" for children.[71] To be sure, the "official" nature of the media as a source of news vied with the unofficial or improvised quality of the news conveyed in rumor:

> I think it was when I was in third or fourth grade of elementary school that "Kuchi-sake-onna" was popular. I remember it as being a thoroughly frightening experience. When you went to school, you would get all sorts

> of information. She could run 100 meters in 3 seconds. She was wearing a mask, and if she removed it her mouth was slit from ear to ear. She was holding a scythe. She couldn't turn corners quickly, so if she was chasing you, it was best to turn into a side street.
>
> At the time, I took all of this very seriously and was frightened. At recess, everybody would be talking in the hallway and we would hear the sound of somebody running up the stairway—we were all seriously terrified.
>
> After a few days, when my mother showed me a bold headline in the newspaper that read "Kuchi-sake-onna Is a Bald-Faced Lie," I began to have some suspicions. Now when I think back, it seems so stupid, but at the time I was really terrified.[72]

At the same time the media could also help "prove" the veracity of the word-of-mouth rumor:

> It was about the time I was in second grade—I really believed it wasn't a rumor but something real. When a boy in my class brought in a newspaper clipping with a picture of Kuchi-sake-onna's face, I was terrified. And also, when I heard about Kuchi-sake-onna, I was frightened to walk home from school by myself on the empty streets toward evening. Because of the threat of Kuchi-sake-onna appearing, the teacher warned us, "Don't walk alone on dark streets." There was a special program about Kuchi-sake-onna on television, and somebody said on the news that they had arrested Kuchi-sake-onna—when I think back on it now, it seems my life was really shaken up by the whole Kuchi-sake-onna thing.[73]

Clearly, then, mass media and word of mouth intersected and overlapped, creating in Kuchi-sake-onna a plaything suitable not only for children but for adults as well. In early 1979 the woman with the slit mouth was the talk of the town: the *Asahi shinbun,* one of Japan's major national newspapers, identified *Kuchi-sake-onna* (along with *rabbit hutches*) as a buzzword (hayari kotoba) for the first half of the year.[74] Within six months of her initial appearance, Kuchi-sake-onna had become a media darling, a celebrity yōkai born and bred within a national context. The fact that almost anybody who lived in Japan in 1979 is familiar with her not only reflects the ubiquity of her playful media presence but also suggests that her presence said something very serious about the cultural concerns of the moment. Even faster than a literary or filmic text, a legend will disappear if it fails to resonate within the social, cultural, economic, and political circumstances of the moment; the fact that we even *have* a text (or texts) is testimony to Kuchi-sake-onna's cultural relevance.

I have noted that the quest for Kuchi-sake-onna's historical origins and folkloric ancestors tended to limit academic interpretation of her immediate sociocultural relevance—her "circumstantial origins."[75] This is not to say that her meaning as a reflection of the concerns of her particular moment was entirely overlooked. Indeed, one debate touched on critical contemporary issues by associating Kuchi-sake-onna with the so-called *kyōiku mama,* or "education mama." The term *education mama* is succinctly described by anthropologist Anne Allison as

> a mother so committed to furthering the education of her child that she does everything from sharpening pencils . . . and pouring tea for a studying child to consulting with teachers; investigating the range of subjects, tutors, and *juku* (cram schools) available; and boning up on subjects where her child is deficient. [It] . . . is a term both of respect and reprobation: respect for those mothers who are successful in seeing children through the competitions of the Japanese school system and reprobation for the pressure they consequently must exert on children whose days, nights, and energies are consumed by study.[76]

Kuchi-sake-onna, some Japanese scholars have suggested, may represent a sort of education mama turned monster: the image of her confronting children on their way home from school, or on the twilit streets between school and supplementary lessons at juku, was born of anxieties felt by children about pressures exerted by their own mothers.[77] As a frightening woman standing on the street corner, Kuchi-sake-onna is a projection of children's apprehensions: the absolute control exerted by the mother inside the household is internalized by the child and carried forth into the outside world, creating a fantasy of constant surveillance and discipline. She represents mother-as-demon, panoptic, inescapable, driving the child beyond her or his natural capacities.

Pressures on young children to perform academically became increasingly intense during the 1970s, with rates of juku attendance steadily rising. In the legend, it is often en route to juku that children are confronted, and Kuchi-sake-onna herself is usually portrayed as being in her twenties or thirties, an appropriate age for the mother of a young child. But the very neatness with which the images of the Kuchi-sake-onna and the education mama can be conflated reflects the difficulty of interpreting a cultural product as varied as this one: while undeniably resonant, the association of the two female figures is also a function of the polyvocality and mutability of the narrative. The correlation obtains primarily when particular motifs (i.e., her appearance as a young mother, her accosting of children) are emphasized. In short, although the education mama may be one influence on the construction of Kuchi-sake-onna, it certainly is not the only one.[78]

Indeed, any pervasive legend or rumor articulates anxieties across a number of social strata and concerning a range of salient issues. Undoubtedly, Kuchi-sake-onna reflects the alienation felt by children in an urban environment; the lonely twilit streets become liminal spaces of mystery and fear in the urban or suburban landscape. According to one interpretation, the legend functions as a barometer of increasing urban anxiety and can be read specifically as an ominous harbinger of the so-called *tōrima jiken,* a series of arbitrary acts of violence committed against innocent passersby starting in 1980—as if the fear of strangers articulated by the rumor became a self-fulfilling prophecy in the ensuing years.[79] Certainly the late 1970s and early 1980s witnessed intense social and cultural change after the end of Japan's high economic growth period, and surely the strains of these circumstances nourished the legend. But tempting as it may be to see a legend as a manifestation of a vague set of sociocultural transitions, I concur with Satō Kenji that anxiety or discontent "can probably be found at any time or during any historical period."[80]

The Good, the Bad, and the Ugly

One way we can meaningfully explore Kuchi-sake-onna's place in the particular sociohistorical moment is by zeroing in on her voice as a young adult woman. She does not simply embody vague fears or mysteries regarding women: she also speaks of the specific role of women in Japan during the 1970s, an avenue of consideration all but overlooked in both academic and popular discourse. The drive to associate her with the yōkai of the past, and with the playful images of Mizuki Shigeru, has distracted attention from what she had to say about gender, normative standards of beauty, and particularly the women's liberation movement of the 1970s.

As we have seen, descriptions of Kuchi-sake-onna's image and behavior vary. However, several key motifs are present in almost every recorded version of the legend: she is a young woman; her mouth is slit from ear to ear; she asks, "Am I pretty?"; and a mask covers her mouth. Although methods of escape, types of weapon, clothing, and so on are all subject to variation, the four elements vary only nominally (e.g., she asks, "Atashi bijin ka?" [Am I a beauty?] instead of "Watashi kirei?") and might be considered definitive traits of Kuchi-sake-onna. Taken one by one, these four motifs provide a perspective on her meaning as a monster born of the trauma and concerns of the particular moment.

The fact that Kuchi-sake-onna is a woman links her to earlier female yōkai as well as to the contemporary notion of the education mama. But such similarities are not based on a genealogical line of demonic women or some essentialist female nature; rather, they indicate that, during a range of different historical moments, similar attitudes have prevailed. Kuchi-sake-onna, more particularly, is always portrayed as a *young* woman and often described as quite attractive, factors that reflect specific attitudes toward gender in 1970s Japan. Komatsu Kazuhiko, one of the few scholars to seriously consider what Kuchi-sake-onna says as a young woman within her particular historical context, suggests that, "If a man with a mask were to walk up to people on a street at night, stop them, and ask, 'Am I handsome?' *[Ore bidanshi ka?]*, it just would not cause the same vivid sense of fear as 'Kuchi-sake-onna'; rather, it would even have a sense of the comic about it."[81] The humor denoted here critically exposes taken-for-granted assumptions regarding the different values set for men and women. "Kuchi-sake-onna arouses people's terror," Komatsu continues, "because she works powerfully on their tacit understanding with regard to how much effort women must expend on their own 'beauty,' how much they are controlled by it, as well as how difficult it is for a woman not considered beautiful to live in this world."[82]

Bound up with the image of Kuchi-sake-onna as an attractive young woman is the sexual iconography of her slit mouth. The feminist film theorist Barbara Creed has elucidated the role of the "monstrous-feminine," and particularly the motif of the vagina with teeth, or *vagina dentata,* in horror films.[83] The relevance of this motif to Kuchi-sake-onna—with the clean white cotton gauze of the mask covering a hidden slit, and the simultaneous desire and fear associated with seeing what is normally concealed—does not take a great stretch of the imagination. Psychoanalytically, Kuchi-sake-onna might be the paradigmatic "dyadic mother," a "maternal figure of the pre-Oedipal period who threatens symbolically to engulf the infant." Similarly, the gigantic mouth suggests "the oral sadistic mother," a cannibalistic female demon "feared by both female and male infants who imagine that, just as they derive pleasure from feeding/eating at the mother's breast, the mother might in turn desire to feed on them."[84]

Creed argues that a woman's genitals can be frightening not only because they "appear castrated" but also because they "appear castrating."[85] With her gaping red-lipped mouth (sometimes portrayed with sharp teeth), Kuchi-sake-onna articulates a visceral image of the castrating mother, the femme fatale, the insatiable sexual predator; she invokes the intimate connection between desire *(Am I pretty?)* and disgust *(Even like this?)*, between the pleasure principle and the death drive. And just as the mouth threatens to dismember and devour, so too the accompanying knife or scythe conveys a similar symbolic power to mutilate (castrate).

Encountered on the street, Kuchi-sake-onna is a pervert, a female flasher, exposing sexuality to innocent children. Although I translate the line "kore demo" as "even like this," it might also be rendered as "even *this*"; she performs a cynical bait-and-switch tactic whereby the desire for the "pretty" is replaced with "*this,*" a representation of the desired in its most sexualized, extreme—*un*pretty—form. To the young boy, she embodies the threat of female sexuality, playing off anxieties of emasculation and castration; to the young girl, she is an eerie figure of warning, unveiling adult sexuality in its starkest, most visceral reality. Indeed, the conflation here between mouth and vagina is clear in the comments of a male college student in 1979: "The mouth of Kuchi-sake-onna is genital-like. And what's more, it's ridiculously huge and gaudy and unclean, so I don't want to be touched by it!"[86]

Consistent in almost all versions of the legend is the line "Am I pretty?" Komatsu posits a connection between Kuchi-sake-onna and Japan's oldest frightening female, Izanami, a deity who dies giving birth to the fire god. When her husband, Izanagi, ventures after her into the underworld *(yomi)*, he discovers to his horror that she has been transformed into a frightening maggot-infested figure. Komatsu also links Kuchi-sake-onna to the famous Dōjōji woman of legend, whose lust for a young monk transforms her into a gigantic snake. Although his observations fit the trope of treating Kuchi-sake-onna as an avatar of earlier demonic women, Komatsu critically highlights the importance of the beauty/ugliness binary manifest in these narratives of good (= beautiful) women gone bad (= ugly).[87]

Of course, the beauty or "prettiness" problematized by Kuchi-sake-onna slips easily in and out of metaphor, the notion of physical attractiveness blending with a general social attractiveness (= conformity) of behavior. In this light, Kuchi-sake-onna's terrible transformation upon removing the mask reflects a fear of women unmasking themselves in male society: what appears at first glance to be an attractive—or at least "normal"—face suddenly reveals an ugly and dangerous hidden truth. Significantly, it is the mouth that is deemed threatening, for agency is most powerfully asserted through the mouth and the voice it projects.

Kuchi-sake-onna's transformation from an attractive young woman into a terrifying threat occurs with the removal of her mask, a literal unveiling that works as the pivot point of the narrative. Her mask is distinct from, for example, the masks used in *nō* and *kyōgen* theater and numerous local ritual or religious performances. These are usually full facial masks worn in the ritualized space of the stage or the shrine. Kuchi-sake-onna's mask *(masuku)*, on the other hand, covers only half her face; rather than replacing the mouth with a different one, the white gauze erases it completely. Available at any pharmacy or convenience store, this type of mask is usually worn when the subject is ill and does not want to transmit germs, or inversely, worn to protect oneself from contagion when others are ill. The public use of such masks in Japan can be traced back to 1918, when they were proposed as a prophylactic against the Spanish influenza.[88] Even today, the use of masks to prevent the spread of germs is common in Japan; additionally, they are marketed as filters against common allergens and, most notably, became internationally visible during the SARS outbreak of 2002.

As a method for preventing contagion, the mask permits the wearer to participate in the traffic of everyday life. But even here the mask is an ambiguous sign. On the one hand, it serves as a form of stigmatization, signifying that the individual wearer is ill (unclean) and must be separated—if only by thin gauze—from the rest of society. On the other hand, it can also suggest that the wearer is healthy but that those around her, or the environment itself, are unclean and dangerous. In either case, the mask signifies disease, either of the individual or of the society or environment; it functions as a thin and pliable boundary indicating only that someone or something is unhealthy or polluted, but does not specify the location or form of pollution.

During the 1960s and 1970s, as the media began to report on the negative effects of rapid economic growth, this ambiguous association of the mask with disease and pollution became part of the cultural imaginary. Environmentally induced health problems ("pollution illnesses," as one mayor called them), such as Minamata disease (mercury poisoning) and *itai-itai* disease (cadmium poisoning), garnered more and more media attention; citizen protests became increasingly frequent, and in 1971 a government Environmental Agency was formed to respond officially to pollution- and health-related concerns.[89] During this period, children in some areas might be seen wearing "pollution masks" on their way to school.[90] The simple white mask came to be emblematic of the human side of environmental destruction.

Within this context, the Kuchi-sake-onna legend becomes a symbolically charged allegory of the suffering incurred during Japan's postwar drive toward economic success. Her mutilated face is the visage of the populace, with a bitter smile hacked out by sacrifice, disfigured through overwork and environmentally wrought disease. Or, as the countenance of the land, she is cut and made ugly through the overharvesting of natural resources and overconstruction of roadways and factories. Or as the Japan shown to other nations, she is a brave face put on to cover the disfigurement etched by sacrifices made for economic growth. She inquires, sheepishly but with pride, whether she now looks "pretty." In all these allegories, the mask signifies that something is wrong; its sudden removal shockingly reveals a hideous truth, poignantly questioning the hope embodied by the figure of the young woman. *(Even like this? = Was it worth it?)* The target of Kuchi-sake-onna's attack is almost always a child, as if the monstrous victim/victimizer is warning about the future or, perhaps, pointing out that it was for the sake of the children that the sacrifices of her own generation were made.

But we can add here one more critical, if usually overlooked, symbolic association of the mask: it is a mark of protest. It can conceal the identity of a wearer engaged in behavior that deviates from sociocultural standards. The mask as sign of deviance obtains not only semiotically but also historically: in postwar public demonstrations in Japan, such as the student movement of the 1960s, protests against the U.S.–Japan Security Treaty (in 1960 and again in 1970), the women's liberation movement of the 1970s, and the decades-long protests against the expansion of Narita International Airport, participants often covered their mouths with masks or white towels. These images were unavoidable in the 1970s: Narita airport protests, for example, made headlines in May 1977, when demonstrators clashed with riot police (resulting in some four hundred injuries and the death of one protester), and again in March 1978, when protesters broke into a control tower.[91] In the Japan of 1979, then, along with its associations with disease and pollution, a mask signified protest and recalcitrance—marking Kuchi-sake-onna as a figure of resistance.

By considering these four defining (and overlapping) characteristics of the Kuchi-sake-onna image—gender (she is a woman), sexuality (the slit mouth), aesthetic consciousness ("Am I pretty?"), and resistance (the mask)—we can better understand her meaning within the specific historical moment. The 1970s were the heyday of the women's liberation movement in Japan. With the public protests of such groups as Chūpiren, an organization dedicated to the legalization of the birth control pill, images of masked women holding placards appeared frequently in the popular press.[92] Not surprisingly, women who organized against male hegemony were often defeminized and demonized: in men's entertainment weeklies, for example, women's liberation activities were described under headlines such as "Ugly Women Are Causing a Commotion" (*Busu no onna domo ga sawaideru*) and "Coven of Witches" (*Majo no shūdan*).[93] This demonic image cut both ways: some female activists appropriated *witch*, for example, as just the right word "for women who choose to find their own way of living."[94] At least in certain popular culture venues, then, the image of Kuchi-sake-onna can be read as a lingering remnant of the transgressive voice, both feared and desired, of the 1970s women's liberation movement.

Perhaps then it is not surprising that one media outlet in which the legend appeared consistently in the summer of 1979 was women's weekly magazines. Although such magazines targeted a female readership, the editorial board, reporters, and advertisers were primarily male. These magazines served simultaneously as forums for women's concerns and as sites through which a male-dominated (corporate) society tacitly promoted its own image for women. Not only did Kuchi-sake-onna show up with comparative frequency in these magazines, but her appearance in a format specifically targeting a female readership also raises questions as to what she had to say as a gendered subject. Chock full of advertisements and articles for makeup, weight-loss techniques, cosmetic surgery, and "aesthetic treatments," these popular weeklies represent a critical site for discourses on normative female beauty. In their pages, Kuchi-sake-onna's story assumes a particular poignancy, highlighting the dominant ideologies of women's appearance and providing a subtle but resonant critique of these ideologies.[95]

An episode described in the July 5, 1979, issue of *Josei jishin* (Woman Herself), for example, vividly demonstrates how Kuchi-sake-onna speaks of gender, sexuality, aesthetic consciousness, and resistance, expressing the loneliness of women's struggles against an objectifying male gaze. After introducing the cosmetic surgery motif mentioned earlier, the article quotes a male farmer from "near Narita airport":

> They say she comes out by a lonely road near the airport. You see there was this man from one of the neighborhood farms, and he's walking along the road at about 9:00 at night, and there's this pretty good-looking woman standing there. Nice big eyes. So he calls out to her. After all, she's wearing a neckerchief and all, so he thinks she's a prostitute. . . . What? No! It wasn't me. . . . I said I heard this from somebody! So anyway, he goes closer and this woman, from behind her mask, she says, "Give me

> candy." So the guy who had approached her thinks, Ah ha, this one's a little funny in the head. . . . He thinks he can do her for cheap, and he says, "If I buy you some candy, will you go to a hotel with me?"

The article goes on to report that "for a moment the beautiful woman said nothing, stared intently at the man, and then suddenly removed her mask! Not only did the man lose any desire to fool around with her, but he left his farm implements where they were and escaped to his house."[96]

While there is a tawdry and titillating undertone to the article, it can also be read as a critique of dominant male attitudes. Affecting "the male/subject—female/object structuring of the symbolic order," the man immediately assumes that an unknown woman walking alone must be a prostitute;[97] he bargains for her as a commodity, hoping to purchase her for the price of some candy. Upon removal of her mask, however, the vectors of power are instantly reversed, and the woman transforms into an agent of social critique. It is significant that the narrative is set near Narita airport, notorious as the site of violent protest; the informant concludes: "It is also said that this is the curse [tatari] of the airport riots." The episode represents a coalescence of several vital aspects of Kuchi-sake-onna's role: she speaks of a moment of protest, turns a perceived vulnerability into a source of power, stares back at the male gaze, and silently articulates a critical female subjectivity.

The expression *Kuchi ga saketemo iwanai,* which might be translated as "Even if [my] mouth were slit, [I] would not speak," is invoked when somebody promises to keep a secret.[98] The expression is constructed on the premise that a slit mouth will inevitably, naturally, speak, and that the voice which flows forth will betray truths that others would prefer to remain concealed. As a female subject defined by a slit mouth, Kuchi-sake-onna represents a figure who will not, *cannot,* keep her mouth shut; she is to be feared not only because of her monstrous potential to devour but also because of her monstrous potential to speak, to voice concerns that some would prefer to conceal. Within the context of an evolving feminist movement, Kuchi-sake-onna becomes a powerful icon, oppressed and demonized but simultaneously embodying a determination to express herself within the restrictive hegemony of a society that continues to objectify women. At least in the pages of women's weekly magazines, Kuchi-sake-onna represents the potential of a female voice.[99]

I have argued from the outset that Kuchi-sake-onna is polyvocal. To be sure, my own interpretation here highlights just one of her many voices—one that has gone practically unnoticed. The very notion of closely considering a textual version of her legend surprises some scholars, such as Nomura Jun'ichi, who suggests that reading Kuchi-sake-onna as a "text" elevates it to "a classical [kotenteki] existence," a fact about which he is "unbearably delighted."[100] Ironically, of course, such comments reflect the privileging of the "classical" over the contemporary and suggest a desire for continuity with the past—the very tendencies that have limited interpretation of this meaningful yōkai. Almost as soon as she garnered public attention, Kuchi-sake-onna came to be treated, not as a this-worldly figure speaking sharply about late 1970s social norms, but rather as an otherworldly figure, a present-day avatar of age-old mysteries that refuse to go away. Ultimately, the critical voice that emerged from her gaping mouth fell on deaf ears, as both academic and popular discourses generally treated her as simply a modern, urbanized reconfiguration of the monsters of Japan's pastoral past.

It is too bad that this occurred, for the legend of Kuchi-sake-onna provides a valuable case study for understanding the discursive construction of yōkai throughout all the moments we have examined. By exploring how she emerges meaningfully and politically from specific sociocultural contexts—how she speaks of gender, sexuality, and the environment—we better see how yōkai of all ages are shaped by the timely, particular concerns of the people who tell of them. We can also see the way they easily traverse boundaries between "serious" social critique and "playful" entertainment. Furthermore, by examining how a frightening woman is removed from her specific context and folded into the transcendent category of "yōkai," we can imagine a similar process for many of the yōkai encountered in this book.

The legend of Kuchi-sake-onna circulated with great vibrancy for about six months, after which the excitement surrounding this frightening woman began to die down.[101] But she has certainly never disappeared. In early-twenty-first-century Japan, she has become legendary. For scholars, she provides a paradigmatic contemporary legend or rumor; in popular culture she is a stock character in horror movies, listed alongside other yōkai in bestiary-like compendia, and still occasionally discussed by schoolchildren. Now, already, a sense of nostalgia clings to her.

YŌKAI NATION

Mizuki Shigeru's productions and the legend of Kuchi-sake-onna were by no means the only manifestations of yōkai-like phenomena in the popular imaginary of the second half of the twentieth century. Horror manga, children's books about yōkai, even a renewed interest in Kokkuri were part of growing up in Japan during this period.[102] But by far the most pervasive yōkai images were those created by Mizuki, and the most frightening and far-reaching yōkai rumor was that of Kuchi-sake-onna. In Mizuki's work, an encyclopedically complete otherworld—where everyday signs are traces of not-so-everyday possibilities—lurks just on the other side of history, constantly threatening to irrupt into the present. And Kuchi-sake-onna herself is a disruptive invader from this otherworld who brings a touch of the not-so-ordinary to contemporary urban and suburban Japan and tempts us to believe that what we see in front of us is not necessarily all there is.

The media in which Mizuki and Kuchi-sake-onna thrived provided a space for disparate versions of reality to be brought together. In this way too, the late twentieth century parallels the late eighteenth, as Sekien's representations demanded neither belief nor disbelief, but provoked a titillating ambiguity. The proliferation of print and electronic media during the postwar period inspired a sense of possibility with regard to the mysterious and the weird. Pressed into the mold of a yōkai, Kuchi-sake-onna reattached the nostalgic notion of yōkai to the living notion of the fushigi. Her rapid inscription by Mizuki located her within the visual taxonomy he was developing for earlier yōkai; in the popular imagination, she was akin to any one of Mizuki's images, yet endowed with a living relevance, a believability (at least for a time), not as something that *used* to haunt the small towns of pre-Meiji and prewar Japan, but as a terrifying creature you might just run into as dusk descended on the streets of suburbia.

Kuchi-sake-onna's explosive popularity helped infuse the terrain once more with a fresh sense of mystery. The liminal, dangerous no-man's-land of the mountains and forests surrounding Yanagita's Tōno was now manifest in the expanses between home and school in the conurbations of late industrial Japan. As Mizuki's otherworld acted as a foil for the present, so Kuchi-sake-onna helped to rekindle a little of the carnivalesque world of possibility in the mundane urbanized landscape.

In the end, both Mizuki's work and Kuchi-sake-onna were energized by a lively media environment through which they received national distribution. Yanagita may have set out to collect the fragments of yōkai beliefs scattered around the landscape, but Mizuki helped to reassemble these fragments and breathe life into them. His manga and anime reanimated the yōkai of Sekien and Yanagita, painting them onto the canvas of the nation. And on this canvas, primed by an ever-expanding web of mass media and communication systems, a new yōkai, with one foot in the nostalgic dreams of the past and one foot firmly planted in present-day concerns, could be born. In a sense, while Mizuki worked to illustrate a yōkai-infested landscape, Kuchi-sake-onna, propelled to stardom by the mass media, emerged to haunt its every corner.

Like Gojira stamping across postwar Japan, Kuchi-sake-onna and Mizuki's monsters left their footprints throughout the land. Unlike Gojira, however, they did not destroy the cities they infiltrated, but enlivened them; unlike Gojira, they did not achieve international fame but remained domestic actors, manifestations of the weird and mysterious whose perambulations helped to define the nation itself. The 1960s through the 1980s witnessed a growing obsession with yōkai, the beginnings of a so-called "yōkai boom" that continues to this day. During the waning years of the twentieth century and the beginning of the twenty-first, yōkai increasingly garnered the attention of academics, artists, writers, and fans almost obsessively dedicated to documenting what Mizuki would call an "other mysterious world" *[betsu no fushigi na sekai]*.[103] The ongoing popularity of yōkai reflects not only a modern persistence of mystery but also a postmodern persistence of a desire for mystery, a fetishizing of an alternative space in which the imagination can expand. And this alternative space, as Mizuki and Kuchi-sake-onna demonstrate, is very close at hand: the Japanese nation, it turns out, is a yōkai nation.

CHAPTER 6

Yōkai Culture

Past, Present, Future

It is said that without living for three hundred years,
a human being cannot understand yōkai.

Mizuki Shigeru

By exploring discourses and practices surrounding the weird and mysterious, the preceding chapters trace how interpretations of yōkai reflect changes in broader cultural paradigms. For the early to mid-Tokugawa period, natural history provides a lens through which we can understand not only encyclopedic texts that include strange creatures in their purview but also the playful bestiaries devoted exclusively to portraying such creatures. The Meiji period can be perceived through the optic of science, as rational thinking was deployed both to debunk yōkai phenomena and to inspire a new sense of enchantment. For the early twentieth century, the museum provides the governing metaphor, with yōkai preserved as relics to be cherished as part of a shared cultural heritage. Finally, yōkai in the late twentieth century, when Japan was coming to terms with its new place as a world economic power, can be viewed through the trope of the media—both the mass media in which they proliferated and their mediumistic role for negotiating broader social concerns.

I reiterate here that these heuristic tropes are never mutually exclusive: within and between each phase they overlap and influence each other. During the Tokugawa period, for example, mass media was arguably as important to yōkai production and popularity as it was during the late Shōwa period; inversely, the natural-history style of presentation that began in the 1600s persisted in the encyclopedic compendia of late Shōwa and beyond. In some cases, the overlap and influence was not between successive moments but between moments broken up by generations—

as with Mizuki's reinscription of Sekien's images some two hundred years after their original popularity.

The project of elucidating specific historical paradigms and the sinews that connect them is always teleological: a light shone backward from a moving vehicle, illuminating the twists and bumps of the path already traveled. My own contribution to the discourse is, inevitably, circumscribed by the scope of this light. As somebody who did not grow up with yōkai or the discourses surrounding them, however, I hope I have been able to productively reinterpret some of the landmarks of the historical terrain and can briefly observe some of the prominent features of the current landscape.

J-HORROR

In the 1980s and 1990s, yōkai continued to gather momentum in both academic and popular media. The phrase *yōkai boom* is now so commonly used as to be a cliché. One element of this putative boom, however, is the continued production of new yōkai. The excitement inspired by Kuchi-sake-onna, for example, was complemented by a slew of other monstrous rumors—such as that of the *jinmenken* (human-faced dog) that became a short-lived media sensation in 1989, and Toire-no-Hanako-san (Hanako of the Toilet), a ghostly young girl haunting elementary school bathrooms. For children, the schoolhouse was a particularly fertile spawning ground for frightening, yōkai-infested stories. The folklorist and middle school teacher Tsunemitsu Tōru (b. 1948) began collecting and publishing these so-called *gakkō no kaidan,* or "eerie tales of the schoolhouse," inspiring not only serious academic discussion but also a series of books, adaptations for television, and a popular film, *Gakkō no kaidan* (1995, dir. Hirayama Hideyuki), that was rapidly followed by three sequels.[1]

Perhaps because of their association with concerns specific to Japanese schoolchildren, the *Gakkō no kaidan* movies, although popular in Japan, were not widely released in other countries. I suggest, however, that they were instrumental to the development of the so-called J-horror genre, Japanese horror films that would explode onto the global market in the late 1990s. Many of the people who worked on the early *Gakkō no kaidan* productions, particularly the television adaptations, went on to become influential in the J-horror world. Like kaijū eiga of the 1950s and 1960s, Japanese horror cinema has created an aesthetic with profit potential in an international market. Also similar to kaijū eiga, some of these films have been remade in American versions, as if a Hollywood filter is needed to translate the cultural aspects of Japanese horror for consumption by a non-Japanese audience.

Whether such buffering is actually necessary, the issue of cultural relevancy is worth considering within the yōkai context. The most influential of the new wave of Japanese horror is *Ringu* (1998, dir. Nakata Hideo), the film version just one node in a web of intertwining media manifestations, including a 1991 novel by Suzuki Kōji, several television adaptations, manga versions, and numerous cinematic sequels made in Japan, Korea, and the United States. The plot of the first *Ringu* film concerns a cursed video that has been circulating among schoolchildren; viewers of this viral video have seven days to live—unless they copy the tape and show it to somebody else, thus transferring the curse but also ensuring the proliferation of dangerous videos. A paradigmatic image from the film is of the monstrous girl Sadako, her black hair covering her face, crawling out of the television set to frighten (to death) her victims. Just as with the very earliest hyakkiyagyō, simply looking upon the demon (or her video) can cause your demise.

Ringu not only draws on earlier sources of Japanese horror, such as the Oiwa-san-style imagery of this Sadako character, but is also actually related to historical events (the backstory is loosely derived from the so-called senrigan incident of 1911).[2] Furthermore, the film is deeply aware of folkloric processes: the plot is set in motion when the main protagonist, a journalist, sets out to investigate an urban legend circulating among schoolchildren (not surprisingly, passing reference is made to Kuchi-sake-onna). While in some ways, then, *Ringu* develops naturally from the *Gakkō no kaidan* movies that came before it, the Sadako character, like Gojira half a century before her, is as much a product of tradition as of technology. The media of television and video cassettes take on a frightening, otherworldly potential: Sadako crawling out of the television becomes a terrifying (in)version of Mizuki's Terebi-kun crawling in and out of a televisual otherworld.

Indeed, perhaps what is so compelling, and globally translatable, about *Ringu* is that the film does not concern a haunted Japanese landscape so much as the haunting of contemporary technologies that transcend particular landscapes: television, video, film, the very media that allow us to access the story in the first place.[3] In so many of the most popular J-horror films, communication technologies—videos, televisions, cell phones, computer monitors—are construed as liminal and often dangerous apparatuses providing Kokkuri-like portals for communication between different worlds. At least part of J-horror's international appeal is this ability to play with themes that are not limited to a Japanese cultural context. Within this milieu, the sort of traditional yōkai we have examined may simply have too much cultural and historical baggage to leap easily onto the global stage.

HOME AND NATION

As Sadako and her J-horror compatriots make a name for themselves internationally, back home the more traditional yōkai continue to exert their powers as nostalgic icons of the hometown, or furusato. They remain paradigmatic of local Japan: small communities throughout the nation have adopted yōkai (particularly the ubiquitous kappa) as mascots for village revitalization *(mura okoshi)*.[4] By extension, these yōkai also represent Japan as a nation, featuring in advertisements for a range of products from a major brand of sake to Tokyo-Mitsubishi Bank's DC Card (a credit card), with its paired mascots—a kappa and a tanuki. In their explicitly commercial conceptions, yōkai are no longer frightening or mysterious—the DC Card kappa, for example, is not a slimy water creature threatening to kill unsuspecting children but a cute and (almost) cuddly cartoon character.

It is noteworthy that all these yōkai are implicitly Japanese figures. As icons of a shared rural history, even in their manga-influenced contemporary form, they represent characters from a presumed national memory. Yōkai are all the more desirable as representatives of a lost Japanese nation because, as denizens from an *other*worldly past, they can be invoked without also calling up distasteful *this*-worldly memories of, for example, colonialist and militarist ventures. At a time when, as one scholar of social memory puts it, "much of the current preoccupation with the past is less about a paradise lost than skeletons in the closet,"[5] the very otherworldliness of yōkai ensures that they remain untainted, uncontroversial, and remarkably safe for fetishistic consumption. Perhaps this is one reason for the ongoing yōkai boom: yōkai are spooky, but they are fun-spooky and, ultimately, much less threatening than the serious ghosts of the human past still haunting the present.

THE NEW YŌKAIGAKU

In scholarship on yōkai, too, we continue to find a constant inscription of these creatures onto the tableau of Japan as nation, a theme that runs from the *Kinmōzui* and the *Wakan sansaizue* through Enryō and Yanagita and the efforts to explain Kuchi-sake-onna as a modern avatar of earlier Japanese monsters. In the 1980s and 1990s, the anthropologist and folklorist Komatsu Kazuhiko (b. 1947) emerged as the driving force in a revitalized academic yōkaigaku. In one sense, Komatsu's work develops naturally from this historic quest to interpret yōkai within the context of comprehending Japan and Japanese culture. The subtitle of his 1994 work *Yōkaigaku shinkō* (New Considerations of Yōkaigaku) exemplifies this paradigm: *Yōkai kara miru Nihonjin no kokoro* might be translated as "the heart of the Japanese people as seen through yōkai." While this invocation of the Japanese heart and people gestures strategically to the historical and nostalgic associations of yōkai, Komatsu's project simultaneously transcends the confining logic of the national. In essence, he is inserting a broader, more universalist strain into the desire to understand yōkai:

> The new yōkaigaku is a discipline that researches the yōkai that humans imagine (create), that is, yōkai as cultural phenomena. Just as with animals, plants, and minerals, the form and attributes of yōkai existence cannot be studied without considering their relationship with human beings; they always reside within this relationship with humans, within the world of human imagination. Accordingly, the study of yōkai is nothing other than the study of the people who have engendered yōkai. In short, yōkaigaku is "yōkai culture studies" *[yōkai bunka-gaku]*, a "human-ology" *[ningen-gaku]* that seeks to comprehend human beings through yōkai.[6]

Just as Yanagita sought to establish minzokugaku as a unique field of inquiry in the early twentieth century, Komatsu develops yōkaigaku as a multidisciplinary humanistic study drawing on diverse fields of literature, anthropology, history, art, sociology, and psychology. Although much of his own work is deeply engaged with Japanese history and culture, he introduces a wide range of theoretical literature and foreign scholarship (and scholars) into the yōkaigaku project in an effort to compare and contrast Japanese yōkai culture with the "yōkai culture of other countries."[7] Within the new yōkaigaku, then, we can see two simultaneous—sometimes complementary, sometimes contradictory—directions of inquiry: a broad, universalist quest to understand the weird and mysterious within human culture; and a narrower, particularist pursuit of the weird and mysterious in Japan. I also see one more related trend: many recent discussions of yōkaigaku begin with a historical survey of the discipline itself. That is, the lineage of the intellectual discourse, starting particularly with Inoue Enryō, has itself become an important subject of study within the larger framework of yōkai studies. These three aspects of the new yōkaigaku—the national, the universal, and the meta—also resonate within more popular manifestations of yōkai culture today.

YŌKAI COMMUNITY

In 1994, the same year Komatsu introduced his new yōkaigaku, Studio Ghibli released an animated film titled *Heisei tanuki gassen Pompoko* (Tanuki Battle of the Heisei Era: Pompoko) directed by Takahata Isao. The story revolves around the plight of a tribe of tanuki living in the Tama Hills on the outskirts of Tokyo. Humans are planning to build a new suburb that will destroy the tanuki's native home. In a desperate attempt to thwart the encroachment of civilization, the older tanuki teach the younger tanuki the shape-shifting magic of old. Here we have a vivid, animated representation of the clash of metaphorical (and real) landscapes, and a storyline uncannily reminiscent of the legends prominent during that earlier moment of urbanization at the beginning of the twentieth century.

The tanuki transform themselves into a dazzling array of humans, trees, snakes, and, most strikingly, other yōkai. In the elaborately staged "Operation Yōkai" *(yōkai sakusen),* they attempt to intimidate the human residents by parading through the suburban streets in the guise of numerous monsters extracted from folklore or directly modeled on woodblock prints and the hyakkiyagyō picture scrolls. The scene is a fascinating reminder of the trope of pandemonium and parade—through this literal parade of yōkai, the tanuki cause, for just a few minutes, pandemonium. At the same time, however, they also create an enjoyable spectacle; crowds throng the streets, applauding their ghostly antics.

But this nostalgic return to the shape-shifting referential ecology of the past is short-lived. When the parade ends, a small boy complains, "Is it over already?" His mother tells him to go to bed and not to forget to brush his teeth—the mundane human world returns, and the enchantment of the yōkai parade is all but forgotten. Ultimately, the tanuki end up frustrated because the humans refuse to believe in their magic. Eerily recalling Yanagita's concerns from many years earlier, some of the tanuki complain that their tricks would certainly have been understood in the rural regions of Shikoku, but were completely lost on Tokyo's urbanized residents. To add insult to injury, not only are the tanuki's efforts unrecognized and ineffective, but credit for the yōkai parade is taken by a new local theme park, called Wonderland. Once more, the lament of the tanuki goes unheard, and this time their shape-shifting magic is co-opted not by the human hypnotists of late Meiji but by the commercial otherworld of a theme park—a cynically confined place of enchantment in the late-industrial Japanese landscape.

By invoking picture scrolls and other yōkai, *Heisei tanuki gassen Pompoko* also articulates a postmodern reflexivity, with the history of the subject itself paraded across the screen. We find a similar reference to yōkai discourse in the work of best-selling mystery writer Kyōgoku Natsuhiko (b. 1963), who has achieved extraordinary popularity and acclaim since his 1994 debut novel, and who won the prestigious Naoki Prize for popular fiction in 2003 for *Nochi no kōsetsu hyaku-monogatari* (Subsequent Hyaku-monogatari Rumors).[8] Like his mentor and source of creative influence, Mizuki Shigeru, Kyōgoku explicitly looks to the Tokugawa period for thematic inspiration. Some of his stories are set in the distant past, while others are more contemporary, but one of the governing conceits of his work is the referential homage he pays to Sekien. He has even produced several short-story collections named after the works in Sekien's *Hyakkiyagyō* series; each story is prefaced with a reproduction of one of Sekien's drawings, and the theme of the narrative itself is loosely based on the title yōkai.[9]

Set in the 1950s, Kyōgoku's most famous series of novels concern the cantankerous owner of a used bookshop, Kyōgoku-dō (the name of the shop as well as the hero), who solves mysteries through an Enryō-like rationalistic consideration of facts bolstered by eclectic knowledge of an array of subjects, including folklore, religion, philosophy, and psychology. In a sense, Kyōgoku-dō represents Komatsu's multidisciplinary yōkaigaku scholar, probing yōkai not only to solve the specific mystery in the novel but also for insight into the greater mysteries of humanity. Each novel in the series takes its title and theme from one of Sekien's yōkai and features a Sekien illustration on the frontispiece. The first of these novels, for example, is titled *Ubume no natsu* (Summer of the Ubume) and concerns a mysterious pregnancy—an issue, of course, appropriate to the yōkai of the title.

In the process of bringing logic to bear on the situation and eventually disenchanting the mystery, Kyōgoku-dō casually drops the names of "Meiji period philosophy professor Inoue Enryō" and "Venerable Yanagita."[10] The offhand inclusion of these figures, who may (in Yanagita's case) or may not (in Enryō's case) be familiar to the general public, paints the work with a scholarly authenticity and also intimates that Kyōgoku-dō the character and Kyōgoku the author are heirs to a long line of serious yōkai professionals. The mention of these historical characters in a popular fictional work provides readers with a set of shared referents—that is, not only the yōkai themselves but also a cast of historically real yōkai researchers. Furthermore, by setting these novels in the 1950s, a time of intense recovery and rebuilding, Kyōgoku also suggests a continuity with the past, as if the emerging landscape of postwar Japan is built on a communal memory of yōkai.

Another present-day venue that both reflects and inspires popular interest in yōkai is *Kai* (The Strange), a semiannual journal that began publication in 1997. Started by Kyōgoku, Mizuki, and the eclectic writer Aramata Hiroshi (b. 1947), and put out by Kadokawa Shoten Publishing, *Kai* is both playful and scholarly in its approach, printing an assortment of academic articles, roundtable discussions, manga, photographs, and short fiction all devoted to yōkai. I mention these various media here to underscore the interrelatedness of intellectual inquiry and popular enthusiasm, and also to suggest that interest in yōkai has come, more than ever, to represent a separate realm of knowledge replete with a coterie of hobbyists and aficionados. Yōkai enthusiasts are part of an imagined community, connected not only through a vague interest in the weird and mysterious but also through a particular knowledge of Sekien's images, Mizuki's manga, and now Kyōgoku's fiction and Komatsu's analyses.

Paradigmatic of both this imagined community and the body of shared knowledge that defines its members is a pocket date book for the year 2005 produced by the editors of *Kai*.[11] This compact vinyl-covered book includes a schedule of yōkai events both old (e.g., the Namahage ritual of Akita Prefecture) and new (e.g., the Kitarō Wooden Sandal Festival in Sakaiminato); a calendar with reminders of yōkai-relevant dates throughout the year; a mini dictionary of yōkai; and even a time line of yōkai-related occurrences throughout Japanese history. The date book also includes the wit and wisdom of Mizuki, venerable patriarch of the community: every other page of the calendar section features a "famous utterance," some expressly about yōkai ("There are places that humans don't know and can't see—that's where yōkai live"), and others typical of his dry irreverent humor ("Humans who work seriously are stupid!").

We also find here a perfect example of the contradictory rhetoric surrounding the notion of yōkai as universal (global) versus particularistic (national) phenomenon. Despite a quotation by Mizuki stating that "with yōkai there are no national borders," the almanac is restricted to the weird and mysterious wonders of Japan and even includes a reference section with Japanese emperors and reign dates and several maps of old Japan.

While the text allows yōkai lovers to enrich their everyday lives with knowledge of a supplementary, or doppelganger, realm to shadow their daily schedules—complete with its own history, its own set of events, its own conflicts and questions—in the end, it seems, the space of yōkai is not an other*world* but an other *Japan*.

In short, experiences of the weird and mysterious in the abstract are undoubtedly universal, but at least in the popular imagination, yōkai are always already imbedded in the referential landscape of the Japanese nation. Although Mizuki Shigeru is a household name in Japan, he is surprisingly unknown among Western fans of manga and anime. This is partly because, in contrast to, for example, the internationally acclaimed anime of Miyazaki Hayao (b. 1941) with their charmingly mystical characters and vaguely folkloric references, Mizuki's work is profoundly connected to the specific yōkai of Japan, bound to a particularistic history, and indelibly tied to national and cultural knowledges that are much more difficult for the uninitiated to access.[12]

This brings us to the 2005 film *Yōkai daisensō* (Great Yōkai War), directed by Miike Takashi (b. 1960), from a novel by Aramata Hiroshi and featuring cameo performances by Mizuki, Kyōgoku, the mystery novelist Miyabe Miyuki (b. 1960), and other *Kai* regulars. Although the title is identical to the 1968 film discussed earlier, and it features a similar war between a monstrous villain and a panoply of sympathetic yōkai characters, the 2005 movie is by no means a simple remake of the earlier one. Set in contemporary Japan, the plot revolves around a young boy from Tokyo who moves with his mother to his grandfather's home in the countryside. The rural furusato (filmed on location in Sakaiminato!) is a nostalgic repository of mysterious rituals and still-living yōkai. The boy gets caught up in an epic battle of good yōkai against machine-like monsters whose energy comes from discarded human refuse—reminiscent of the tsukumogami from centuries earlier. The movie is a multimillion-dollar spectacle combining live action, stop-motion puppetry, and computer graphics to animate an entire parade/pandemonium of yōkai characters (1.2 million according to the filmmakers), some canonical and some newly invented, some frightening and some comically absurd. Promoted as a blockbuster event through which "the resurgence of the hyakkiyagyō is throwing all of Japan into a whirlpool of excitement,"[13] *Yōkai daisensō* was screened at the Venice and Toronto film festivals and released internationally.

To succeed in the international market, presumably Miike would have to develop the same sort of hybrid aesthetic that is found in Miyazaki

Hayao's anime, to which *Yōkai daisensō* has been compared in the American press.[14] And indeed, *Yōkai daisensō* does fuse a cheerfully tongue-in-cheek tenor with J-horror techniques and references to kaijū eiga and a host of other films—including the *Lord of the Rings* series (2001–2003), *Gremlins* (1984), *Gamera,* and *Yōkai daisensō*'s 1968 namesake. But for all its good-natured high jinks, the film is a dubious candidate for success outside Japan; it must tread a fine line between the universally (or translatably) spooky or funny and detailed information about yōkai and their milieu. Certainly, these "grotesque and comical creatures," as the *New York Times* describes them, may be appreciated as "visual marvels" by an international audience,[15] but can they ever have the same historical and cultural depth they have for viewers raised with Mizuki's manga? Furthermore, inside jokes and references permeate the script in ways that would be incomprehensible to anybody but a devoted yōkai aficionado. One of the characters, for instance, is a writer for *Kai,* and not only is the action set in Sakaiminato, but also scenes take place on Mizuki Road and in the Mizuki Shigeru Memorial Hall (Kinenkan). At the end of the film, Mizuki himself makes a brief appearance as a giant-faced king of yōkai—who literally gets the last word.[16]

Yōkai daisensō did not turn out to be an overwhelming success in the international market. But it did expose non-Japanese, especially children, to an exciting parade of weird and mysterious creatures. The question remains as to how (or whether) yōkai will be transformed as Japanese popular culture becomes more and more conspicuous in the global marketplace. How will yōkai negotiate the fractured, multiethnic, multilingual, internet-linked terrain of transnational culture? Will they resonate primarily in an Asian market, or will they transcend traditional regional economies and cultures? Will they ever, like Harry Potter and his friends, appeal to a worldwide constituency without losing the flavor of their place of origin? Will some yōkai characters assume a generic globalized personality, akin to products like Sanrio's Hello Kitty, while other "real" yōkai remain a niche interest, located only in Japan, and tied exclusively to a national discourse?

OTHERWORLDS, COLLECTIONS, AND THE MYSTERIOUS BODY

To date, one of the most prominent and explicitly commercial incursions of Japanese monsters into the world economy is the Pokémon phenomenon. Pokémon (literally "pocket monsters") is an interactive form of entertainment that can be experienced in a number of different fashions, from the handheld electronic Game Boy to the television series to the trading of cards among friends. While the popularity of this multiplatform game deserves much more space than I can devote to it here, I can point out that a number of the pocket monsters, though certainly not all, seem modeled in part on "real" yōkai (e.g., the *nokocchi* derived from the tsuchinoko).

More significant, however, the Pokémon world shares critical structural affinities with yōkai culture—particularly the collusion of ludic and encyclopedic modes. The original version, for example, includes some 150 monsters, each with a distinct name, habitat, and set of characteristics. Success in the game is predicated on mastery of the facts about all the beasts in the pantheon. Handbooks and catalogs list, illustrate, organize, and describe these creatures in classic hakubutsugaku-style: "Pokémon of the prairies," "Pokémon of the mountains," "Pokémon of the forests," and the like. As if to further bolster the authority of this discourse, the "Pokémon world" is endowed with its own history and even an academic discipline reminiscent of yōkaigaku, appropriately called "Pokémon-gaku," or Pokémon-ology.[17]

In the way children play Pokémon, then, we find a familiar compulsion toward taxonomy, through which the denizens of an otherworld are named, located, defined, described, and made to come alive. This passion for order and classification is evident also in manga, film, video games, and fiction, as well as in many of the scholarly articles found in *Kai* and other venues. By applying real-world signifying practices to things as elusive as yōkai, we create an authentic, authorized system in which they can reside: a doppelganger universe, fully rendered and complete but somehow separate from our own. "'The otherworld [ikai],'" Komatsu suggests, "is the world on the other side of our 'lived world *[seikatsu sekai]*.'" This can be understood temporally (the world of the past, future, prelife, after death) or spatially (in the mountains, across the river, in the ocean).[18] On occasion this otherworld interfaces directly with ours, its yōkai agents causing mischief or fear or grief or laughter; it is these occasional irruptions—the sighting of a kappa, the movement of Kokkuri—that alert us to this world just beyond our own.

The otherworld of yōkai is just one manifestation of a more fundamental longing for something beyond what is immediately visible and available. Traditional and Internet role-playing games, the wizarding world of Harry Potter, multiplatform entertainments such as Pokémon and Yu-Gi-Oh!, and online virtual communities such as Second Life, all nurture a fantasy of something unseen but always there, something somehow more exciting than the mundane present place and time. They offer a dream of continued mystery and the hope of transcendence.

This desire to imagine an otherworld as a self-contained system, separate from (but always relevant to) this world, also affords insight into the fetishism of collecting. A natural extension of the taxonomical need for systems is the collector's impulse. Like the hakubutsugaku hobbyists so many years earlier, the enthusiasts who obsessively read Komatsu, Kyōgoku, and *Kai* are collectors. In some cases they collect objects—books, pictures, figurines—but many of them simply collect details: information not limited to the yōkai themselves but extending to the main human interpreters of the yōkai world. Data about Sekien, Enryō, Yanagita, and Mizuki are part and parcel of this world. Like sports fans who compulsively assemble statistics, many yōkai lovers seem to take pride in their encyclopedic recall of names and characteristics and historical and folkloric records. A 2005 issue of *Kai* exemplifies this categorizing, collecting impulse. Dedicated to the release of *Yōkai daisensō,* it includes a section titled "Yōkai meikan" (Yōkai Directory) featuring encyclopedic entries for the yōkai (i.e., hitotsume-kozō, mokumokuren, kawatarō) appearing in the film; each listing is complete with background information and still shots from the movie. The encyclopedic mode of articulation persists, providing enthusiasts with yet one more version, one more unit of information, to add to their collections.[19]

"The collection," Susan Stewart tells us, "is a form of art as play, a form involving the reframing of objects within a world of attention and manipulation of context. Like other forms of art, its function is not the restoration of context of origin but rather the creation of a new context, a context standing in a metaphorical, rather than contiguous, relation to the world of everyday life."[20] In contemporary yōkai discourse, specific historical and cultural contexts may be sacrificed for continuity of subject matter. All those things relating to yōkai—in the present as well as the past—can be assembled into an autonomous world. Sekien's creations from almost two and a half centuries ago are as relevant and alive here as Mizuki's manga. Himamushi-nyūdō and Kuchi-sake-onna, despite the cultural and historic particularities of their origins, sit side by side in the yōkai collector's display case. In the cabinet of wonders, memories from different times and places are brought together and placed in a singular new order, on parade.

Through carefully studying this parade, working to redraw the connections between the objects on display and rediscover the temporal and spatial contexts out of which they emerged, we can discern again the voices, past and present, of those who have played with notions of the mysterious and the weird. At the heart of the study, however, there remains still the mysterious body, the thing that is ultimately impossible to identify, define, qualify, or display. In the end, only the clamorous voices can be captured as they rise up around the ungraspable form.

Notes

CHAPTER 1. INTRODUCTION TO THE WEIRD

1. Ishizaka Masao, "Watashi mimashita, tsuchi-no-ko to neko no kenka," *Shūkan pureibōi,* October 24, 2000, p. 54. For more on tsuchinoko-related activities in Yoshii, see www.city.akaiwa.lg.jp/tutinoko (in Japanese).

Please note that, unless otherwise indicated, all translations from Japanese sources are my own.

2. "Yōkai: Nihonshi himotoku tegakari," *Nihon keizai shinbun,* August 17, 2002, p. 36. The database (in Japanese) can be accessed at www.nichibun.ac.jp/youkaidb/. Strictly speaking there were two related workshop series, both organized by Professor Komatsu Kazuhiko of the International Research Center for Japanese Studies (Kokusai Nihon bunka kenkyū sentā): "Nihon ni okeru kaii, kaidan bunka no seiritsu to hensen ni kansuru gakusaiteki kenkyū," from 1998 to 2000, and "Nihon ni okeru kaii, kaidan oyobi yōkai bunka ni kansuru sōgoteki kenkyū," from 1999 to 2001. I had the opportunity to observe and participate in these meetings from October 1999 through March 2001.

3. Jeffrey Jerome Cohen, "Monster Culture (Seven Theses)," in *Monster Theory: Reading Culture,* ed. Jeffrey Jerome Cohen (Minneapolis: University of Minnesota Press, 1994), 2.

4. See Michel Foucault, *The Archeology of Knowledge and the Discourse on Language,* trans. A. M. Sheridan Smith (New York: Pantheon Books, 1972).

5. N. Katherine Hayles, *How We Became Posthuman: Virtual Bodies in Cybernetics, Literature, and Informatics* (Chicago: University of Chicago Press, 1999), 14.

6. Implicitly bound up with cultural practice is a political (and socioeconomic) contrast between "elite" and "common." Such words reflect distinctions found in the discourse of each time period I explore, often signifying different levels of

academic education—that is, the extent to which an individual is trained in current (often institutional) regimes of knowledge. Those privy to such education might be called "elite"; the vast majority who are not are the "common" people. In the practices and discourses surrounding yōkai, the interaction between these two extremes often provides the most valuable insight.

7. Gerald Figal coins the word *monsterology* in his insightful discussion of Inoue Enryō and the place of yōkaigaku within modernity. While I agree with Figal that *monsterology* "captures the nineteenth-century scientific quaintness, sensationalism, and seriousness of the pursuit," I prefer to use *yōkaigaku,* because it retains the difficult and often ambiguous associations of yōkai without introducing the added cultural nuances of the English word *monster.* Figal, *Civilization and Monsters: Spirits of Modernity in Modern Japan* (Durham, NC: Duke University Press, 1999), 41.

8. Komatsu Kazuhiko, "Yōkai: Kaisetsu," in *Yōkai,* ed. Komatsu Kazuhiko (Kawade shobō shinsha, 2000), 435–36. For more on early usages of *yōkai,* see also Kyōgoku Natsuhiko, "Yōkai to iu kotoba ni tsuite (sono 2)," *Kai* 12 (December 2001): 296–307.

9. Komatsu, "Yōkai: Kaisetsu," 436; for Edo-period meanings of *bakemono,* see Adam Kabat (Adamu Kabatto), "Bakemono zukushi no kibyōshi no kōsatsu: Bakemono no gainen o megutte," in *Yōkai,* ed. Komatsu Kazuhiko (Kawade shobō shinsha, 2000), 141–64. A clear distinction between stable-form yōkai and *henge,* in which transformative powers are stressed, is made by Ema Tsutomu (see chapter 4).

10. The events that led to the deification of Michizane are outlined in Robert Borgen, *Sugawara no Michizane and the Early Heian Court* (Cambridge, MA: Council on East Asian Studies, Harvard University, 1986), 307–25.

11. Doris G. Bargen, *A Woman's Weapon: Spirit Possession in* The Tale of Genji (Honolulu: University of Hawai'i Press, 1997), 19. Bargen specifically distinguishes more generic forms of mono-no-ke from their manifestation in *Genji,* in which they "always take an invisible form imagined to signify human spirits" (21).

12. Marian Ury, "A Heian Note on the Supernatural," *Journal of the Association of Teachers of Japanese* 22, no. 2 (November 1988): 189.

13. Although she does not describe the "supernatural" in the same way I have here, Ury notes that medieval tales of random encounters with the supernatural resemble "the folklore of modern crime." Ibid.

14. Quoted in Komatsu Kazuhiko, *Hyōrei shinkō ron* (Kōdansha gakujutsu bunko, 1994), 329. For more on tsukumogami, see Komatsu Kazuhiko, *Nihon yōkai ibunroku* (Shōgakkan, 1995), 175–212; *Ikai to Nihonjin: Emonogatari no sōzōryoku* (Kadokawa sensho, 2003), 149–62; also Shibusawa Tatsuhiko, "Tsukumogami," in *Yōkai,* ed. Komatsu Kazuhiko (Kawade shobō shinsha, 2000), 65–78.

15. Komatsu, *Hyōrei shinkō ron,* 329–32.

16. For a concise discussion of the lineage of the various *Hyakkiyagyō emaki,* see Tanaka Takako, "*Hyakkiyagyō emaki* wa nao mo kataru," in *Zusetsu: Hyakkiyagyō emaki o yomu,* ed. Tanaka Takako et al. (Kawade shobō shinsha, 1999), 17–33. For a much more detailed exploration of hyakkiyagyō in its his-

torical context, see Tanaka Takako, *Hyakkiyagyō no mieru toshi* (Chikuma gakugei bunko, 2002).

17. The word translated here as "demons" is *oni*. Oni were associated with epidemics and misfortune in general but eventually (certainly by the Edo period) came to be characterized iconographically as horned anthropomorphic figures. For recent research see Minami Kiyohiko, *Oni no ezōshi: Sono minzokugaku to keizaigaku* (Sōbunsha, 1998); Komatsu Kazuhiko, ed., *Oni* (Kawade shobō shinsha, 2000).

18. "Pandemonium" is how *hyakkiyagyō* is translated in a catalogue of Kawanabe Kyōsai's work: Oikawa Shigeru, ed., *Kyōsai no gekiga, kyōgaten* (Tōkyō shinbun, 1996). For more on this translation, see my essay "Hyakki yakukō," in *Kai* 11 (July 2001): 304–5.

19. Michel Foucault, *The Order of Things: An Archaeology of the Human Sciences* (New York: Vintage Books, 1994), xv–xvi. Borges's list has become an almost clichéd example of an "exotic" system of classification, but as Zhang Longxi notes, "we may certainly attribute the Chinese encyclopedia to Borges the mythmaker and writer of fantastic tales, and realize that the incomprehensible passage Foucault quoted is nothing more than a good-natured joke, a fictitious representation of fictitious writing itself." Zhang Longxi, "The Myth of the Other: China in the Eyes of the West," *Critical Inquiry* 15, no. 1 (Autumn 1988): 112. Borges himself hints at the ambiguity of his reference, describing the "Chinese encyclopedist" as "unknown (or apocryphal)." See "The Analytical Language of John Wilkins," in *Other Inquisitions, 1937–1952*, trans. Ruth L. C. Simmons (Austin: University of Texas, 1964), 104. Interestingly, it seems the fabulous discourses of Borges's imagination have contaminated the "very real" categories of Foucault's analysis.

20. Harriet Ritvo, *The Platypus and the Mermaid and Other Figments of the Classifying Imagination* (Cambridge, MA: Harvard University Press, 1997), 137.

21. Komatsu Kazuhiko, *Yōkaigaku shinkō: Yōkai kara miru Nihonjin no kokoro* (Shōgakkan, 1994), 31.

22. Yi-Fu Tuan, *Landscapes of Fear* (Minneapolis: University of Minnesota Press, 1979), 5.

23. Physiologically this shift from general anxiety to specific alarm might be understood in terms of the interaction between the "rational fear system" and the "primitive fear system." For a summary of the processes involved, see Rush W. Dozier Jr., *Fear Itself: The Origin and Nature of the Powerful Emotion That Shapes Our Lives and Our World* (New York: Thomas Dunne Books, 1998), 3–57.

24. See Steven Schneider, "Monsters as (Uncanny) Metaphors: Freud, Lakoff, and the Representation of Monstrosity in Cinematic Horror," in *Horror Film Reader*, ed. Alain Silver and James Ursini (New York: Limelight Editions, 2000), 180–82. Schneider is developing a notion from George Lakoff, "The Contemporary Theory of Metaphor," in *Metaphor and Thought*, ed. Andrew Ortony, 2nd ed. (New York: Cambridge University Press, 1993), 202–51.

25. Benson Saler, "On What We May Believe about Beliefs," in *Religion in Mind: Cognitive Perspectives on Religious Belief, Ritual, and Experience*, ed. Jensine Andresen (Cambridge: Cambridge University Press, 2001), 48.

26. Inoue Enryō, *Inoue Enryō, Yōkaigaku zenshū*, ed. Tōyō Daigaku Inoue

Enryō kinen gakujutsu sentā (Kashiwa shobō, 2000), 4:57. The phrase used by Enryō is *shinkōshin no kōhaku*, which might be translated literally as "the thickness and thinness of the belief feeling."

27. Eric Schwitzgebel, "In-Between Believing," *Philosophical Quarterly* 51, no. 202 (January 2001): 78. For a response to Schwitzgebel's argument, see Darrell Patrick Rowbottom, "In-Between Believing and Degrees of Belief," *Teorema* 26, no. 1 (2007): 131–37.

28. See Loren Coleman and Jerome Clark, *Cryptozoology A to Z* (New York: Simon and Schuster, 1999). The tsuchinoko was rated by cryptozoologists as one of the "Top Cryptozoology Stories of 2000": www.lorencoleman.com/top_cryptozoology_2000.html. Cryptozoology is also interested in sightings of more mundane rare creatures, such as wolverines in the state of Michigan.

29. For more on the question of legends and beliefs, much of which is relevant to yōkai, see Linda Dégh and Andrew Vázsonyi, "Legend and Belief," in *Folklore Genres,* ed. Dan Ben-Amos (Austin: University of Texas Press, 1976), 93–123; Linda Dégh, *Legend and Belief: Dialectics of a Folklore Genre* (Bloomington: Indiana University Press, 2001). For supernatural belief in everyday life, see Gillian Bennett, *Traditions of Belief: Women, Folklore, and the Supernatural Today* (London: Penguin Books, 1987). Recent research in cognitive psychology not only notes the persistence of belief in the supernatural (in its broadest sense) but also suggests its naturalness within human evolutionary processes. See Paul Bloom, *Descartes's Baby: How the Science of Child Development Explains What Makes Us Human* (New York: Basic Books, 2004); Pascal Boyer, *Religion Explained: The Evolutionary Origins of Religious Thought* (New York: Basic Books, 2001).

30. Benson Saler, "Beliefs," 63. Saler is summarizing here the ideas of Pascal Boyer, in *The Naturalness of Religious Ideas: A Cognitive Theory of Religion* (Berkeley: University of California Press, 1994).

31. Michael Saler, "'Clap if You Believe in Sherlock Holmes': Mass Culture and the Re-Enchantment of Modernity, c. 1890–c. 1940," *Historical Journal* 46, no. 3 (2003): 607.

32. Yanagita Kunio, *Teihon Yanagita Kunio shū* (Chikuma shobō, 1969), 5:125.

33. Komatsu, *Yōkaigaku shinkō,* 162–73, 33–40. See also *Ijinron: Minzoku shakai no shinsei* (Seidosha, 1985), 228–33.

34. Although issues of belief are embedded in many of the texts considered in the chapters that follow, I generally avoid cultural forms that deal explicitly with the religious, because the rubric of organized religion presupposes a system of belief. Similarly, while the discourse and practice of religious professionals is linked to popular understandings of the spiritual, their constant ideological engagement with belief sets their work apart as a realm of specialist conversation. I am more concerned with the way yōkai quietly inform the lives of people not otherwise focused on questions of belief; I explore how yōkai gain access to sites not considered sacred—spaces of play or urban landscapes, for example, where mystery is not customarily expected.

35. Emile Durkheim, *The Elementary Forms of the Religious Life* (1912; reprint, New York: Free Press, 1965), 39.

36. For a discussion of the use of *supernatural* in Western theological and

anthropological discourse, see Benson Saler, "Supernatural as a Western Category," *Ethos* 5, no. 1 (1977): 31–53.

37. Stephen Greenblatt, *Marvelous Possessions: The Wonder of the New World* (Chicago: University of Chicago Press, 1991), 22.

38. Sigmund Freud, "The 'Uncanny,'" in *Writings on Art and Literature* (Stanford: Stanford University Press, 1997), 195. Hereafter cited parenthetically in the text.

39. Marilyn Ivy has also effectively applied the *unheimlich* concept to notions of the hometown, or *furusato*, in Japan. See *Discourses of the Vanishing: Modernity, Phantasm, Japan* (Chicago: University of Chicago Press, 1995), 105–8.

40. Mladen Dolar notes, "It seems that Freud speaks about a 'universal' of human experience when he speaks of the uncanny, yet his own examples tacitly point to its location in a specific historical conjuncture, to the particular historical rupture brought about by the Enlightenment." "'I Shall Be with You on Your Wedding-Night': Lacan and the Uncanny," *October* 58 (Fall 1991): 7. Terry Castle also points out that the eighteenth-century and Enlightenment mentality "'invented the uncanny': that the very psychic and cultural transformations that led to the subsequent glorification of the period as an age of reason or enlightenment . . . also produced[,] like a kind of side effect, a new human experience of strangeness, anxiety, and intellectual impasse." *The Female Thermometer: Eighteenth-Century Culture and the Invention of the Uncanny* (New York: Oxford University Press, 1995), 8.

41. Tzvetan Todorov, *The Fantastic: A Structural Approach to a Literary Genre* (Ithaca, NY: Cornell University Press, 1975); Rosemary Jackson, *Fantasy: The Literature of Subversion* (London: Routledge, 1981). On fantastic literature in Japan, see Susan J. Napier, *The Fantastic in Japanese Literature: The Subversion of Modernity* (London: Routledge, 1996).

42. Todorov, *The Fantastic*, 25.

43. Todorov himself concludes that the literature of the fantastic has been replaced by psychoanalysis, which explains those things for which there once were monsters. Ibid., 160–61.

44. Andrew Tudor, "Why Horror? The Peculiar Pleasures of a Popular Genre," *Cultural Studies* 11, no. 3 (1997): 446.

45. See James Twitchell, *Dreadful Pleasures: An Anatomy of Modern Horror* (New York: Oxford University Press, 1985), 65–104; Robin Wood, "An Introduction to the American Horror Film," in *American Nightmare: Essays on the Horror Film*, ed. Andrew Britton, Richard Lippe, Tony Williams, and Robin Wood (Toronto: Festival of Festivals, 1979), 9; Barbara Creed, *The Monstrous-Feminine: Film, Feminism, Psychoanalysis* (London: Routledge, 1993); Carol Clover, *Men, Women, and Chain Saws: Gender in the Modern Horror Film* (Princeton: Princeton University Press, 1992). Also of interest are Judith Halberstam, *Skin Shows: Gothic Horror and the Technology of Monsters* (Durham, NC: Duke University Press, 1995); Noël Carroll, *The Philosophy of Horror or Paradoxes of the Heart* (New York: Routledge, 1990). While these texts provide important insights into horror, the gothic, and the monstrous, they focus almost exclusively on Western (especially English-language) literature and film.

46. Tudor, "Why Horror?" 461 (emphasis in original).
47. Todorov, *The Fantastic*, 42.
48. Robert I. Levy, Jeannette Marie Mageo, and Alan Howard, "Gods, Spirits, and History: A Theoretical Perspective," in *Spirits in Culture, History, and Mind*, ed. Jeannette Marie Mageo and Alan Howard (London: Routledge, 1996), 12–13.
49. First coined by John Napier, the term *Goblin Universe* is explained as including "all beings or creatures which human beings have reported from their experience but which have not been catalogued as real by natural science." Marjorie M. Halpin, "Investigating the Goblin Universe," in *Manlike Monsters on Trial: Early Records and Modern Evidence*, ed. Marjorie M. Halpin and Michael M. Ames (Vancouver: University of British Columbia Press, 1980), 5.
50. For the platypus, see Ritvo, *The Platypus and the Mermaid*, 3–15. An exhibition at the Kawasaki City Museum focused on these more corporeal manifestations of elusive animals (including the tsuchinoko) in Japan, labeling them *genjū*, literally "fantastic beasts." See Kawasaki-shi Shimin Myūjiamu, *Nihon no genjū: Mikakunin seibutsu shutsugen roku* (Kawasaki: Kawasaki-shi Shimin Myūjiamu), 2004.
51. David D. Gilmore, *Monsters: Evil Beings, Mythical Beasts, and All Manner of Imaginary Terrors* (Philadelphia: University of Pennsylvania Press, 2003), 6, 16.
52. Frank Cawson, *The Monsters in the Mind: The Face of Evil in Myth, Literature, and Contemporary Life* (Sussex: Book Guild, 1995), 157.
53. Cohen notes, "Any kind of alterity can be inscribed across (constructed through) the monstrous body, but for the most part monstrous difference tends to be cultural, political, racial, economic, sexual." "Monster Culture," 7. Several essays in Cohen's edited volume deal with this conception of monstrosity. For more on monstrous births and prodigies, see Lorraine Daston and Katherine Park, *Wonders and the Order of Nature, 1150–1750* (New York: Zone Books, 1998), 173–214; Marie-Hélène Huet, *Monstrous Imagination* (Cambridge: Harvard University Press), 1993; Rosi Braidotti, "Signs of Wonder and Traces of Doubt: On Teratology and Embodied Differences," in *Between Monsters, Goddesses, and Cyborgs: Feminist Confrontations with Science, Medicine, and Cyberspace*, ed. Nina Lykke and Rosi Braidotti (London: Zed Books, 1996), 135–52. Very little theoretical literature in Japan considers yōkai from the perspective of monstrous birth, the notable exception being discussions of the *kudan*, a human-faced cow whose appearance is imbued with ominous portent. See Satō Kenji, *Ryūgen higo: Uwasabanashi o yomitoku sahō* (Yūshindō, 1995), 147–209; also Kihara Hirokatsu, "Hakken: Yōkai-kudan," *Kai* 17 (October 2004): 2–7, 230–35.
54. Peter Stallybrass and Allon White, eds., *The Politics and Poetics of Transgression* (Ithaca, NY: Cornell University Press, 1986), 8.
55. Michel de Certeau, *The Mystic Fable*, vol. 1, *The Sixteenth and Seventeenth Centuries*, trans. Michael B. Smith (Chicago: University of Chicago Press, 1992), 143. Interestingly, such hybrid construction is the very method by which new Japanese (and Chinese) characters are often created—as combinations of existing graphs invoked for their phonetic content, semantic content, or both. This is noted by Richard E. Strassberg in correlation to the hybrid creatures that

inhabit the Chinese text called the *Shanhaijing*. See Richard E. Strassberg, ed. and trans., *A Chinese Bestiary: Strange Creatures from the Guideways through Mountains and Seas* (Berkeley: University of California Press, 2002).

56. Benedict Anderson, *Imagined Communities: Reflections on the Origins and Spread of Nationalism*, rev. ed. (London: Verso, 1991), 24. See also 187–88. Anderson is developing a concept (and phrase) from Walter Benjamin. See Benjamin, *Illuminations: Essays and Reflections*, trans. Harry Zohn (New York: Schocken Books, 1968), 262–63.

57. Stallybrass and White, *Politics and Poetics of Transgression*, 5 (emphasis in original).

CHAPTER 2. NATURAL HISTORY OF THE WEIRD

Epigraph: Engelbert Kaempfer, *Kaempfer's Japan: Tokugawa Culture Observed*, ed. and trans. Beatrice M. Bodart-Bailey (Honolulu: University of Hawai'i Press, 1999), 70.

1. See Katsuhisa Moriya, "Urban Networks and Information Networks," in *Tokugawa Japan: The Social and Economic Antecedents of Modern Japan*, ed. Chie Nakane and Shinzaburō Oishi (Tokyo: University of Tokyo Press, 1990), 97–123; Peter Kornicki, *The Book in Japan: A Cultural History from the Beginnings to the Nineteenth Century* (Honolulu: University of Hawai'i Press, 2001), 169–276; Ikegami Eiko, *Bonds of Civility: Aesthetic Networks and the Political Origins of Japanese Culture* (Cambridge: Cambridge University Press, 2005); Mary Elizabeth Berry, *Japan in Print: Information and Nation in the Early Modern Period* (Berkeley: University of California Press, 2006); Marcia Yonemoto, *Mapping Early Modern Japan: Space, Place, and Culture in the Tokugawa Period (1603–1868)* (Berkeley: University of California Press, 2003); Donald H. Shively, "Popular Culture," in *The Cambridge History of Japan*, vol. 4, ed. John Whitney Hall (Cambridge: Cambridge University Press, 1991), 706–69; Richard Rubinger, *Popular Literacy in Early Modern Japan* (Honolulu: University of Hawai'i Press, 2007).

2. Although I use *encyclopedic* as the most appropriate term to refer to this discourse, the Japanese words for "encyclopedia"—*hyakkazenshū* or *hyakkajiten*—were not in common parlance until the Meiji period. See Carol Gluck, "The Fine Folly of the Encyclopedists," in *Currents in Japanese Culture: Translations and Transformations*, ed. Amy Vladeck Heinrich (New York: Columbia University Press, 1997), 234. My objective here is not to present a history of encyclopedias in Japan but rather to examine the development of a way of perceiving the world that reflects the encyclopedias and natural histories produced during the Tokugawa period. For more about the history of Japanese encyclopedias in general, see Gluck, "Fine Folly of the Encyclopedists," 223–51. For more on the Western encyclopedic tradition, see Richard Yeo, *Encyclopedic Visions: Scientific Dictionaries and Enlightenment Culture* (Cambridge: Cambridge University Press, 2001).

3. Berry, *Japan in Print*, 15.

4. Masao Maruyama, *Studies in the Intellectual History of Tokugawa Japan,* trans. Mikiso Hane (Princeton: Princeton University Press, 1974), 15. Herman Ooms asserts that, through ignoring the "process by which an ideology is put into place," scholars have overemphasized the hegemony of "orthodox neo-Confucianism." He argues that "Hayashi Razan was primarily responsible for making all later generations believe that political thought in early Tokugawa Japan was neo-Confucian, and that the bakufu was its active sponsor." *Tokugawa Ideology: Early Constructs, 1570–1680* (Ann Arbor: Center for Japanese Studies, University of Michigan, 1998), 72–73.

5. Nishimura Saburō, *Bunmei no naka no hakubutsugaku: Seiyō to Nihon* (Kinokuniya shoten, 1999), 1:102–5. As Hayashi Razan puts it, "All creatures, plants, animals and inanimate objects owe their existence to the will of heaven and earth. Thus not a single object lacks within it the principles of heaven." Razan quoted in John David Lu, ed., *Sources of Japanese History* (New York: McGraw-Hill, 1973), 1:236. Zhu Xi himself had outlined the connections between knowledge of the world and proper behavior within it: "The extension of knowledge consists in the investigation of things. When things are investigated, knowledge is extended; when knowledge is extended, the will becomes sincere, the mind rectified; when the mind is rectified, personal life is cultivated; when personal life is cultivated, the family will be regulated; when the family is regulated, the state will be in order; and when the state is in order, there will be peace in the world." Quoted in Maruyama, *Studies in the Intellectual History of Tokugawa Japan,* 25. For Zhu Xi, the "investigation of things" was not an end in itself, but rather a first step in an eightfold process of morality. For a concise explanation of the "Doctrine of Extension of Knowledge through the Investigation of Things," see Siu-chi Huang, *Essentials of Neo-Confucianism: Eight Major Philosophers of the Song and Ming Period* (Westport, CT: Greenwood Press, 1999), 138–40.

6. One of the more prominent earlier texts is the twenty-volume *Wamyō ruijūshō* of 931–937. For more on pre-Edo-period honzōgaku in Japan, see Yabe Ichirō, *Edo no honzō: Yakubutsugaku to hakubutsugaku* (Saiensusha, 1991), 15–42.

7. Nishimura notes that there is some evidence that Razan, Fujiwara Seika, and others may have read the text earlier than 1607, and that the set delivered to Ieyasu was not the first to be imported in Japan. *Bunmei no naka no hakubutsugaku,* 105–8.

8. Yabe, *Edo no honzō,* 51–52.

9. Ibid., 208–9. The *Honzō kōmoku* was not the first Chinese honzōgaku text to break with the so-called three-tier system common to its predecessors, but it was innovative in the precision and detailed nature of its categorization. See also Nishimura, *Bunmei no naka no hakubutsugaku,* 195–96, 202; Yamada Keiji, "Honzō ni okeru bunrui no shisō," in *Higashi Ajia no honzō to hakubutsu no sekai,* vol. 1, ed. Yamada Keiji (Kyoto: Shibunkaku shuppan, 1995), 12–15.

10. Ueno Masuzō, "Jobun: Edo hakubutsugaku no romanchishizumu," in *Edo hakubutsugaku shūsei: Saishiki,* ed. Shimonaka Hiroshi (Heibonsha, 1994), 8. The difference between honzōgaku and hakubutsugaku is fuzzy at best, and made all the more problematic by the different labels applied to the study historically:

for example, although Kaibara Ekiken (1630–1714) would today be considered a practitioner of hakubutsugaku, he would have labeled himself a scholar of honzōgaku. See ibid.; also Sugimoto Tsutomu, *Edo no hakubutsugakusha-tachi* (Kōdansha gakujutsu bunkō, 2006), 106–25, 374–77.

11. Gluck, "The Fine Folly of the Encyclopedists," 230.

12. Ronald P. Toby notes that the Wanli Era (1573–1620) of the late Ming period was especially prolific, and encyclopedias were produced "for both elite and popular audiences." The importation of such encyclopedias to Japan was "influential in the emergence of a Japanese encyclopedism." See "Imagining and Imaging 'Anthropos' in Early-Modern Japan," *Visual Anthropology Review* 14, no 1 (Spring–Summer 1998): 38. See also Tadao Sakai, "Confucianism and Popular Educational Works," in *Self and Society in Ming Thought*, ed. William Theodore de Bary and Conference on Ming Thought (New York: Columbia University Press, 1970), 331–66.

13. Berry, *Japan in Print*, 23–24.

14. Although older indigenous honzōgaku texts such as the *Wamyō ruijūshō* or Razan's *Shinkan tashikihen* might be labeled "encyclopedias," the *Kinmōzui* was the first *illustrated* encyclopedia. Yabe, *Edo no honzō*, 56–57. Nishimura notes that it was the second edition that Kaempfer took home to Europe. *Bunmei no naka no hakubutsugaku*, 113.

15. Shively perceptively translates the title as "Illustrations and Definitions to Train the Untutored." "Popular Culture," 720.

16. Nishimura, *Bunmei no naka no hakubutsugaku*, 112–13; Yabe, *Edo no honzō*, 57–59.

17. Yabe, *Edo no honzō*, 59. For a schematic of the contents and organization of the *Kinmōzui*, see Sugimoto Tsutomu's commentary in the facsimile edition, Nakamura Tekisai, *Kinmōzui* (Waseda Daigaku shuppanbu, 1975), 265. See also Toby, "Imagining and Imaging 'Anthropos' in Early-Modern Japan," 32–35.

18. Many of these "kinmōzui" texts are reproduced in Asakura Haruhiko, ed., *Kinmōzui shūsei*, 25 vols. (Ōzorasha, 1998). For a discussion of derivative texts, including parodies, see Kurashima Toshihito's "Kaisetsu," 25:5–18.

19. *Tanuki* (often conflated with *mujina*) is sometimes (mis)translated as "badger." The Linnaean classification of the tanuki is *Nyctereutes procyonoides*. For more on the tanuki, see Nakamura Teiri, *Tanuki to sono sekai* (Asahi shinbunsha, 1990).

20. Research on kitsune is extensive. For a brief discussion, see Komatsu Kazuhiko, *Nihon yōkai ibunroku* (Shōgakkan, 1995), 44–79. On the relationship of the fox to Edo-period Inari belief, see Komatsu Kazuhiko, *Akuryōron: Ikai kara no messēji* (Chikuma shobō, 1997), 203–14; also Karen Smyers, *The Fox and the Jewel: Shared and Private Meanings in Contemporary Japanese Inari Worship* (Honolulu: University of Hawai'i Press, 1999), 14–28. For an analysis of the fox's shape-shifting proclivities, see Michael Bathgate, *The Fox's Craft in Japanese Religion and Folklore: Shapeshifters, Transformations, and Duplicities* (New York: Routledge, 2004). For a review of lore relating to both kitsune and tanuki, see U. A. Casal, "The Goblin Fox and Badger and Other Witch Animals of Japan," *Folklore Studies* 18 (1959): 1–93; also M. W. de Visser, "The Fox and

Badger in Japanese Folklore," pt. 3, *Transactions of the Asiatic Society of Japan* 36 (1908): 1–159. De Visser suggests that in Chinese texts the term *kori* (Chinese, *huli*) referred exclusively to foxes (1).

21. Nakamura, *Kinmōzui,* 75.

22. Berry, *Japan in Print,* 15.

23. Toby, "Imagining and Imaging 'Anthropos' in Early-Modern Japan," 35. Toby also comments on the confusing nature of Tekisai's categorization within the human category (34). See also Robert Eskildsen, "Telling Differences: The Imagery of Civilization and Nationality in Nineteenth Century Japan" (PhD diss., Stanford University, 1998), 47–117.

24. George Lakoff, *Women, Fire, and Dangerous Things: What Categories Reveal about the Mind* (Chicago: University of Chicago Press, 1987), 35–37. For more on folkbiology and folk taxonomy, see Scott Atran, *Cognitive Foundations of Natural History: Toward an Anthropology of Science* (Cambridge: Cambridge University Press, 1990), 1–80; also Douglas L. Medin and Scott Atran, eds., *Folkbiology* (Cambridge, MA: MIT Press), 1999. For an insightful discussion of the classification of the wolf in Japan, see Brett L. Walker, *The Lost Wolves of Japan* (Seattle: University of Washington Press, 2005), 25–56.

25. Tekisai may also have been loath to categorize something as distinctly "supernatural" because Shushigaku ordered the world along specific natural principles, without creating a separate space for the *super*natural. Zhu Xi's own opinion of ghosts (Chinese, *guei*) and spirits (Chinese, *shen*) is somewhat ambiguous. Although he admits that the "ancient sages" believed in them, he also suggests, "Let us comprehend what is comprehensible. What we cannot comprehend, we'll set aside and await the time when we understand thoroughly what we do every day in our lives. That is when the *li* of ghosts and spirits will also become clear." Julia Ching, *The Religious Thought of Chu Hsi* (Oxford: Oxford University Press, 2000), 62.

26. See Yonemoto for a brief description of the organization of the *Wakan sansaizue. Mapping Early Modern Japan,* 107.

27. Nishimura, *Bunmei no naka no hakubutsugaku,* 116.

28. Michel Foucault, *The Order of Things: An Archeology of the Human Sciences* (New York: Vintage Books, 1994), 129. Foucault's observations about pre-seventeenth-century European natural history could apply as well to Chinese and Japanese texts: "To write the history of a plant or animal was as much a matter of describing its elements or organs as of describing the resemblances that could be found in it, the virtues that it was thought to possess, the legends and stories with which it had been involved, its place in heraldry, the medicaments that were concocted from its substance, the foods it provided, what the ancients recorded of it, and what travellers might have said of it" (129).

29. Robert M. Maniquis, "Encyclopedia and Society: Order, Disorder, and Textual Pleasure," in *The Encyclopedia and the Age of Revolution,* ed. Clorinda Donato and Robert M. Maniquis (Boston: G.K. Hall and Co., 1992), 79. Although they developed in distinct historical and cultural milieus, there is a remarkable affinity between the *Wakan sansaizue* project and the "Western tradition," in which "there has been a conviction that it is possible, and worthwhile, to collate knowledge that is representative of some larger whole. The ideal imag-

ined here is a work that summarizes and organises the knowledge contained in many books." Yeo, *Encyclopedic Visions*, 2.

30. All quotations from the *Wakan sansaizue* are from the two-volume *kanbun* facsimile edition (Terajima Ryōan, *Wakan sansaizue* [Nihon zuihitsu taisei kankōkai, 1929]) with reference to the eighteen-volume modern Japanese translation (Terajima Ryōan, *Wakan sansaizue* [Heibonsha, 1994]). Citations are included parenthetically in the text with the *kanbun* edition volume and page first, followed by the volume and page of the modern edition. I have also consulted a Tokugawa-period edition in the Stanford University East Asia Library.

31. The entry continues with practical information about the curative powers of various parts of the kitsune's body. The liver of a male fox, for example, can revive somebody who has died suddenly; the procedure of crushing the liver in hot water and pouring it into the patient's mouth must be performed soon after death for it to be effective.

32. The kappa has a long and complex history. The vernacular and dialectal variants of its name include *kawatarō, kawarō, suiko, medochi,* and many others. For a discussion of the many names and characteristics associated with the creature, see Ishikawa Jun'ichirō, *Shinpan kappa no sekai* (Jiji tsūshinsha, 1985), 41–64.

33. Yabe notes this same tendency not to distinguish between hearsay *(denbun)* and firsthand observation in the influential work of the natural historian Matsuoka Gentatsu (1668–1746). *Edo no honzō*, 74. Gluck suggests that in the encyclopedic context the conflation of documentation and hearsay would not be unusual: "The tradition of esoteric transmission of knowledge from master to disciple meant that instead of identifying the source of the quotation, Japanese compilers sometimes resorted to locutions like 'it has been said since ancient times' or 'according to a certain source' to provide authority for their selections." "The Fine Folly of the Encyclopedists," 232.

34. See Nakamura Teiri, *Kappa no Nihonshi* (Nihon Editāsukūru shuppanbu, 1996), 173–76.

35. James E. Combs, *Play World: The Emergence of the New Ludenic Age* (Westport, CT: Praeger, 2000), 7.

36. Timon Screech, *The Lens within the Heart: The Western Scientific Gaze and Popular Imagery in Later Edo Japan* (Honolulu: University of Hawai'i Press, 2002), 22. See also H. D. Harootunian, "Late Tokugawa Culture and Thought," in *The Cambridge History of Japan*, vol. 5, ed. Marius B. Jansen (Cambridge: Cambridge University Press, 1989), 168–258.

37. The quote is from Combs, *Play World*, 15.

38. There was a shift in emphasis here, from Razan's nonempiricist use of documents to a fieldwork-based approach reliant on direct observation. By researching indigenous flora and fauna, this nativist project also encouraged the investigation of regional folklore—whether medical remedy or local legend—and gave new value to indigenous sources and beliefs. In fact, much of the information collected during this period is considered more important for studies of folklore and dialect than of natural history. See Nishimura, *Bunmei no naka no hakubutsugaku*, 129–33.

39. Ibid., 133–34.

40. Ibid., 136–46. See also Yabe and Sugimoto for more on this text and Hiraga Gennai's involvement with honzōgaku (Yabe, *Edo no honzō,* 135–42; Sugimoto, *Edo no hakubutsugakusha-tachi,* 77–88).

41. Nishimura, *Bunmei no naka no hakubutsugaku,* 147.

42. Harootunian, "Late Tokugawa Culture," 169. Harootunian is referring to an idea presented by Hayashiya Tatsusaburō, who identifies *ki* ("strange, curious, and eccentric") and *i* ("different, uncommon, and foreign") as terms symbolic of the attitudes of the times.

43. For Edo-period misemono, see Kawazoe Yū, *Edo no misemono* (Iwanami shoten, 2000); Andrew L. Markus, "The Carnival of Edo: Misemono Spectacles from Contemporary Accounts," *Harvard Journal of Asiatic Studies* 45, no. 2 (December 1985): 499–541. Markus defines his subject in a way that dovetails neatly with the fetishization of the strange in the product conventions: "private exhibitions of unusual items, individuals, or skills, conducted for a limited span of time inside a temporary enclosure for the purpose of financial gain" (501). For more on the relationship between hakubutsugaku, product conventions, misemono, and yōkai, see Kagawa Masanobu, *Edo no yōkai kakumei* (Kawade shobō shinsha, 2006), 130–38.

44. For the construction of mummified mermaids in Japan, see Aramata Hiroshi, *Kaii no kuni Nippon* (Shūeisha, 1997), 330–40.

45. More accurately such a gathering was called a *hyaku-monogatari kaidan kai.*

46. *Wakan kaidan hyōrin,* quoted in Tachikawa Kiyoshi, ed., *Hyaku-monogatari kaidan shūsei* (Kokusho kankōkai, 1995), 354. Most *hyaku-monogatari* collections include fewer than one hundred tales; the number may simply denote a large amount rather than a specific number. Sumie Jones suggests that the use of one hundred "may indicate a threat that there were always more to be told and that the wealth of dark and irrational ghost stories could not be exhausted." See "The Other Side of the Hakone: Ghosts, Demons, and Desire for Narrative in Edo Literature," in *The Desire for Monogatari: Proceedings of the Second Midwest Research/Pedagogy Seminar on Japanese Literature,* ed. Eiji Sekine (West Lafayette, IN: U.S.-Japan Friendship Commission and Purdue University, 1994), 57. Nakazawa Shin'ichi suggests that one hundred is not just a signifier of quantity but also "clearly possesses a qualitative meaning" underscoring the profusion of different yōkai and a sense of wonder at their variety. The classification and ordering of yōkai, he argues, was a "pleasure" discovered by the people of the Edo period and represents a sensibility that distinguishes them from previous generations. "Yōkai-ga to hakubutsugaku," in *Yōkai,* ed. Komatsu Kazuhiko (Kawade shobō shinsha, 2000), 79.

47. Asai Ryōi, *Otogibōko,* in *Shin Nihon koten bungaku taikei* (Iwanami shoten, 2001), 75:395.

48. Komatsu Kazuhiko, "Hyaku-monogatari kaidan to yōkai kenkyū," in *Shutendōji no kubi* (Serika shobō, 1997), 251.

49. Tachikawa, *Hyaku-monogatari,* 81.

50. Noriko T. Reider, "The Emergence of *Kaidan-shū:* The Collection of Tales of the Strange and Mysterious in the Edo Period," *Asian Folklore Studies* 60, no. 1 (2001): 79–99. For a recent English translation of *Ugetsu monogatari* with

valuable introductory notes, see Ueda Akinari, *Tales of Moonlight and Rain*, trans. Anthony H. Chambers (New York: Columbia University Press, 2007). For more on the *kaidan* aesthetic, see Takada Mamoru, *Edo gensō bungakushi* (Chikuma gakugei bunko, 1999), 9–24. Tachikawa and Komatsu both argue that the origins of the written collections can be found in the oral practice (Tachikawa, *Hyaku-monogatari kaidan shūsei*, 354; Komatsu, "Hyaku-monogatari," 251), but Takeda Tadashi notes the difficulty of ascertaining the relationship between the oral and written. See "Hyaku-monogatari: Sono seiritsu to hirogari," in *Yōkai*, ed. Komatsu Kazuhiko (Kawade shobō shinsha, 2000), 112–18.

51. In one sense, there was really nothing new about hyaku-monogatari—compilations of weird tales in Japan go back at least as far as the ninth-century *Nihon ryōiki*, the earliest known collection of *setsuwa*. As Komine Kazuaki notes, however, in collections of setsuwa tales, weird narratives were always treated as a single type of tale within a wider selection—not until the Tokugawa period did they become a separate genre. "Yōkai no hakubutsugaku," *Kokubungaku: Kaishaku to kyōzai no kenkyū* 41, no. 4 (March 1996): 82.

52. Komatsu, "Hyaku-monogatari," 251.

53. This is the word often used to characterize the tales. See, for example, the preface of *Konjaku hyaku-monogatari hyōban* of 1687, which describes "the mysterious *[fushigi]* and frightening *[osoroshiki]* things of hyaku-monogatari." Tachikawa Kiyoshi, ed., *Zoku hyaku-monogatari kaidan shūsei* (Kokusho kankōkai, 1993), 6.

54. Komine argues similarly that, although each yōkai presumably has a story associated with it, detailed individual descriptions allow them to be ordered, catalogued, and presented as a unified category. "Yōkai no hakubutsugaku," 86.

55. *Gazu hyakkiyagyō*, 1776; *Konjaku gazu zoku hyakki*, 1779; *Konjaku hyakki shūi*, 1781; *Hyakki tsurezure bukuro*, 1784. All four texts are reproduced in Inada Atsunobu and Tanaka Naohi, eds., *Toriyama Sekien gazu hyakkiyagyō* (Kokusho kankōkai, 1999). All subsequent references are noted parenthetically in the text and refer to this facsimile edition.

56. Evidence suggests that the *Shanhaijing* had found its way to Japan by the tenth century. See Takada Mamoru, "'Hyakkiyagyō' sōsetsu: Jo ni kaete," in *Toriyama Sekien gazu hyakkiyagyō*, ed. Inada Atsunobu and Tanaka Naohi (Kokusho kankōkai, 1999), 11–12. Although the extent of its circulation is unclear, it is cited in the *Wakan sansaizue*, and several Japanese versions were published during the Edo period, including the *Kaiichōjū zusetsu* (date unknown), an annotated picture scroll deriving most of its creatures from the *Shanhaijing*. See Itō Seiji, ed., *Kaiichōjū zusetsu* (Kōsakusha, 2001). The *Shanhaijing*'s direct influence on Sekien is questionable: most of his yōkai are not found in that text. As Sekien himself notes, however, it certainly provided inspiration for his work: "Since in China *(Morokoshi)* there was the *Shanhaijing*, and in our own country there was Motonobu's *Hyakkiyagyō*, I have learned from them and soil the paper with my own pen." Inada and Tanaka, *Toriyama Sekien gazu hyakkiyagyō*, 92. The Motonobu referred to here is Kanō Motonobu (1476–1559), founder of the Kanō school of painting, of which Sekien was a member. *Hyakkiyagyō* probably refers to one of the Muromachi-period picture scrolls known by that name. Although none of these are generally attributed to Kanō Motonobu him-

self, models for Sekien's own work are known to have been passed down within the Kanō school. For more on "Hyakkiyagyō emaki," see Tanaka Takako et al., eds., *Zusetsu: Hyakkiyagyō emaki o yomu* (Kawade shobō shinsha, 1999), 17–33; and Tanaka Takako, *Hyakkiyagyō no mieru toshi* (Chikuma gakugei bunko, 2002). For a translation and thorough discussion of the *Shanhaijing,* see Richard E. Strassberg, ed. and trans., *A Chinese Bestiary: Strange Creatures from the Guideways through Mountains and Seas* (Berkeley: University of California Press, 2002). For more on the influence of *Shanhaijing* and derivative works on Sekien, see Kagawa, *Edo no yōkai kakumei,* 124–27.

57. In what seems to be an homage to the Muromachi-period *Hyakkiyagyō emaki,* Sekien includes a rising sun at the conclusion of his second set of books. See Inada and Tanaka, *Toriyama Sekien gazu hyakkiyagyō,* 172–73. This is the only explicit gesture to narrative in the series.

58. Kornicki, *The Book in Japan,* 44.

59. Tanaka Hatsuo suggests that one effect of Sekien's dividing up of the yōkai into distinct characters on separate pages is that, rather than a stationary viewer witnessing a procession as in the picture scrolls, the viewer is the one proceeding through the demons. Tanaka Hatsuo, ed., *Gazu hyakkiyagyō* (Watanabe shoten, 1967), 211. Tada Katsumi suggests that Sekien's friendship with Hiraga Gennai may have influenced his decision to portray yōkai in catalog rather than picture-scroll form. *Hyakki kaidoku* (Kōdansha, 1999), 21–22. Although I agree with Tada, I would also stress Sekien's immersion in a broader cultural milieu in which the encyclopedic mode was a powerful expressive form. Nakazawa also discusses the structural similarities between yōkai pictures in general (including picture scrolls) and hakubutsugaku. "Yōkai-ga," 79–86. I would emphasize that this affinity is most pertinent to Sekien's nonnarrative, condensed presentation.

60. Tada, *Hyakki kaidoku,* 19–22.

61. See Kyōgoku Natsuhiko and Tada Katsumi, eds., *Yōkai zukan* (Kokusho kankōkai, 2000), 130–39.

62. This may be a portrayal of the tanuki thumping its own belly, an action associated with the legendary version of the creature.

63. See Miyata Noboru, *Yōkai no minzokugaku: Nihon no mienai kūkan* (Iwanami shoten, 1985), 119–67. The association of yōkai with borders and liminal spaces/times is discussed in chapter 4.

64. Ibid., 22–24. Miyata goes on to explain that a man who has encountered the ubume will often discover that he has developed great physical strength. The version recounted here is only one of many; the legend is widespread and has many localized variations. In fact, the ubume is documented as far back as the *Konjaku monogatari shū;* see *Nihon koten bungaku taikei* (Iwanami shoten, 1965), 25:539–41. For more on the ubume image, see Tada, *Hyakki kaidoku,* 27–34; also Shibuya Yōichi, "Bakemono zōshi no kenkyū: Yōkai kenkyū e no shikiron" (undergraduate thesis, Chiba University, Chiba City, 2000), 24–30. For a discussion of the ubume and similar legends within a religious context, see Hank Glassman, "At the Crossroads of Birth and Death: The Blood-Pool Hell and Postmortem Fetal Extraction," in *Death and the Afterlife in Japanese Buddhism,* ed. Mariko Walter and Jacqueline Stone (Honolulu: University of Hawai'i Press, 2008), 175–206.

65. Nihon daijiten kankōkai, *Nihonkoku daijiten* (Shogakkan, 1976), 3:7.

66. In the *Wakan sansaizue,* the ubume is in a section on "birds of the mountains." The bird characters were associated with the ubume before the *Wakan sansaizue,* at least as early as the 1687 *Kokin hyakumonogatari hyōban* (Tachikawa, *Zoku,* 32–34). Shibuya posits that Sekien's use of the bird characters suggests that the knowledge of ubume from hakubutsugaku was so widespread that his readers required no further explanation. "Bakemono zōshi no kenkyū," 26.

67. It is likely that this second set of three volumes was originally meant to be published together with the first set of texts in 1776. Yumoto Kōichi, *Edo no yōkai emaki* (Kōbunsha, 2003), 19–23.

68. Sekien was particularly close to poet and writer Ōta Nanpo (1749–1823). Tada, *Hyakki kaidoku,* 19–20.

69. Sekien's work might also be read within the context of a genre of visual humor known as *kyōga,* mad or comical pictures, that was also developing at this time. For more on kyōga, see Shimizu Isao, *Edo no manga* (Kōdansha gakujutsu bunko, 2003), 66–69.

70. For a detailed interpretation of this yōkai, see Tada, *Hyakki kaidoku,* 174–77. Murakami Kenji also suggests the mokumokuren was most likely a fabrication on the part of Sekien. *Yōkai jiten* (Mainichi shinbunsha, 2000), 332.

71. There are also variations, such as the *hemamushyo-nyūdō,* in which ヨ is added as part of the ear. For more on this and similar rebuses *(moji-e),* see Shimizu, *Edo no manga,* 16–17.

72. The interpretations in this paragraph are derived primarily from Tada, *Hyakki kaidoku,* 189–91.

73. Kagawa points out that the creation of new yōkai was already part of parodic practice at this time; a parodic "yōkai dictionary" and a comical work listing yōkai names for male and female genitalia were already circulating by the time Sekien's first catalog was published. For more on these parodies and a careful analysis of Sekien's wordplay, see *Edo no yōkai kakumei,* 173–80. Additionally, so-called *mitate* works that parodied encyclopedias and natural history texts (including *Kinmōzui* and *Wakan sansaizue*) were popular before and after Sekien's work. See Kagawa, *Edo no yōkai kakumei,* 157–61.

74. Saeki Umetomo, ed., *Kokin waka shū,* in *Nihon koten bungaku taikei* (Iwanami shoten, 1980), 8:93.

75. The many yōkai-related rumors recorded in the *Mimi bukuro* collection of the early 1800s reflect the vitality of supernatural phenomena in an urban setting. See Negishi Yasumori, *Mimi bukuro,* 3 vols. (Iwanami shoten, 1991). For a general account of Edo-period urban yōkai, see Hirosaka Tomonobu, *Edo kaiki ibunroku* (Kirinkan, 1999).

76. Tada, *Hyakki kaidoku,* 20. Shibuya also suggests that the majority of Sekien's yōkai images can be labeled either fiction or, as modifications of folkloric tradition, folklorism. "Bakemono zōshi no kenkyū," 5.

77. See Kagawa, *Edo no yōkai kakumei,* 149–56. Melinda Takeuchi notes that in art "the depiction of supernatural themes reached an apogee during the nineteenth century, an age when artists vied with each other to satisfy the public's quickened appetite for images of the bizarre and the macabre." "Kuniyoshi's Minamoto Raikō and the Earth Spider: Demons and Protest in Late Tokugawa

Japan," *Ars Orientalis* 17 (1987): 5. For more on the kibyōshi genre, which flourished between 1775 and 1806, see Adam L. Kern, *Manga from the Floating World: Comicbook Culture and the* Kibyōshi *of Edo Japan* (Cambridge: Harvard University Asia Center, 2006). For the relationship of kibyōshi with yōkai, see Adam Kabat [Adamu Kabatto], *Edo bakemono zōshi* (Shogakkan, 1999); *Ōedo bakemono saiken* (Shōgakkan, 2000); "Bakemono zukushi no kibyōshi no kōsatsu: Bakemono no gainen o megutte," in *Yōkai*, ed. Komatsu Kazuhiko (Kawade shobō shinsha, 2000), 141–64. Kabat also outlines the way yōkai during this period were commodified as cute "characters," such as Tōfu-kozō (Tofu Boy). See *Edo kokkei bakemono zukushi* (Kōdansha, 2003), 5–83; also *Ōedo bakemono zufu* (Shōgakkan, 2000), 29–56.

78. Kagawa Masanobu, "Yōkai to goraku," *Kai* 11 (August 2001): 306–7. See also Kagawa, *Edo no yōkai kakumei*, 181–239; Yumoto, *Edo no yōkai emaki*, 70–89; Iwata Noriko, "Bakemono to asobu: 'Nankenkeredomo bakemono sugoroku,'" *Tōkyō-to Edo-Tōkyō hakubutsukan hōkoku* 5 (February 2000): 39–52.

79. Yōkai karuta was still produced as late as the Taishō period. Tada Katsumi, *Edo yōkai karuta* (Kokusho kankōkai, 1998), 3–5. See also Kagawa (*Edo no yōkai kakumei*, 189–92), who notes the correlation between the game and a hakubutsugaku sensibility. Karuta (Portuguese: *Carta*) apparently entered Japan from Europe in the sixteenth century and came to be played in a number of different ways. One of the best-known forms, still played today, is based on the collection of poems *Hyakunin isshu* (One Hundred Poems by One Hundred Poets); players must match the beginning of a famous poem with its concluding verses. For more about karuta, see Yamaguchi Kakutarō, "Nihonjin to karuta," *Gekkan bunkazai* (January 1975): 12–19.

80. Berry, *Japan in Print*, 211.

81. Ibid. Berry suggests that the "conjuncture of territory, state, and culture" often attributed to the Meiji period can also be found (differently) in the Tokugawa period and is exemplified by what she calls the "library of public information" (212). See 209–51 for an important discussion of nation during the early modern period.

82. Jorge Luis Borges, *Labyrinths: Selected Stories and Other Writings* (New York: New Directions, 1964), 18. This infiltration of a fictitious encyclopedia into the real world is of course neatly reflected in the infiltration of Borges's fictitious "Chinese encyclopedia" into Foucault's *The Order of Things* and the discourses it has inspired.

83. Nakazawa, "Yōkai-ga," 83.

84. There is evidence that this tradition of paying respects was already established two years after the play's debut. Yokoyama Yasuko, *Yotsuya kaidan wa omoshiroi* (Heibonsha, 1997), 238. See also Jones, "Other Side of the Hakone," 61–62. For more on the local legends upon which the play was based, see Hirosaka, *Edo kaii ibunroku*, 137–44.

85. For *Kappa no shirigodama*, see Kabat, *Ōedo bakemono saiken*, 151–82. Takagi Shunzan's *Honzō zusetsu*, with illustrations of plants, animals, and humans, was not published until the Meiji period. See Aramata Hiroshi, ed., *Takagi Shunzan, Honzō zusetsu*, 3 vol. (Riburo poruto, 1988); also *Zōhoban zukan no hakubutsushi* (Shūeisha, 1995), 337–44. Handwritten accounts of kappa sight-

ings, complete with detailed illustrations, include the early-nineteenth-century *Kappa jissetsu*. I am grateful to the United States Library of Congress for allowing me access to this text.

86. See Wilburn Nels Hansen, *Strange Tidings from the Realm of the Immortals: Hirata Atsutane's Ethnography of the Other World* (PhD diss., Stanford University, 2006).

CHAPTER 3. SCIENCE OF THE WEIRD

1. Stefan Tanaka, *New Times in Modern Japan* (Princeton: Princeton University Press, 2004), 13.

2. See Timon Screech, *The Lens within the Heart: The Western Scientific Gaze and Popular Imagery in Later Edo Japan* (Honolulu: University of Hawai'i Press, 2002); also W. F. Vande Walle and Kazuhiko Kasaya, eds., *Dodonaeus in Japan: Translation and the Scientific Mind in the Tokugawa Period* (Leuven, Belgium: Leuven University Press, 2001).

3. See Gerald Figal, *Civilization and Monsters: Spirits of Modernity in Modern Japan* (Durham, NC: Duke University Press, 1999). Also see Itakura Kiyonobu, *Yōkai hakase: Enryō to yōkaigaku no tenkai* (Kokusho kankōkai, 1983); Tanaka, *New Times in Modern Japan*, 69–76; Hirano Imao, *Den Enryō* (Sōfūsha, 1974); Kathleen M. Staggs, "'Defend the Nation and Love the Truth': Inoue Enryō and the Revival of Meiji Buddhism," *Monumenta Nipponica* 38, no. 3 (Autumn 1983): 251–81; Jason Ānanda Josephson, "When Buddhism Became a 'Religion': Religion and Superstition in the Writings of Inoue Enryō," *Japanese Journal of Religious Studies* 33, no. 1 (2006): 143–68. Biographical information is derived from these sources, particularly Itakura.

4. Itakura, *Yōkai hakase*, 6–8. Enryō's thinking can also be characterized as combining Western rationalism and Japanese traditionalism. Niita Shunzō, "Enryō ni okeru keimō shisō no nijūsei ni tsuite," in *Inoue Enryō to seiyō shisō*, ed. Saitō Shigeo (Tōyō Daigaku Inoue Enryō kenkyūkai dainibukai, 1988), 163.

5. Miura Setsuo, "Kaisetsu: Inoue Enryō to yōkaigaku no tanjō," in *Inoue Enryō, Yōkaigaku zenshū*, ed. Tōyō Daigaku Inoue Enryō kinen gakujutsu sentā (Kashiwa shobō, 2001), 6:472. For more on Enryō's education, see Staggs, "'Defend the Nation and Love the Truth.'"

6. Itakura, *Yōkai hakase*, 16. See also Niita, "Enryō ni okeru keimō shisō no nijūsei ni tsuite," 170–71.

7. Itakura suggests Enryō's yōkai research began when he was a second-year university student. *Yōkai hakase*, 20. Within a few years, he was actively collecting data from around the country: in August of 1884, a newspaper in Niigata Prefecture reported that Inoue Enryō, a fourth-year philosophy student at the University of Tokyo, had arrived to research local monsters *(kaibutsu)*. See *Nihon rikken seitō shinbun*, August 17, 1884, in *Chihō hatsu Meiji yōkai nyūsu*, ed. Yumoto Kōichi (Kashiwa shobō, 2001), 83. The origin of Enryō's obsession with yōkai is disputed, but some locate it in the pleasure he took in hearing yōkai stories as a child. See Miura, "Kaisetsu," 468–69.

8. Ichiyanagi Hirotaka makes this comparison to the British group; see "'Yōkai' to iu ba: Inoue Enryō, 'yōkaigaku' no ichi," in *Nihon shisō no kanō-*

sei, ed. Suzuki Tadashi and Yamaryō Kenji (Satsuki shobō, 1997), 85–87. For more on the Society, see Renée Haynes, *The Society for Psychical Research, 1882–1982* (London: MacDonald and Co., 1982); see also Deborah Blum, *Ghost Hunters: William James and the Search for Scientific Proof of Life after Death* (New York: Penguin Books, 2006). For a list of the original members of the Fushigi kenkyūkai, see Itakura, *Yōkai hakase*, 24; Figal, *Civilization and Monsters*, 44–45; Tanaka, *New Times in Modern Japan*, 70. Miura reproduces Enryō's original minutes from the meetings. "Kaisetsu," 476–77.

9. Inoue, quoted in Itakura, *Yōkai hakase*, 25.

10. Miura, "Kaisetsu," 477–83. The word *yōkaigaku* also appears as the name of a course Enryō taught at Tetsugakukan in 1891. See ibid., 480.

11. Inoue Enryō, *Yōkaigaku kōgi*, in *Inoue Enryō, Yōkaigaku zenshū*, ed. Tōyō Daigaku Inoue Enryō kinen gakujutsu sentā (Kashiwa shobō, 1999), 1:19–20.

12. Figal elucidates Enryō's involvement in enforcing nationalistic aims through education, noting that, "the cooptation of folk knowledge for the regulation of Japanese bodies within a single national body *[kokutai]* involved in this instance the attachment of this folk knowledge to sites of knowledge, such as schools, that were becoming institutionalized under state control." *Civilization and Monsters*, 92.

13. See *Inoue Enryō, Yōkaigaku zenshū*, ed. Tōyō Daigaku Inoue Enryō kinen gakujutsu sentā (Kashiwa shobō, 2000), 4:63–180; 4:181–306.

14. Inoue, *Yōkaigaku* 4:111.

15. Itakura, *Yōkai hakase*, 3.

16. For an example of the ludic qualities of his lectures, see "Yōkai dan," in *Inoue Enryō, Yōkaigaku zenshū*, ed. Tōyō Daigaku Inoue Enryō kinen gakujutsu sentā (Kashiwa shobō, 2001), 6:408–23. It would be unfair to characterize Enryō only according to the more sensationalist aspects of his yōkaigaku project. He was a prolific scholar actively involved in the reform of Buddhism (see Josephson, "When Buddhism Became a 'Religion'"), the promotion of psychology and Western philosophy, and the development of correspondence education. See Staggs, "'Defend the Nation and Love the Truth'"; Ogura Takeharu, *Inoue Enryō no shisō* (Kōgura shobō, 1986); Tōyō Daigaku sōritsu 100 shūnen kinen ronbunshū hensan iinkai, ed., *Inoue Enryō no kyōiku rinen: Atarashii kengaku no seishin o motomete* (Tōyō Daigaku, 1987); and the essays in Saitō Shigeo, ed., *Inoue Enryō to seiyō shisō* (Tōyō Daigaku Inoue Enryō kenkyūkai dainibukai, 1988).

17. Inoue, *Yōkaigaku kōgi*, 57–59.

18. Ibid., 21.

19. Inoue Enryō, "Shinkai," in *Inoue Enryō, Yōkaigaku zenshū*, ed. Tōyō Daigaku Inoue Enryō kinen gakujutsu sentā (Kashiwa shobō, 2000), 5:507–8.

20. Enryō describes the revelation of shinkai in Buddhist terms of *jiriki* and *tariki*. *Yōkaigaku kōgi*, 277–78. The analogy between shinkai and Spencer's "Unknowable" is made by Ichiyanagi and by Figal, who also notes the correlation between shinkai and Kant's "noumenon." Ichiyanagi, "'Yōkai' to iu ba," 83; Figal, *Civilization and Monsters*, 43. For more on Enryō's notion of the absolute, see Josephson, "When Buddhism Became a 'Religion,'" 158–60.

21. Enryō elaborates on these distinctions throughout his oeuvre. For a convenient diagram of this typology, see *Yōkaigaku kōgi,* 282.

22. Lorraine Daston and Katherine Park, *Wonders and the Order of Nature, 1150–1750* (New York: Zone Books, 1998), 14.

23. Tanaka perceptively translates Enryō's *Yōkaigaku kōgi* as "Studies in Wonderology." *New Times in Modern Japan,* 70.

24. Enryō's trajectory conforms to the unilinear evolutionary biases of his contemporaries in the West (Tylor, Frazer, etc.), in which cultures "progress" from animism, to belief in a distinct deity figure (or figures), and finally to modern scientific interpretations of nature. And like many of his contemporaries in the West, Enryō posits a scientific modernity without destroying religious belief—in his case, he reserves the higher mysteries of the universe, those which cannot be explained through the scientific paradigm, for his ultimate category of shinkai. See Inoue Enryō, *Yōkai gendan,* in *Inoue Enryō, Yōkaigaku zenshū,* ed. Tōyō Daigaku Inoue Enryō kinen gakujutsu sentā (Kashiwa shobō, 2000), 4:17. Subsequent citations from *Yōkai gendan* are noted parenthetically in the text.

25. Miyatake Gaikotsu, *Meiji kibun* (Kawade shobō shinsha, 1997), 53.

26. A form of Kokkuri is still played in Japan today and was particularly popular among schoolchildren in the mid-1970s. More recently, the practice was featured in a 1997 horror film entitled simply *Kokkuri-san* (dir. Takahisa Zeze). Although this latter version of Kokkuri is related to the Meiji incarnation, the playing method (most likely influenced by the Ouija board) is different; in some cases the name has also been changed to "Angel-san" or "Cupid-san." For more on the later versions of the game, see Imaizumi Toshiaki, "Kokkuri-san ni kansuru shakai shinrigakuteki chōsa: 1930 nendai kara 1992 nen made no ryūkō shi," *Shūkyō to shakai* 1, no. 6 (1995): 29–48; Nakata Jun, "'Kokkuri' wa naze fumetsu nano ka," *Gendai* (September 1997): 299–305; Ichiyanagi Hirotaka, "Gakkō no kaidan no riarizumu," in *Aera mook: Dōwagaku ga wakaru,* ed. Sekido Mamoru (Asahi shinbunsha, 1999), 86–89; Ichiyanagi, "Shinrei o kyōiku suru: Tsunoda Jirō 'Ushiro no Hyakutarō' no tōsō," *Nihon bungaku* (November 2001): 30–38.

27. The description here is derived from a number of sources, most prominent among them Enryō's *Yōkai gendan.* Although Enryō's monograph is colored by his anti-yōkai ideology, it is a remarkably rigorous ethnographic document, providing descriptions of Kokkuri from a network of informants living throughout the country.

28. Ryōkū Yajin, *Seiyō kijutsu Kokkuri kaidan,* 1st ed. (Iiguru shobō, March 1887), 7.

29. This explanation is supported by Enryō's data from Nagoya/Gifu, in which a variant name is noted as "Okatabuki," an appellation constructed of an honorific *o* prefixed to the nominal form of the verb *katabuku* (variant of *katamuku*), meaning "to tilt or lean" (*Yōkai gendan,* 22). See also Ryōkū, *Seiyō kijutsu Kokkuri kaidan,* 11.

30. These characters appeared by June 1886, in Kojima Hyakuzō, *Jinshin denki no zuga* (Osaka, n.p., 1886). They can also be found in newspaper accounts of the phenomenon as early as July 1886: "Kami oroshi to Kokkuri no ryūkō," *Asahi Shinbun,* July 16, 1886, in *Meiji nyūsu jiten* (Mainichi komyunikēshonzu

shuppanbu, 1986), 3:230. For a discussion of variant graphs associated with *Kokkuri*, see Enryō, *Yōkai gendan*, 19; also Inoue Enryō, "Shinrigaku bumon," *Yōkaigaku kōgi*, in *Inoue Enryō, Yōkaigaku zenshū*, ed. Tōyō Daigaku Inoue Enryō kinen gakujutsu sentā (Kashiwa shobō, 1999), 2:546. Ryōkū asserts that the original set of characters applied to Kokkuri is 告理. 告 *(koku)* is associated with the meaning to "tell" or "inform." 理 *(ri)* is associated with reason and logic. *Seiyō kijutsu Kokkuri kaidan*, 11. The compound 告理, therefore, can be interpreted as meaning "to tell or inform the reason or workings of something," which is what Kokkuri does with regard to the future. Another possible derivation (or at least association) is the expression *Mukuri-Kokuri*. Mukuri refers to Mongolia (Mōko) and Kokuri to Koguryo, the ancient kingdom on the Korean Peninsula; the term likely originated in reference to the Mongolian invasions of Japan in 1274 and 1281. The association with a foreign otherworld and the fear of invasion, as in the expression "a demon from Mukuri-Kokuri has come" (Mukuri-Kokuri *no oni ga kita;* Matsumura Akira, *Daijirin*, 2nd ed. [Sanseido, 1995], 2055), may have deepened Kokkuri's mysterious connotations. There is, however, no mention of this connection in the contemporary literature. I am grateful to Professor Ronald Toby for bringing this expression to my attention. Personal communication, November 3, 2001.

31. References to fox possession can be found as far back as the *Nihon ryōiki*, and numerous records exist throughout the Tokugawa period. See Hiruta Genshirō, "Kitsune tsuki no shinseishi," in *Tsukimono*, ed. Komatsu Kazuhiko (Kawade shobō shinsha, 2000), 67–90.

32. For more on inugami, see Kagawa Masanobu, "Tōkō kyohi to tsukimono no shinkō: Gendai ni ikiru 'inugami tsuki,'" in *Tsukimono*, ed. Komatsu Kazuhiko (Kawade shobō shinsha, 2000), 238–63. See also Sekien's portrayal in Inada Atsunobu and Tanaka Naohi, eds., *Toriyama Sekien gazu hyakkiyagyō* (Kokusho kankōkai, 1999), 34. Much has been written on tengu; see, for example, the articles in Komatsu Kazuhiko, ed., *Tengu to yamamba* (Kawade shobō shinsha, 2000). For a study in English, based extensively on Enryō's work, see M. W. de Visser, "The Tengu," *Transactions of the Asiatic Society of Japan* 36, no. 2 (1908): 25–99. For kami-kakushi and Hirata Atsutane, see Carmen Blacker, "Supernatural Abductions in Japanese Folklore," *Asian Folklore Studies* 26, no. 2 (1967): 111–48; also Wilburn Nels Hansen, *Strange Tidings from the Realm of the Immortals: Hirata Atsutane's Ethnography of the Other World* (PhD diss., Stanford University, 2006).

33. As mentioned in chapter 2, the word *kori* 狐狸 means literally "kitsune and tanuki" but refers in a general way to these creatures' proclivities for shifting shape and "deceiving *[bakasu]*" people. Accordingly *kori* also denotes a trickster or deceptive person. See Matsumura, *Daijirin*, 949. Though the relationship between *kori* and *Kokkuri* is unclear, the insertion of the *ku* between *ko* and *ri* draws on the meaning of *kori*, and adds the association of another yōkai (狗 = ku), simultaneously creating a word *(kokkuri)* that describes the nodding motion of the apparatus.

34. Ryōkū, *Seiyō kijutsu Kokkuri kaidan*, 18–21.

35. Enryō also cites a practice in the Nihonbashi district of Tokyo in which the characters for the three yōkai are separately written on slips of paper and in-

serted into the apparatus. *Yōkai gendan*, 27. Ryōkū notes, "In some places [people] write the three characters with their fingers on the underside of the tray." *Seiyō kijutsu Kokkuri kaidan*, 25.

36. Ichiyanagi Hirotaka, *"Kokkuri-san" to "Senrigan": Nihon kindai to shinreigaku* (Kōdansha, 1994), 27.

37. Kojima, *Jinshin denki no zuga*. This pamphletlike document has no pagination.

38. Ryōkū, *Seiyō kijutsu Kokkuri kaidan*, 17.

39. For several of these other theories, see *Yōkai gendan*, 33–34.

40. In *Yōkai gendan*, Enryō confines himself to this brief explanation and one example from the Western context. In a later (1893–1894) work on psychology, however, he goes into much greater detail, discussing the Fox sisters and other spiritualists. See *Yōkaigaku zenshū* 2:541–45. In North America and Europe, part of the broad appeal of Spiritualism may have been its relatively egalitarian nature, representing a transition from common poltergeist and haunted house phenomena, in which specific ghosts haunted specific locations, to a paradigm in which "*any* spirit could be summoned from *any* sitting room." Kenneth Pimple, "Ghosts, Spirits, and Scholars: The Origins of Modern Spiritualism," in *Out of the Ordinary: Folklore and the Supernatural*, ed. Barbara Walker (Logan: Utah State University Press, 1995), 80. Practices such as table-turning provided an exciting forum for informal experimentation and research: see C. P. Nicholls, *Table Moving: Its causes and phenomena, with directions how to experiment* (London: J. Wesley, [186?]). For more on Spiritualism and psychical research in nineteenth-century Europe and North America, see William Benjamin Carpenter, *Mesmerism, Spiritualism, &c., Historically & Scientifically Considered; Being Two Lectures Delivered at the London Institution; with Preface and Appendix* (New York: D. Appleton and Company, 1895); Alison Winter, *Mesmerized: Powers of Mind in Victorian Britain* (Chicago: University of Chicago Press, 1998); Janet Oppenheim, *The Other World: Spiritualism and Psychical Research in England, 1850–1914* (Cambridge: Cambridge University Press, 1985); Haynes, *Society for Psychical Research*, 1982; Blum, *Ghost Hunters*, 2006. For Spiritualism in Japan, see Helen Hardacre, "Asano Wasaburō and Japanese Spiritualism in Early Twentieth-Century Japan," in *Japan's Competing Modernities: Issues in Culture and Democracy, 1900–1930*, ed. Sharon A. Minichiello (Honolulu: University of Hawai'i Press, 1998), 133–53; see also Lisette Gebhardt, "The 'Other World' in the Light of a New Science: Spiritism in Modern Japan," in *Practicing the Afterlife: Perspectives from Japan*, ed. Susanne Formanek and William R. LaFleur (Vienna: Verlag der Österreichischen Akademie der Wissenschaften, 2004), 383–96.

41. Frank Podmore, *Modern Spiritualism: A History and a Criticism* (London: Methuen and Co., 1902), 2:7.

42. Mary Louise Pratt, *Imperial Eyes: Travel Writing and Transculturation* (London: Routledge, 1992), 6.

43. An example of this paradigm in a colonialist context can be found in the autobiography of the great French magician Eugene Robert-Houdin (1805–1871). Robert-Houdin describes how, during his travels through Algeria, he set out to "startle and even terrify them by the display of a supernatural power."

By using electricity and electromagnetism, he controlled whether or not a small box could be lifted up by a volunteer, and thus made a local "Hercules" seem "weaker than a woman." *The Memoirs of Robert-Houdin*, trans. Lascelles Wraxall (New York: Dover Publications, 1964), 266–68.

44. Komatsu Kazuhiko, "Tsukimono: Kaisetsu," in *Tsukimono*, ed. Komatsu (Kawade shobō shinsha, 2000), 436–37. Komatsu does not refer to Kokkuri here but is discussing more traditional forms of shamanism in Japan. His distinction is between "uncontrolled" *(seigyo sarenai)* possession, by which he means possession that occurs without the will of the possessed, and "controlled" *(seigyo sareta)* possession, in which "a religious practitioner we call a 'shaman' can cause, when she so desires, her own body or somebody else's body to be possessed by either a good or evil spirit."

45. Kawamura Kunimitsu documents in a modern context the process by which several women have become professional miko. See *Miko no minzokugaku: 'Onna no chikara' no kindai* (Seikyūsha, 1993), 123–51; also Carmen Blacker, *The Catalpa Bow: A Study of Shamanistic Practices in Japan* (London: George Allen and Unwin, 1975).

46. Ryōkū, *Seiyō kijutsu Kokkuri kaidan*, 3.

47. Ichiyanagi, *"Kokkuri-san" to "Senrigan,"* 27.

48. See Kawamura Kunimitsu, *Genshi suru kindai kūkan: Meishin, byōki, zashikirō, aruiwa rekishi no kioku* (Seikyūsha, 1997), 61–121; Susan Burns [S. Bānzu], "Toritsukareta shintai kara kanshi sareta shintai e: Seishin igaku no hassei," *Edo no shisō* 6 (May 1997): 48–62; and Figal, *Civilization and Monsters*, 96–99. Burns notes that, in particular, the second and third decades of Meiji witnessed an increase in psychiatric hospitals; by 1900 there were eight such facilities in Tokyo, three in Kyoto, two in Osaka, and one in Hakodate (59).

49. Kawamura, *Miko*, 35–38.

50. The extent to which these laws were enforced is unclear, but there is evidence of at least one case in 1880 in which a shaman was punished. Ibid., 36.

51. Ibid., 38. Elsewhere, Kawamura notes that, in 1876, newspaper articles on fox possession appeared for the first time, indicating that such occurrences had become rarer and therefore newsworthy. See *Genshi suru*, 61–65. Though shamanic practices never disappeared completely in Japan, Blacker points out that, until the Religious Bodies Law of 1945 granted freedom of religious activities, many miko "practiced their calling only furtively and in secret." *Catalpa Bow*, 127–28.

52. See Donald Campbell, "Science's Social System of Validity-Enhancing Collective Belief Change and the Problems of Social Sciences," in *Metatheory in Social Science*, ed. D. Fiske and R. Shweder (Chicago: University of Chicago Press, 1986), 108–35; Mark A. Schneider, *Culture and Enchantment* (Chicago: University of Chicago Press, 1993). My explanation here is based on my own adaptation of the notion to fit the yōkai case.

53. Schneider, *Culture and Enchantment*, 5–6.

54. For more on the political objectives and motivations of Enryō's ideology, see Figal, *Civilization and Monsters*, 77–104.

55. Basil Hall Chamberlain, *Japanese Things: Being Notes on Various Subjects Connected with Japan* (Rutland, VT: Charles E. Tuttle Co., 1971), 158. Cham-

berlain does not mention the word *Kokkuri,* but notes that "table-turning" was in fashion from 1887 to 1888.

56. Enryō's internalizing of the demons is reminiscent of the burgeoning of Western psychological practices in which thoughts and ideas themselves came to be considered dangerous phantasmagoria. See Terry Castle, *The Female Thermometer: Eighteenth Century Culture and the Invention of the Uncanny* (New York: Oxford University Press, 1995), 168–89.

57. Although most of his informants describe the movement as a nodding or tilting, Enryō himself often writes of Kokkuri's spinning or rotation *(kaiten).* Presumably he is referring to a pivoting action that may occur when the apparatus tilts to one side or lifts up a leg. Enryō's rhetoric may also have been influenced by his familiarity with Western discourse on table-turning, which often refers to the spinning of the table.

58. Carpenter also describes the operations of the nerves in detail, and Enryō's *fukaku kindō* and *yoki ikō* seem to be direct translations of Carpenter's "unconscious muscular activities" and "expectant attention." See Carpenter, *Principles of Mental Physiology* (New York: D. Appleton and Co., 1883), 32–38. Enryō does not cite Carpenter in *Yōkai gendan,* but in his later "Shinrigaku bumon," he quotes an extended passage from *Principles of Mental Physiology* (which he calls *Shinrisho*). See *Inoue Enryō, Yōkaigaku zenshū,* 2:569–70; Carpenter, *Principles,* 284–85.

59. Inoue Enryō, "Meishin to shūkyō," in *Inoue Enryō, Yōkaigaku zenshū,* ed. Tōyō Daigaku Inoue Enryō kinen gakujutsu sentā (Kashiwa shobō, 1999–2001), 5:270.

60. See Christoph Asendorf, *Batteries of Life: The History of Things and Their Perception in Modernity,* trans. Don Reneau (Berkeley: University of California Press, 1993), 153–77.

61. John Bovee Dods, *Philosophy of Electro-Biology, or Electrical Psychology . . . ,* compiled and edited by G. W. Stone (London: H. Bailliere, 1852), 2, 26–27.

62. Winter, *Mesmerized,* 265.

63. Ibid., 263.

64. Ibid., 266. Faraday's experiments demonstrated that the cause of the table's movements was not electricity but the unconscious force exerted on the table by participants. These experiments were reported over several months in a number of popular magazines and newspapers; they greatly influenced Carpenter's (and therefore Enryō's) later writings on the subject. See ibid., 290–92; Carpenter, *Principles,* 293–95. Carpenter's own notion of "ideo-motor action," introduced with regard to table-turning in 1852, was itself an influence on Faraday. Winter, *Mesmerized,* 292. See also Michael Faraday, "Professor Faraday on Table-Moving," *Athenaeum* (July 2, 1853): 801–3.

65. Ichiyanagi Hirotaka, *Saiminjutsu no Nihon kindai* (Seikyūsha, 1997), 42; see Screech, *The Lens within the Heart,* 44–47, for the Edo-period fascination with erekiteru.

66. Shimokawa Kōshi and Katei sōgō kenkyūkai, eds., *Meiji Taishō kateishi nenpyō 1868–1925* (Kawade shobō shinsha, 2000), 130–32. See also Ishii Kendō, *Meiji jibutsu kigen* (Chikuma gakugei bunko, 1997), 8:192–96.

67. Kikkawa Takeo, *Nihon denryoku gyō to Matsunaga Yasuzaemon* (Nagoya: Nagoya Daigaku shuppankai, 1995), 28.

68. A famous example is the *denki buran*, or "electric brandy," served since 1882 at the Kamiya Bar in the Asakusa district of Tokyo. The name gave the drink a certain cachet appropriate to a Western-style bar; undoubtedly the high alcohol content (45 percent) also contributed to the suitability of the appellation. See the Kamiya Bar Web site, www.kamiya-bar.com/02.html.

69. My analysis is based primarily on the first edition of the text (published in March 1887), in the possession of Waseda University in Tokyo. Unless otherwise noted, page numbers for subsequent quotations refer to this edition and are cited parenthetically. I have also consulted the third edition (published in June 1887, after *Yōkai gendan*), archived at the National Diet Library. This text is slightly longer (forty-six pages) and contains some changes, particularly concerning Kokkuri's importation into Japan. Ichiyanagi's discussion appears to rely primarily on this later edition. Both editions were priced at twenty sen.

70. Ryōkū, *Seiyō kijutsu Kokkuri kaidan*, 3rd ed., 17–20. Ryōkū disputes Enryō's Shimoda explanation, claiming that Kokkuri was originally introduced into the entertainment districts by a Japanese student of physics who had studied in the United States. The allusion to Enryō is not found in the first edition of Ryōkū (March 1887), indicating that it was inserted into the later edition in response to *Yōkai gendan*, published May 2 of the same year.

71. "Human-electricity" is written parenthetically in English with a katakana gloss. Although the direct source of the "human electricity" concept is unclear, such notions—often associated with hypnotism and medical treatment—had been popular in the United States and Britain from mid century. See Dods, *Philosophy of Electro-Biology;* Winter, *Mesmerized,* 81–84.

72. A remarkably similar example is given in Suzuki Manjirō, *Dōbutsu denki gairon* (Jūjiya, 1885), 6–7, believed to be the first text to introduce mesmerism to Japan.

73. Max Weber, "Science as a Vocation," in *From Max Weber: Essays in Sociology,* ed. H. H. Gerth and C. Wright Mills (New York: Oxford University Press, 1958), 155. Weber's "disenchantment of the world" may have been taken from Schiller. See Alex Owen, *The Place of Enchantment: British Occultism and the Culture of the Modern* (Chicago: University of Chicago Press, 2004), 10–11.

74. This pamphlet-style broadsheet is archived at the National Diet Library. Its price is marked at 2 *sen,* 5 *ri.*

75. Richard Bauman and Charles L. Briggs, *Voices of Modernity: Language Ideologies and the Politics of Inequality* (Cambridge: Cambridge University Press, 2003), 4. Bauman and Briggs are summarizing the ideas in Bruno Latour, *We Have Never Been Modern* (Cambridge: Harvard University Press, 1993).

76. Oppenheim, *Other World,* 111–58.

77. Ryōkū also notes that, "in one region, the custom that was very popular . . . was to play the *shamisen* and sing, etc., really raising a commotion until by the end they were chanting, 'Kokkuri-sama, please come down.'" *Seiyō kijutsu Kokkuri kaidan,* 14.

78. Shōyō was personally acquainted with Enryō and an original member of the Fushigi kenkyūkai.

79. Also called Konishi Gikei; dates unknown.

80. Tsubouchi Shōyō, "Kaki no heta," *Shōyō senshū bessatsu* (Dai ichi shobō, 1977), 4:472–73.

81. Figal, *Civilization and Monsters*, 199.

82. *Meiji nyūsu jiten*, 230. The article, titled "Kami oroshi to Kokkuri ryūkō," appeared in the *Asahi shinbun* of July 16, 1886.

83. Schneider, *Culture and Enchantment*, 39–40.

84. "Seiyō no Kokkuri-san," *Yomiuri Shinbun*, Sunday supplement, May 17, 1903, p. 1. The article is based on a report by Inoue Enryō.

CHAPTER 4. MUSEUM OF THE WEIRD

Epigraph: Michel de Certeau, *The Practice of Everyday Life*, trans. Steven Rendall (Berkeley: University of California Press, 1984), 108.

1. Kōjin Karatani, *Origins of Modern Japanese Literature* (Durham, NC: Duke University Press, 1993), 21. Karatani does not explicitly discuss the train in this context, but he locates the "discovery of the landscape" in the third decade of Meiji, as trains were becoming an increasing presence throughout Japan.

2. Matsutani Miyoko, *Gendai no minwa: Anata mo katarite, watashi mo katarite* (Chūkōshinsho, 2000), 34–35. Stories of kitsune and tanuki causing mischief along the train tracks were widely distributed. See Matsutani Miyoko, *Gendai minwakō* (Rippū shobō, 1985), 3:13–47; Nomura Jun'ichi, *Edo Tōkyō no uwasa-banashi: 'Konna ban' kara 'Kuchi-sake-onna' made* (Taishūkan shoten, 2005), 200–210.

3. The relationship of modern academia with hypnosis *(saiminjutsu)*, clairvoyance *(senrigan)*, thoughtography *(nensha)*, etc., was complex and controversial. Particularly notorious were the parapsychological investigations of Fukurai Tomokichi (1869–1952), an assistant professor at Tokyo Imperial University. After the so-called senrigan incident of 1911, in which the subject of clairvoyance experiments committed suicide, Fukurai was forced to resign his position. See Ichiyanagi Hirotaka, *Saiminjutsu no Nihon kindai* (Seikyūsha, 1997), 103–55; Ichiyanagi, *"Kokkuri-san" to "Senrigan": Nihon kindai to shinreigaku* (Kōdansha, 1994), 100–184; Matsuyama Iwao, *Uwasa no enkinhō* (Kōdansha, 1997), 153–84. Parapsychology also found a place in some organized religious movements during this time. See Helen Hardacre, "Asano Wasaburō and Japanese Spiritualism in Early Twentieth-Century Japan," in *Japan's Competing Modernities: Issues in Culture and Democracy, 1900–1930*, ed. Sharon A. Minichiello (Honolulu: University of Hawai'i Press, 1998), 133–53; also Lisette Gebhardt, "The 'Other World' in the Light of a New Science: Spiritism in Modern Japan," in *Practicing the Afterlife: Perspectives from Japan*, ed. Susanne Formanek and William R. LaFleur (Vienna: Verlag der Österreichischen Akademie der Wissenschaften, 2004), 383–96.

4. Tomi Suzuki, *Narrating the Self: Fictions of Japanese Modernity* (Stanford: Stanford University Press, 1996), 10.

5. This chapter does not explicitly engage with Japanese Naturalism *(shizenshugi)* and the so-called I-novel *(watakushi shōsetsu)*, but my use of "self" (denoted variously in Japanese as *jiga, jibun, jiko, watakushi*) reflects discourses that

surrounded these ideas in the early twentieth century. I assume a process—of discovery, construction, definition—reflecting the position of "self" as "a master signifier whose signifieds remained vague and fluid." Suzuki, *Narrating*, 40. That is, self is a discursive construction similar to the modern notion of the "subject," which "is not self-contained, as it were, but is immediately cast into conflict with forces that dominate it in some way or another—social formations, language, political apparatuses, and so on." Paul Smith, *Discerning the Subject* (Minneapolis: University of Minnesota Press, 1988), xxxiv. The narrators in these stories by Sōseki and Ōgai find themselves in a world in which such "social formations, language, [and] political apparatuses" are in a particular flux. The self is *subjected* to the ideology of modernity and constituted by a dialectic between putatively exterior forces and an interiority that is itself a product of other ideologies (traditions, "superstitions," "premodern" knowledge). This is complicated by the fact that Sōseki and Ōgai (and their major protagonists) are intellectual elites central to the creation and promulgation of the very ideologies through which their own subjectivities are constituted. An implicit awareness of this complex subject position lies at the heart of the struggle experienced in these stories. Similarly, the discursive construction of national identity in which Yanagita and others were engaged can be thought of as the constitution of a communal self, fraught with the same sort of contradictions and ambiguities as the process of defining individual selfhood. Throughout this book I invoke such dualisms as self/other and modern/premodern because they are heuristically valuable (and often contemporaneously relevant) for framing the multifarious discourses explored, but I underscore that such terms are always implicitly within quotation marks, never absolute or freestanding but always contingent and interconnected.

6. "Koto no sorane" originally appeared in *Shichinin* 7 (May 1905): 25–69. All references in the current chapter are from Natsume Sōseki, "Koto no sorane," *Natsume Sōseki zenshū*, vol. 2 (Chikuma shobō, 1995), and are noted parenthetically. The word *sorane* in the title refers to sounds that are not really there—what I translate as "empty sounds," but which could also perhaps be rendered as "imagined sounds." An English translation of the story creatively but appropriately translates the title as "Hearing Things": see Natsume Sōseki, *Ten Nights of Dream, Hearing Things, The Heredity of Taste*, trans. Aiko Itō and Graeme Wilson (Rutland, VT: Charles E. Tuttle, 1974).

7. Inoue Enryō may have been the model for Tsuda. See Gerald Figal, *Civilization and Monsters: Spirits of Modernity in Modern Japan* (Durham, NC: Duke University Press, 1999), 39.

8. Similar accounts of what are sometimes called "crisis apparitions"—when a person mysteriously appears to others on the day of his or her death—are common. For examples from Japan, see Matsutani, *Gendai minwakō* 4:335–68.

9. For a detailed discussion of Gokurakusui and other locations mentioned in Sōseki's text, see Takeda Katsuhiko, *Sōseki no Tōkyō* (Waseda Daigaku shuppanbu, 1997), 5–32.

10. The quote is from Michel de Certeau, *The Practice of Everyday Life*, trans. Steven Rendall (Berkeley: University of California Press, 1984), 103.

11. The narrator's uncertainty about what to believe, his movement between

a mystic and scientific landscape is reminiscent of Freud's discussion of the uncanny: "Nowadays we no longer believe in them, we have *surmounted* these modes of thought; but we do not feel quite sure of our new beliefs, and the old ones still exist within us ready to seize upon any confirmation. As soon as something actually happens in our lives which seems to confirm the old, discarded beliefs we get a feeling of the uncanny." Sigmund Freud, "The 'Uncanny,'" in *Writings on Art and Literature* (Stanford: Stanford University Press, 1997), 224.

12. For more on "nerves" (shinkei) in the Meiji cultural imagination, see Kawamura Kunimitsu, *Genshi suru kindai kūkan: Meishin, byōki, zashikirō, aruiwa rekishi no kioku* (Seikyūsha, 1997), 100–121; also Daniel Cuong O'Neill, "Ghostly Feelings in Meiji and Early Taishō Literature" (PhD diss., Yale University, 2002), 20–60. For O'Neill's analysis of "Koto no sorane," see 84–105.

13. J. Thomas Rimer, *Mori Ōgai* (Boston: Twayne Publishers, 1975), 20.

14. "Hebi," in *Mori Ōgai zenshū* (Chikuma shobō, 1995), 3:22. Hereafter cited parenthetically in the text. An English translation can also be found in *Youth and Other Stories*, ed. J. Thomas Rimer (Honolulu: University of Hawai'i Press, 1994), 88–101.

15. "Masui," in *Mori Ōgai zenshū* (Chikuma shobō, 1995), 1:188. Hereafter cited parenthetically in the text.

16. Ōgai uses the German word here with no gloss or explanation.

17. Apparently the story is based on an incident experienced by Ōgai's wife; Isogai is modeled on a medical professor who had deep ties to the imperial household. Superficially, if not transparently, Ōgai disguised the referentiality of his narrative by titling it "Masui," a medical term for hypnosis common earlier in Meiji, rather than using "Saimin" or "Saiminjutsu," which were more common when he wrote the story. After the publication of "Masui," Ōgai was apparently reprimanded by Prime Minister Katsura Tarō (1848–1913). See Ichiyanagi, *Saiminjutsu*, 122–38.

18. For more on ero-guro-nansensu in its cultural context, see Jim Reichert, "Deviance and Social Darwinism in Edogawa Ranpo's Erotic-Grotesque Thriller *Kotō no oni*," *Journal of Japanese Studies* 27, no. 1 (Winter 2001): 113–41; also Miriam Silverberg, *Erotic Grotesque Nonsense: The Mass Culture of Japanese Modern Times* (Berkeley: University of California Press, 2006).

19. Ichiyanagi, *Saiminjutsu*, 122.

20. Ibid., 138.

21. "Kompira," in *Mori Ōgai zenshū* (Chikuma shobō, 1995), 1:392. A translation can be found in *Youth and Other Stories*, 102–35.

22. For more on the historical basis of the story and characters, see Higashi Masao, *Hyaku-monogatari no hyaku-kai* (Kadokawa shoten, 2001), 167–71.

23. "Hyaku-monogatari," in *Mori Ōgai zenshū* (Chikuma shobō, 1995), 3:121. Hereafter noted parenthetically in the text. The story has also been translated as "Ghost Stories," in *Youth and Other Stories*, ed. J. Thomas Rimer (Honolulu: University of Hawai'i Press, 1994), 182–96.

24. Of Shitomi's occupation the reader is told only that he indulges in photography. Although the significance of photography in early-twentieth-century Japan is manifold, by mentioning it in the sentence immediately following the

narrator's equation of the effect of hyaku-monogatari with "visual illusion," Ōgai draws a parallel between old forms of illusion and the new technological form known as photography.

25. The Norwegian title, *Gengangere*, is more literally rendered as "Those-Who-Walk-Again." The play was originally published in December 1881 and translated into German in 1884. See Henrik Ibsen, *Ghosts and Other Plays*, trans. Peter Watts (London: Penguin Books, 1964), 291. Ōgai's own interest in Ibsen is well known. *Ghosts* was the second complete Ibsen play he translated; he published it in December of 1911. As "Hyaku-monogatari" was published in October of the same year, one would imagine that his translation work significantly influenced—perhaps inspired—the story. Interestingly, however, unless they had read or seen a European-language version of *Ghosts*, most readers would not have understood Ōgai's references to it until the later publication of his translation and subsequent performance in January of 1912.

26. Ibsen, *Ghosts and Other Plays*, 61.

27. Ibsen is relevant here too: in *Ghosts*, Osvald, a young man stricken with disease from the transgressions of his father, desires constant nursing by the young and beautiful Regina. Ōgai makes this association explicit by mentioning Ibsen again when he ponders the curious relationship of Shikamaya and Tarō ("Hyaku-monogatari," 139).

28. For a discussion of this introspective musing, see Richard John Bowring, *Mori Ōgai and the Modernization of Japanese Culture* (Cambridge: Cambridge University Press, 1979), 133.

29. Freud, "The 'Uncanny,'" 212.

30. Even in its Tokugawa-period manifestation, the practice of hyaku-monogatari was characterized by longing—as narrative after narrative was recounted in order to create a desired "authentic" experience of the mystic.

31. The quote is from Susan Stewart, *On Longing: Narratives of the Miniature, the Gigantic, the Souvenir, the Collection* (Durham, NC: Duke University Press, 1993), 23.

32. This latter translation, most prominent in the work of H. D. Harootunian, also gestures to the links between nativist scholarship of the Edo period and the burgeoning nationalism of the interwar period during which minzokugaku began to flourish. Although I do not focus on Yanagita's minzokugaku per se, many issues treated here are pertinent to the development of this controversial discipline. For more in English, see for example Figal, *Civilization and Monsters;* Marilyn Ivy, *Discourses of the Vanishing: Modernity, Phantasm, Japan* (Chicago: University of Chicago Press, 1995); Alan S. Christy, "Representing the Rural: Place as Method in the Formation of Japanese Native Ethnology, 1910–1945" (PhD diss., University of Chicago, 1997); H. D. Harootunian, *Overcome by Modernity: History, Culture, and Community in Interwar Japan* (Princeton: Princeton University Press, 2000); Mariko Asano Tamanoi, "Gender, Nationalism, and Japanese Native Ethnology," *positions* 4, no. 1 (1996): 59–86; Ronald A. Morse, *Yanagita Kunio and the Folklore Movement: The Search for Japan's National Character and Distinctiveness* (New York: Garland Publishing, 1990); Kawada Minoru, *The Origin of Ethnography in Japan: Yanagita Kunio and His Times*, trans. Toshiko Kishida-Ellis (London: Kegan Paul International, 1993).

33. H. D. Harootunian, *Things Seen and Unseen: Discourses and Ideology in Tokugawa Nativism* (Chicago: University of Chicago Press, 1988), 416.

34. For more on *Tōno monogatari* as a literary text, particularly its position with respect to Naturalism, see Iwamoto Yoshiteru, *Mō hitotsu no Tōno monogatari* (Tōsui shobō, 1983), 103–19; Figal, *Civilization and Monsters*, 127–30, 134–37; Ivy, *Discourses of the Vanishing*, 92–97.

35. Ivy, *Discourses of the Vanishing*, 72.

36. Yanagita Kunio, *Tōno monogatari*, in *Teihon Yanagita Kunio shū* (Chikuma shobō, 1970), 4:6. Hereafter noted parenthetically.

37. Flat description was a technique used by Tayama Katai (1871–1930) and the Naturalists. For more on Yanagita's version, see Figal, *Civilization and Monsters*, 122–26; Iwamoto, *Mō hitotsu no Tōno monogatari*, 103–19. For a discussion of Yanagita's early writing on literary style, see Melek Ortabasi, "Sketching Out the Critical Tradition: Yanagita Kunio and the Reappraisal of Realism," *Japanese Poeticity and Narrativity Revisited: Proceedings of the Association for Japanese Literary Studies* 4 (Summer 2003): 184–93.

38. See Iwamoto, *Mō hitotsu no Tōno monogatari*; Ivy, *Discourses of the Vanishing*, 66–97; Figal, *Civilization and Monsters*, 105–12.

39. See Ivy, *Discourses of the Vanishing*, 70–71.

40. Michel de Certeau with Dominique Julia and Jacques Revel, "Beauty of the Dead: Nissard," in *Heterologies: Discourse on the Other*, by Michel de Certeau, trans. Brian Massumi (Minneapolis: University of Minnesota Press, 1997), 123.

41. Ibid., 136.

42. Harootunian, *Overcome*, 316.

43. Karatani, *Origins of Modern Japanese Literature*, 33.

44. Clifford's comments on salvage ethnography could easily be applied to Yanagita's minzokugaku: "I do not wish to deny specific cases of disappearing customs and languages, or to challenge the value of recording such phenomena. I do, however, question the assumption that with rapid change something essential ('culture'), a coherent differential identity, vanishes. And I question, too, the mode of scientific and moral authority associated with salvage, or redemptive, ethnography. It is assumed that the other society is weak and 'needs' to be represented by an outsider (and that what matters in its life is past, not present or future). The recorder and interpreter of fragile custom is custodian of an essence, unimpeachable witness to authenticity." James Clifford, "On Ethnographic Allegory," in *Writing Culture: The Politics and Poetics of Ethnography*, ed. James Clifford and George E. Marcus (Berkeley: University of California Press, 1986), 112–13.

45. Harootunian, *Overcome*, 319.

46. Figal, *Civilization and Monsters*, 215. See also Figal's discussion (116–17) of "Yūmeidan" (Discussions of the Hidden World; 1905), Yanagita's first scholarly essay on yōkai, which includes specific critical references to Enryō.

47. Miyata Noboru, *Yōkai no minzokugaku: Nihon no mienai kūkan* (Iwanami shoten, 1985), 46–47; also Ichiyanagi Hirotaka, "'Yōkai' to iu ba: Inoue Enryō, 'yōkaigaku' no ichi," in *Nihon shisō no kanōsei*, ed. Suzuki Tadashi and Yamaryō Kenji (Satsuki shobō, 1997), 83–84.

48. "Genkaku no jikken," in *Teihon Yanagita Kunio shū* (Chikuma shobō, 1970), 4:330–31. Hereafter cited parenthetically in the text.

49. Figal poses the possibility "that the literariness of *Tōno monogatari* or even the poetry he wrote prior to it opened the way to an alternative form of human science." *Civilization and Monsters*, 137.

50. Harootunian, *Overcome*, 323.

51. See Ivy, *Discourses of the Vanishing*, 94.

52. "Yōkai dangi," in *Teihon Yanagita Kunio shū* (Chikuma shobō, 1970), 4:376.

53. See Yanagita, "Hitotsume-kozō," in *Teihon Yanagita Kunio shū* (Chikuma shobō, 1969), 5:113–59. Hereafter cited parenthetically in the text. In this essay, Yanagita clearly states his archeological methodology of minzokugaku: "Since customs, popular beliefs, and legends are created by humans, they must have meaning in a human way. Even when something seems to be meaningless to a person today, all the more deeply is the thing buried" (153). "Hitotsume-kozō" was first published in August 1917 in *Tōkyō nichi nichi shinbun*. It was reprinted in 1934 along with a number of other essays in a separate volume titled *Hitotsume kozō sono ta*. This essay should not be confused with another, much shorter essay, also titled "Hitotsume-kozō," that was originally published several months earlier and reprinted later (see *Teihon* 4:411–12). Translating the word *kozō* is difficult: although strictly speaking it refers to a Buddhist acolyte, it is also commonly used to signify a boy and may have a slightly derogative or casual tone, as in "kid" or "rascal."

54. Akasaka Norio discusses this essay and Yanagita's view of human sacrifice, what he calls the "folklore of cruelty," with respect to Minakata Kumagusu's perspective on similar issues. *Yanagita Kunio no yomikata: Mō hitotsu no minzokugaku wa kanō ka* (Chikuma shinsho, 1994), 38–51. See also Iijima Yoshiharu, *Hitotsume kozō to hyōtan: Sei to gisei no fōkuroa* (Shinyōsha, 2001), 18–43.

55. Yanagita's willingness to deal with unattractive aspects of Japanese culture was not consistent throughout his career.

56. Harootunian *Overcome*, 309, 308. Harootunian is describing the broader "task" of minzokugaku's investigation of "stories, beliefs, and artifacts," of which yōkai are only one part.

57. The work can be found in *Ema Tsutomu chosaku shū*, vol. 6 (Chūōkōron sha, 1977). Hereafter cited parenthetically in the text.

58. Ema describes the discipline: "The study of fūzoku is both the study of the things [koto] upon which abstract spiritual phenomena are based, and the study of the things [mono] upon which concrete phenomena are based. Within this there are two sides: the individual thing and the social thing. The first subject of study is the social thing, and afterward the individual thing. Since society is a collective of individuals, however, society cannot exist without the individual; while taking up each individual's fūzoku and researching that particular fūzoku, we simultaneously research the social fūzoku in order to take as our object the trends and fashions of each time period." See "Nihon fūzoku bunkashi," in *Ema Tsutomu chosaku shū* (Chūōkōron sha, 1975), 1:7–8. For another attempt at definition and brief historical discussion, see Nihon fūzokushi gakkai, ed., *Nihon fūzokushi jiten* (Kōbundō, 1994), 555–58. The study of customs and

everyday life was also the purview of *kōgengaku*, or "modernology," a discipline developed by Kon Wajirō (1888–1973). Kōgengaku's focus on documenting the present distinguishes it from the historical approach taken by Ema's fūzokushigaku. For more on kōgengaku, see Miriam Silverberg, "Constructing the Ethnography of Modernity," *Journal of Asian Studies* 51, no. 1 (February 1992), 30–54; also Silverberg, *Erotic Grotesque Nonsense*.

59. See, for example, Ema's complex taxonomical chart of the different categories and subcategories of yōkai-henge (*Ema Tsutomu chosaku shū* 6:394–95).

60. Ema's classifications are almost obsessive in their detail. "This-worldly" and "transmigratory" henge, for example, can each be divided further into "spiritual" (*seishinteki*) or "material" (*jittaiteki*) transformations. And even a yūrei is not just a yūrei but is more accurately delineated as "shiryō; ikiryō; yūrei. A shiryō is when, after death, the spirit performs actions without assuming a temporary form. An ikiryō is when the spirit of a living person separates and travels and performs actions. And a yūrei is when after death, the 'empty shell' of the body's form acts" (ibid., 374).

61. Komatsu Kazuhiko, *Yōkaigaku shinkō: Yōkai kara miru Nihonjin no kokoro* (Shōgakkan, 1994), 14.

62. Other than "Hitotsume-kozō," Yanagita's most substantial early essays on yōkai can be found in his *Santō mindan shū*, originally published in 1914; see *Teihon Yanagita Kunio shū* (Chikuma shobō, 1970), 27:41–179. Other relevant pre-Ema essays include "Tanuki to demonorojii," of 1918 (*Teihon* 22:467–73), and "Yūrei shisō no hensen," of 1917 (*Teihon* 15:562–68). In 1956, Yanagita released *Yōkai dangi* (Discussions of Monsters), a collection of thirty essays published originally in a variety of sources—from scholarly journals to newspapers—between 1910 and 1939. (Some essays originally appeared under pseudonyms.) See *Teihon* 4:287–438. In the preface, Yanagita explains that yōkai were among his earliest concerns, and that even now, in the midst of "this glittering new culture" (289), the mysterious has not been explained away.

63. Komatsu, *Yōkaigaku shinkō*, 15.

64. The glossary is reprinted as the final "essay" in the *Yōkai dangi* collection. See "Yōkai meii," *Teihon Yanagita Kunio shū* (Chikuma shobō, 1970), 4:424–38. Hereafter cited parenthetically in the text.

65. The distinction here concerns the difference between legend *(densetsu)* and folktale *(mukashibanashi* or *minwa)*. Simply put, legend usually implies belief on the part of either, or both, the teller and the listener and often includes specific details regarding time and place. Folktales, on the other hand, are usually told as fictional stories for purposes of entertainment and are separated from everyday "true" discourse by codified rhetorical markers ("once upon a time"; "mukashi mukashi" [long, long ago]). Yanagita's point is that the tales told as legends have lost the element of belief and come to be told as folktales for purposes of entertainment. See also "Yōkai dangi," *Teihon* 4:301–3. In his glossary, Yanagita is most interested in yōkai that still exist in legend.

66. Freely translated, *obake* might be "monster," while *yūrei* would be "ghost." Yanagita uses *obake* and *bakemono* interchangeably. Although he never states this explicitly, he includes all these labels under the broader rubric of *yōkai*.

67. Komatsu, *Yōkaigaku shinkō,* 16–17.

68. The word *reiraku* might also be translated as "fallen" or "reduced," but "degraded" captures the simple sense of a downgrading in status along with the loss of dignity implied by such a fall. See Yanagita, "Hitotsume-kozō," 5:125.

69. "Tanuki to demonorojii," *Teihon* 22:467–73.

70. Tessa Morris-Suzuki, *Re-Inventing Japan: Time, Space, Nation* (Armonk: M. E. Sharpe, 1998), 72.

71. Yanagita outlines his ideas on the greetings of twilight in "Yōkai dangi" (4:291–307) and again in "Kawatare-toki" (*Teihon Yanagita Kunio shū* [Chikuma shobō, 1970] 4:308–10).

72. See particularly "Yōkai koi" (in *Teihon Yanagita Kunio shū* [Chikuma shobō, 1970], 4:311–24) and "Obake no koe" (in *Teihon* 4:325–28). In her discussion of schoolgirl speech, Miyako Inoue illustrates how eavesdropping and similar "citational practices" constitute the male intellectual "as a listening subject uniquely situated in the context of late-nineteenth- and early-twentieth-century modernizing Japan." *Vicarious Language: Gender and Linguistic Modernity in Japan* (Berkeley: University of California Press, 2006), 40. In a similar fashion, Yanagita's recording of children's games makes yōkai (and the children who play with them) into modernity's Other and, simultaneously, establishes his (and his readers') own modern subject position.

73. "Tanuki to demonorojii," *Teihon* 22:471–72.

74. Stefan Tanaka, *New Times in Modern Japan* (Princeton: Princeton University Press, 2004), 76.

75. Terada Torahiko, "Bakemono no shinka," in *Terada Torahiko zuihitsushū* (Iwanami bunko, 1993), 2:204.

76. As evidenced by his mention of Yanagita in this fictional text, Akutagawa was conversant not only with kappa beliefs but also with the folkloric discourse about these beliefs. See Akutagawa Ryūnosuke, *Kappa* (Iwanami shoten, 1996), 34.

77. Reichert, "Deviance and Social Darwinism," 114.

78. Komatsu Kazuhiko, interview by author, mini disk recording, Kyoto, Japan, November 27, 2000.

CHAPTER 5. MEDIA OF THE WEIRD

1. See, for example, William Tsutsui, *Godzilla on My Mind: Fifty Years of the King of Monsters* (New York: Palgrave Macmillan, 2004); William M. Tsutsui and Michiko Ito, eds., *In Godzilla's Footsteps: Japanese Pop Culture Icons on the Global Stage* (New York: Palgrave Macmillan, 2006); Kobayashi Toyomasa, *Gojira no ronri* (Chūkei shuppan, 1992); Takahashi Toshio, *Gojira no nazo: Kaijū shinwa to Nihonjin* (Kōdansha, 1998); Yoshikuni Igarashi, *Bodies of Memory: Narratives of War in Postwar Japanese Culture, 1945–1970* (Princeton: Princeton University Press, 2000), 114–22; Anne Allison, *Millennial Monsters: Japanese Toys and the Global Imagination* (Berkeley: University of California Press, 2006), 40–51.

2. Generally, *kaijū* evokes a corporeality distinct from the elusive, shape-shifting image usually associated with yōkai. In a survey I conducted of fifteen yōkai en-

thusiasts, including a number of published researchers, fourteen classified Gojira as kaijū as opposed to yōkai (March 30, 2001). Saitō Jun posits that the associations of kaijū change with historical context; movies such as *King Kong* and *Gojira* have played a large part in influencing the current conception. See "Yōkai to kaijū," in *Yōkai henge*, ed. Tsunemitsu Tōru (Chikuma shobō, 1999), 66–101.

3. Tsutsui explains that "the design of the Godzilla suit was drawn from picture books of dinosaurs—as well as some illustrations in an issue of *Life* magazine—and the distinctive physical appearance of the monster was formed from a fossil-record-be-damned fusion of Tyrannosaurus rex, Iguanodon, and Stegosaurus." *Godzilla on My Mind*, 23.

4. Igarashi, *Bodies of Memory*, 117.

5. For an overview of Gojira sequels and other kaijū eiga, see Tsutsui, *Godzilla on My Mind*, 177–204.

6. Abe Kazue, *Yōkaigaku nyūmon* (Yūsankaku, 1971), 3.

7. "Rabbit hutches" *(usagi-goya)* was noted by the *Asahi* newspaper as being one of the "buzzwords" *(hayari kotoba)* for the first half of 1979. "Hayari kotoba hakusho: 79nen zenhan," *Asahi shinbun*, evening ed., July 10, 1979, p. 7.

8. Jennifer Robertson, *Native and Newcomer: Making and Remaking a Japanese City* (Berkeley: University of California Press, 1991), 26.

9. Adachi Noriyuki, *Yōkai to aruku: Hyōden, Mizuki Shigeru* (Bungei shunjū, 1994), 58.

10. For more on the relationship of kami shibai to the manga industry, see Fujishima Usaku, *Sengo manga no minzokugakushi* (Kawai Shuppan, 1990), 2–18. Kashi-hon manga existed before the war but especially flourished in the 1950s, when kashi-hon shops were nicknamed "libraries for the common folk" *(shomin no toshokan)*. Adachi suggests that the rapid decline of the kashi-hon manga industry was presaged by the increase of televisions in private households, particularly spurred by the royal wedding of 1959. *Yōkai to aruku*, 42–43. For more on the rise and fall of kashi-hon manga, see Fujishima, who suggests that economic security contributed to an increasing interest in more professionally produced comics. *Sengo manga no minzokugakushi*, 46–76.

11. See Mizuki Shigeru, *Gensō sekai e no tabi, yōkai wandārando* (Chikuma bunko, 1995), 3:11–42. "Terebi-kun" was originally published in *Bessatsu shōnen magajin* of August 15, 1965, but has been reprinted numerous times.

12. In the episode ("Kitarō no tanjō") concerning Kitarō's birth, the eyeball that becomes Medama-oyaji is the sole remnant of Kitarō's father after he melts away through disease. The eyeball remains to watch over Kitarō as he grows up in the human world. See Mizuki Shigeru, *Chūkō aizōban Gegege no Kitarō* (Chūōkōronsha, 1994), 1:5–49; originally published in March 1966 in *Garo*, a monthly manga anthology. With his monstrous but caring father, Kitarō might be contrasted with that other charming boy-hero of postatomic manga and anime, Tezuka Osamu's Tetsuwan Atom (Astro Boy), a high-tech robot created by a human technocrat father. Both Kitarō and Atom are outsiders in human society (the one a yōkai, the other a robot), and both represent a kind of nostalgia, Kitarō for a mysterious utopian past and Atom for a techno-haunted utopian future. For more on Tetsuwan Atom, see Allison, *Millennial Monsters*, 51–65.

13. Mizuki Shigeru, *Nonnonbā to ore* (Chikuma bunko, 1997), 28.

14. Yanagita, "Yōkai meii," *Teihon Yanagita Kunio shū* (Chikuma shobō, 1970), 4:428. Although Yanagita lists this yōkai as a *suna-kake-baba* (with a short final vowel), Mizuki presents it with a long final vowel, "babā."

15. Ibid., 431.

16. Similarly, Kyōgoku Natsuhiko discusses the transformation of another Mizuki character, Konaki-jijii (Old Man Crying Like a Baby) from a local phenomenon into a "national 'character.'" "Tsūzoku 'yōkai' gainen no seiritsu ni kansuru ichi kōsatsu," in *Nihon yōkaigaku taizen,* ed. Komatsu Kazuhiko (Shōgakkan, 2003), 547. By tracing Konaki-jijii back to its point of origin in Shikoku, researchers have charted the way in which a "word used on the family level" (551) to denote a particular old man who could imitate the crying of a baby develops, through Yanagita and eventually Mizuki, into a nationally known yōkai figure (547–52); also Higashi Masao, *Yōkai densetsu kibun* (Gakken, 2005), 246–58.

17. Having said this, I should note that Kitarō has also appeared in an encyclopedic format, where Mizuki explains, "This is a made-up story, but having thought about it for many years, this yōkai took shape in my head. All the yōkai in this book actually might exist (well, you can't actually see them, but . . .) so I wanted to put [Kitarō] into this group." Mizuki Shigeru, *Yōkai gadan* (Iwanami shoten, 1994), 152.

18. Mizuki Shigeru, *Zusetsu Nihon yōkai taizen* (Kōdansha, 1994), 337.

19. Mizuki Shigeru, "Me ni mienai mono o miru," in *Yōkai tengoku* (Chikuma bunko, 1996), 66. Emphasis in original.

20. Mizuki, *Zusetsu Nihon yōkai taizen,* 447.

21. Ibid., 391.

22. Donald Keene, trans., *Essays in Idleness: The Tsurezuregusa of Kenkō* (New York: Columbia University Press, 1967), 50–51.

23. Inada Atsunobu and Tanaka Naohi, eds. *Toriyama Sekien gazu hyakkiyagyō* (Kokusho kankōkai, 1999), 273. Sekien's entry is typically packed with verbal and visual punning. Tada Katsumi suggests that the appearance of the tenjō-name itself is a play on the Edo-period fire companies: the monster's clothing, mane, and fingers resemble a *matoi,* the frilly flaglike banner carried by the firemen: "Etoki gazu hyakkiyagyō no yōkai," *Kai* 12 (December 2001): 320–21.

24. Mizuki Shigeru, *Zoku yōkai jiten* (Tōkyōdō shuppan, 1984), 152–53.

25. Komatsu discusses the geographic and cultural similarities between Mizuki's Sakaiminato and Yanagita's Tōno. *Yōkaigaku shinkō: Yōkai kara miru Nihonjin no kokoro* (Shōgakkan, 1994), 53–61, 77–94.

26. All citations here are taken from a 1997 edition and noted parenthetically in the text.

27. Iwai Hiromi, *Kurashi no naka no yōkai* (Bunka shuppankyoku, 1986), 139–40. Iwai includes Sekien's illustration.

28. Komatsu, *Yōkaigaku shinkō,* 63. Murakami Kenji suggests that the tenjō-name is a Sekien invention that plays off notions of ceilings as boundaries between this world and the other. *Yōkai jiten* (Mainichi shinbunsha, 2000), 235.

29. Adachi, *Yōkai to aruku,* 19.

30. Ibid., 285–87.

31. "As a child," Mizuki explains, "whenever I heard a yōkai story, I would

draw an image in my head. In other words, having heard of it, the shape would take form; so when I first had a chance to look at Sekien's illustrations, I knew most of the yōkai without even looking at the names." "Yōkai no 'katachi' konjaku," in *Yōkai tengoku* (Chikuma bunko, 1996), 46.

32. Jorge Luis Borges, *Labyrinths: Selected Stories and Other Writings* (New York: New Directions, 1964), 18.

33. For example, Mizuki illustrates the scene in which Nonnonbā points out stains on the ceiling—although he does not draw the tenjō-name itself. Mizuki Shigeru, *Komikku Shōwa-shi* (Kōdansha komikkusu, 1994), 1:57–58. See figure 19, page 175.

34. The final volume of the series includes, appropriately, two parallel datelines—one for the Shōwa period and one for Mizuki Shigeru. *Komikku Shōwa-shi* (Kōdansha komikkusu, 1994), 8:270–73.

35. Mizuki Shigeru, *Musume ni kataru otōsan no senki* (Kawade shobō shinsha, 1995), 148–49. Hereafter cited parenthetically in the text.

36. Mizuki's lionization of the local people is unusual; most other Japanese memoirists of the war in Rabaul write disparagingly of the natives and their lifestyle. See Iwamoto Hiromitsu, "Japanese and New Guinean Memories of Wartime Experiences at Rabaul" (paper delivered at the symposium "Remembering the War in New Guinea," Australian National University, Canberra, October 19–21, 2000). http://ajrp.awm.gov.au/ajrp/remember.nsf/pages/NT00002B7E.

37. Mizuki Shigeru, *Rabauru jūgunkōki: Topetoro to no gojūnen* (Chūōkōron shinsha, 2002), 18.

38. Ibid., 150.

39. Komatsu, *Yōkaigaku shinkō*, 66.

40. Mizuki Shigeru, *Umareta toki kara 'yōkai' datta* (Kōdansha, 2002), 147.

41. See the discussion of this episode in Kyōgoku Natsuhiko, Tada Katsumi, and Murakami Kenji, *Yōkai baka* (Shinchō OH! bunko, 2001), 241–42.

42. Mizuki Shigeru, *Yōkai nandemo nyūmon* (Shōgakkan, 1974), 10.

43. Ibid., 11.

44. From Shizuoka Prefecture, cited in Saitō Shūhei, "Uwasa no fōkuroa: Kuchi-sake-onna no denshō oboegaki," *Kenkyū kiyō* 7 (March 30, 1992): 90.

45. The Kuchi-sake-onna narrative could arguably be referred to by any number of terms: contemporary legend, urban legend, rumor, anecdote, memorate, or simply hearsay. For the purposes of the present discussion, I generally use the expression "contemporary legend" (or simply "legend"). For more on such terminology, see Gary Alan Fine, *Manufacturing Tales: Sex and Money in Contemporary Legends* (Knoxville: University of Tennessee Press, 1992), 1–4; Patricia A. Turner, *I Heard It through the Grapevine: Rumor in African-American Culture* (Berkeley: University of California Press, 1993), 1–5. For terminology within Japanese folkloristics, see Miyamoto Naokazu, "'Kodomo no ryūgen' kenkyū: Otona no miru kodomo no genjitsu to kodomo no genjitsu" (PhD diss., Kanagawa University Graduate School of History and Folk Culture Studies, Yokohama, 1998), 5–10.

46. Asakura Kyōji, "Ano 'Kuchi-sake-onna' no sumika o Gifu sanchū ni mita!" in *Uwasa no hon*, vol. 92 of *Bessatsu takarajima*, ed. Ishii Shinji (JICC Shuppan kyoku, 1989), 138–40. Asakura bases his information on a report from

Shūkan asahi, which claims the rumor started in the town of Yaotsuchō in Gifu Prefecture. See Hiraizumi Etsurō, "Zenkoku no shō-chū-gakusei o osoresaseru 'Kuchi-sake-onna' fūsetsu no kiki kaikai," *Shūkan asahi,* June 29, 1979, pp. 16–20.

47. Kinoshita Tomio, "Gendai no uwasa kara kōtōdenshō no hassei mekanizumu o saguru: 'Kuchi-sake-onna' no uwasa o daizai toshite," in *Ryūgen, uwasa, soshite jōhō: Uwasa no kenkyūshū taisei,* ed. Satō Tatsuya (Shibundō, 1999), 14.

48. It is difficult to locate the engine of Kuchi-sake-onna's initial diffusion across the country, but evidence suggests that it involved a combination of word of mouth and media. Miyamoto notes that, while younger children heard the rumor first from classmates, university students often heard it first from media sources. "'Kodomo no ryūgen' kenkyū," 17, 20. Asakura suggests that mass media had a particularly large impact in the Osaka area. "Ano 'Kuchi-sake-onna,'" 140. Early print media reports of the legend include *Gifu nichi nichi shinbun,* January 26, 1979; "Kuchi-sake-onna densetsu ga kyō ni tassuru," *Shūkan asahi,* March 23, 1979, pp. 35–36; "Kakuchi ni tobu kimyō na uwasa," *Shūkan shinchō,* April 5, 1979, pp. 128–29.

49. Example from Tokyo in Saitō, "Uwasa no fōkuroa," 92–93.

50. Ibid., 91.

51. Nomura Jun'ichi, *Nihon no sekenbanashi* (Tōkyō shoseki, 1995), 51.

52. "'Kuchi-sake-onna' tte honto?" *Asahi shinbun,* July 8, 1979, p. 32.

53. Asakura, "Ano 'Kuchi-sake-onna,'" 140. Asakura lists specific place names for these occurrences but does not provide sources for this information.

54. Kinoshita, "Gendai no uwasa," 19–23; Miyamoto, "'Kodomo no ryūgen' kenkyū," 19–20.

55. Tanaka Kakuei, *Nihon rettō kaizō ron* (Nikkan kōgyō shinbunsha, 1973), 1–2.

56. See Marilyn Ivy, *Discourses of the Vanishing: Modernity, Phantasm, Japan* (Chicago: University of Chicago Press, 1995), 29–65.

57. "Nihon no shōgakusei ga furue-agatta 'kuchi-sake-onna' no 'rūtsu,'" *Shūkan bunshū,* June 28, 1979, p. 34.

58. Toguri Hiroshi, "'Kuchi-sake-onna' ga imadoki chōryō suru kai," *Shūkan yomiuri,* July 1, 1979, p. 27. The "candy-buying ghost" *(ame-kai yūrei)* is a widely distributed legend in which the ghost of a woman who died pregnant or during childbirth buys candy for her unborn child.

59. The number three appears again and again in the Kuchi-sake-onna cycle—there are often three sisters, for example, and Kuchi-sake-onna comes to be associated with place-names containing the character for *three* (e.g., Sangenjaya, Mitaka). See Nomura, *Nihon no sekenbanashi,* 69; Nomura Jun'ichi, *Edo Tōkyō no uwasa-banashi: 'Konna ban' kara 'Kuchi-sake-onna' made* (Taishūkan shoten, 2005), 125–28.

60. See Nomura, *Edo Tōkyō,* 129–34.

61. Miyata Noboru, *Yōkai no minzokugaku: Nihon no mienai kūkan* (Iwanami shoten, 1985), 22–27.

62. Ibid., 32–33.

63. Satō Kenji, "Uwasa-banashi no shisōshi," in *Uwasa no hon,* vol. 92 of *Bessatsu takarajima,* ed. Ishii Shinji (ICC Shuppan kyoku, 1989), 264.

64. Nomura, *Nihon no sekenbanashi*, 63.

65. The quote is from Nomura, *Edo Tōkyō*, 130.

66. The evolutionary biologist Richard Dawkins first posited the "meme" notion in 1976 to explain how ideas and behaviors are transmitted through imitation in a process analogous to genetics. See *The Selfish Gene* (New York: Oxford University Press, 1976), 203–15.

67. Hiraizumi, "Zenkoku no shō-chū-gakusei," 16–20. The information provided in this article seems to have become accepted fact in subsequent discourse; it is cited, for example, by Asakura and Miyamoto.

68. See, for example, Mizuki, *Zoku yōkai jiten*, 79; Mizuki, *Zusetsu Nihon yōkai taizen*, 182.

69. All quotations from Hiraizumi, "Zenkoku no shō-chū-gakusei," 19–20.

70. The group's name was Pomādo & Kompeitō, and the record was scheduled to be released on August 5, 1979. *Asahi geinō*, July 19, 1979, p. 34; *Shūkan pureibōi*, July 24, 1979, p. 76. A week later, however, *Shūkan pureibōi* featured a follow-up article explaining that the advertising director of King Records had received a phone call from a woman claiming to be Kuchi-sake-onna herself and accusing King Records of attempting to profit from her "distinct physical characteristics." See "Kuchi-sake-onna o shōbai ni suru nante yūki ga iru no da to iu ohanashi," *Shūkan pureibōi*, July 31, 1979, p. 74. According to a King Records executive, the recording was completed but never released (personal communication, 2000). In 2005, however, the single was included on a CD by Teichiku Entertainment featuring a number of "character" related songs.

71. Nakano Osamu, "'Asobi' o shimetsusaseru bunka: 'Kuchi-sake-onna' no haikai," *is* (September 10, 1979): 42–43.

72. Example from Tokyo cited in Saitō, "Uwasa no fōkuroa," 94. The notion that rumor serves as an "improvised" form of information that competes with "official" news sources is the basis of Shibutani's argument in his seminal work, Tamotsu Shibutani, *Improvised News: A Sociological Study of Rumor* (Indianapolis: Bobbs-Merrill, 1966).

73. Example from Tokyo cited in Saitō, "Uwasa no fōkuroa," 93–94.

74. "Hayari kotoba hakusho: 79nen zenhan," p. 7.

75. The distinction between historical and circumstantial origins is discussed by Barbara Allen Bogart, "The 'Image on Glass': Technology, Tradition, and the Emergence of Folkore," in *Contemporary Legend: A Reader*, ed. Gillian Bennett and Paul Smith (New York: Garland Publishing, 1996), 134.

76. Anne Allison, *Permitted and Prohibited Desires: Mothers, Comics, and Censorship in Japan* (Boulder, CO: Westview Press, 1996), 106.

77. See, for example, Miyata, *Yōkai no minzokugaku*, 20.

78. Komatsu Kazuhiko, "'Kuchi-sake-onna' no imiron," in *Oni no tamatebako: Minzoku shakai no kōkan* (Seigensha, 1986), 231. For more on the education-mama debate, see Miyamoto, "'Kodomo no ryūgen' kenkyū," 24–37; Kinoshita, "Gendai no uwasa," 18–19; 22–23. For a psychoanalytic interpretation of the legend, see Akiyama Satoko, "'Kuchi-sake-onna' to shōjo shinri," *Asahi shinbun*, June 25, 1979, p. 15.

79. Nakamura Mareaki, *Kaidan no shinrigaku: Gakkō ni umareru kowai hanashi* (Kōdansha, 1994), 194–98.

80. Satō Kenji, *Ryūgen higo: Uwasabanashi o yomitoku sahō* (Yūshindō, 1995). 182–83.

81. Komatsu, "'Kuchi-sake-onna,'" 232. For an overview of historic female yōkai, see Miyata Noboru, *Hime no minzokugaku* (Seidosha, 1993), 177–88.

82. Komatsu, "'Kuchi-sake-onna' no imiron," 232.

83. See Barbara Creed, *The Monstrous-Feminine: Film, Feminism, Psychoanalysis* (London: Routledge, 1993). For more on the vagina dentata motif, see Jill Raitt, "The *Vagina Dentata* and the *Immaculatus Uterus Divini Fontis*," *Journal of the American Academy of Religion* 48, no. 3 (1980): 415–31; also Elizabeth Grosz, *Space, Time, and Perversion: Essays on the Politics of Bodies* (London: Routledge, 1995), 187–205.

84. Creed, *Monstrous-Feminine,* 109.

85. Ibid., 110.

86. Quoted in Fukasaku Mitsusada, "Tsune ni kienai Nihonjin no animizumu: 'Kuchi-sake-onna' ga kakemawatta ura de," *Gekkan kyōiku no mori* (September 1979): 31. Komatsu explicitly makes this link: "Kuchi-sake-onna is a monster of the female genitalia": "'Kuchi-sake-onna,'" 237–38.

87. Komatsu, "'Kuchi-sake-onna,'" 236–38. The story of Izanami and Izanagi is in both the *Kojiki* and *Nihonshoki.* For analysis of the setsuwa and nō versions of the Dōjōji legend, see Susan B. Klein, "Woman as Serpent: The Demonic Feminine in the Noh Play *Dōjōji,*" in *Religious Reflections on the Human Body,* ed. Jane Marie Law, 100–136 (Bloomington: Indiana University Press, 1995).

88. Masks were originally required only of soldiers and policemen, but eventually the general public was also encouraged to wear them. Shimokawa Kōshi and Katei sōgō kenkyūkai, eds., *Meiji Taishō kateishi nenpyō 1868–1925* (Kawade shobō shinsha, 2000), 429. As early as 1880 a black masklike device called a "respirator" *(resupirātoru)* was advertised as a way to keep healthy in cold and damp weather. See Miyatake Gaikotsu, *Miyatake Gaikotsu chosaku shū* (Kawade shobō shinsha, 1994), 1:69.

89. See Jeffrey Broadbent, *Environmental Politics in Japan: Networks of Power and Protest* (Cambridge: Cambridge University Press), 1998; Timothy S. George, *Minamata: Pollution and the Struggle for Democracy in Postwar Japan* (Cambridge, MA: Harvard University Asia Center), 2001.

90. Esashi Akiko, ed., *Shashin, kaiga shūsei Nihon no onnatachi: Jidai o ikiru* (Nihon tosho sentā, 1996), 1:155.

91. Shimokawa Kōshi and Katei sōgō kenkyūkai, eds., *Shōwa, Heisei kateishi nenpyō 1926–2000* (Kawade shobō shinsha, 2001), 445, 451.

92. Chūpiren, short for Chūzetsu kinshihō ni hantai shi piru kaikin o yōkyū suru josei kaihō rengō, was founded June 14, 1972. Although it was not the most important organization in the liberation movement, its skillful use of the media made it highly visible. Ehara Yumiko, "Feminizumu no 70 nendai to 80 nendai," in *Feminizumu ronsō: 70 nendai kara 90 nendai e,* ed. Ehara Yumiko (Keisei shobō, 1990), 7. The low-dosage birth control pill was not legalized for general use in Japan until September 1999.

93. Ariga Takashi, "Karakai no minzoku 'ūman ribu wa busuna onna no ōsawagi' to iu zasshihōdō no shisei ni miru karakai no dentō" (paper presented at

the annual meeting of the Japanese Folklore Association, Nagano, Japan, October 1, 2000).

94. Mizoguchi Akiyo, Saeki Yōko, and Miki Sōko, eds., *Shiryō Nihon ūman ribu shi* (Kyoto: Uimenzu bukkustoa shōkado, 1995), 3:325. The period in which Kuchi-sake-onna thrived (1978–1979) was a particular time of transition within Japanese feminism, from the more conspicuous media-visible manifestation of the women's liberation movement to the more academic and theoretical women's studies *(joseigaku)*. Ehara notes that this transition was demarcated by the publication of two important feminist books in 1979. "Feminizumu no 70 nendai to 80 nendai," 8–9.

95. The yearbook of the Japanese publishing industry cites three magazines as examples of weekly publications within the broader category of "women's magazines" *(joseishi)*: *Josei jishin, Josei sebun,* and *Shūkan josei.* In 1979, weeklies accounted for 42 percent of total sales in this category. Shuppan nenkan henshūbu, ed., *Shuppan nenkan* (Shuppan nyūsusha, 1980), 64. Statistics for the second half of 1979 are as follows: *Josei jishin* = 705,399 copies; *Josei sebun* = 576,855 copies; and *Shūkan josei* = 439,897 copies. See *Shuppan nenkan* (Shuppan nenkan henshū bu, 1981), 1719. Recent (2001) data from the *Josei jishin* editorial department suggest that readers are generally female and range from their teens to their sixties, although 60 percent are married women in their late twenties through thirties (personal communication, 2001). That the ubiquitous (and now pejorative) term *OL* or *office lady* originated in *Josei jishin* is testimony to the distribution and influence of this particular medium. *OL* first made an appearance in the May 17, 1965, issue of the magazine as a replacement for *BG* (business girl). See Ochiai Emiko, "Bijyuaru imēji toshite no onna: Sengo josei zasshi ga miseru sei yakuwari," in *Nihon no feminizumu 7: Hyōgen to media,* ed. Inoue Teruko, Ueno Chizuko, and Ehara Yumiko (Iwanami shoten, 1995), 108. For more on the readership of women's magazines in general, see Inoue Teruko, "Masukomi to josei no gendai," in *Kōza joseigaku 1: Onna no imēji,* ed. Joseigaku kenkyūkai (Keisō shobō, 1984), 43.

96. "'Kuchi-sake-onna' sōdō de shōmei sareta dema no mōi," *Josei jishin,* July 5, 1979, pp. 46–48.

97. The quote is from Leslie Rabine, "A Woman's Two Bodies: Fashion Magazines, Consumerism, and Feminism," in *On Fashion,* ed. Shari Benstock and Suzanne Ferris (New Brunswick: Rutgers University Press, 1994), 65.

98. I am grateful to Professor Komma Tōru of Kanagawa University for bringing this expression and its relevance to my attention.

99. For an extended analysis of Kuchi-sake-onna as she appears in women's weekly magazines, see my article "The Question of the Slit-Mouthed Woman: Contemporary Legend, the Beauty Industry, and Women's Weekly Magazines in Japan," *Signs: Journal of Women in Culture and Society* 32, no. 3 (Spring 2007): 699–726.

100. Nomura, *Edo Tōkyō,* 120–21.

101. Ichiyanagi suggests that the period of Kuchi-sake-onna's popularity—approximately six months—reflects the length of one cycle of a television drama at the time. Ichiyanagi Hirotaka, "Kuchi-sake-onna no 'jikan,'" in *Akane* (Akane henshū sōinkai, 2000), 22.

102. Children's manga or books concerning yōkai include Satō Arifumi, *Ichiban kuwashii Nihon yōkai zukan* (Rippū shobō, 1972); and *Yōkai, yūrei daihyakka* (Keibunsha, 1982). For a sense of the abundance and influence of these works during the 1970s and 1980s, see Kyōgoku, Tada, and Murakami, *Yōkai baka*.

103. Mizuki, *Umareta toki kara*, 150.

CHAPTER 6. YŌKAI CULTURE

Epigraph: Quoted in Kai henshūbu, ed., *Hikkei yōkai koyomi* (Kadokawa shoten, 2004), 67.

1. See Tsunemitsu Tōru, *Gakkō no kaidan: Kōshō bungei no tenkai to shosō* (Kyoto: Mineruva, 1993). The legend of Toire-no-Hanako-san was also thematized for an eponymous film (1995, dir. Matsuoka Jōji) and *Shinsei Toire-no-Hanako-san* (1998, dir. Tsutsumi Yukihiko); in both movies a modern version of Kokkuri is played.

2. See chapter 4, n. 3.

3. Gore Verbinski, who directed the 2002 Hollywood remake, first viewed the Japanese version of *Ringu* on a "really poor quality" copy of a copy of a copy—a fact that poignantly, if ironically, highlights the very mode of urban-legend-like exchange on which the film is structured. Quoted in David Kalat, *J-Horror: The Definitive Guide to* The Ring, The Grudge, *and Beyond* (New York: Vertical, 2007), 6. For more on Japanese horror films, including *Ringu*, within a global context, see Jay McRoy, ed., *Japanese Horror Cinema* (Edinburgh: Edinburgh University Press, 2005).

4. See Saitō Tsugio, *Yōkai toshi keikaku ron: Obake kara no machi zukuri* (Sairyūsha, 1996); also see my article, "The Metamorphosis of the Kappa: Transformation from Folklore to Folklorism in Japan," *Asian Folklore Studies* 57 (Fall 1998): 1–24.

5. Vered Vinitzky-Seroussi, "Social Memory and Commemoration: Some 'After the Fact' Thoughts," in *Perspectives on Social Memory in Japan*, ed. Tsu Yun Hui, Jan Van Bremen, and Eyal Ben-Ari (Folkestone, U.K.: Global Oriental, 2005), 233.

6. Komatsu Kazuhiko, *Yōkaigaku shinkō: Yōkai kara miru Nihonjin no kokoro* (Shōgakkan, 1994), 8.

7. Ibid.

8. If future scholars seek watershed dates in the history of yōkai, certainly 1994 will be among them, as it coincidently (?) witnessed the publication of Kyōgoku's debut novel, Komatsu's *Yōkaigaku shinkō*, and Takahata's *Heisei tanuki gassen Pompoko*.

9. See, for example, Kyōgoku Natsuhiko, *Hyakkiyagyō: In* (Kodansha, 1999), which includes stories titled "Mokumokuren" and "Himamushi-nyūdō."

10. Kyōgoku Natsuhiko, *Ubume no natsu* (Kōdansha bunko, 1998), 31–33. Originally published in 1994.

11. Kai henshūbu, ed., *Hikkei yōkai koyomi*.

12. This is not to say that the films of Miyazaki Hayao (particularly *Tonari*

no totoro [*My Neighbor Totoro*, 1988], *Mononoke-hime* [*Princess Mononoke*, 1997], and *Sen to Chihiro no kami-kakushi* [*Spirited Away*, 2001]) are unconnected to Japanese history and landscape. My point is that Miyazaki's characters rarely index specific historically traceable yōkai but rather cobble together a variety of folkloric motifs to create new characters. Although the image of Totoro, for example, draws on traditional animistic notions of nature, nowhere in the historic and folkloric record does an identical figure exist. Miyazaki also freely appropriates non-Japanese sources for his creations; his witch-like Yubaba in *Spirited Away* is arguably influenced as much by the Russian folkloric figure of Baba Yaga as it is by Japanese yamamba (mountain woman) traditions, and *Totoro* itself may be a (mis)pronunciation of *troll*. (Accordingly, I also note that Miyazaki's work, though certainly receiving academic attention from film, anime, literature, and religion scholars, seems generally to fall outside mainstream yōkai scholarship.) Perhaps the eclectic nature of Miyazaki's characters is the very thing that enables them to negotiate national borders with such success.

Inversely, *Heisei tanuki gassen Pompoko*, although produced by Studio Ghibli and directed by Miyazaki's partner, Takahata Isao, has received very little recognition outside Japan and was released internationally on DVD only in 2005 (by Disney, under the title *Pompoko*), eleven years after its initial production. This lack of attention is due in part to the obscurity, for international audiences, of the yōkai characters and the many direct references to folklore. As Susan Napier notes, *Heisei tanuki gassen Pompoko* "could have been made only in a Japanese context." "Confronting Master Narratives: History as Vision in Miyazaki Hayao's Cinema of De-assurance," *positions* 9, no. 2 (2001): 491. Perhaps it is no coincidence that Takahata Isao directed the first two television versions of Mizuki's *Gegege no Kitarō*, and that a yōkai expert named Mizuki-sensei makes a brief appearance in *Pompoko*.

13. "Kono meibamen o minogasu na! Hikken no hairaito shiin," *Kai* 19 (July 2005): 2. *Yōkai daisensō* was produced by Kadokawa Group Holdings, the media house behind *Kai*, *Ringu*, and numerous other yōkai- and horror-related books, manga, and movies.

14. A. O. Scott, "A Motley Crew of Spirits Recruit a Boy to Be Savior in 'The Great Yōkai War,'" *New York Times*, June 30, 2006.

15. Ibid.

16. In one scene, the protagonist flips through an issue of *Kai*—with postmodern self-referentiality, the particular volume shown (vol. 15) contains several references to the film itself.

17. See Tawara Seiji ed., *Poketto monsutā zukan* (Ascii, 1997); also Nakazawa Shin'ichi, *Poketto no naka no yasei* (Iwanami shoten, 1997), 83–105; Joseph Tobin, ed., *Pikachu's Global Adventure: The Rise and Fall of Pokémon* (Durham, NC: Duke University Press, 2004); and Anne Allison (*Millennial Monsters: Japanese Toys and the Global Imagination* [Berkeley: University of California Press, 2006]), who discusses not only Pokémon but also the broader global impact of Japanese toys and popular culture.

Regarding the incursion of traditional yōkai into other cultures, it is also worth noting the tanuki's quiet infiltration into American popular literature, as a protagonist in Tom Robbins's *Villa Incognito* (New York: Bantam Books, 2003).

18. Komatsu, *Yōkaigaku shinkō*, 230.

19. "Dokusen kōkai! Kai teki kanshō no tame no yōkai meikan," *Kai* 19 (July 2005): 24–55.

20. Susan Stewart, *On Longing: Narratives of the Miniature, the Gigantic, the Souvenir, the Collection* (Durham, NC: Duke University Press, 1993), 151–52.

Bibliography

Unless otherwise noted, all Japanese works are published in Tokyo.

Abe Kazue. *Yōkaigaku nyūmon*. Yūsankaku, 1971.

Adachi Noriyuki. *Yōkai to aruku: Hyōden, Mizuki Shigeru*. Bungei shunjū, 1994.

Akasaka Norio. *Yanagita Kunio no yomikata: Mō hitotsu no minzokugaku wa kanō ka*. Chikuma shinsho, 1994.

Akiyama Satoko. "'Kuchi-sake-onna' to shōjo shinri." *Asahi shinbun*, June 25, 1979, p. 15.

Akutagawa Ryūnosuke. *Kappa*. Iwanami shoten, 1996.

Allison, Anne. *Millennial Monsters: Japanese Toys and the Global Imagination*. Berkeley: University of California Press, 2006.

———. *Permitted and Prohibited Desires: Mothers, Comics, and Censorship in Japan*. Boulder, CO: Westview Press, 1996.

Anderson, Benedict. *Imagined Communities: Reflections on the Origins and Spread of Nationalism*. Rev. ed. London: Verso, 1991.

Aramata Hiroshi. *Kaii no kuni Nippon*. Shūeisha, 1997.

———, ed. *Takagi Shunzan, Honzō zusetsu*. 3 vols. Riburo poruto, 1988.

———. *Zōhoban zukan no hakubutsushi*. Shūeisha, 1995.

Ariga Takashi. "Karakai no minzoku 'ūman ribu wa busuna onna no ōsawagi' to iu zasshihōdō no shisei ni miru karakai no dentō." Paper presented at the annual meeting of the Japanese Folklore Association [Nihon minzokugakkai], Nagano, Japan, October 1, 2000.

Asahi geinō, July 19, 1979, p. 34.

Asai Ryōi. *Otogibōko*. Vol. 75, *Shin Nihon koten bungaku taikei*. Iwanami shoten, 2001.

Asakura Haruhiko, ed. *Kinmōzui shūsei*. 25 vols. Ōzorasha, 1998.

Asakura Kyōji. "Ano 'Kuchi-sake-onna' no sumika o Gifu sanchū ni mita!" In

Uwasa no hon, vol. 92 of *Bessatsu takarajima*, edited by Ishii Shinji, 132–49. JICC Shuppan kyoku, 1989.

Asendorf, Christoph. *Batteries of Life: The History of Things and Their Perception in Modernity.* Translated by Don Reneau. Berkeley: University of California Press, 1993.

Atran, Scott. *Cognitive Foundations of Natural History: Toward an Anthropology of Science.* Cambridge: Cambridge University Press, 1990.

Bakhtin, Mikhail M. *Rabelais and His World.* Translated by Helene Iwolsky. Bloomington: Indiana University Press, 1984.

Bargen, Doris G. *A Woman's Weapon: Spirit Possession in* The Tale of Genji. Honolulu: University of Hawai'i Press, 1997.

Bathgate, Michael. *The Fox's Craft in Japanese Religion and Folklore: Shapeshifters, Transformations, and Duplicities.* New York: Routledge, 2004.

Bauman, Richard, and Charles L. Briggs. *Voices of Modernity: Language Ideologies and the Politics of Inequality.* Cambridge: Cambridge University Press, 2003.

Benjamin, Walter. *Illuminations: Essays and Reflections.* Translated by Harry Zohn. New York: Schocken Books, 1968.

Bennett, Gillian. *Traditions of Belief: Women, Folklore, and the Supernatural Today.* London: Penguin Books, 1987.

Berry, Mary Elizabeth. *Japan in Print: Information and Nation in the Early Modern Period.* Berkeley: University of California Press, 2006.

Best, Joel, and Gerald Horiuchi. "The Razor Blade in the Apple: The Social Construction of Urban Legends." In *Contemporary Legend: A Reader,* edited by Gillian Bennett and Paul Smith, 113–31. New York: Garland Publishing, 1996.

Blacker, Carmen. *The Catalpa Bow: A Study of Shamanistic Practices in Japan.* London: George Allen and Unwin, 1975.

———. "Supernatural Abductions in Japanese Folklore." *Asian Folklore Studies* 26, no. 2 (1967): 111–48.

Bloom, Paul. *Descartes's Baby: How the Science of Child Development Explains What Makes Us Human.* New York: Basic Books, 2004.

Blum, Deborah. *Ghost Hunters: William James and the Search for Scientific Proof of Life after Death.* New York: Penguin Books, 2006.

Bogart, Barbara Allen. "The 'Image on Glass'": Technology, Tradition, and the Emergence of Folkore." In *Contemporary Legend: A Reader,* edited by Gillian Bennett and Paul Smith, 133–50. New York: Garland Publishing, 1996.

Borgen, Robert. *Sugawara no Michizane and the Early Heian Court.* Cambridge, MA: Council on East Asian Studies, Harvard University, 1986.

Borges, Jorge Luis. "The Analytical Language of John Wilkins." In *Other Inquisitions, 1937–1952,* translated by Ruth L. C. Simmons. Austin: University of Texas, 1964.

———. *Labyrinths: Selected Stories and Other Writings.* New York: New Directions, 1964.

Bowring, Richard John. *Mori Ōgai and the Modernization of Japanese Culture.* Cambridge: Cambridge University Press, 1979.

Boyer, Pascal. *The Naturalness of Religious Ideas: A Cognitive Theory of Religion.* Berkeley: University of California Press, 1994.

———. *Religion Explained: The Evolutionary Origins of Religious Thought.* New York: Basic Books, 2001.
Braidotti, Rosi. "Signs of Wonder and Traces of Doubt: On Teratology and Embodied Differences." In *Between Monsters, Goddesses, and Cyborgs: Feminist Confrontations with Science, Medicine, and Cyberspace,* edited by Nina Lykke and Rosi Braidotti, 135–52. London: Zed Books, 1996.
Broadbent, Jeffrey. *Environmental Politics in Japan: Networks of Power and Protest.* Cambridge: Cambridge University Press, 1998.
Burns, Susan [S. Bānzu]. "Toritsukareta shintai kara kanshi sareta shintai e: Seishin igaku no hassei." *Edo no shisō* 6 (May 1997): 48–62.
Campbell, Donald. "Science's Social System of Validity-Enhancing Collective Belief Change and the Problems of Social Sciences." In *Metatheory in Social Science,* edited by D. Fiske and R. Shweder, 108–35. Chicago: University of Chicago Press, 1986.
Carpenter, William Benjamin. *Mesmerism, Spiritualism, &c., Historically & Scientifically Considered; Being Two Lectures Delivered at the London Institution; with Preface and Appendix.* New York: D. Appleton and Company, 1895.
———. *Principles of Mental Physiology.* New York: D. Appleton and Company, 1883.
Carroll, Noël. *The Philosophy of Horror or Paradoxes of the Heart.* New York: Routledge, 1990.
Casal, U. A. "The Goblin Fox and Badger and Other Witch Animals of Japan." *Folklore Studies* 18 (1959): 1–93.
Castle, Terry. *The Female Thermometer: Eighteenth-Century Culture and the Invention of the Uncanny.* New York: Oxford University Press, 1995.
Cawson, Frank. *The Monsters in the Mind: The Face of Evil in Myth, Literature, and Contemporary Life.* Sussex: Book Guild, 1995.
Chamberlain, Basil Hall. *Japanese Things: Being Notes on Various Subjects Connected with Japan.* Rutland, VT: Charles E. Tuttle Co., 1971.
Chigiri Mitsutoshi. *Oni no kenkyū.* Tairiku shobō, 1978.
Ching, Julia. *The Religious Thought of Chu Hsi.* Oxford: Oxford University Press, 2000.
Christy, Alan S. "Representing the Rural: Place as Method in the Formation of Japanese Native Ethnology, 1910–1945." PhD diss., University of Chicago, 1997.
Clifford, James. "On Ethnographic Allegory." In *Writing Culture: The Politics and Poetics of Ethnography,* edited by James Clifford and George E. Marcus, 98–121. Berkeley: University of California Press, 1986.
Clover, Carol. *Men, Women, and Chain Saws: Gender in the Modern Horror Film.* Princeton: Princeton University Press, 1992.
Cohen, Jeffrey Jerome, ed. *Monster Theory: Reading Culture.* Minneapolis: University of Minnesota Press, 1994.
Coleman, Loren, and Jerome Clark. *Cryptozoology A to Z.* New York: Simon and Schuster, 1999.
Combs, James E. *Play World: The Emergence of the New Ludenic Age.* Westport, CT: Praeger, 2000.

Cook, James W. *The Arts of Deception: Playing with Fraud in the Age of Barnum.* Cambridge, MA: Harvard University Press, 2001.

Creed, Barbara. *The Monstrous-Feminine: Film, Feminism, Psychoanalysis.* London: Routledge, 1993.

Daston, Lorraine, and Katherine Park. *Wonders and the Order of Nature, 1150–1750.* New York: Zone Books, 1998.

Dawkins, Richard. *The Selfish Gene.* New York: Oxford University Press, 1976.

de Certeau, Michel. *The Mystic Fable,* Vol. 1, *The Sixteenth and Seventeenth Centuries.* Translated by Michael B. Smith. Chicago: University of Chicago Press, 1992.

———. *The Practice of Everyday Life.* Translated by Steven Rendall. Berkeley: University of California Press, 1984.

de Certeau, Michel, with Dominique Julia and Jacques Revel. "Beauty of the Dead: Nissard." In *Heterologies: Discourse on the Other,* by Michel de Certeau, translated by Brian Massumi, 119–36. Minneapolis: University of Minnesota Press, 1997.

Dégh, Linda. *Legend and Belief: Dialectics of a Folklore Genre.* Bloomington: Indiana University Press, 2001.

Dégh, Linda, and Andrew Vázsonyi. "Legend and Belief." In *Folklore Genres,* edited by Dan Ben-Amos, 93–123. Austin: University of Texas Press, 1976.

de Visser, M. W. "The Fox and Badger in Japanese Folklore." Pt. 3. *Transactions of the Asiatic Society of Japan* 36 (1908): 1–159.

———. "The Tengu." *Transactions of the Asiatic Society of Japan* 36, no. 2 (1908): 25–99.

Dods, John Bovee. *Philosophy of Electro-Biology, or Electrical Psychology . . .* Compiled and edited by G. W. Stone. London: H. Bailliere, 1852.

"Dokusen kōkai! Kai teki kanshō no tame no yōkai meikan." *Kai* 19 (July 2005): 24–55.

Dolar, Mladen. "'I Shall Be with You on Your Wedding-Night': Lacan and the Uncanny." *October* 58 (Fall 1991): 5–23.

Dozier, Rush W., Jr. *Fear Itself: The Origin and Nature of the Powerful Emotion That Shapes Our Lives and Our World.* New York: Thomas Dunne Books, 1998.

Durkheim, Emile. *The Elementary Forms of the Religious Life.* 1912. Reprint, New York: Free Press, 1965.

Ehara Yumiko. "Feminizumu no 70 nendai to 80 nendai." In *Feminizumu ronsō: 70 nendai kara 90 nendai e,* edited by Ehara Yumiko, 1–46. Keisei shobō, 1990.

Ema Tsutomu. *Ema Tsutomu chosaku shū.* Vol. 6. Chūōkōron sha, 1977.

———. "Nihon fūzoku bunkashi." In *Ema Tsutomu chosaku shū.* Vol. 1. Chūōkōron sha, 1975.

Esashi Akiko, ed. *Shashin, kaiga shūsei Nihon no onnatachi: Jidai o ikiru.* Vol. 1. Nihon tosho sentā, 1996.

Eskildsen, Robert. "Telling Differences: The Imagery of Civilization and Nationality in Nineteenth Century Japan." PhD diss., Stanford University, 1998.

Faraday, Michael. "Professor Faraday on Table-Moving." *Athenaeum* (July 2, 1853): 801–3.

Figal, Gerald. *Civilization and Monsters: Spirits of Modernity in Modern Japan.* Durham, NC: Duke University Press, 1999.
Fine, Gary Alan. *Manufacturing Tales: Sex and Money in Contemporary Legends.* Knoxville: University of Tennessee Press, 1992.
Foster, Michael Dylan. "Hyakki yakukō." In *Kai* 11 (July 2001): 304–5.
———. "The Metamorphosis of the Kappa: Transformation from Folklore to Folklorism in Japan." *Asian Folklore Studies* 57 (Fall 1998): 1–24.
———. "The Otherworlds of Mizuki Shigeru." In *Mechademia.* Vol. 3, *Limits of the Human* (Minneapolis: University of Minnesota Press, 2008).
———. "The Question of the Slit-Mouthed Woman: Contemporary Legend, the Beauty Industry, and Women's Weekly Magazines in Japan." *Signs: Journal of Women in Culture and Society* 32, no. 3 (Spring 2007): 699–726.
———. "Strange Games and Enchanted Science: The Mystery of Kokkuri." *Journal of Asian Studies* 65, no. 2 (May 2006): 251–75
Foucault, Michel. *The Archaeology of Knowledge and the Discourse on Language.* Translated by A. M. Sheridan Smith. New York: Pantheon Books, 1972.
———. *The Order of Things: An Archeology of the Human Sciences.* New York: Vintage Books, 1994.
Freud, Sigmund. "The 'Uncanny.'" In *Writings on Art and Literature,* 193–233. Stanford: Stanford University Press, 1997.
Fujishima Usaku. *Sengo manga no minzokugakushi.* Kawai Shuppan, 1990.
Fukasaku Mitsusada. "Tsune ni kienai Nihonjin no animizumu: 'Kuchi-sake-onna' ga kakemawatta ura de." *Gekkan kyōiku no mori* (September 1979): 24–31.
Gebhardt, Lisette. "The 'Other World' in the Light of a New Science: Spiritism in Modern Japan." In *Practicing the Afterlife: Perspectives from Japan,* edited by Susanne Formanek and William R. LaFleur, 383–96. Vienna: Verlag der Österreichischen Akademie der Wissenschaften, 2004.
George, Timothy S. *Minamata: Pollution and the Struggle for Democracy in Postwar Japan.* Cambridge, MA: Harvard University Asian Center, 2001.
Gifu nichi nichi shinbun, January 26, 1979.
Gilmore, David D. *Monsters: Evil Beings, Mythical Beasts, and All Manner of Imaginary Terror.* Philadelphia: University of Pennsylvania Press, 2003.
Glassman, Hank. "At the Crossroads of Birth and Death: The Blood-Pool Hell and Postmortem Fetal Extraction." In *Death and the Afterlife in Japanese Buddhism,* edited by Mariko Walter and Jacqueline Stone, 175–206. Honolulu: University of Hawai'i Press, 2008.
Gluck, Carol. "The Fine Folly of the Encyclopedists." In *Currents in Japanese Culture: Translations and Transformations,* edited by Amy Vladeck Heinrich, 224–51. New York: Columbia University Press, 1997.
Greenblatt, Stephen. *Marvelous Possessions: The Wonder of the New World.* Chicago: University of Chicago Press, 1991.
Grosz, Elizabeth. *Space, Time, and Perversion: Essays on the Politics of Bodies.* London: Routledge, 1995.
Halberstam, Judith. *Skin Shows: Gothic Horror and the Technology of Monsters.* Durham, NC: Duke University Press, 1995.

Halpin, Marjorie M. "Investigating the Goblin Universe." In *Manlike Monsters on Trial: Early Records and Modern Evidence,* edited by Marjorie M. Halpin and Michael M. Ames, 3–26. Vancouver: University of British Columbia Press, 1980.

Hansen, Wilburn Nels. *Strange Tidings from the Realm of the Immortals: Hirata Atsutane's Ethnography of the Other World.* PhD diss., Stanford University, 2006.

Hardacre, Helen. "Asano Wasaburō and Japanese Spiritualism in Early Twentieth-Century Japan." In *Japan's Competing Modernities: Issues in Culture and Democracy, 1900–1930,* edited by Sharon A. Minichiello, 133–53. Honolulu: University of Hawai'i Press, 1998.

Harootunian, H. D. "Late Tokugawa Culture and Thought." In *The Cambridge History of Japan.* Vol. 5, edited by Marius B. Jansen, 168–258. Cambridge: Cambridge University Press, 1989.

———. *Overcome by Modernity: History, Culture, and Community in Interwar Japan.* Princeton: Princeton University Press, 2000.

———. *Things Seen and Unseen: Discourses and Ideology in Tokugawa Nativism.* Chicago: University of Chicago Press, 1988.

"Hayari kotoba hakusho: 79nen zenhan." *Asahi shinbun*, evening ed., July 10, 1979, p. 7.

Hayles, N. Katherine. *How We Became Posthuman: Virtual Bodies in Cybernetics, Literature, and Informatics.* Chicago: University of Chicago Press, 1999.

Haynes, Renée. *The Society for Psychical Research, 1882–1982.* London: MacDonald and Co., 1982.

Higashi Masao. *Hyaku-monogatari no hyaku-kai.* Kadokawa shoten, 2001.

———. *Yōkai densetsu kibun.* Gakken, 2005.

Hiraizumi Etsurō. "Zenkoku no shō-chū-gakusei o osoresaseru 'Kuchi-sake-onna' fūsetsu no kiki kaikai." *Shūkan asahi,* June 29, 1979, pp. 16–20.

Hirano Imao. *Den Enryō.* Sōfūsha, 1974.

Hirosaka Tomonobu. *Edo kaiki ibunroku.* Kirinkan, 1999.

Hiruta Genshirō. "Kitsune-tsuki no shinseishi." In *Tsukimono,* edited by Komatsu Kazuhiko, 67–90. Kawade shobō shinsha, 2000.

Huang, Siu-chi. *Essentials of Neo-Confucianism: Eight Major Philosophers of the Song and Ming Period.* Westport, CT: Greenwood Press, 1999.

Huet, Marie-Hélène. *Monstrous Imagination.* Cambridge, MA: Harvard University Press, 1993.

Ibsen, Henrik. *Ghosts and Other Plays.* Translated by Peter Watts. London: Penguin Books, 1964.

Ichiyanagi Hirotaka. "Gakkō no kaidan no riarizumu." In *Aera mook: Dōwagaku ga wakaru,* edited by Sekido Mamoru, 86–89. Asahi shinbunsha, 1999.

———. *"Kokkuri-san" to "Senrigan": Nihon kindai to shinreigaku.* Kōdansha, 1994.

———. "Kuchi-sake-onna no 'jikan.'" In *Akane,* 21–22. Akane henshū sōinkai, 2000.

———. *Saiminjutsu no Nihon kindai.* Seikyūsha, 1997.

———. "Shinrei o kyōiku suru: Tsunoda Jirō 'Ushiro no Hyakutarō' no tōsō." *Nihon bungaku* (November 2001): 30–38.

———. "'Yōkai' to iu ba: Inoue Enryō, 'yōkaigaku' no ichi." In *Nihon shisō no kanōsei*, edited by Suzuki Tadashi and Yamaryō Kenji, 71–90. Satsuki shobō, 1997.

Igarashi, Yoshikuni. *Bodies of Memory: Narratives of War in Postwar Japanese Culture, 1945–1970*. Princeton: Princeton University Press, 2000.

Iijima Yoshiharu. *Hitotsume kozō to hyōtan: Sei to gisei no fōkuroa*. Shinyōsha, 2001.

Ikegami Eiko. *Bonds of Civility: Aesthetic Networks and the Political Origins of Japanese Culture*. Cambridge: Cambridge University Press, 2005.

Imaizumi Toshiaki. "Kokkuri-san ni kansuru shakai shinrigakuteki chōsa: 1930 nendai kara 1992 nen made no ryūkō shi." *Shūkyō to shakai* 1, no. 6 (1995): 29–48.

Inada Atsunobu and Tanaka Naohi, eds. *Toriyama Sekien gazu hyakkiyagyō*. Kokusho kankōkai, 1999.

Inoue Enryō. *Inoue Enryō, Yōkaigaku zenshū*. Edited by Tōyō Daigaku Inoue Enryō kinen gakujutsu sentā. 6 vols. Kashiwa shobō, 1999–2001.

Inoue, Miyako. *Vicarious Language: Gender and Linguistic Modernity in Japan*. Berkeley: University of California Press, 2006.

Inoue Teruko. "Masukomi to josei no gendai." In *Kōza joseigaku 1: Onna no imēji*, edited by Joseigaku kenkyūkai, 42–73. Keisō shobō, 1984.

Ishii Kendō. *Meiji jibutsu kigen*. Vol. 8. Chikuma gakugei bunko, 1997.

Ishikawa Jun'ichirō. *Shinpan kappa no sekai*. Jiji tsūshinsha, 1985.

Ishizaka Masao. "Watashi mimashita, tsuchinoko to neko no kenka." *Shūkan pureibōi*. October 24, 2000, pp. 54–57.

Itakura Kiyonobu. *Yōkai hakase: Enryō to yōkaigaku no tenkai*. Kokusho kankōkai, 1983.

Itō Seiji, ed. *Kaiichōjū zusetsu*. Kōsakusha, 2001.

Ivy, Marilyn. *Discourses of the Vanishing: Modernity, Phantasm, Japan*. Chicago: University of Chicago Press, 1995.

Iwai Hiromi. *Kurashi no naka no yōkai*. Bunka shuppankyoku, 1986.

Iwamoto Hiromitsu. "Japanese and New Guinean Memories of Wartime Experiences at Rabaul." Paper delivered at the symposium "Remembering the War in New Guinea," Australian National University, Canberra, October 19–21, 2000, http://ajrp.awm.gov.au/ajrp/remember.nsf/pages/NT00002B7E.

Iwamoto Yoshiteru. *Mō hitotsu no Tōno monogatari*. Tōsui shobō, 1983.

Iwata Noriko. "Bakemono to asobu: 'Nankenkeredomo bakemono sugoroku.'" *Tōkyō-to Edo-Tōkyō hakubutsukan hōkoku* 5 (February 2000): 39–52.

Jackson, Rosemary. *Fantasy: The Literature of Subversion*. London: Routledge, 1981.

Jones, Sumie. "The Other Side of the Hakone: Ghosts, Demons, and Desire for Narrative in Edo Literature." In *The Desire for Monogatari: Proceedings of the Second Midwest Research/Pedagogy Seminar on Japanese Literature*, edited by Eiji Sekine, 53–78. West Lafayette, IN: U.S.-Japan Friendship Commission and Purdue University, 1994.

Josephson, Jason Ānanda. "When Buddhism Became a 'Religion': Religion and Superstition in the Writings of Inoue Enryō." *Japanese Journal of Religious Studies* 33, no. 1 (2006): 143–68.

Kabat, Adam [Adamu Kabatto]. "Bakemono zukushi no kibyōshi no kōsatsu: Bakemono no gainen o megutte." In *Yōkai*, edited by Komatsu Kazuhiko, 141–64. Kawade shobō shinsha, 2000.

———. *Edo bakemono zōshi*. Shōgakkan, 1999.

———. *Edo kokkei bakemono zukushi*. Kōdansha, 2003.

———. *Ōedo bakemono saiken*. Shōgakkan, 2000.

———. *Ōedo bakemono zufu*. Shōgakkan, 2000.

Kaempfer, Engelbert. *Kaempfer's Japan: Tokugawa Culture Observed*. Edited, translated, and annotated by Beatrice M. Bodart-Bailey. Honolulu: University of Hawai'i Press, 1999.

Kagawa Masanobu. *Edo no yōkai kakumei*. Kawade shobō shinsha, 2006.

———. "Tōkō kyohi to tsukimono no shinkō: Gendai ni ikiru 'inugami tsuki.'" In *Tsukimono*, edited by Komatsu Kazuhiko, 238–63. Kawade shobō shinsha, 2000.

———. "Yōkai to goraku." *Kai* 11 (August 2001): 306–7.

Kai henshūbu, ed. *Hikkei yōkai koyomi*. Kadokawa shoten, 2004.

Kalat, David. *J-Horror: The Definitive Guide to* The Ring, The Grudge, *and Beyond*. New York: Vertical, 2007.

Karatani, Kōjin. *Origins of Modern Japanese Literature*. Durham, NC: Duke University Press, 1993.

Kawada Minoru. *The Origin of Ethnography in Japan: Yanagita Kunio and His Times*. Translated by Toshiko Kishida-Ellis. London: Kegan Paul International, 1993.

Kawamura Kunimitsu. *Genshi suru kindai kūkan: Meishin, byōki, zashikirō, aruiwa rekishi no kioku*. Seikyūsha, 1997.

———. *Miko no minzokugaku: 'Onna no chikara' no kindai*. Seikyūsha, 1993.

Kawasaki-shi Shimin Myūjiamu, ed. *Nihon no genjū: Mikakunin seibutsu shutsugen roku*. Kawasaki: Kawasaki-shi Shimin Myūjiamu, 2004.

Kawazoe Yū. *Edo no misemono*. Iwanami shoten, 2000.

Keene, Donald, trans. *Essays in Idleness: The Tsurezuregusa of Kenkō*. New York: Columbia University Press, 1967.

Kern, Adam L. *Manga from the Floating World: Comicbook Culture and the* Kibyōshi *of Edo Japan*. Cambridge, MA: Harvard University Asia Center, 2006.

Kihara Hirokatsu. "Hakken: Yōkai-kudan." *Kai* 17 (October 2004): 2–7, 230–35.

Kikkawa Takeo. *Nihon denryoku gyō to Matsunaga Yasuzaemon*. Nagoya: Nagoya Daigaku shuppankai, 1995.

Kinoshita Tomio. "Gendai no uwasa kara kōtōdenshō no hassei mekanizumu o saguru: 'Kuchi-sake-onna' no uwasa o daizai toshite." In *Ryūgen, uwasa, soshite jōhō: Uwasa no kenkyūshū taisei*, edited by Satō Tatsuya, 13–30. Shibundō, 1999.

Klein, Susan B. "Woman as Serpent: The Demonic Feminine in the Noh Play *Dōjōji*." In *Religious Reflections on the Human Body*, edited by Jane Marie Law, 100–136. Bloomington: Indiana University Press, 1995.

Kobayashi Toyomasa. *Gojira no ronri*. Chūkei shuppan, 1992.

Kojima Hyakuzō. *Jinshin denki no zuga*. Osaka: n.p., 1886.

Komatsu Kazuhiko. *Akuryōron: Ikai kara no messēji*. Chikuma shobō, 1997.

———. "Hyaku-monogatari kaidan to yōkai kenkyū." In *Shutendōji no kubi*, 248–53. Serika shobō, 1997.
———. *Hyōrei shinkō ron*. Kōdansha gakujutsu bunko, 1994.
———. *Ijinron: Minzoku shakai no shinsei*. Seidosha, 1985.
———. *Ikai to Nihonjin: Emonogatari no sōzōryoku*. Kadokawa sensho, 2003.
———. "'Kuchi-sake-onna' no imiron." In *Oni no tamatebako: Minzoku shakai no kōkan*, 227–40. Seigensha, 1986.
———. *Nihon yōkai ibunroku*. Shōgakkan, 1995.
———, ed. *Oni*. Kawade shobō shinsha, 2000.
———, ed. *Tengu to yamamba*. Kawade shobō shinsha, 2000.
———. "Tsukimono: Kaisetsu." In *Tsukimono*, edited by Komatsu Kazuhiko, 436–37. Kawade shobō shinsha, 2000.
———, ed. *Yōkai*. Kawade shobō shinsha, 2000.
———. *Yōkaigaku shinkō: Yōkai kara miru Nihonjin no kokoro*. Shōgakkan, 1994.
Komine Kazuaki. "Yōkai no hakubutsugaku." *Kokubungaku: Kaishaku to kyōzai no kenkyū* 41, no. 4 (March 1996): 80–87.
Konjaku monogatari shū. In *Nihon koten bungaku taikei*. Vol. 25. Iwanami shoten, 1965.
"Kono meibamen o minogasu na! Hikken no hairaito shiin." *Kai* 19 (July 2005): 2.
Kornicki, Peter. *The Book in Japan: A Cultural History from the Beginnings to the Nineteenth Century*. Honolulu: University of Hawai'i Press, 2001.
"Kuchi-sake-onna o shōbai ni suru nante yūki ga iru no da to iu ohanashi." *Shūkan pureibōi*, July 31, 1979, p. 74.
"'Kuchi-sake-onna' sōdō de shōmei sareta dema no mōi." *Josei jishin*, July 5, 1979, pp. 46–48.
"'Kuchi-sake-onna' tte honto?" *Asahi shinbun*, July 8, 1979, p. 32.
Kyōgoku Natsuhiko. *Hyakkiyagyō: In*. Kodansha, 1999.
———. "Tsūzoku 'yōkai' gainen no seiritsu ni kansuru ichi kōsatsu." In *Nihon yōkaigaku taizen*, edited by Komatsu Kazuhiko, 547–82. Shōgakkan, 2003.
———. *Ubume no natsu*. Kōdansha bunko, 1998.
———. "Yōkai to iu kotoba ni tsuite (sono 2)." *Kai* 12 (December 2001): 296–307.
Kyōgoku Natsuhiko and Tada Katsumi, eds. *Yōkai zukan*. Kokusho kankōkai, 2000.
Kyōgoku Natsuhiko, Tada Katsumi, and Murakami Kenji. *Yōkai baka*. Shinchō OH! bunko, 2001.
Lakoff, George. "The Contemporary Theory of Metaphor." In *Metaphor and Thought*. Edited by Andrew Ortony, 202–51. 2nd ed. New York: Cambridge University Press, 1993.
———. *Women, Fire, and Dangerous Things: What Categories Reveal about the Mind*. Chicago: University of Chicago Press, 1987.
Latour, Bruno. *We Have Never Been Modern*. Cambridge, MA: Harvard University Press, 1993.
Levy, Robert I., Jeannette Marie Mageo, and Alan Howard. "Gods, Spirits, and

History: A Theoretical Perspective." In *Spirits in Culture, History, and Mind,* edited by Jeannette Marie Mageo and Alan Howard, 11–27. London: Routledge, 1996.

Lu, John David, ed. *Sources of Japanese History.* Vol. 1. New York: McGraw-Hill, 1973.

Maniquis, Robert M. "Encyclopedia and Society: Order, Disorder, and Textual Pleasure." In *The Encyclopedia and the Age of Revolution,* edited by Clorinda Donato and Robert M. Maniquis, 77–87. Boston: G. K. Hall and Co., 1992.

Markus, Andrew L. "The Carnival of Edo: Misemono Spectacles from Contemporary Accounts." *Harvard Journal of Asiatic Studies* 45, no. 2 (December 1985): 499–541.

Maruyama, Masao. *Studies in the Intellectual History of Tokugawa Japan.* Translated by Mikiso Hane. Princeton: Princeton University Press, 1974.

Matsumura Akira, ed. *Daijirin.* 2nd ed. Sanseido, 1995.

Matsutani Miyoko. *Gendai minwakō.* Vols. 3–4. Rippū shobō, 1985.

———. *Gendai no minwa: Anata mo katarite, watashi mo katarite.* Chūkōshinsho, 2000.

Matsuyama Iwao. *Uwasa no enkinhō.* Kōdansha, 1997.

McRoy, Jay, ed. *Japanese Horror Cinema.* Edinburgh: Edinburgh University Press, 2005.

Medin, Douglas L., and Scott Atran, eds. *Folkbiology.* Cambridge: MIT Press, 1999.

Meiji nyūsu jiten. Vol. 3. Mainichi komyunikēshonzu shuppanbu, 1986.

Minami Kiyohiko. *Oni no ezōshi: Sono minzokugaku to keizaigaku.* Sōbunsha, 1998.

Miura Setsuo. "Kaisetsu: Inoue Enryō to yōkaigaku no tanjō." In *Inoue Enryō, Yōkaigaku zenshū,* vol. 6, edited by Tōyō Daigaku Inoue Enryō kinen gakujutsu sentā, 464–93. Kashiwa shobō, 2001.

Miyamoto Naokazu. "'Kodomo no ryūgen' kenkyū: Otona no miru kodomo no genjitsu to kodomo no genjitsu." PhD diss., Kanagawa University Graduate School of History and Folk Culture Studies, Yokohama, 1998.

Miyata Noboru. *Hime no minzokugaku.* Seidosha, 1993.

———. *Yōkai no minzokugaku: Nihon no mienai kūkan.* Iwanami shoten, 1985.

Miyatake Gaikotsu. *Meiji kibun.* Kawade shobō shinsha, 1997.

———. *Miyatake Gaikotsu chosaku shū.* Vol. 1. Kawade shobō shinsha, 1994.

Mizoguchi Akiyo, Saeki Yōko, and Miki Sōko, eds. *Shiryō Nihon ūman ribu shi.* Vol. 3. Kyoto: Uimenzu bukkusutoa shōkado, 1995.

Mizuki Shigeru. *Chūkō aizōban Gegege no Kitarō.* 5 vols. Chūōkōronsha, 1994.

———. *Gensō sekai e no tabi, yōkai wandārando.* Vol. 3. Chikuma bunko, 1995.

———. *Komikku Shōwa-shi.* 8 vols. Kōdansha komikkusu, 1994.

———. "Me ni mienai mono o miru." In *Yōkai tengoku,* 65–74. Chikuma bunko, 1996.

———. *Musume ni kataru otōsan no senki.* Kawade shobō shinsha, 1995.

———. *Nonnonbā to ore.* Chikuma bunko, 1997.

———. *Rabauru jūgunkōki: Topetoro to no gojūnen.* Chūōkōron shinsha, 2002.

———. *Umareta toki kara 'yōkai' datta.* Kōdansha, 2002.

———. *Yōkai gadan.* Iwanami shoten, 1994.

———. *Yōkai nandemo nyūmon.* Shōgakkan, 1974.

———. "Yōkai no 'katachi' konjaku." In *Yōkai tengoku,* 43–47. Chikuma bunko, 1996.

———. *Zoku yōkai jiten.* Tōkyōdō shuppan, 1984.

———. *Zusetsu Nihon yōkai taizen.* Kōdansha, 1994.

Mori Ōgai. *Mori Ōgai zenshū.* Vols. 1 and 3. Chikuma shobō, 1995.

———. *Youth and Other Stories.* Edited by J. Thomas Rimer. Honolulu: University of Hawai'i Press, 1994.

Moriya, Katsuhisa. "Urban Networks and Information Networks." In *Tokugawa Japan: The Social and Economic Antecedents of Modern Japan,* edited by Chie Nakane and Shinzaburō Oishi, 97–123. Tokyo: University of Tokyo Press, 1990.

Morris-Suzuki, Tessa. *Re-Inventing Japan: Time, Space, Nation.* Armonk: M. E. Sharpe, 1998.

Morse, Ronald A. *Yanagita Kunio and the Folklore Movement: The Search for Japan's National Character and Distinctiveness.* New York: Garland Publishing, 1990.

Murakami Kenji. *Yōkai jiten.* Mainichi shinbunsha, 2000.

Murakami Tatsugorō. *Saishinshiki saiminjutsu.* Seibidō shoten, 1912.

Nakamura Mareaki. *Kaidan no shinrigaku: Gakkō ni umareru kowai hanashi.* Kōdansha, 1994.

Nakamura Teiri. *Kappa no Nihonshi.* Nihon Editāsukūru shuppanbu, 1996.

———. *Tanuki to sono sekai.* Asahi shinbunsha, 1990.

Nakamura Tekisai. *Kinmōzui.* Waseda Daigaku shuppanbu, 1975.

Nakano Osamu. "'Asobi' o shimetsusaseru bunka: 'Kuchi-sake-onna' no haikai." *is* (September 10, 1979): 42–43.

Nakata Jun. "'Kokkuri' wa naze fumetsu nano ka." *Gendai* (September 1997): 299–305.

Nakazawa Shin'ichi. *Poketto no naka no yasei.* Iwanami shoten, 1997.

———. "Yōkai-ga to hakubutsugaku." In *Yōkai,* edited by Komatsu Kazuhiko, 79–86. Kawade shobō shinsha, 2000.

Napier, Susan J. "Confronting Master Narratives: History as Vision in Miyazaki Hayao's Cinema of De-assurance." *positions* 9, no. 2 (2001): 467–93.

———. *The Fantastic in Japanese Literature: The Subversion of Modernity.* London: Routledge, 1996.

Natsume Sōseki. "Koto no sorane." In *Natsume Sōseki zenshū.* Vol. 2:93–131. Chikuma shobō, 1995.

———. *Ten Nights of Dream, Hearing Things, The Heredity of Taste,* translated by Aiko Itō and Graeme Wilson. Rutland, VT: Charles E. Tuttle, 1974.

Negishi Yasumori. *Mimi bukuro.* 3 vols. Iwanami shoten, 1991.

Nicholls, C. P. *Table Moving: Its causes and phenomena, with directions how to experiment.* London: J. Wesley, [186?].

Nihon daijiten kankōkai. *Nihonkoku daijiten.* Vol. 3. Shōgakkan, 1976.

Nihon fūzokushi gakkai, ed. *Nihon fūzokushi jiten.* Kōbundō, 1994.

"Nihon no shōgakusei ga furue-agatta 'Kuchi-sake-onna' no 'rūtsu.'" *Shūkan bunshū.* June 28, 1979, pp. 32–34.

Niita Shunzō. "Enryō ni okeru keimō shisō no nijūsei ni tsuite." In *Inoue Enryō to seiyō shisō*, edited by Saitō Shigeo. Tōyō Daigaku Inoue Enryō kenkyūkai dainibukai, 1988.

Nishimura Saburō. *Bunmei no naka no hakubutsugaku: Seiyō to Nihon*. Vol. 1. Kinokuniya shoten, 1999.

Nomura Jun'ichi. *Edo Tōkyō no uwasa-banashi: 'Konna ban' kara 'Kuchi-sake-onna' made*. Taishūkan shoten, 2005.

———. *Nihon no sekenbanashi*. Tōkyō shoseki, 1995.

Ochiai Emiko. "Bijyuaru imēji toshite no onna: Sengo josei zasshi ga miseru sei yakuwari." In *Nihon no feminizumu 7: Hyōgen to media*, edited by Inoue Teruko, Ueno Chizuko, Ehara Yumiko, 97–119. Iwanami shoten, 1995.

Ogura Takeharu. *Inoue Enryō no shisō*. Kōgura shobō, 1986.

Oikawa Shigeru, ed. *Kyōsai no gekiga, kyōgaten*. Tōkyō shinbun, 1996.

O'Neill, Daniel Cuong. "Ghostly Feelings in Meiji and Early Taishō Literature." PhD diss., Yale University, 2002.

Ōno Katsura. *Kappa no kenkyū*. San'ichi shobō, 1994.

Ooms, Herman. *Tokugawa Ideology: Early Constructs, 1570–1680*. Ann Arbor: Center for Japanese Studies, University of Michigan, 1998.

Oppenheim, Janet. *The Other World: Spiritualism and Psychical Research in England, 1850–1914*. Cambridge: Cambridge University Press, 1985.

Ortabasi, Melek. "Sketching Out the Critical Tradition: Yanagita Kunio and the Reappraisal of Realism." *Japanese Poeticity and Narrativity Revisited: Proceedings of the Association for Japanese Literary Studies* 4 (Summer 2003): 184–93.

Owen, Alex. *The Place of Enchantment: British Occultism and the Culture of the Modern*. Chicago: University of Chicago Press, 2004.

Pimple, Kenneth. "Ghosts, Spirits, and Scholars: The Origins of Modern Spiritualism." In *Out of the Ordinary: Folklore and the Supernatural*, edited by Barbara Walker, 75–89. Logan: Utah State University Press, 1995.

Podmore, Frank. *Modern Spiritualism: A History and a Criticism*. Vol. 2. London: Methuen and Co., 1902.

Pratt, Mary Louise. *Imperial Eyes: Travel Writing and Transculturation*. London: Routledge, 1992.

Rabine, Leslie. "A Woman's Two Bodies: Fashion Magazines, Consumerism, and Feminism." In *On Fashion*, edited by Shari Benstock and Suzanne Ferris, 59–75. New Brunswick: Rutgers University Press, 1994.

Raitt, Jill. "The *Vagina Dentata* and the *Immaculatus Uterus Divini Fontis*." *Journal of the American Academy of Religion* 48, no. 3 (1980): 415–31.

Reichert, Jim. "Deviance and Social Darwinism in Edogawa Ranpo's Erotic-Grotesque Thriller *Kotō no oni*." *Journal of Japanese Studies* 27, no. 1 (Winter 2001): 113–41.

Reider, Noriko T. "The Emergence of *Kaidan-shū:* The Collection of Tales of the Strange and Mysterious in the Edo Period." *Asian Folklore Studies* 60, no. 1 (2001): 79–99.

Rimer, J. Thomas. *Mori Ōgai*. Boston: Twayne Publishers, 1975.

Ritvo, Harriet. *The Platypus and the Mermaid and Other Figments of the Classifying Imagination*. Cambridge, MA: Harvard University Press, 1997.

Robbins, Tom. *Villa Incognito*. New York: Bantam Books, 2003.
Robert-Houdin, Eugene. *The Memoirs of Robert-Houdin*. Translated by Lascelles Wraxall. New York: Dover Publications, 1964.
Robertson, Jennifer. *Native and Newcomer: Making and Remaking a Japanese City*. Berkeley: University of California Press, 1991.
Rowbottom, Darrell Patrick. "In-Between Believing and Degrees of Belief." *Teorema* 26, no. 1 (2007): 131–37.
Rubinger, Richard. *Popular Literacy in Early Modern Japan*. Honolulu: University of Hawai'i Press, 2007.
Ryōkū Yajin. *Seiyō kijutsu Kokkuri kaidan*. 1st ed. Iiguru shobō, March 1887.
———. *Seiyō kijutsu Kokkuri kaidan*. 3rd ed. Iiguru shobō, June 1887.
Saeki Umetomo, ed. *Kokin waka shū*. In *Nihon koten bungaku taikei*. Vol. 8. Iwanami shoten, 1980.
Saitō Jun. "Yōkai to kaijū." In *Yōkai henge*, edited by Tsunemitsu Tōru, 66–101. Chikuma shobō, 1999.
Saitō Shigeo, ed. *Inoue Enryō to seiyō shisō*. Tōyō Daigaku Inoue Enryō kenkyūkai dainibukai, 1988.
Saitō Shūhei. "Uwasa no fōkuroa: Kuchi-sake-onna no denshō oboegaki." *Kenkyū kiyō* 7 (March 30, 1992): 81–99.
Saitō Tsugio. *Yōkai toshi keikaku ron: Obake kara no machi zukuri*. Sairyūsha, 1996.
Sakai, Tadao. "Confucianism and Popular Educational Works." In *Self and Society in Ming Thought*, edited by William Theodore de Bary and Conference on Ming Thought, 331–66. New York: Columbia University Press, 1970.
Saler, Benson. "On What We May Believe about Beliefs." In *Religion in Mind: Cognitive Perspectives on Religious Belief, Ritual, and Experience*, edited by Jensine Andresen, 47–69. Cambridge: Cambridge University Press, 2001.
———. "Supernatural as a Western Category." *Ethos* 5, no. 1 (1977): 31–53.
Saler, Michael. "'Clap if You Believe in Sherlock Holmes': Mass Culture and the Re-Enchantment of Modernity, c. 1890–c. 1940." *Historical Journal* 46, no. 3 (2003): 599–622.
Satō Arifumi. *Ichiban kuwashii Nihon yōkai zukan*. Rippū shobō, 1972.
Satō Kenji. *Ryūgen higo: Uwasabanashi o yomitoku sahō*. Yūshindō, 1995.
———. "Uwasa-banashi no shisōshi." In *Uwasa no hon*. Vol. 92 of *Bessatsu takarajima*, edited by Ishii Shinji, 261–74. ICC Shuppan kyoku, 1989.
Schneider, Mark A. *Culture and Enchantment*. Chicago: University of Chicago Press, 1993.
Schneider, Steven. "Monsters as (Uncanny) Metaphors: Freud, Lakoff, and the Representation of Monstrosity in Cinematic Horror." In *Horror Film Reader*, edited by Alain Silver and James Ursini, 167–91. New York: Limelight Editions, 2000.
Schwitzgebel, Eric. "In-Between Believing." *Philosophical Quarterly* 51, no. 202 (January 2001): 77–82.
Scott, A. O. "A Motley Crew of Spirits Recruit a Boy to Be Savior in 'The Great Yōkai War.'" *New York Times*, June 30, 2006.
Screech, Timon. *The Lens within the Heart: The Western Scientific Gaze and Popular Imagery in Later Edo Japan*. Honolulu: University of Hawai'i Press, 2002.

"Seiyō no Kokkuri-san." *Yomiuri Shinbun*, Sunday supplement, May 17, 1903, p. 1.

Shibusawa Tatsuhiko. "Tsukumogami." In *Yōkai*, edited by Komatsu Kazuhiko, 65–78. Kawade shobō shinsha, 2000.

Shibutani, Tamotsu. *Improvised News: A Sociological Study of Rumor.* Indianapolis: Bobbs-Merrill, 1966.

Shibuya Yōichi. "Bakemono zōshi no kenkyū: Yōkai kenkyū e no shikiron." Undergraduate thesis, Chiba University, Chiba City, 2000.

Shimizu Isao. *Edo no manga.* Kōdansha gakujutsu bunko, 2003.

Shimokawa Kōshi and Katei sōgō kenkyūkai, eds. *Meiji Taishō kateishi nenpyō 1868–1925.* Kawade shobō shinsha, 2000.

———, eds. *Shōwa, Heisei kateishi nenpyō 1926–2000.* Kawade shobō shinsha, 2001.

Shively, Donald H. "Popular Culture." *The Cambridge History of Japan.* Vol. 4, edited by John Whitney Hall, 706–69. Cambridge: Cambridge University Press, 1991.

Shūkan asahi, March 23, 1979, pp. 35–36.

Shūkan pureibōi, July 24, 1979, p. 76.

Shūkan shinchō, April 5, 1979, pp. 128–29.

Shuppan nenkan henshūbu, ed. *Shuppan nenkan 1981.* Shuppan nyūsusha, 1981.

Silverberg, Miriam. "Constructing the Ethnography of Modernity." *Journal of Asian Studies* 51, no. 1 (February 1992): 30–54.

———. *Erotic Grotesque Nonsense: The Mass Culture of Japanese Modern Times.* Berkeley: University of California Press, 2006.

Smith, Paul. *Discerning the Subject.* Minneapolis: University of Minnesota Press, 1988.

Smyers, Karen. *The Fox and the Jewel: Shared and Private Meanings in Contemporary Japanese Inari Worship.* Honolulu: University of Hawai'i Press, 1999.

Staggs, Kathleen M. "'Defend the Nation and Love the Truth': Inoue Enryō and the Revival of Meiji Buddhism." *Monumenta Nipponica* 38, no. 3 (Autumn 1983): 251–81.

Stallybrass, Peter, and Allon White, eds. *The Politics and Poetics of Transgression.* Ithaca, NY: Cornell University Press, 1986.

Stewart, Susan. *On Longing: Narratives of the Miniature, the Gigantic, the Souvenir, the Collection.* Durham, NC: Duke University Press, 1993.

Strassberg, Richard E., ed. and trans. *A Chinese Bestiary: Strange Creatures from the Guideways through Mountains and Seas.* Berkeley: University of California Press, 2002.

Sugimoto Tsutomu. *Edo no hakubutsugakusha-tachi.* Kōdansha gakujutsu bunko, 2006.

Suzuki Manjirō. *Dōbutsu denki gairon.* Jūjiya, 1885.

Suzuki Tadashi and Yamaryō Kenji, eds. *Nihon shisō no kanōsei.* Satsuki shobō, 1997.

Suzuki, Tomi. *Narrating the Self: Fictions of Japanese Modernity.* Stanford: Stanford University Press, 1996.

Tachikawa Kiyoshi, ed. *Hyaku-monogatari kaidan shūsei.* Kokusho kankōkai, 1995.

———, ed. *Zoku hyaku-monogatari kaidan shūsei*. Kokusho kankōkai, 1993.
Tada Katsumi. *Edo yōkai karuta*. Kokusho kankōkai, 1998.
———. "Etoki gazu hyakkiyagyō no yōkai." *Kai* 12 (December 2001): 320–31.
———. *Hyakki kaidoku*. Kōdansha, 1999.
Takada Mamoru. *Edo gensō bungakushi*. Chikuma gakugei bunko, 1999.
———. "'Hyakkiyagyō' sōsetsu: Jo ni kaete." In *Toriyama Sekien gazu hyakkiyagyō*, edited by Inada Atsunobu and Tanaka Naohi, 7–16. Kokusho kankōkai, 1999.
Takahashi Toshio. *Gojira no nazo: Kaijū shinwa to Nihonjin*. Kōdansha, 1998.
Takeda Katsuhiko. *Sōseki no Tōkyō*. Waseda Daigaku shuppanbu, 1997.
Takeda Tadashi. "Hyaku-monogatari: Sono seiritsu to hirogari." In *Yōkai*, edited by Komatsu Kazuhiko, 109–25. Kawade shobō shinsha, 2000.
Takeuchi, Melinda. "Kuniyoshi's Minamoto Raikō and the Earth Spider: Demons and Protest in Late Tokugawa Japan." *Ars Orientalis* 17 (1987): 5–23.
Tamanoi, Mariko Asano. "Gender, Nationalism, and Japanese Native Ethnology." *positions* 4, no. 1 (1996): 59–86.
Tanaka Hatsuo, ed. *Gazu hyakkiyagyō*. Watanabe shoten, 1967.
Tanaka Kakuei. *Nihon rettō kaizō ron*. Nikkan kōgyō shinbunsha, 1973.
Tanaka, Stefan. *New Times in Modern Japan*. Princeton: Princeton University Press, 2004.
Tanaka Takako. *Hyakkiyagyō no mieru toshi*. Chikuma gakugei bunko, 2002.
Tanaka Takako et al., eds. *Zusetsu: Hyakkiyagyō emaki o yomu*. Kawade shobō shinsha, 1999.
Tawara Seiji, ed. *Poketto monsutā zukan*. Ascii, 1997.
Terada Torahiko. "Bakemono no shinka." In *Terada Torahiko zuihitsushū*. Vol. 2:193–206. Iwanami bunko, 1993.
Terajima Ryōan. *Wakan sansaizue*. 2 vols. Nihon zuihitsu taisei kankōkai, 1929.
———. *Wakan sansaizue*. 18 vols. Heibonsha, 1994.
Tobin, Joseph, ed. *Pikachu's Global Adventure: The Rise and Fall of Pokémon*. Durham, NC: Duke University Press, 2004.
Toby, Ronald P. "Imagining and Imaging 'Anthropos' in Early-Modern Japan." *Visual Anthropology Review* 14, no 1 (Spring–Summer 1998): 19–44.
Todorov, Tzvetan. *The Fantastic: A Structural Approach to a Literary Genre*. Ithaca, NY: Cornell University Press, 1975.
Toguri Hiroshi. "'Kuchi-sake-onna' ga imadoki chōryō suru kai." *Shūkan yomiuri*, July 1, 1979, pp. 26–27.
Tōyō Daigaku sōritsu 100 shūnen kinen ronbunshū hensan iinkai, ed. *Inoue Enryō no kyōiku rinen: Atarashii kengaku no seishin o motomete*. Tōyō Daigaku, 1987.
Tsubouchi Shōyō. "Kaki no heta." In *Shōyō senshū bessatsu*. Vol. 4. Dai ichi shobō, 1977.
Tsunemitsu Tōru. *Gakkō no kaidan: Kōshō bungei no tenkai to shosō*. Kyoto: Mineruva, 1993.
Tsunoda, Ryusaku, William Theodore de Bary, and Donald Keene, eds. *Sources of Japanese Tradition*. New York: Columbia University Press, 1958.
Tsutsui, William. *Godzilla on My Mind: Fifty Years of the King of Monsters*. New York: Palgrave Macmillan, 2004.

Tsutsui, William M., and Michiko Ito, eds. *In Godzilla's Footsteps: Japanese Pop Culture Icons on the Global Stage*. New York: Palgrave Macmillan, 2006.
Tuan, Yi-Fu. *Landscapes of Fear*. Minneapolis: University of Minnesota Press, 1979.
Tudor, Andrew. "Why Horror? The Peculiar Pleasures of a Popular Genre." *Cultural Studies* 11, no. 3 (1997): 443–63.
Turner, Patricia A. *I Heard It through the Grapevine: Rumor in African-American Culture*. Berkeley: University of California Press, 1993.
Twitchell, James. *Dreadful Pleasures: An Anatomy of Modern Horror*. New York: Oxford University Press, 1985.
Ueda Akinari. *Tales of Moonlight and Rain*. Translated by Anthony H. Chambers. New York: Columbia University Press, 2007.
Ueno Masuzō. "Jobun: Edo hakubutsugaku no romanchishizumu." In *Edo hakubutsugaku shūsei: Saishiki*, edited by Shimonaka Hiroshi, 5–21. Heibonsha, 1994.
Ury, Marian. "A Heian Note on the Supernatural." *Journal of the Association of Teachers of Japanese* 22, no. 2 (November 1988): 189–94.
Vande Walle, W. F., and Kazuhiko Kasaya, eds. *Dodonaeus in Japan: Translation and the Scientific Mind in the Tokugawa Period*. Leuven, Belgium: Leuven University Press, 2001.
Vinitzky-Seroussi, Vered. "Social Memory and Commemoration: Some 'After the Fact' Thoughts." In *Perspectives on Social Memory in Japan*, edited by Tsu Yun Hui, Jan Van Bremen, and Eyal Ben-Ari, 231–45. Folkestone, U.K.: Global Oriental, 2005.
Walker, Brett L. *The Lost Wolves of Japan*. Seattle: University of Washington Press, 2005.
Weber, Max. "Science as a Vocation." In *From Max Weber: Essays in Sociology*, edited by H. H. Gerth and C. Wright Mills, 129–56. New York: Oxford University Press, 1958.
Winter, Alison. *Mesmerized: Powers of Mind in Victorian Britain*. Chicago: University of Chicago Press, 1998.
Wood, Robin. "An Introduction to the American Horror Film." In *American Nightmare: Essays on the Horror Film*, edited by Andrew Britton, Richard Lippe, Tony Williams, and Robin Wood, 7–28. Toronto: Festival of Festivals, 1979.
Yabe Ichirō. *Edo no honzō: Yakubutsugaku to hakubutsugaku*. Saiensusha, 1991.
Yamada Keiji. "Honzō ni okeru bunrui no shisō." In *Higashi Ajia no honzō to hakubutsu no sekai*, vol. 1, edited by Yamada Keiji. Kyoto: Shibunkaku shuppan, 1995.
Yamaguchi Kakutarō. "Nihonjin to karuta." *Gekkan bunkazai* (January 1975): 12–19.
Yanagita Kunio. *Teihon Yanagita Kunio shū*. 36 vols. Chikuma shobō, 1968–71.
Yeo, Richard. *Encyclopedic Visions: Scientific Dictionaries and Enlightenment Culture*. Cambridge: Cambridge University Press, 2001.
"Yōkai: Nihonshi himotoku tegakari." *Nihon keizai shinbun*, August 17, 2002, p. 36.
Yōkai, yūrei daihyakka. Keibunsha, 1982.
Yokoyama Yasuko. *Yotsuya kaidan wa omoshiroi*. Heibonsha, 1997.

Yonemoto, Marcia. *Mapping Early Modern Japan: Space, Place, and Culture in the Tokugawa Period (1603–1868).* Berkeley: University of California Press, 2003.

Yumoto Kōichi, ed. *Chihō hatsu Meiji yōkai nyūsu.* Kashiwa shobō, 2001.

———. *Edo no yōkai emaki.* Kōbunsha, 2003.

———, ed. *Zusetsu Bakumatsu-Meiji ryūkō jiten.* Kashiwa shobō, 1998.

Zhang Longxi. "The Myth of the Other: China in the Eyes of the West." *Critical Inquiry* 15, no. 1 (Autumn 1988): 108–31.

Index

Text:	10/13 Sabon
Display:	Sabon
Compositor:	Integrated Composition Systems
Indexer:	Kevin Millham
Printer and binder:	Sheridan Books, Inc.

CPSIA information can be obtained at www.ICGtesting.com
Printed in the USA
BVOW05s0638100915

417391BV00001B/84/P